WHEN THE RIVER RISES

Written by **D.C. Walker**

Art by **Bruno Oliveira**

Letters by **Rob Hebert**

Edits by **Trevor Kress**

Library of Congress Control Number: 2015908274

www.mastermindcomics.com

Rob Hebert, Editor in Chief
Edmond Guidry, President
Trevor Kress, VP Sales

Twitter: @mastermindcomix
Facebook: facebook.com/mastermindcomics
Email: publicity@mastermindcomics.com
Author: @dcwalkerbooks

INSPIRED BY TRUE EVENTS

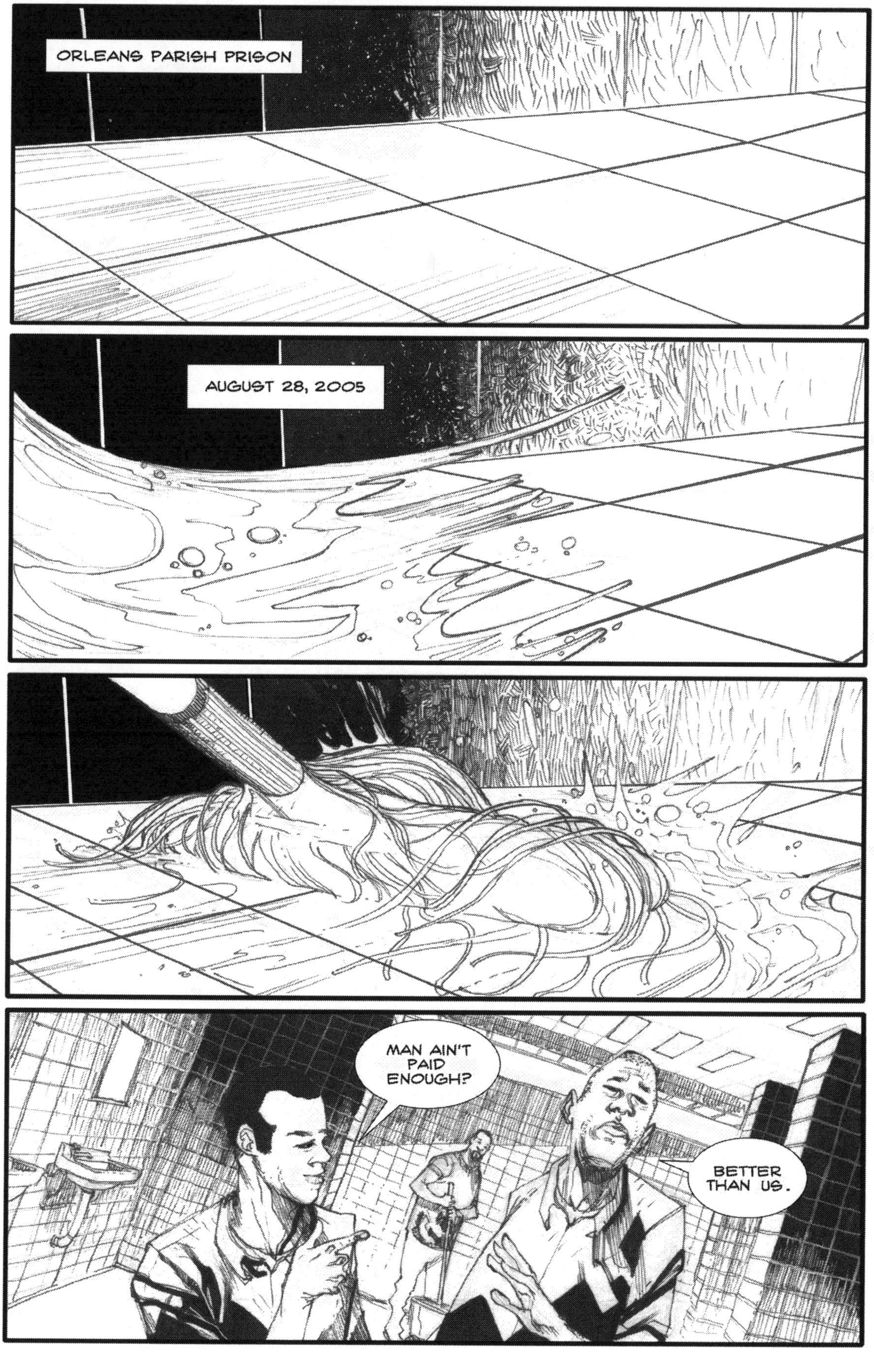
ORLEANS PARISH PRISON
AUGUST 28, 2005
MAN AIN'T PAID ENOUGH?
BETTER THAN US.

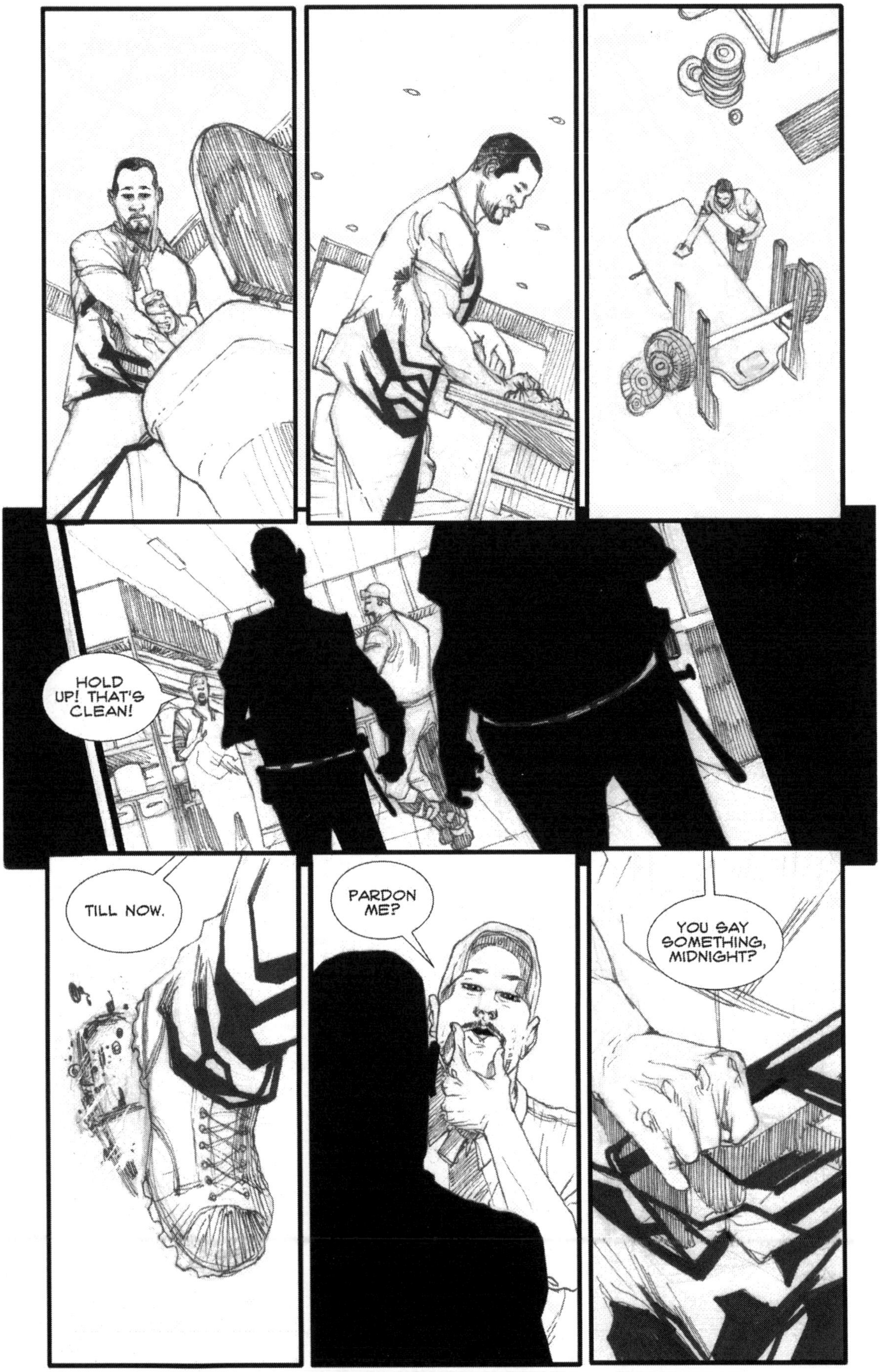
HOLD UP! THAT'S CLEAN!
TILL NOW.
PARDON ME?
YOU SAY SOMETHING, MIDNIGHT?

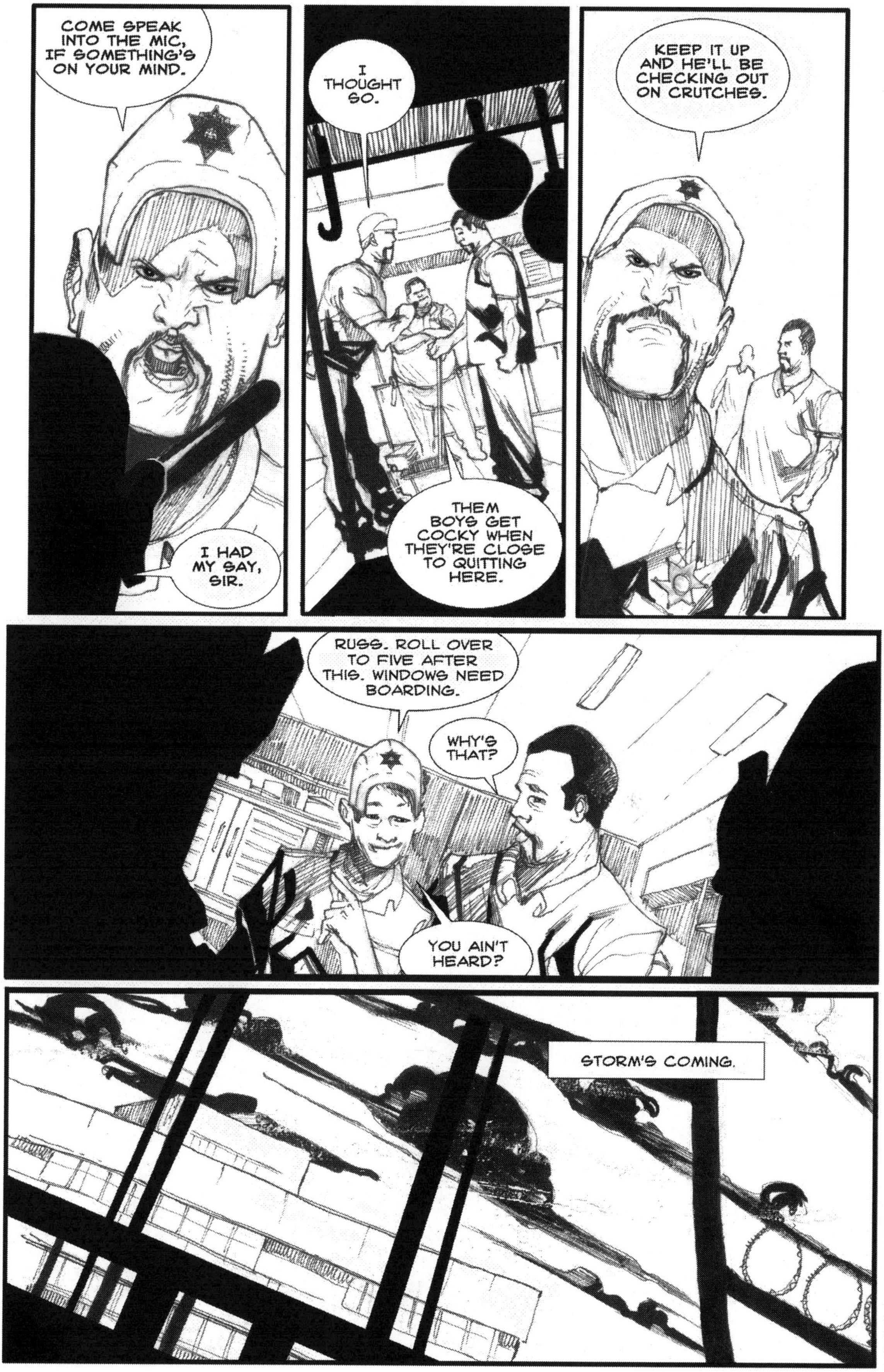
COME SPEAK INTO THE MIC, IF SOMETHING'S ON YOUR MIND.
I HAD MY SAY, SIR.
I THOUGHT SO.
THEM BOYS GET COCKY WHEN THEY'RE CLOSE TO QUITTING HERE.
KEEP IT UP AND HE'LL BE CHECKING OUT ON CRUTCHES.
RUSS. ROLL OVER TO FIVE AFTER THIS. WINDOWS NEED BOARDING.
WHY'S THAT?
YOU AIN'T HEARD?
STORM'S COMING.

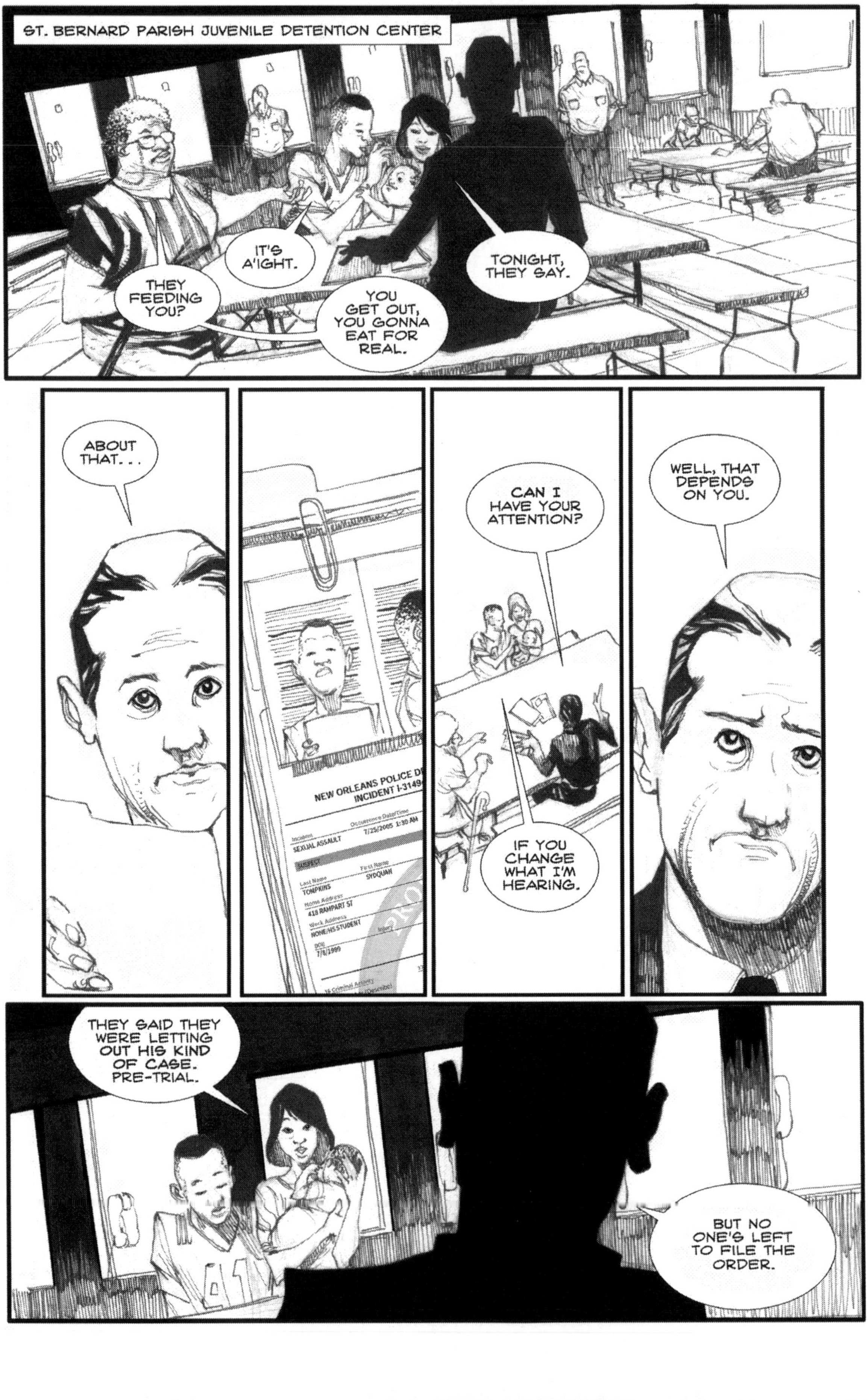

ST. BERNARD PARISH JUVENILE DETENTION CENTER
THEY FEEDING YOU?
IT'S A'IGHT.
YOU GET OUT, YOU GONNA EAT FOR REAL.
TONIGHT, THEY SAY.
ABOUT THAT. . .
NEW ORLEANS POLICE D
INCIDENT I-3149
Occurrence Date/Time
7/25/2005 1:30 AM
Incident
SEXUAL ASSAULT
SUSPECT
Last Name
TOMPKINS
First Name
SYDQUAH
Home Address
418 RAMPART ST
Work Address
NONE/HS STUDENT
DOB
7/8/1999
CAN I HAVE YOUR ATTENTION?
IF YOU CHANGE WHAT I'M HEARING.
WELL, THAT DEPENDS ON YOU.
THEY SAID THEY WERE LETTING OUT HIS KIND OF CASE. PRE-TRIAL.
BUT NO ONE'S LEFT TO FILE THE ORDER.

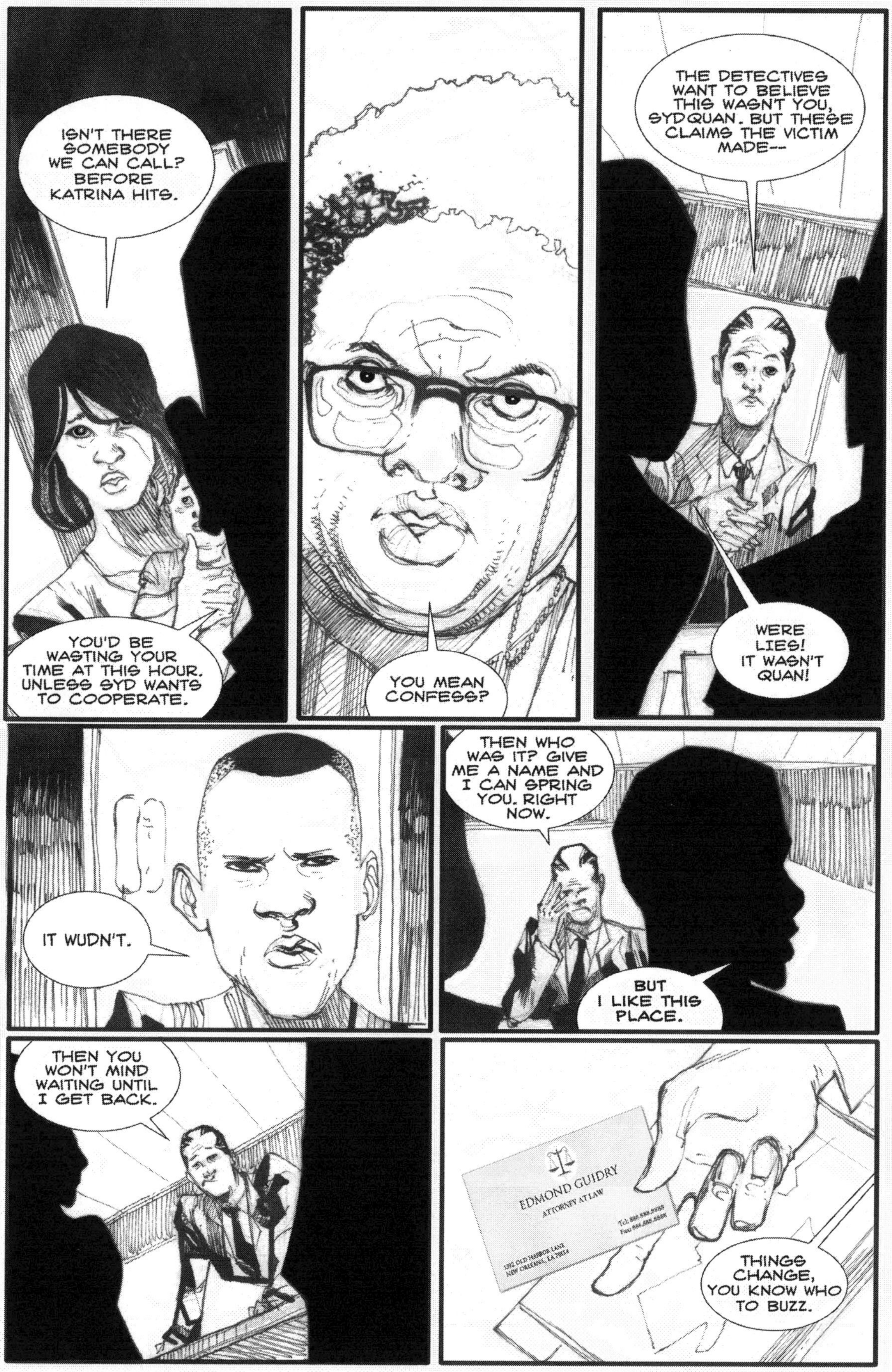
ISN'T THERE SOMEBODY WE CAN CALL? BEFORE KATRINA HITS.
YOU'D BE WASTING YOUR TIME AT THIS HOUR. UNLESS SYD WANTS TO COOPERATE.
YOU MEAN CONFESS?
THE DETECTIVES WANT TO BELIEVE THIS WASN'T YOU, SYDQUAN. BUT THESE CLAIMS THE VICTIM MADE--
WERE LIES! IT WASN'T QUAN!
IT WUDN'T.
THEN WHO WAS IT? GIVE ME A NAME AND I CAN SPRING YOU. RIGHT NOW.
BUT I LIKE THIS PLACE.
THEN YOU WON'T MIND WAITING UNTIL I GET BACK.
EDMOND GUIDRY
ATTORNEY AT LAW
THINGS CHANGE, YOU KNOW WHO TO BUZZ.

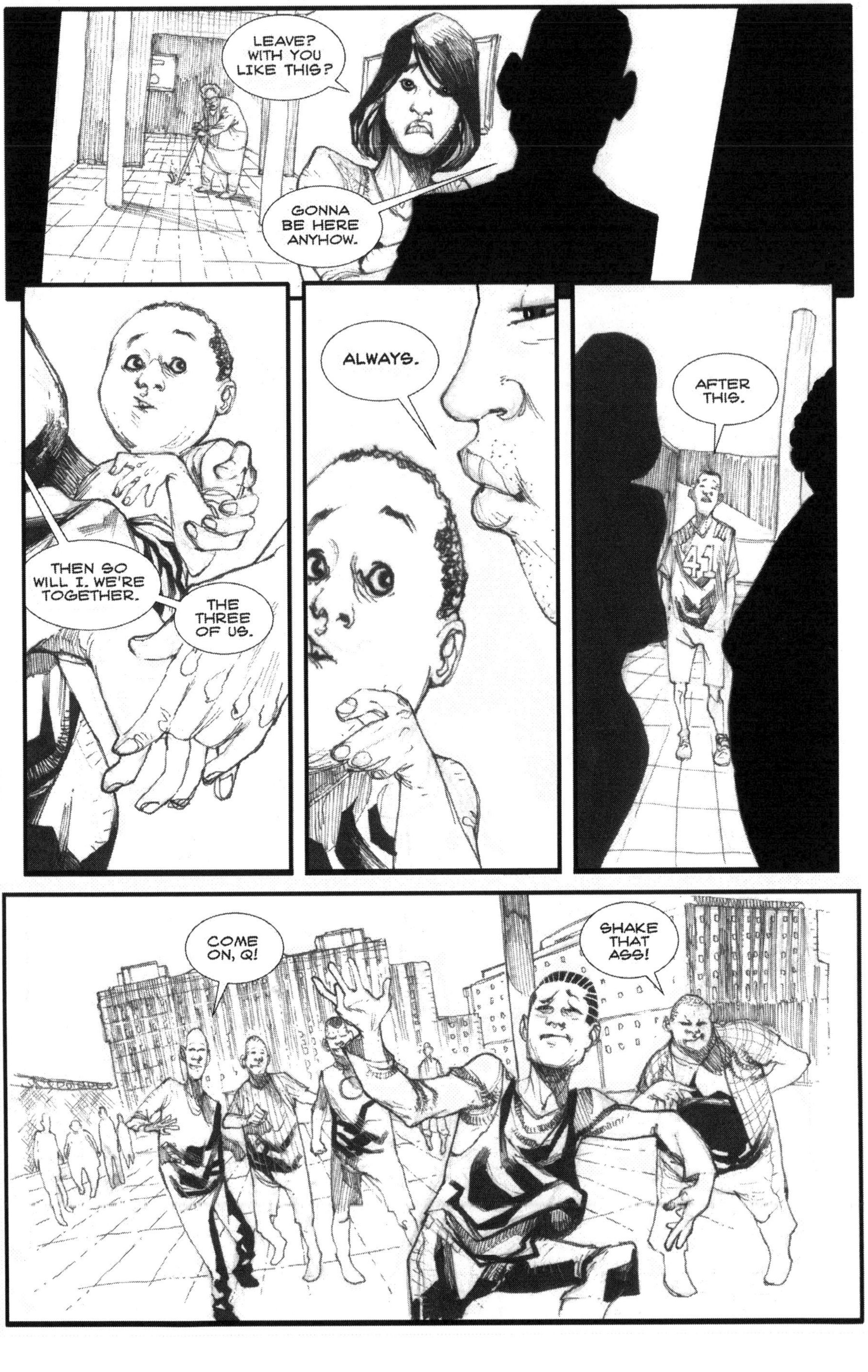
LEAVE? WITH YOU LIKE THIS?
GONNA BE HERE ANYHOW.
THEN SO WILL I. WE'RE TOGETHER.
THE THREE OF US.
ALWAYS.
AFTER THIS.
COME ON, Q!
SHAKE THAT ASS!

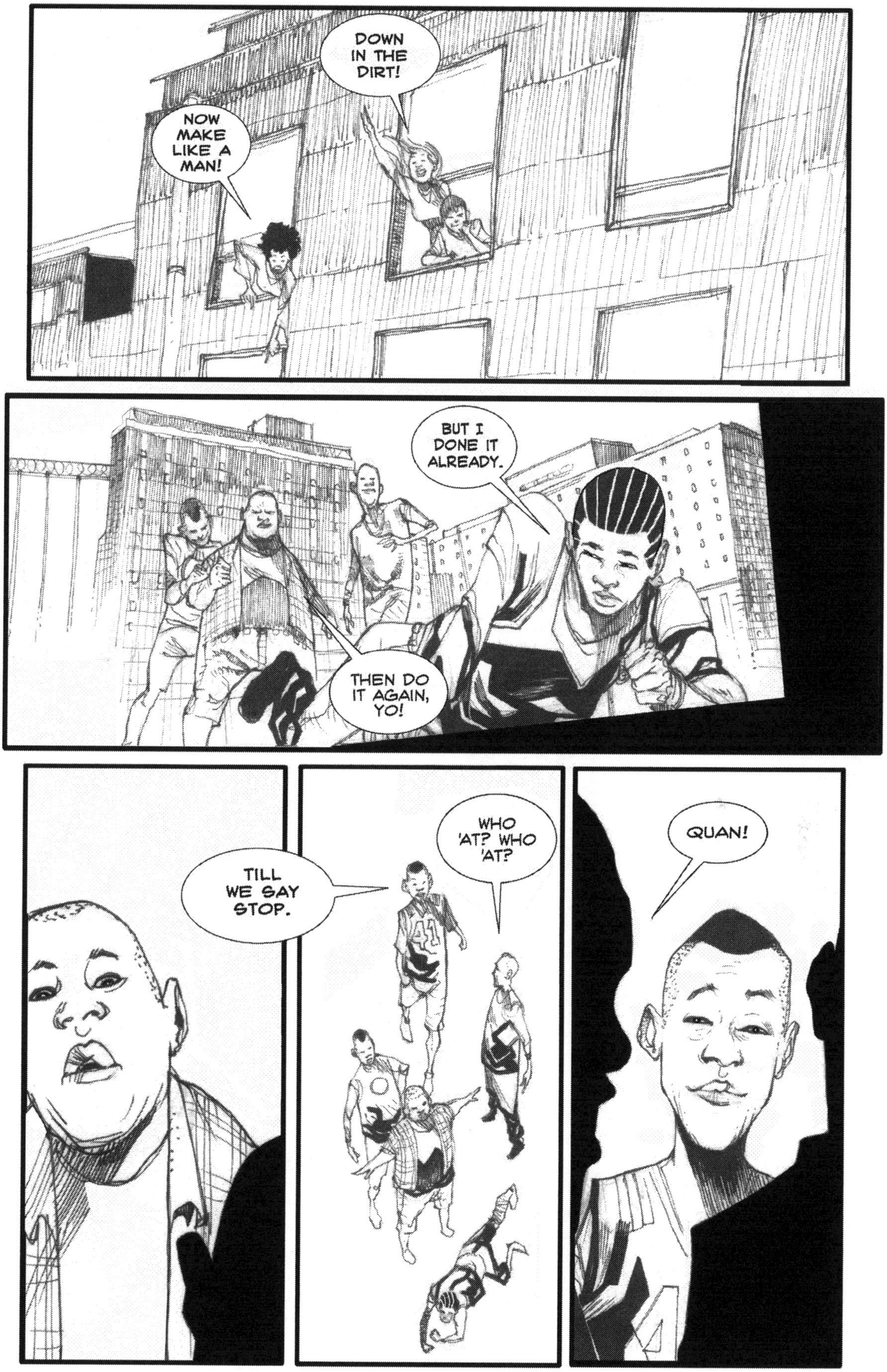
NOW MAKE LIKE A MAN!
DOWN IN THE DIRT!
BUT I DONE IT ALREADY.
THEN DO IT AGAIN, YO!
TILL WE SAY STOP.
WHO 'AT? WHO 'AT?
QUAN!

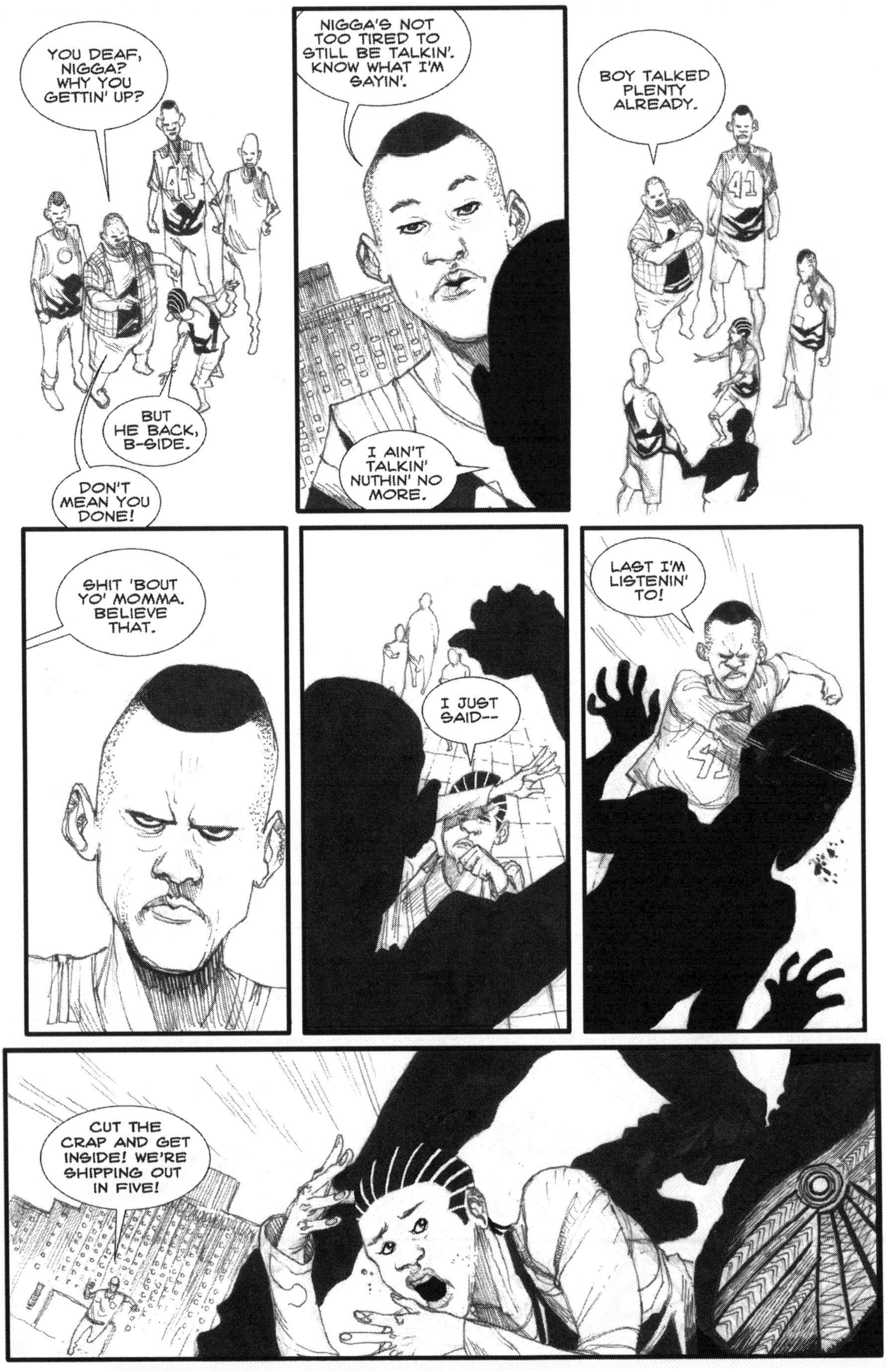
YOU DEAF, NIGGA? WHY YOU GETTIN' UP?
BUT HE BACK, B-SIDE.
DON'T MEAN YOU DONE!
NIGGA'S NOT TOO TIRED TO STILL BE TALKIN'. KNOW WHAT I'M SAYIN'.
I AIN'T TALKIN' NUTHIN' NO MORE.
BOY TALKED PLENTY ALREADY.
SHIT 'BOUT YO' MOMMA. BELIEVE THAT.
I JUST SAID--
LAST I'M LISTENIN' TO!
CUT THE CRAP AND GET INSIDE! WE'RE SHIPPING OUT IN FIVE!

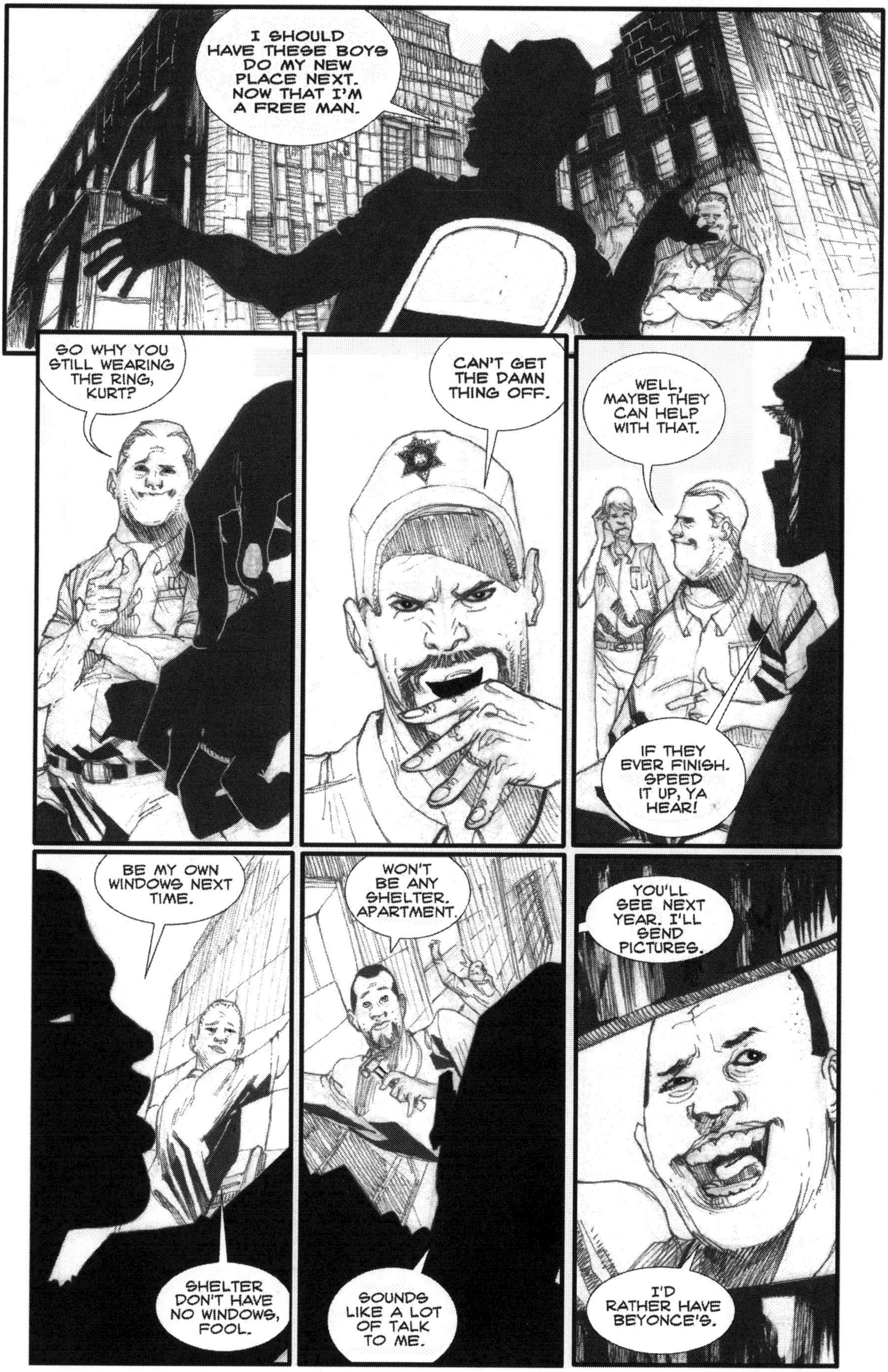
I SHOULD HAVE THESE BOYS DO MY NEW PLACE NEXT. NOW THAT I'M A FREE MAN.
SO WHY YOU STILL WEARING THE RING, KURT?
CAN'T GET THE DAMN THING OFF.
WELL, MAYBE THEY CAN HELP WITH THAT.
IF THEY EVER FINISH. SPEED IT UP, YA HEAR!
BE MY OWN WINDOWS NEXT TIME.
SHELTER DON'T HAVE NO WINDOWS, FOOL.
WON'T BE ANY SHELTER. APARTMENT.
SOUNDS LIKE A LOT OF TALK TO ME.
YOU'LL SEE NEXT YEAR. I'LL SEND PICTURES.
I'D RATHER HAVE BEYONCE'S.

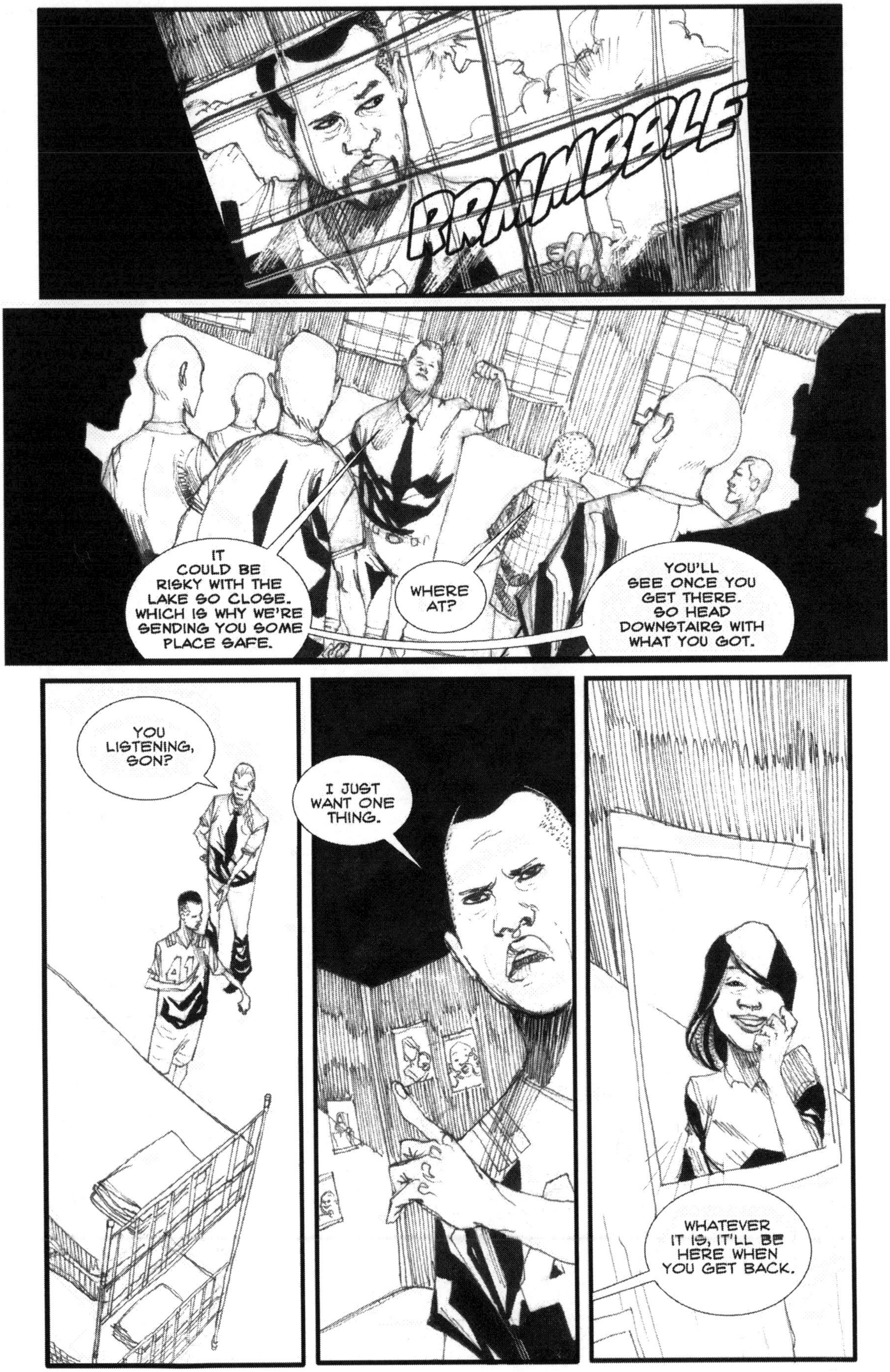
RRMMBBLE
IT COULD BE RISKY WITH THE LAKE SO CLOSE. WHICH IS WHY WE'RE SENDING YOU SOME PLACE SAFE.
WHERE AT?
YOU'LL SEE ONCE YOU GET THERE. SO HEAD DOWNSTAIRS WITH WHAT YOU GOT.
YOU LISTENING, SON?
I JUST WANT ONE THING.
WHATEVER IT IS, IT'LL BE HERE WHEN YOU GET BACK.

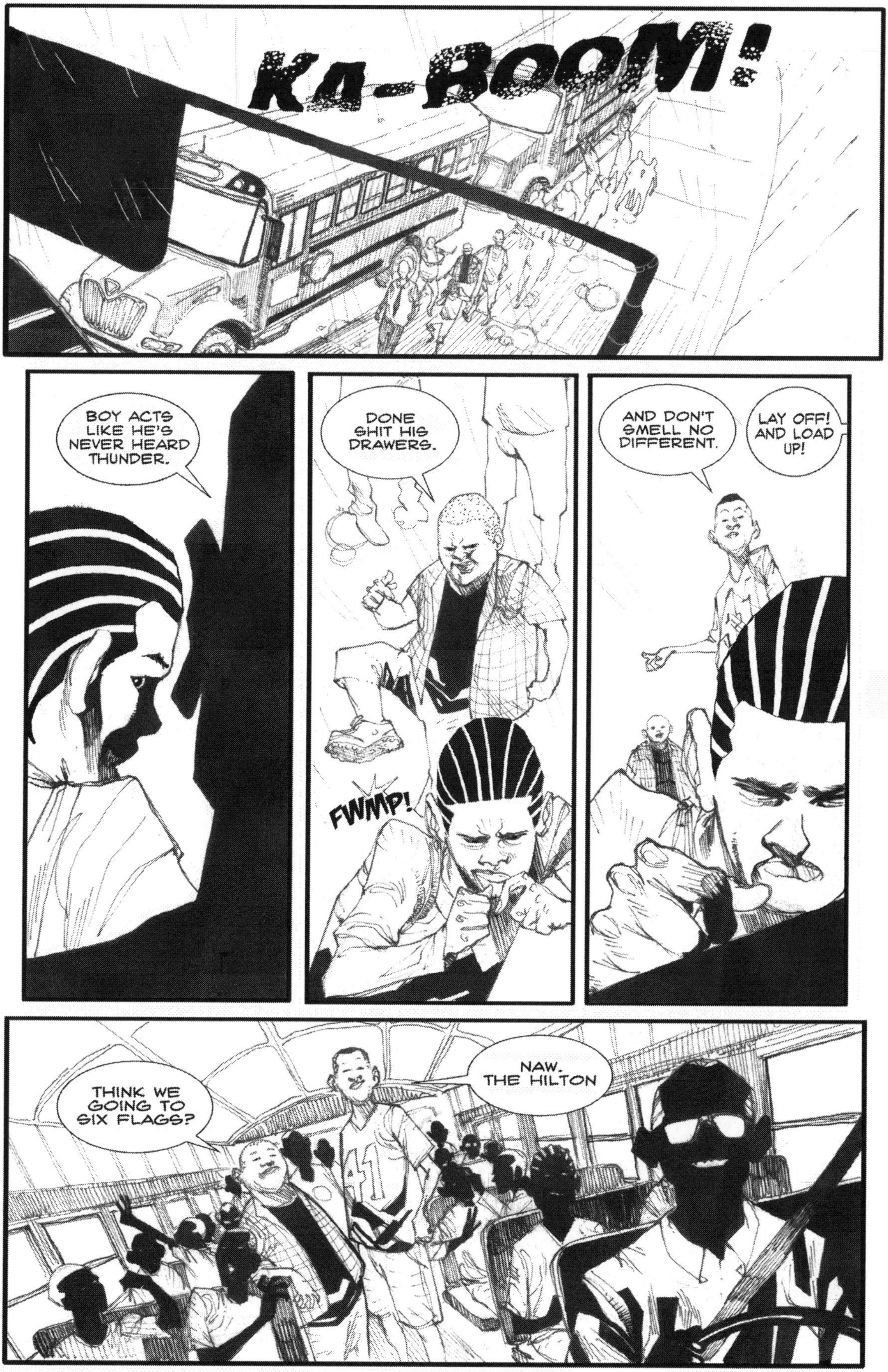
KA-BOOM!
BOY ACTS LIKE HE'S NEVER HEARD THUNDER.
DONE SHIT HIS DRAWERS.
FWMP!
AND DON'T SMELL NO DIFFERENT.
LAY OFF! AND LOAD UP!
THINK WE GOING TO SIX FLAGS?
NAW. THE HILTON
41

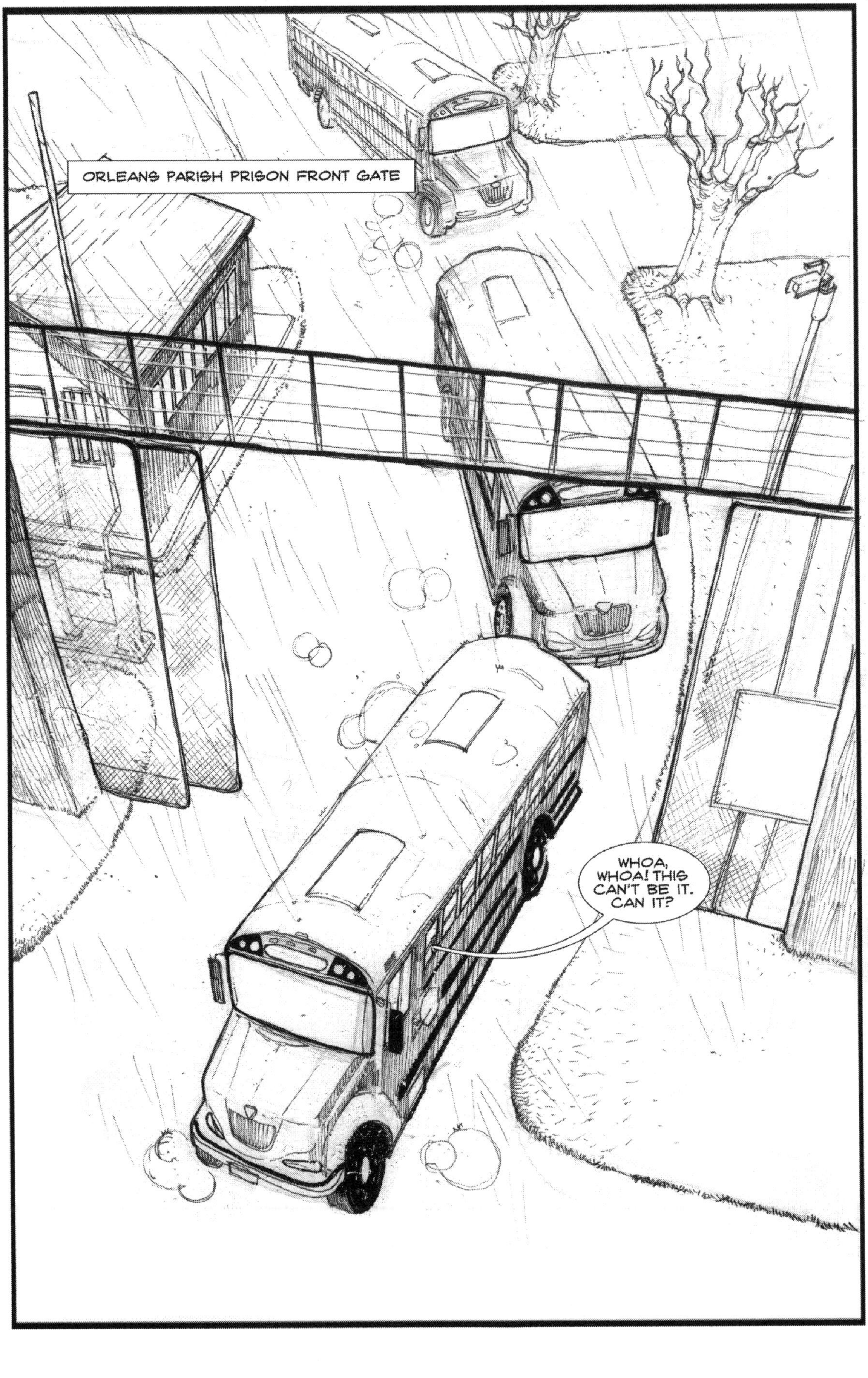
ORLEANS PARISH PRISON FRONT GATE
WHOA, WHOA! THIS CAN'T BE IT. CAN IT?

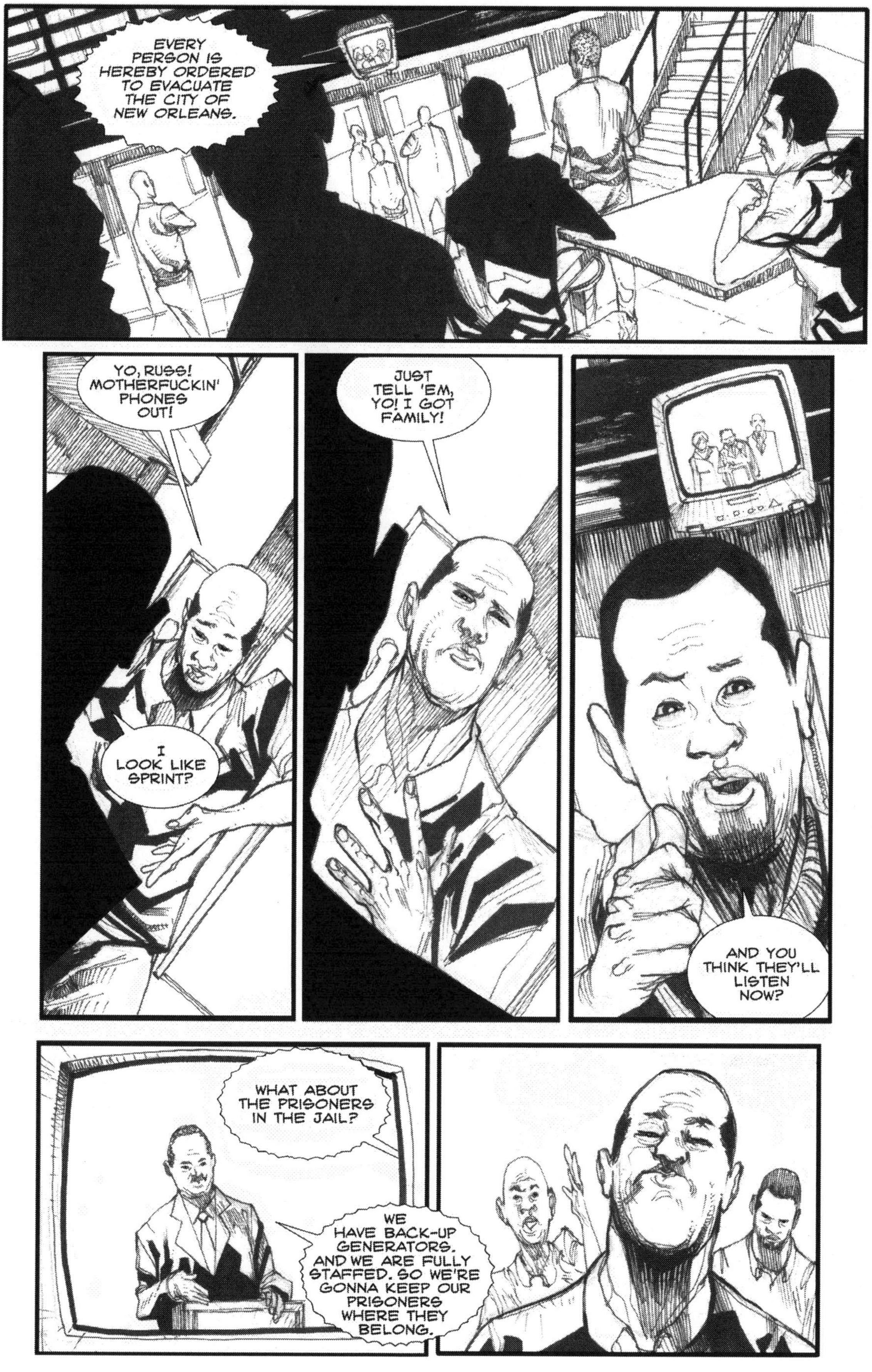
EVERY PERSON IS HEREBY ORDERED TO EVACUATE THE CITY OF NEW ORLEANS.
YO, RUSS! MOTHERFUCKIN' PHONES OUT!
I LOOK LIKE SPRINT?
JUST TELL 'EM, YO! I GOT FAMILY!
AND YOU THINK THEY'LL LISTEN NOW?
WHAT ABOUT THE PRISONERS IN THE JAIL?
WE HAVE BACK-UP GENERATORS. AND WE ARE FULLY STAFFED. SO WE'RE GONNA KEEP OUR PRISONERS WHERE THEY BELONG.

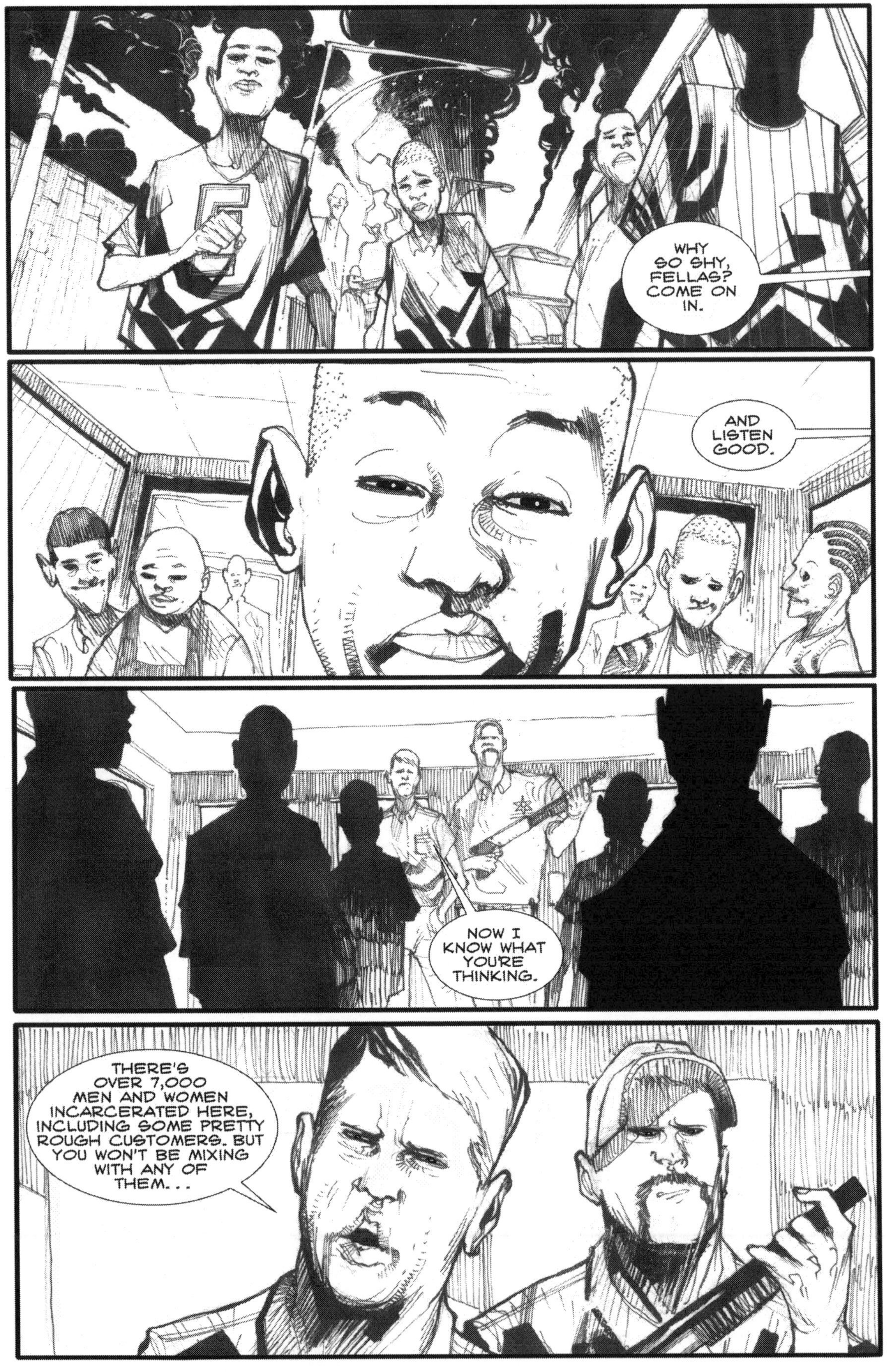
WHY SO SHY, FELLAS? COME ON IN.
AND LISTEN GOOD.
NOW I KNOW WHAT YOU'RE THINKING.
THERE'S OVER 7,000 MEN AND WOMEN INCARCERATED HERE, INCLUDING SOME PRETTY ROUGH CUSTOMERS. BUT YOU WON'T BE MIXING WITH ANY OF THEM. . .

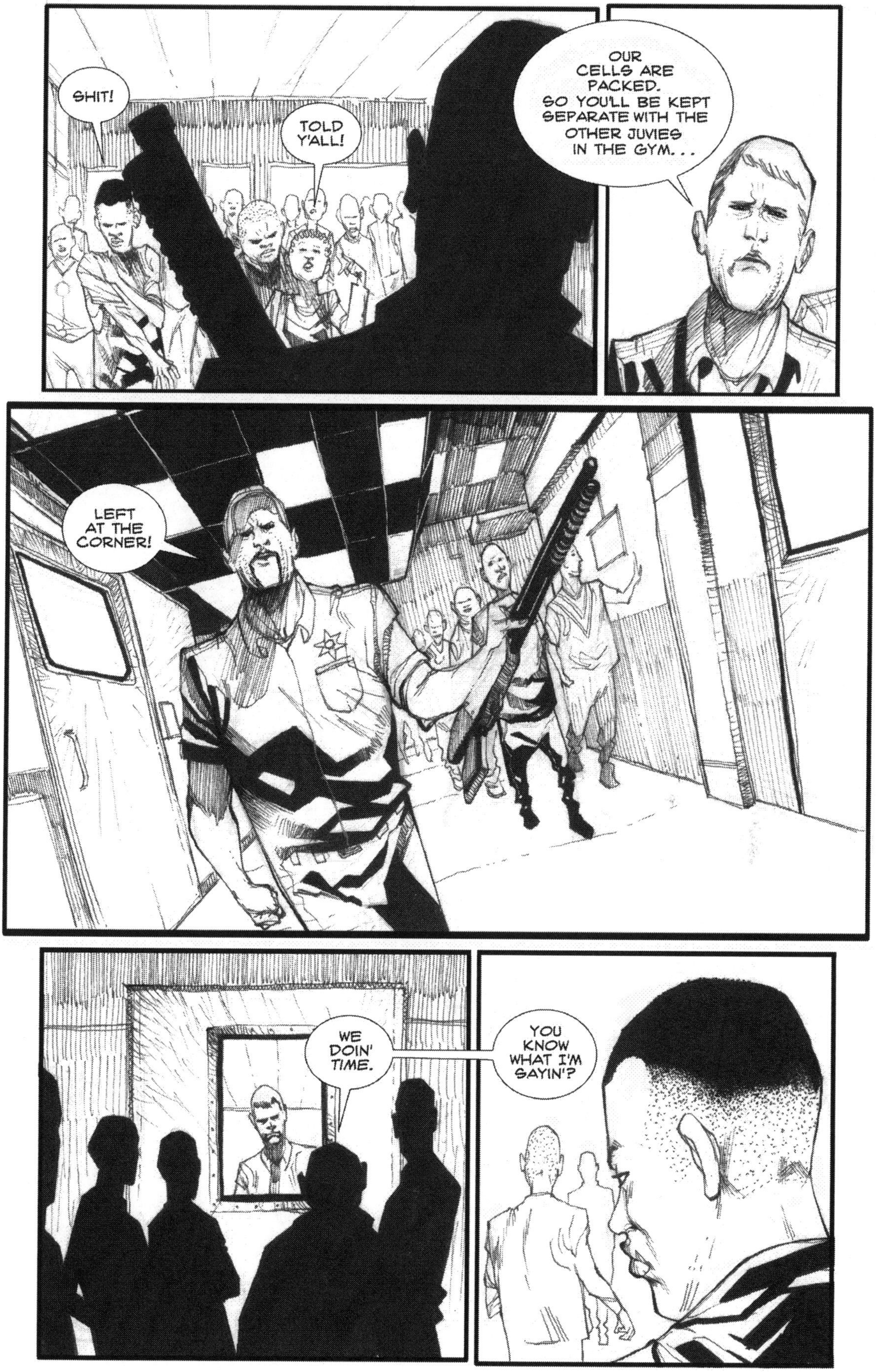
SHIT!
TOLD Y'ALL!
OUR CELLS ARE PACKED. SO YOU'LL BE KEPT SEPARATE WITH THE OTHER JUVIES IN THE GYM. . .
LEFT AT THE CORNER!
WE DOIN' TIME.
YOU KNOW WHAT I'M SAYIN'?

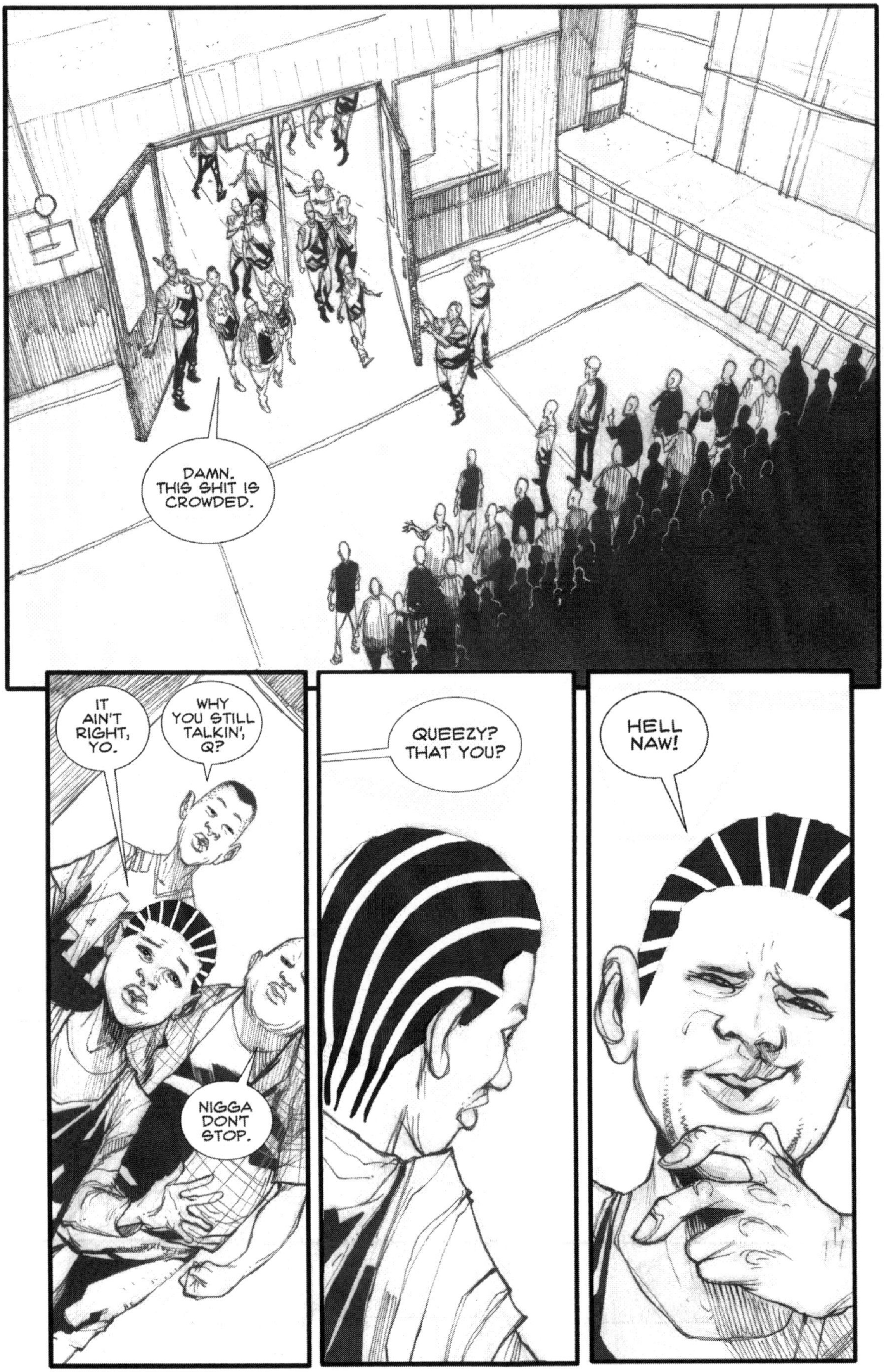
DAMN. THIS SHIT IS CROWDED.
IT AIN'T RIGHT, YO.
WHY YOU STILL TALKIN', Q?
NIGGA DON'T STOP.
QUEEZY? THAT YOU?
HELL NAW!

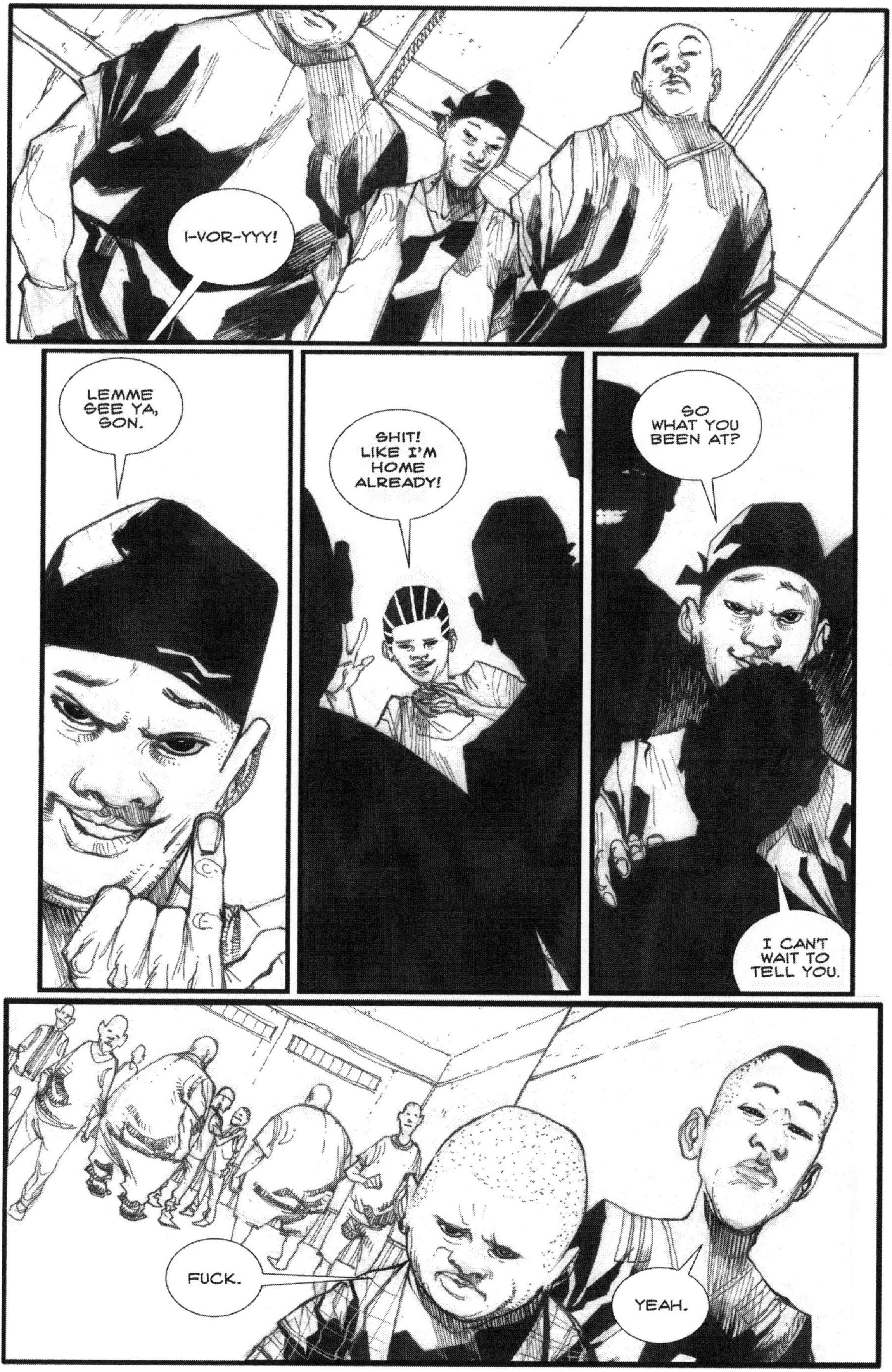
I-VOR-YYY!
LEMME SEE YA, SON.
SHIT! LIKE I'M HOME ALREADY!
SO WHAT YOU BEEN AT?
I CAN'T WAIT TO TELL YOU.
FUCK.
YEAH.

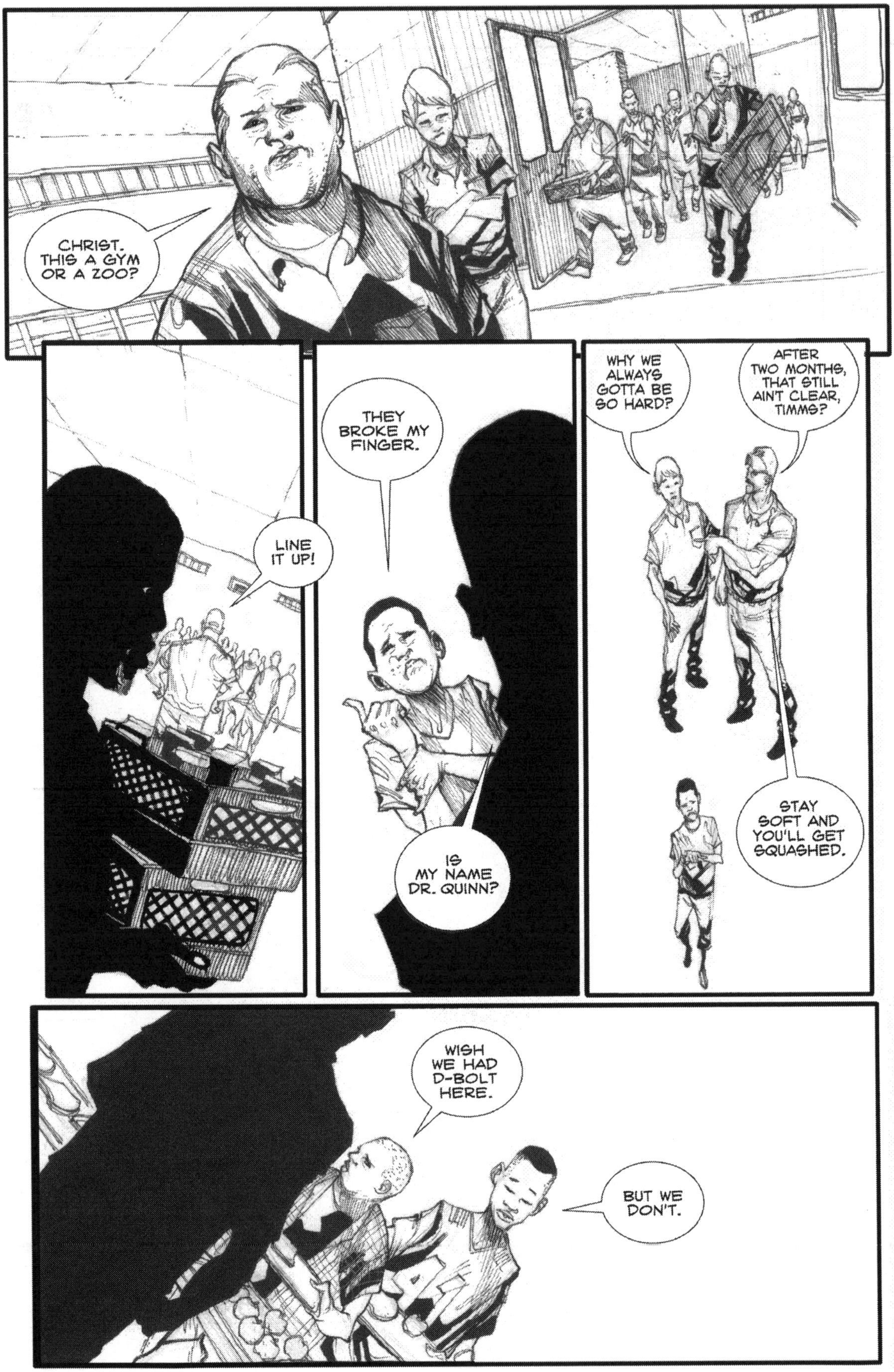
CHRIST. THIS A GYM OR A ZOO?
LINE IT UP!
THEY BROKE MY FINGER.
IS MY NAME DR. QUINN?
WHY WE ALWAYS GOTTA BE SO HARD?
AFTER TWO MONTHS, THAT STILL AIN'T CLEAR, TIMMS?
STAY SOFT AND YOU'LL GET SQUASHED.
WISH WE HAD D-BOLT HERE.
BUT WE DON'T.

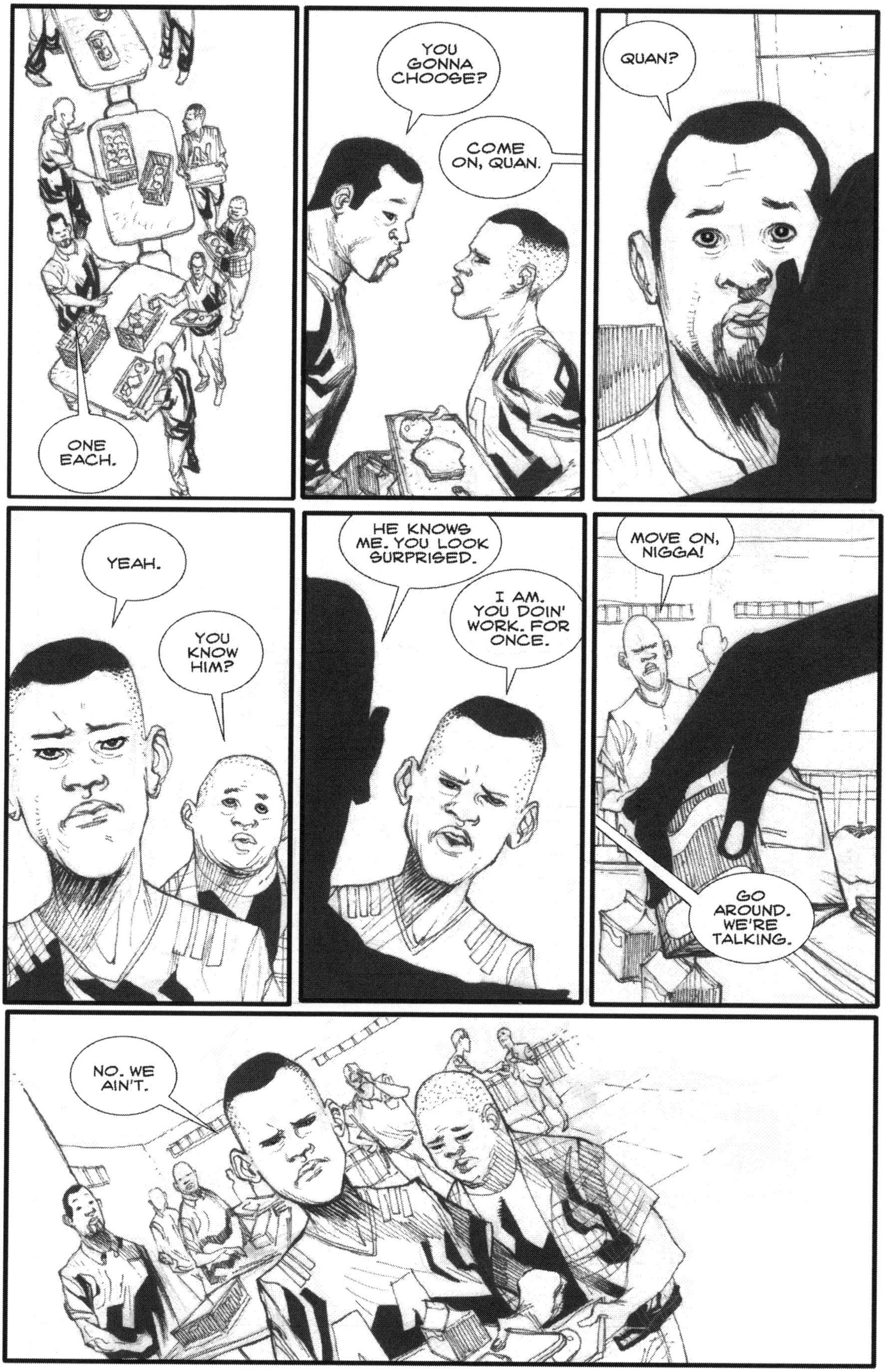
ONE EACH.
YOU GONNA CHOOSE?
COME ON, QUAN.
QUAN?
YEAH.
YOU KNOW HIM?
HE KNOWS ME. YOU LOOK SURPRISED.
I AM. YOU DOIN' WORK. FOR ONCE.
MOVE ON, NIGGA!
GO AROUND. WE'RE TALKING.
NO. WE AIN'T.

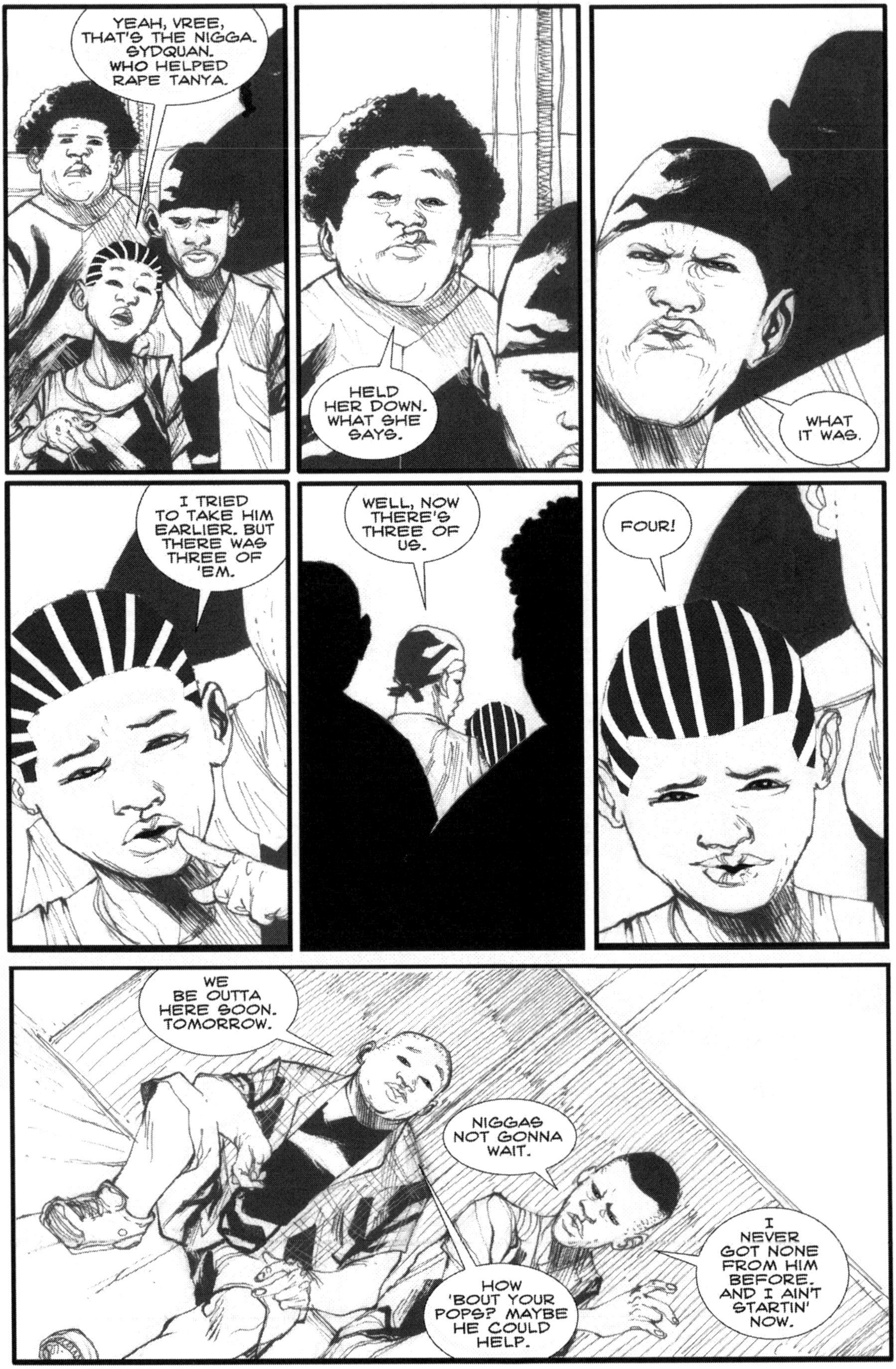
YEAH, VREE, THAT'S THE NIGGA. SYDQUAN. WHO HELPED RAPE TANYA.
HELD HER DOWN. WHAT SHE SAYS.
WHAT IT WAS.
I TRIED TO TAKE HIM EARLIER. BUT THERE WAS THREE OF 'EM.
WELL, NOW THERE'S THREE OF US.
FOUR!
WE BE OUTTA HERE SOON. TOMORROW.
NIGGAS NOT GONNA WAIT.
HOW 'BOUT YOUR POPS? MAYBE HE COULD HELP.
I NEVER GOT NONE FROM HIM BEFORE. AND I AIN'T STARTIN' NOW.

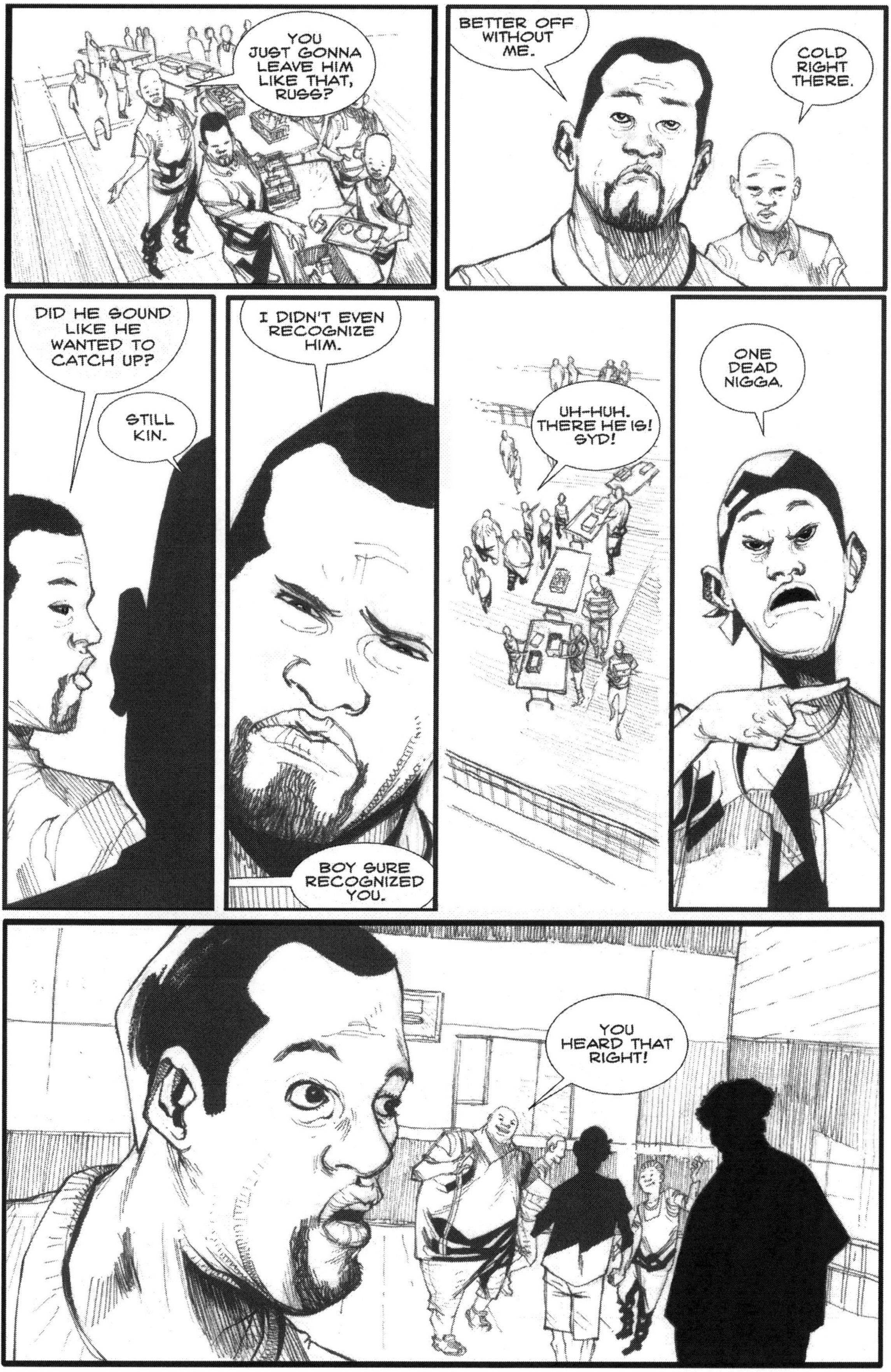
YOU JUST GONNA LEAVE HIM LIKE THAT, RUSS?
BETTER OFF WITHOUT ME.
COLD RIGHT THERE.
DID HE SOUND LIKE HE WANTED TO CATCH UP?
STILL KIN.
I DIDN'T EVEN RECOGNIZE HIM.
BOY SURE RECOGNIZED YOU.
UH-HUH. THERE HE IS! SYD!
ONE DEAD NIGGA.
YOU HEARD THAT RIGHT!

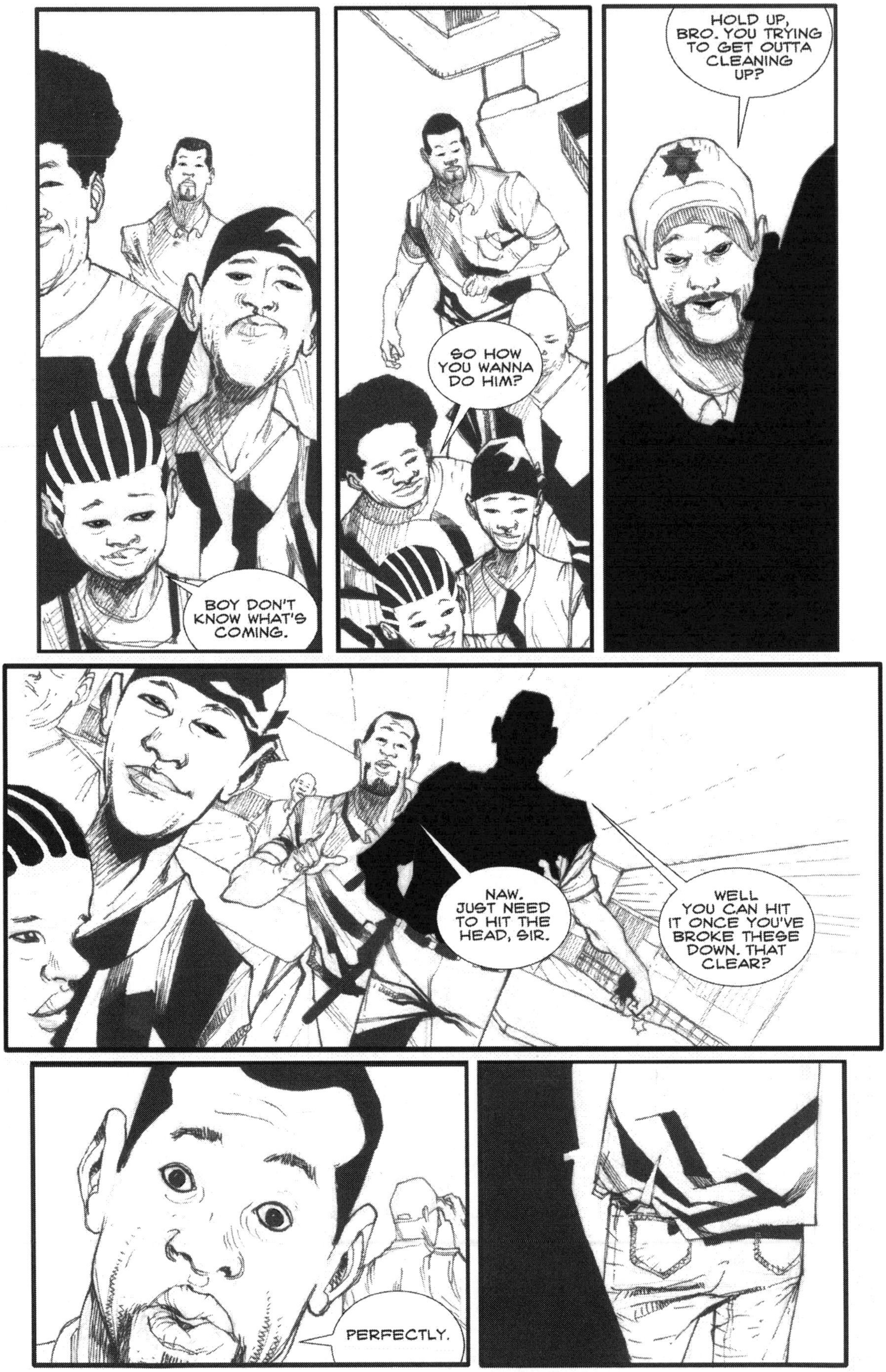
BOY DON'T KNOW WHAT'S COMING.
SO HOW YOU WANNA DO HIM?
HOLD UP, BRO. YOU TRYING TO GET OUTTA CLEANING UP?
NAW. JUST NEED TO HIT THE HEAD, SIR.
WELL YOU CAN HIT IT ONCE YOU'VE BROKE THESE DOWN. THAT CLEAR?
PERFECTLY.

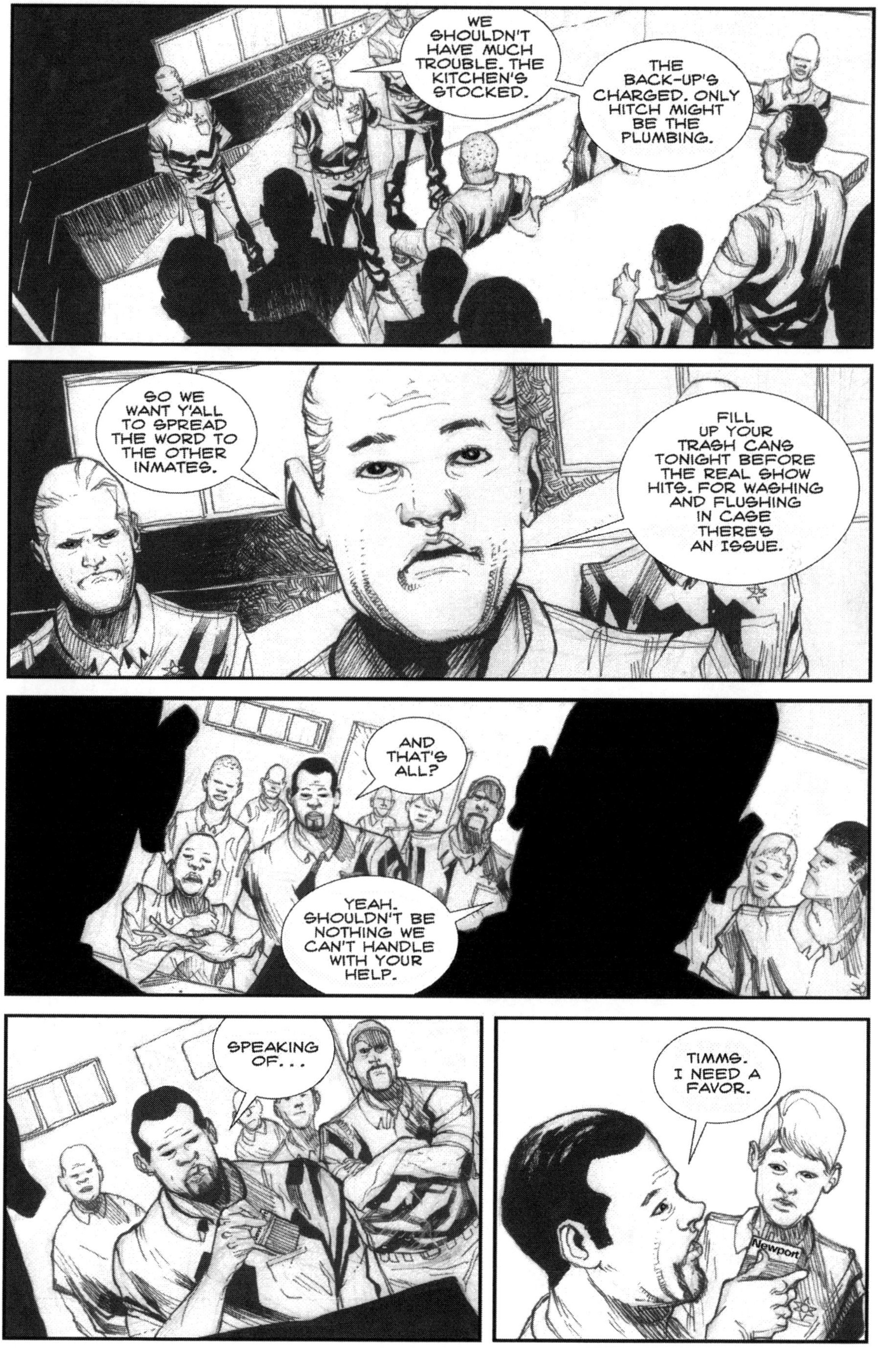
WE SHOULDN'T HAVE MUCH TROUBLE. THE KITCHEN'S STOCKED.
THE BACK-UP'S CHARGED. ONLY HITCH MIGHT BE THE PLUMBING.
SO WE WANT Y'ALL TO SPREAD THE WORD TO THE OTHER INMATES.
FILL UP YOUR TRASH CANS TONIGHT BEFORE THE REAL SHOW HITS. FOR WASHING AND FLUSHING IN CASE THERE'S AN ISSUE.
AND THAT'S ALL?
YEAH. SHOULDN'T BE NOTHING WE CAN'T HANDLE WITH YOUR HELP.
SPEAKING OF. . .
TIMMS. I NEED A FAVOR.
Newport

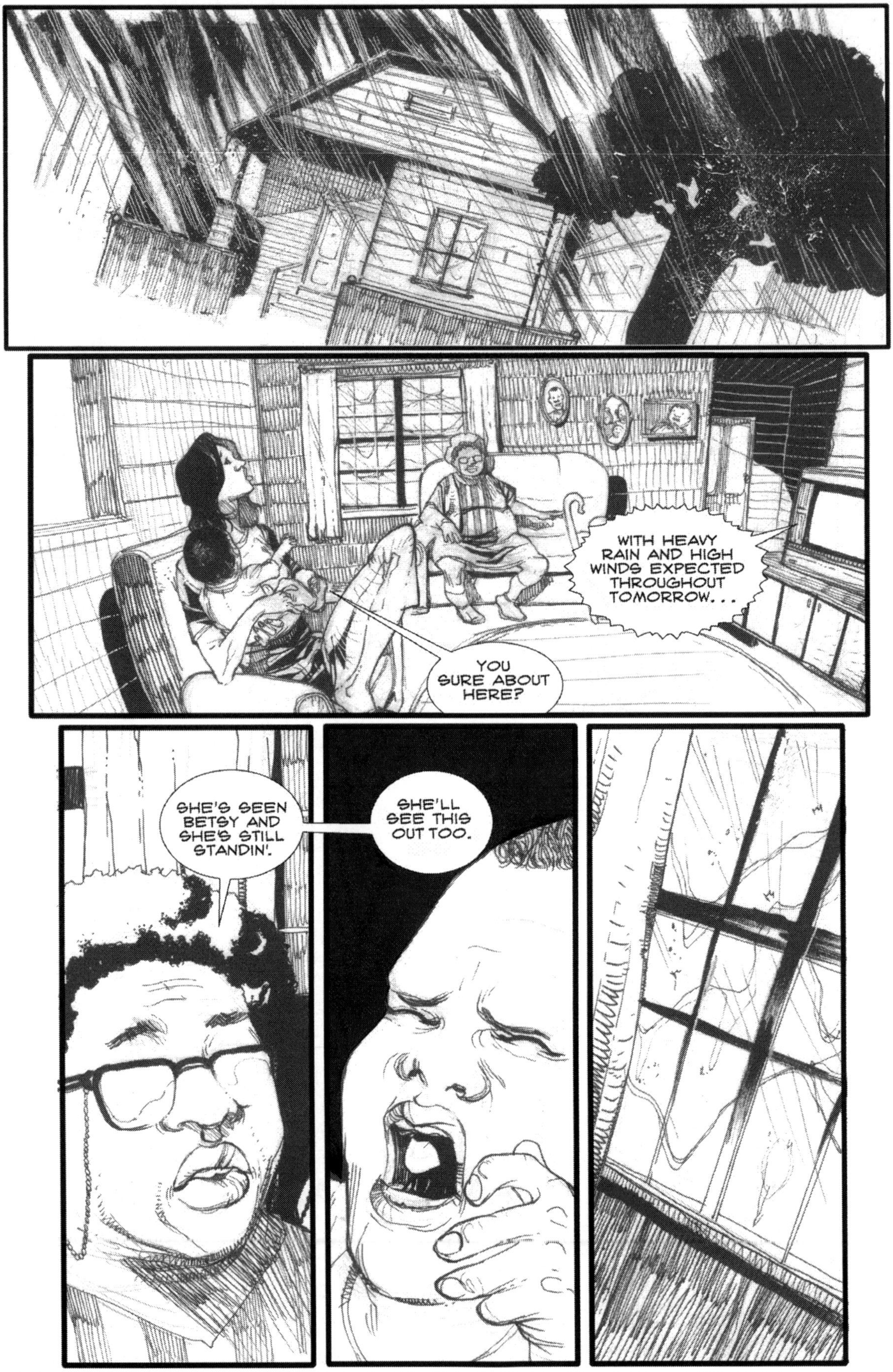
WITH HEAVY RAIN AND HIGH WINDS EXPECTED THROUGHOUT TOMORROW...
YOU SURE ABOUT HERE?
SHE'S SEEN BETSY AND SHE'S STILL STANDIN'.
SHE'LL SEE THIS OUT TOO.

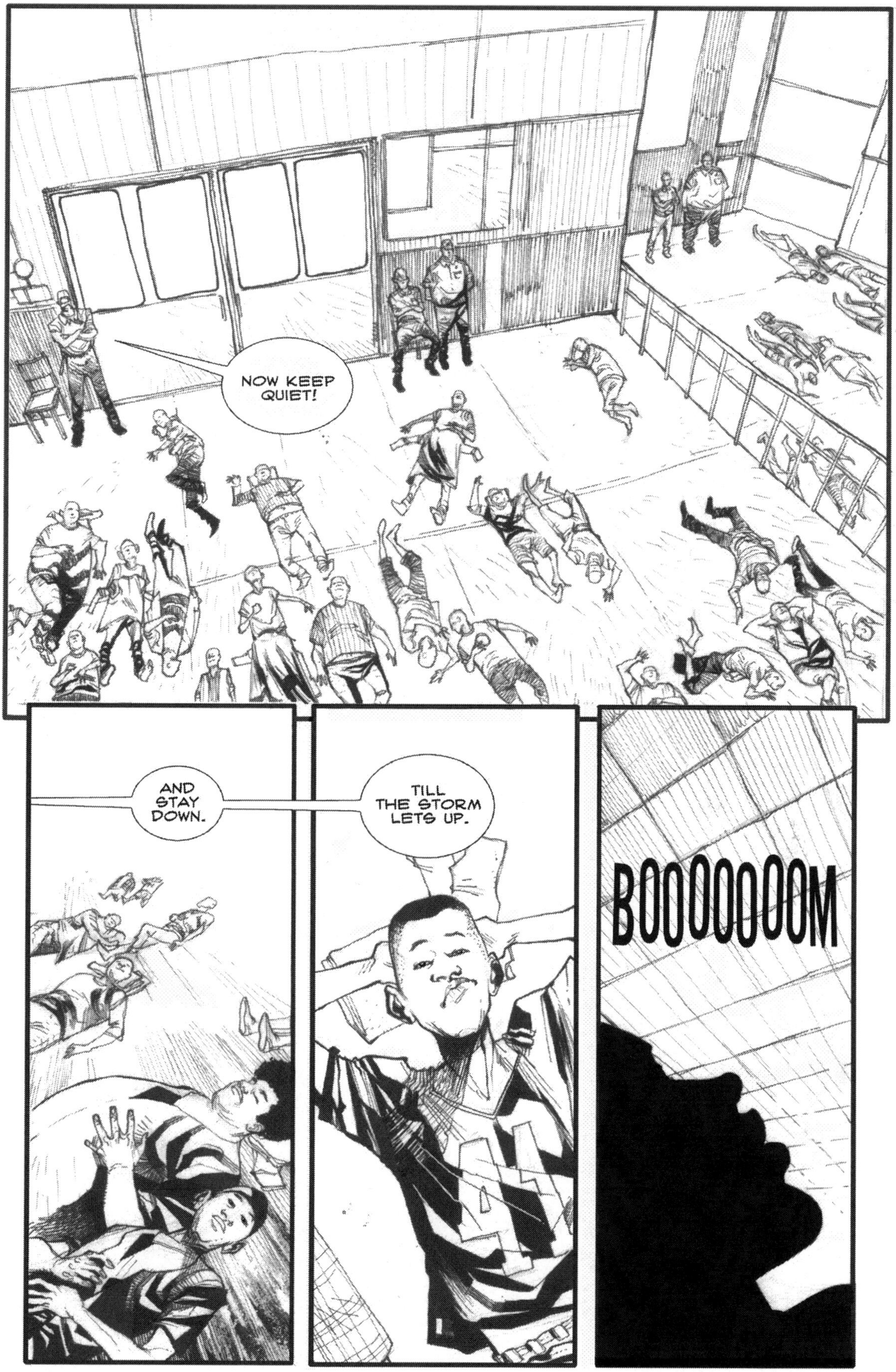
NOW KEEP QUIET!
AND STAY DOWN.
TILL THE STORM LETS UP.
BOOOOOOOM

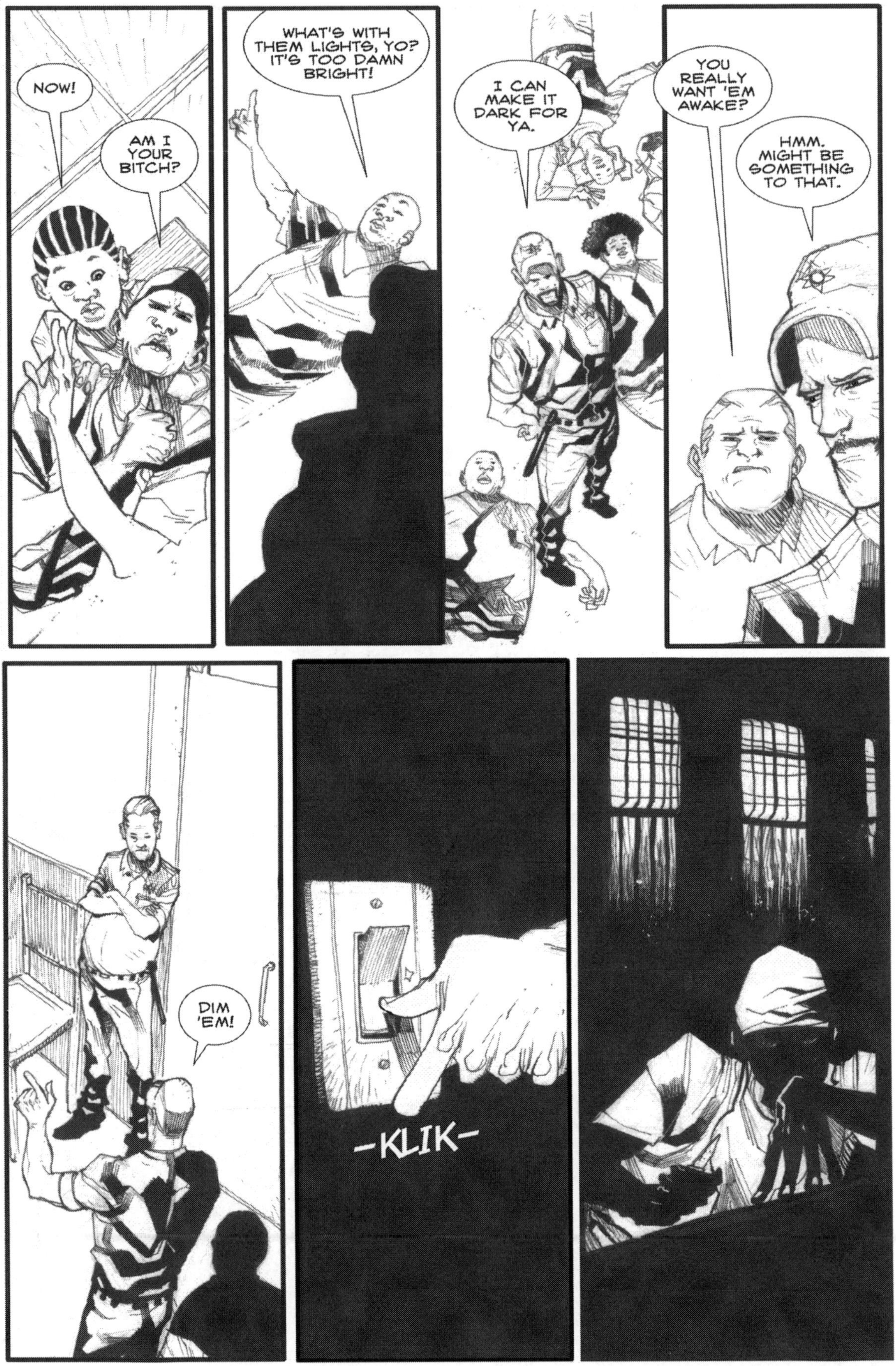
NOW!
AM I YOUR BITCH?
WHAT'S WITH THEM LIGHTS, YO? IT'S TOO DAMN BRIGHT!
I CAN MAKE IT DARK FOR YA.
YOU REALLY WANT 'EM AWAKE?
HMM. MIGHT BE SOMETHING TO THAT.
DIM 'EM!
-KLIK-

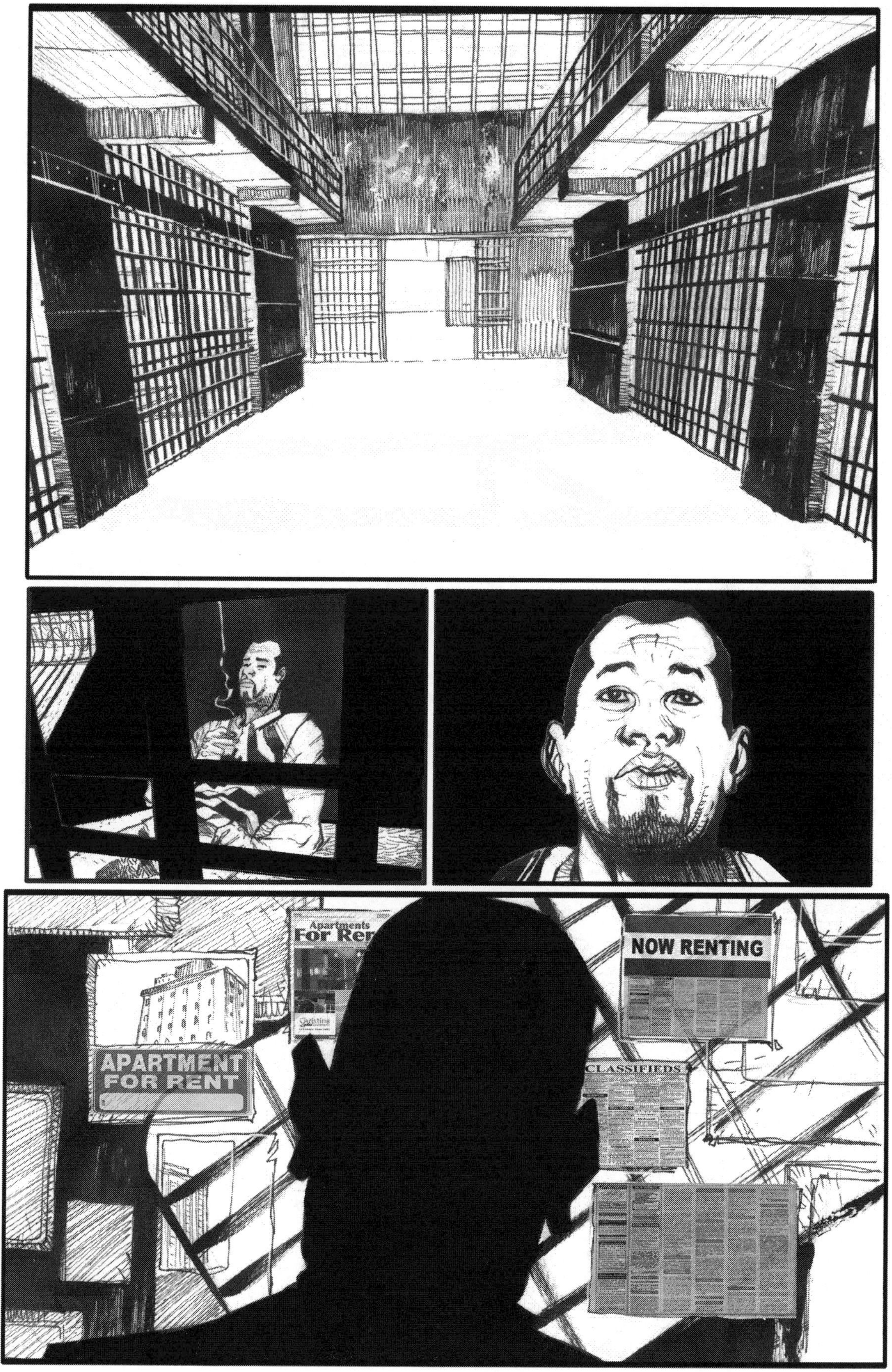

Apartments
NOW RENTING
APARTMENT FOR RENT
CLASSIFIEDS

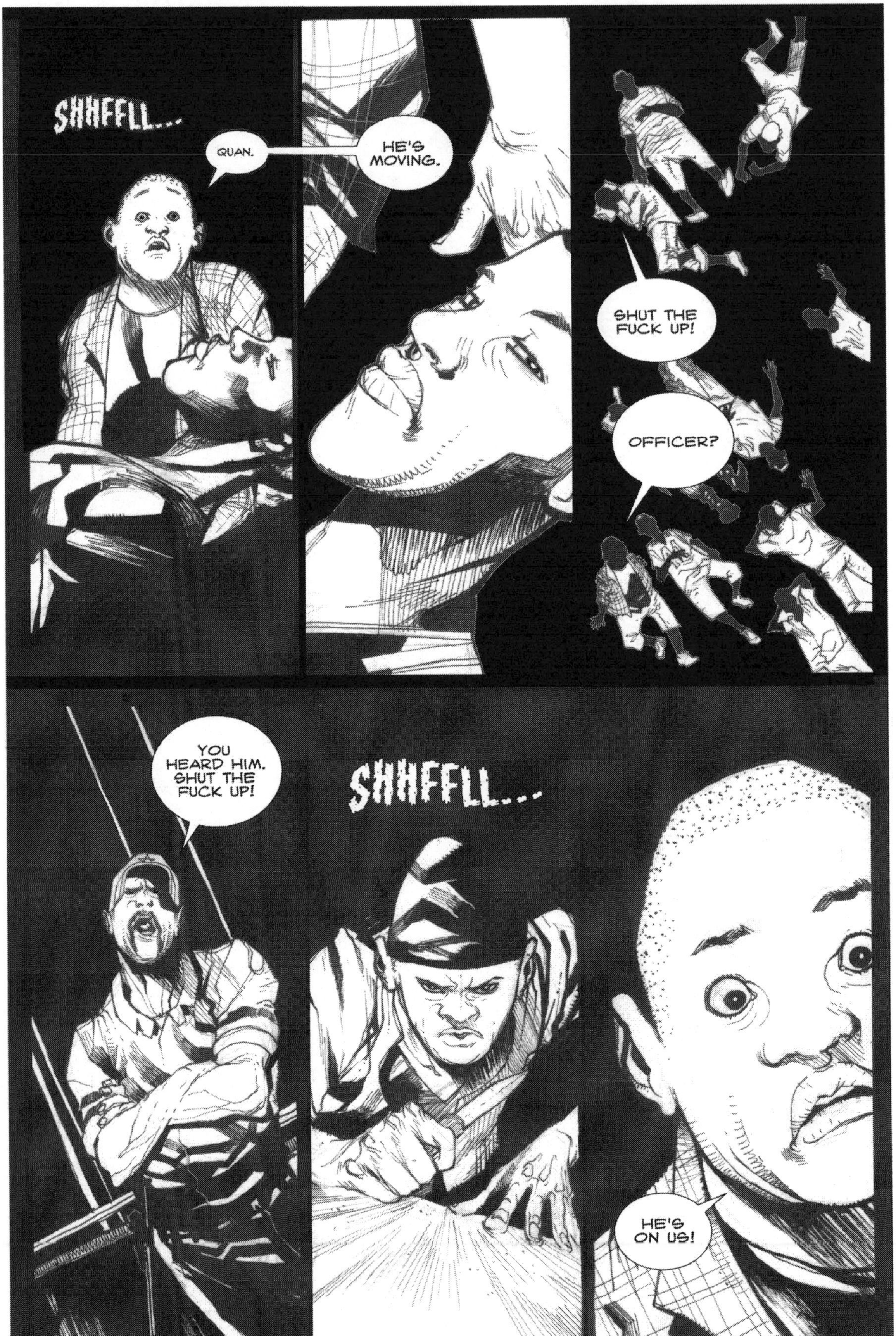
SHHFFLL...
QUAN.
HE'S MOVING.
SHUT THE FUCK UP!
OFFICER?
YOU HEARD HIM. SHUT THE FUCK UP!
SHHFFLL...
HE'S ON US!

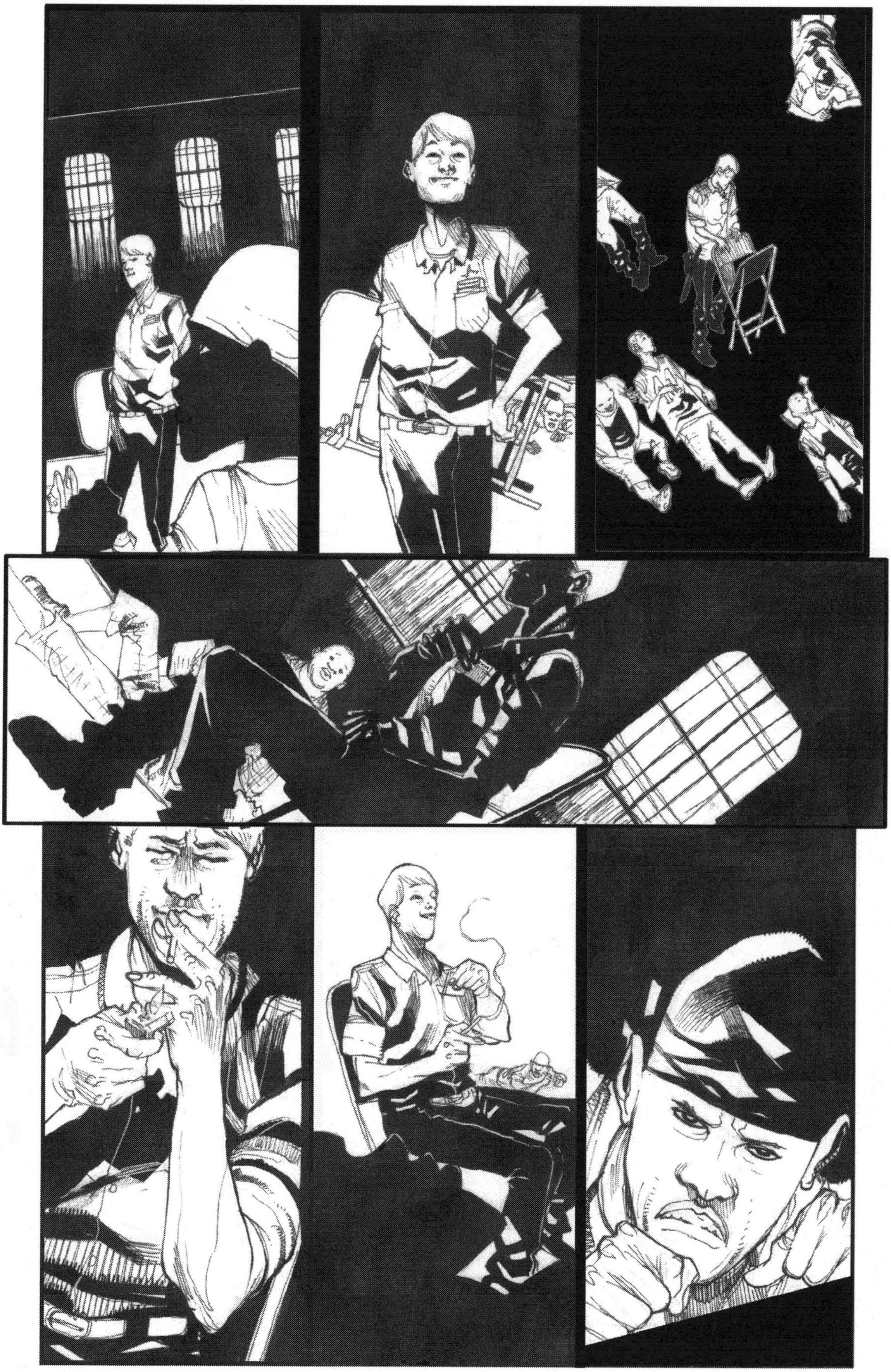

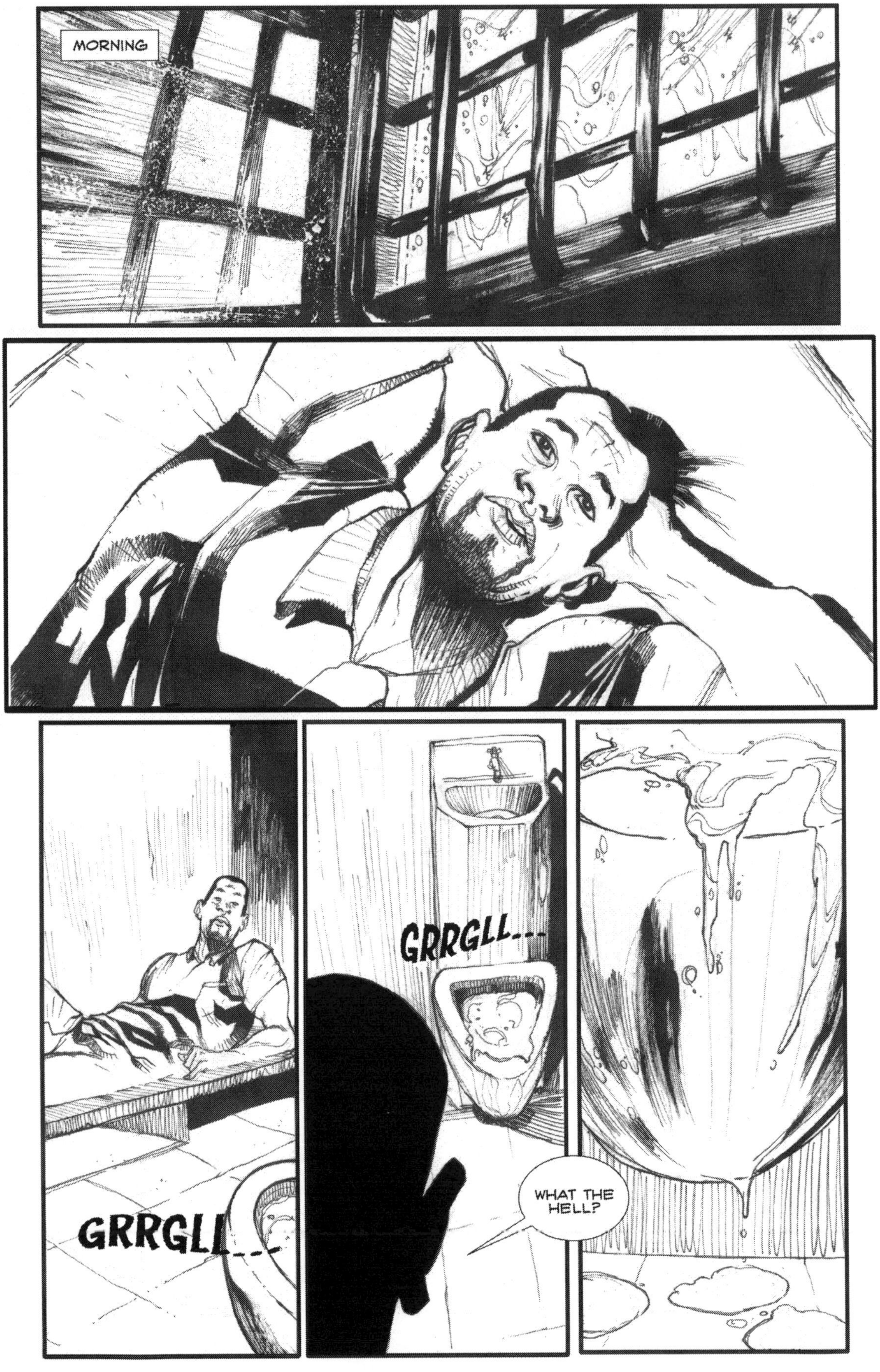
MORNING
GRRGLL...
GRRGLL...
WHAT THE HELL?

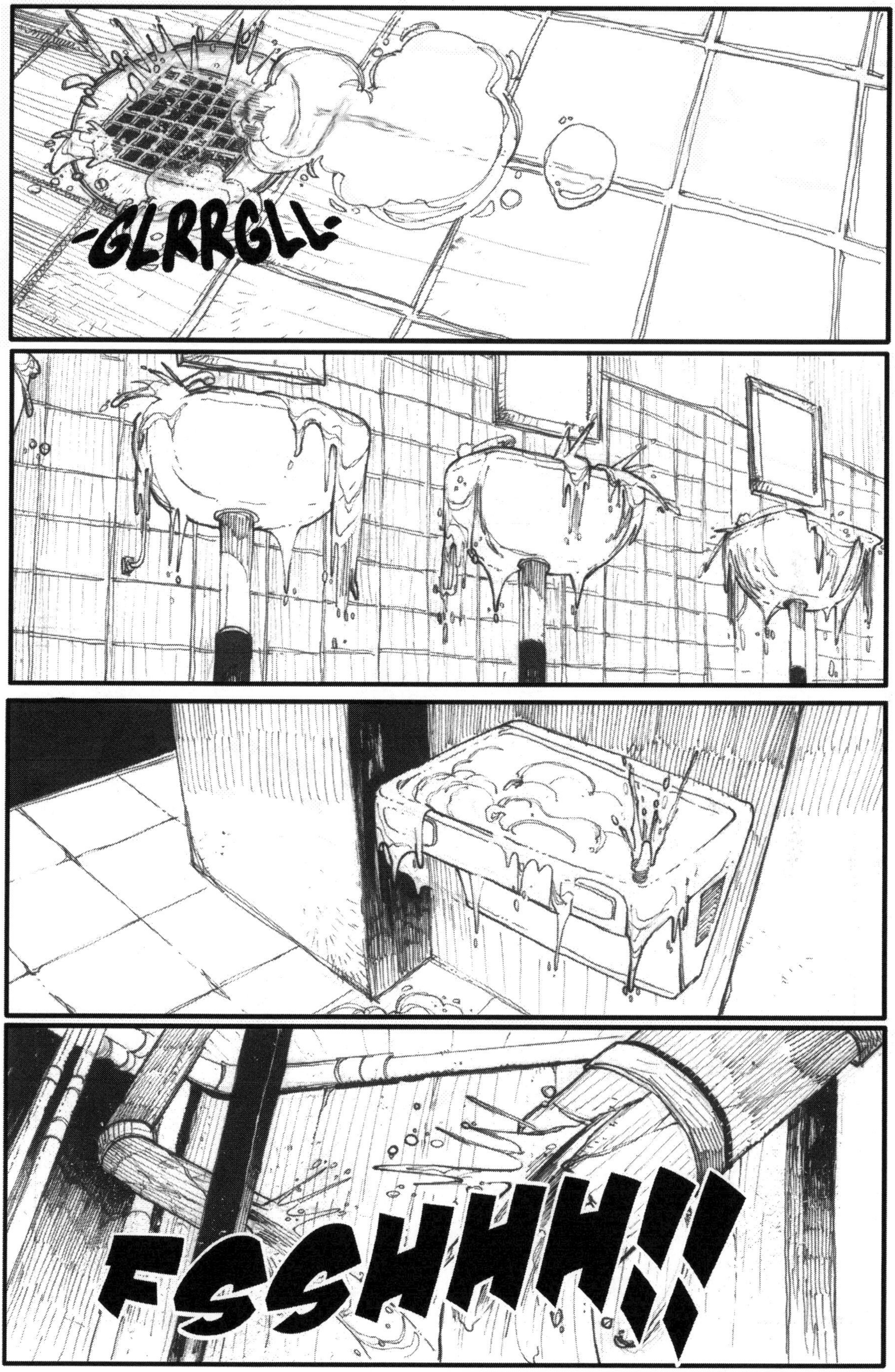
-GLRRGLL-
FSSHHH!!

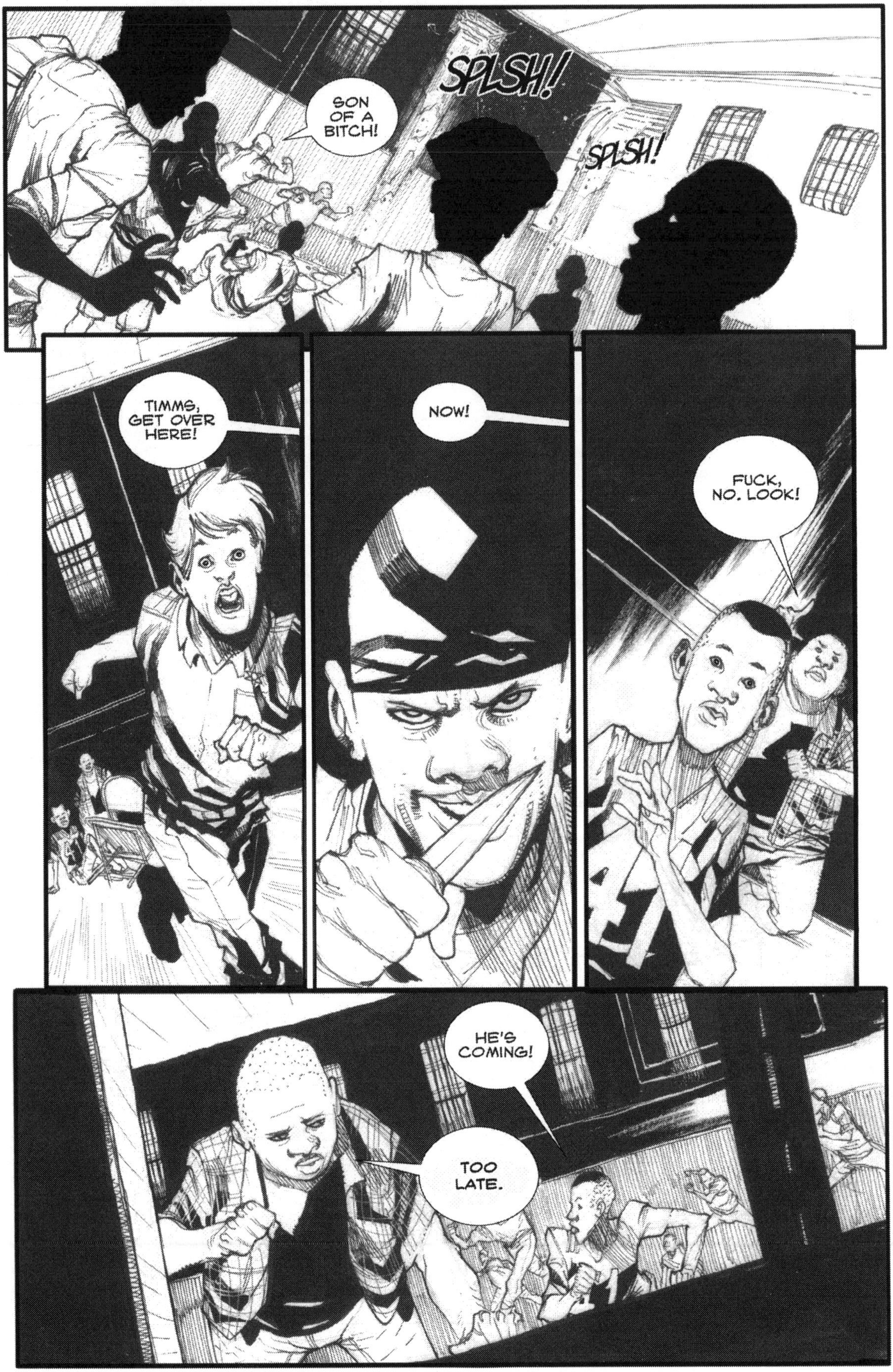
SON OF A BITCH!
SPLSH!
SPLSH!
TIMMS, GET OVER HERE!
NOW!
FUCK, NO. LOOK!
HE'S COMING!
TOO LATE.

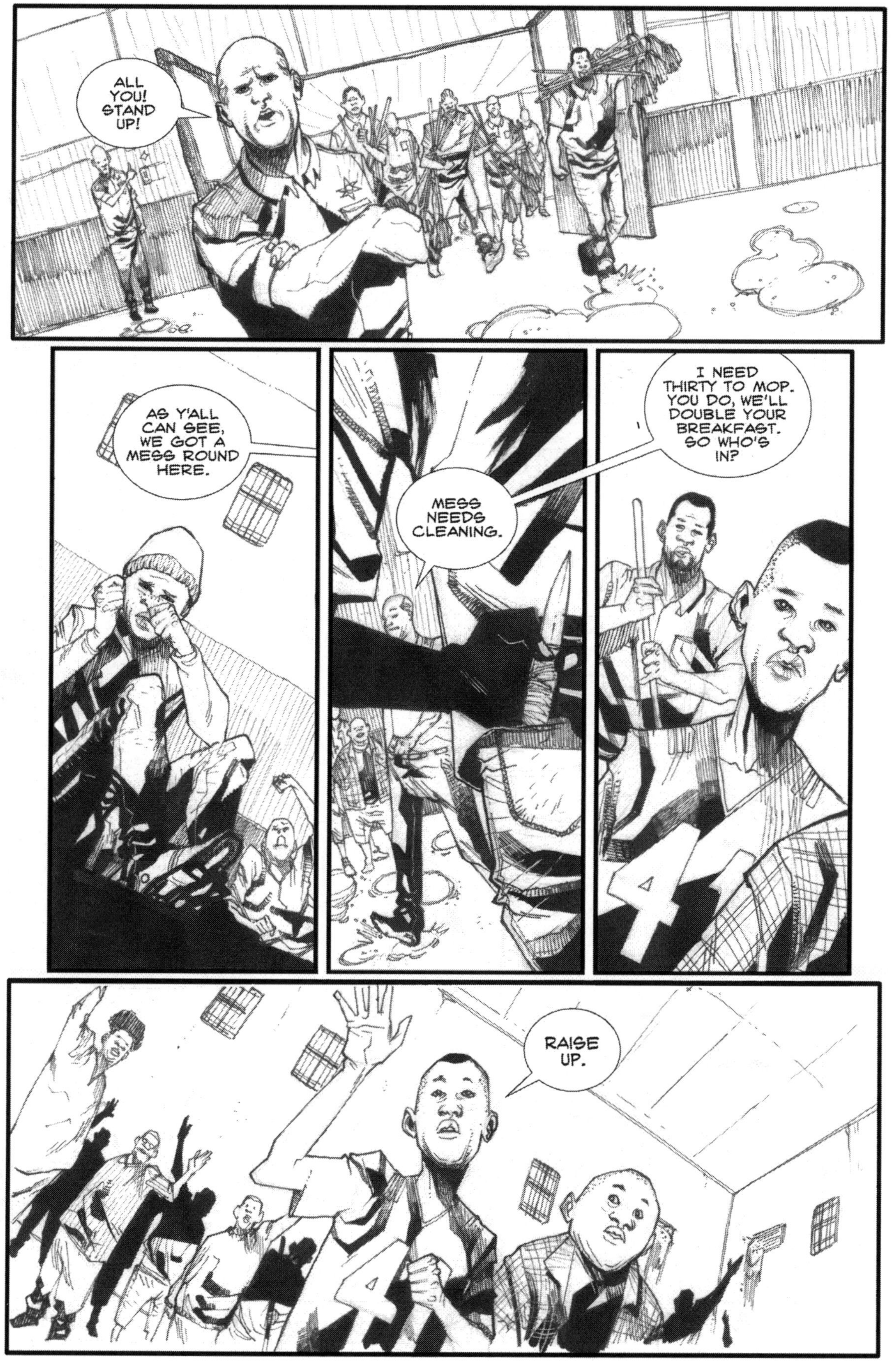
ALL YOU! STAND UP!
AS Y'ALL CAN SEE, WE GOT A MESS ROUND HERE.
MESS NEEDS CLEANING.
I NEED THIRTY TO MOP. YOU DO, WE'LL DOUBLE YOUR BREAKFAST. SO WHO'S IN?
RAISE UP.

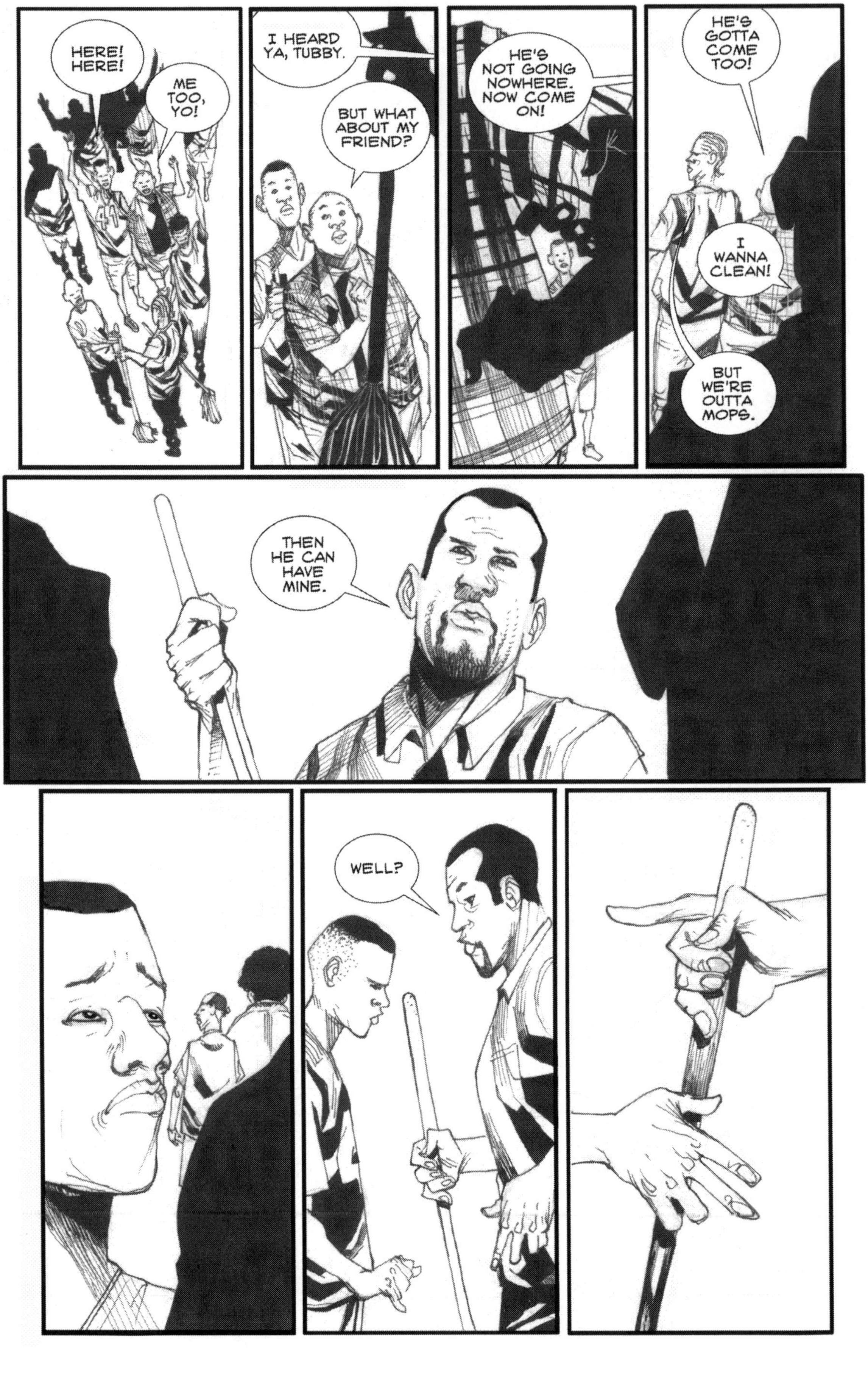
HERE! HERE!
ME TOO, YO!
I HEARD YA, TUBBY.
BUT WHAT ABOUT MY FRIEND?
HE'S NOT GOING NOWHERE. NOW COME ON!
HE'S GOTTA COME TOO!
I WANNA CLEAN!
BUT WE'RE OUTTA MOPS.
THEN HE CAN HAVE MINE.
WELL?

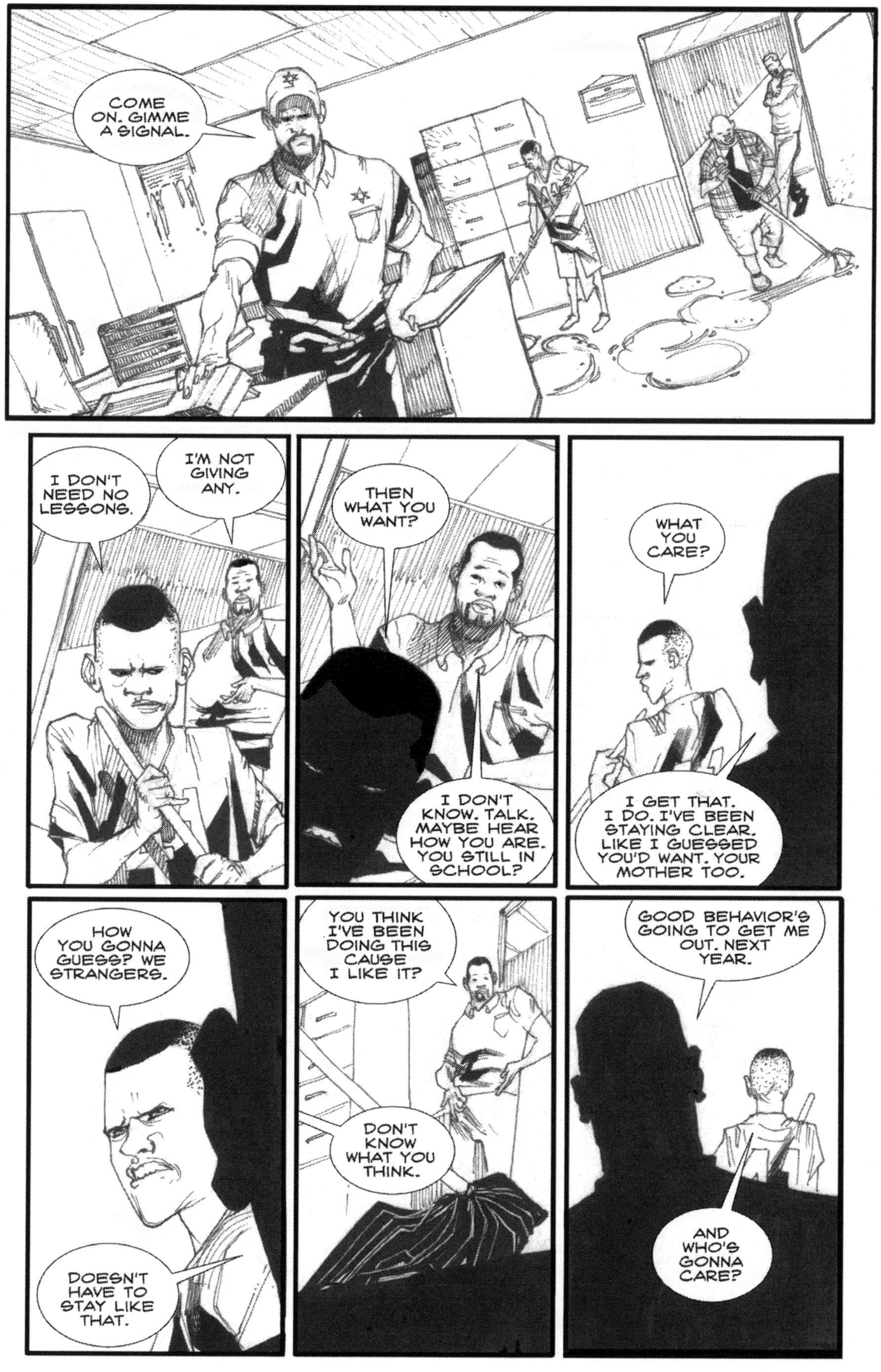
COME ON. GIMME A SIGNAL.
I DON'T NEED NO LESSONS.
I'M NOT GIVING ANY.
THEN WHAT YOU WANT?
I DON'T KNOW. TALK. MAYBE HEAR HOW YOU ARE. YOU STILL IN SCHOOL?
WHAT YOU CARE?
I GET THAT. I DO. I'VE BEEN STAYING CLEAR. LIKE I GUESSED YOU'D WANT. YOUR MOTHER TOO.
HOW YOU GONNA GUESS? WE STRANGERS.
DOESN'T HAVE TO STAY LIKE THAT.
YOU THINK I'VE BEEN DOING THIS CAUSE I LIKE IT?
DON'T KNOW WHAT YOU THINK.
GOOD BEHAVIOR'S GOING TO GET ME OUT. NEXT YEAR.
AND WHO'S GONNA CARE?

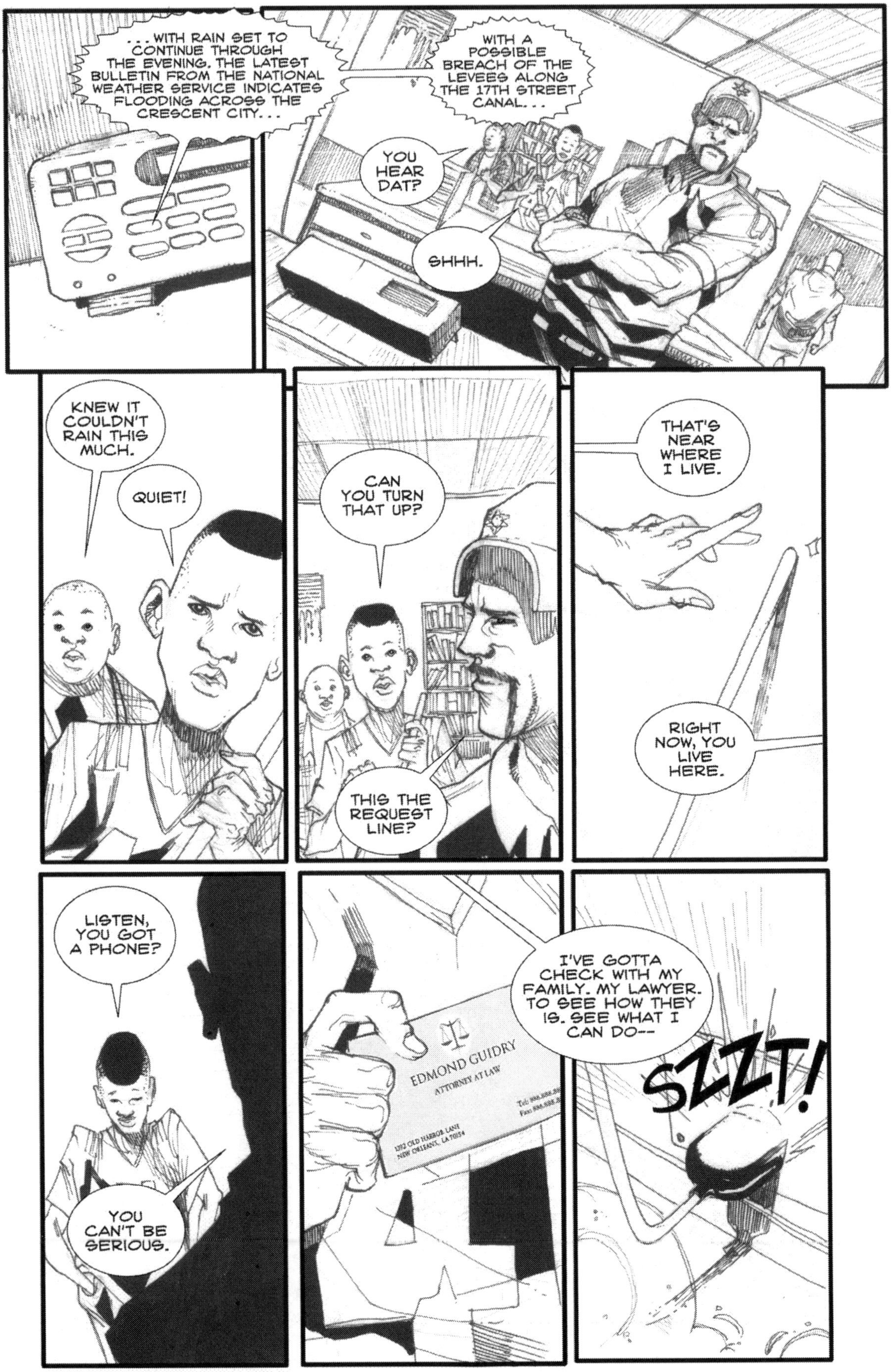
...WITH RAIN SET TO CONTINUE THROUGH THE EVENING. THE LATEST BULLETIN FROM THE NATIONAL WEATHER SERVICE INDICATES FLOODING ACROSS THE CRESCENT CITY...
WITH A POSSIBLE BREACH OF THE LEVEES ALONG THE 17TH STREET CANAL...
YOU HEAR DAT?
SHHH.
KNEW IT COULDN'T RAIN THIS MUCH.
QUIET!
CAN YOU TURN THAT UP?
THIS THE REQUEST LINE?
THAT'S NEAR WHERE I LIVE.
RIGHT NOW, YOU LIVE HERE.
LISTEN, YOU GOT A PHONE?
YOU CAN'T BE SERIOUS.
EDMOND GUIDRY
ATTORNEY AT LAW
I'VE GOTTA CHECK WITH MY FAMILY. MY LAWYER. TO SEE HOW THEY IS. SEE WHAT I CAN DO--
SZZT!

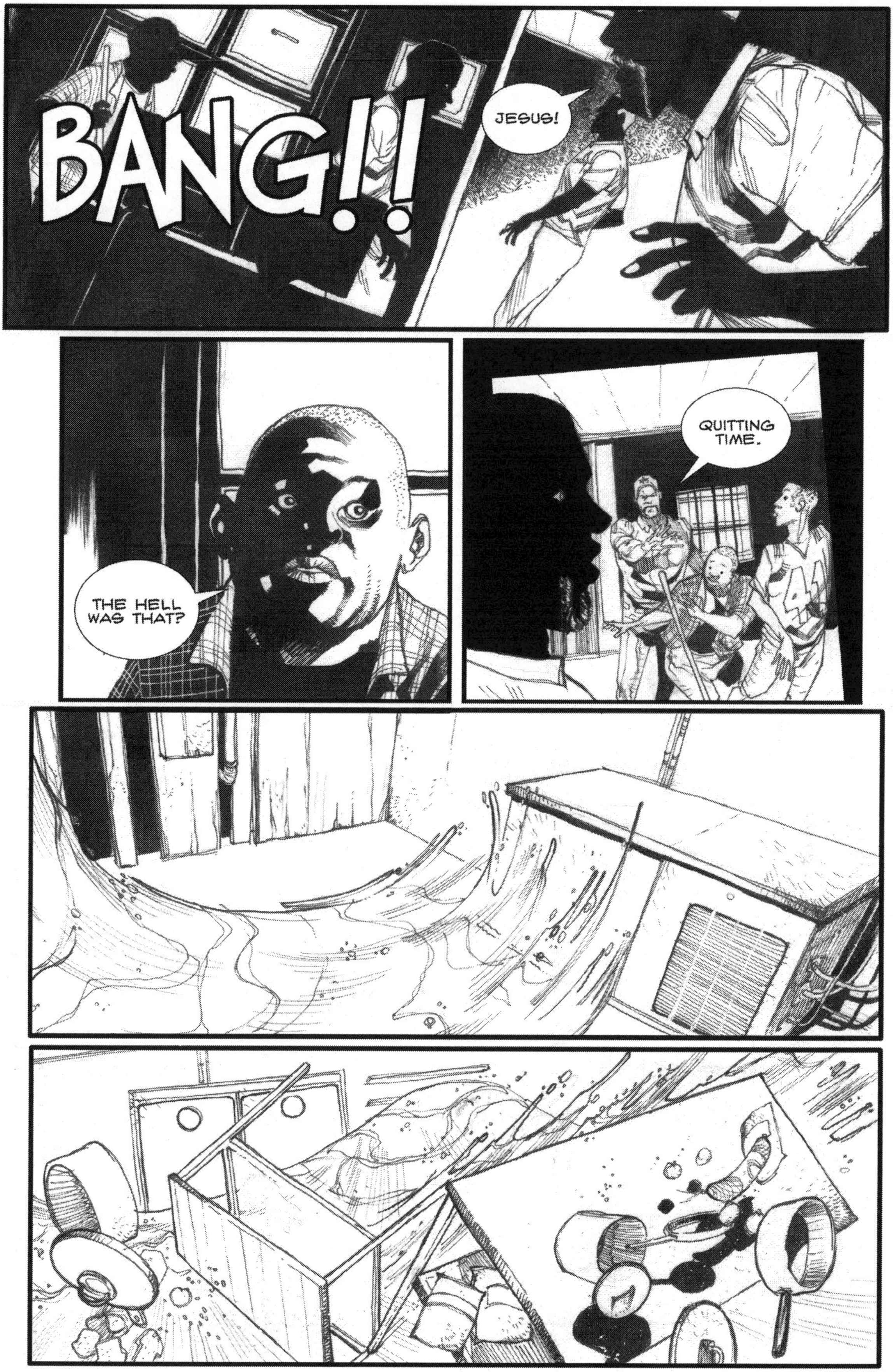
BANG!!
JESUS!
THE HELL WAS THAT?
QUITTING TIME.

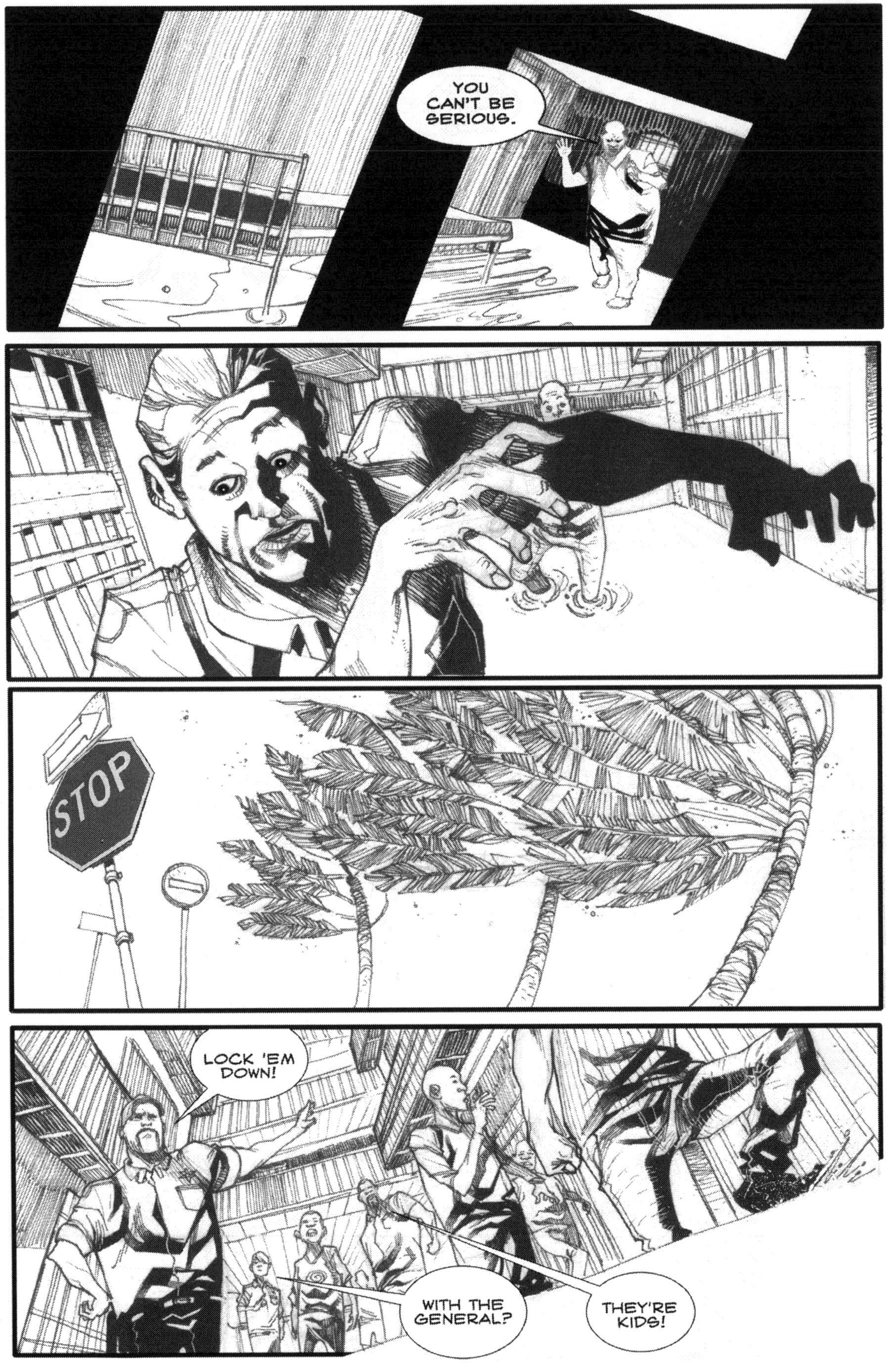
YOU CAN'T BE SERIOUS.
STOP
LOCK 'EM DOWN!
WITH THE GENERAL?
THEY'RE KIDS!

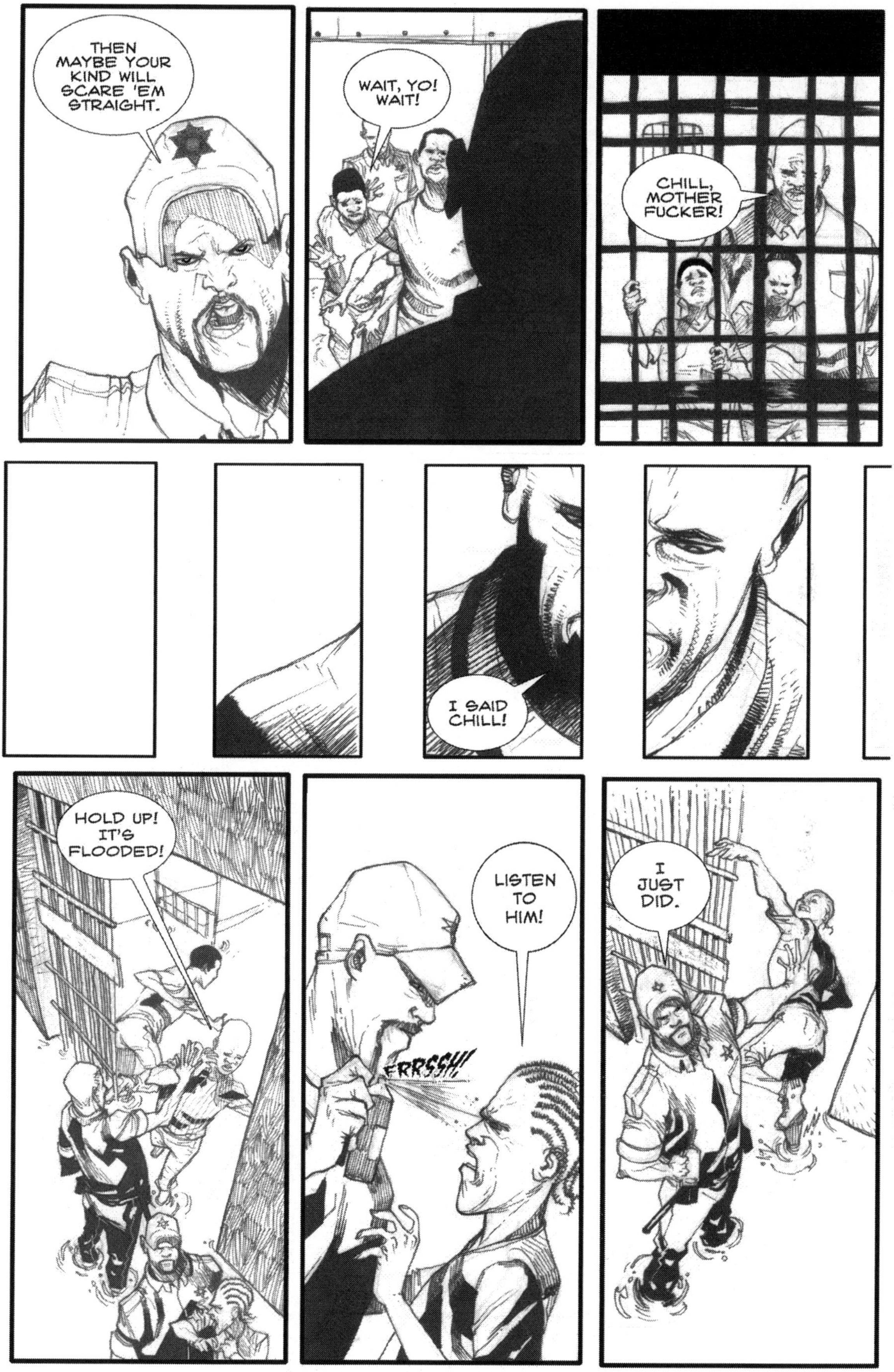
THEN MAYBE YOUR KIND WILL SCARE 'EM STRAIGHT.
WAIT, YO! WAIT!
CHILL, MOTHER FUCKER!
I SAID CHILL!
HOLD UP! IT'S FLOODED!
LISTEN TO HIM!
FRRSSH!!
I JUST DID.

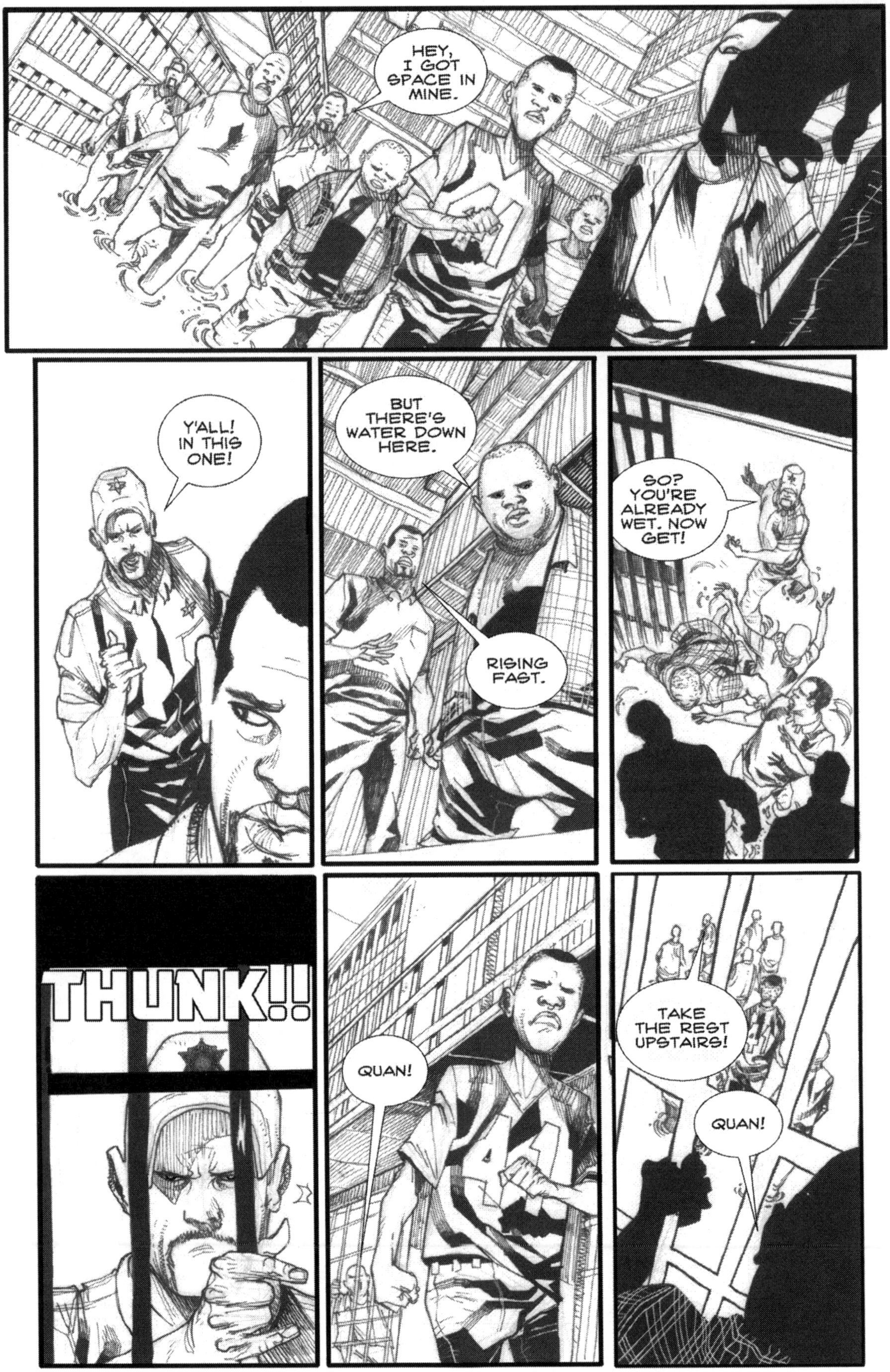
HEY, I GOT SPACE IN MINE.
Y'ALL! IN THIS ONE!
BUT THERE'S WATER DOWN HERE.
RISING FAST.
SO? YOU'RE ALREADY WET. NOW GET!
THUNK!!
QUAN!
TAKE THE REST UPSTAIRS!
QUAN!

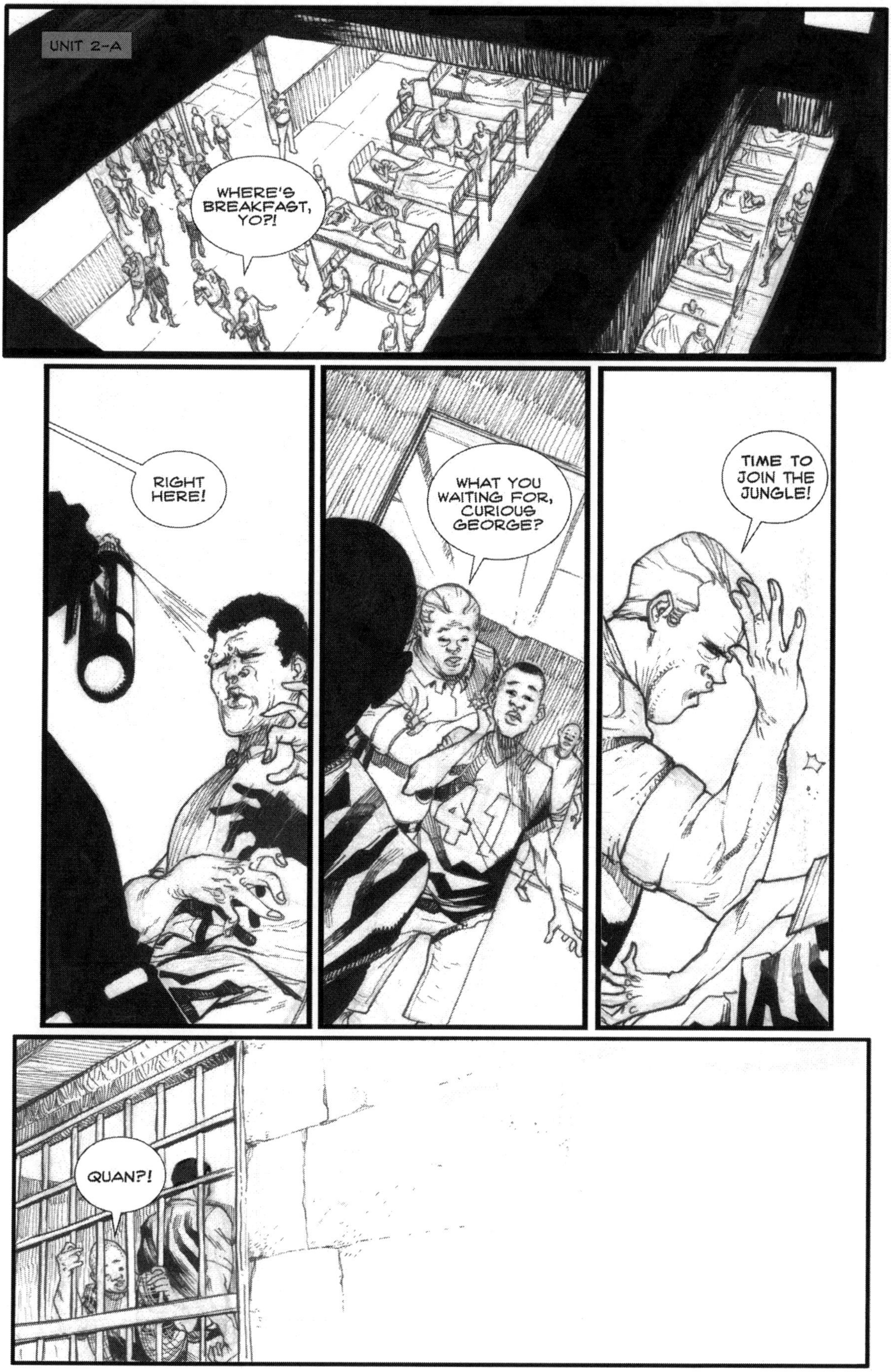
UNIT 2-A
WHERE'S BREAKFAST, YO?!
RIGHT HERE!
WHAT YOU WAITING FOR, CURIOUS GEORGE?
TIME TO JOIN THE JUNGLE!
QUAN?!

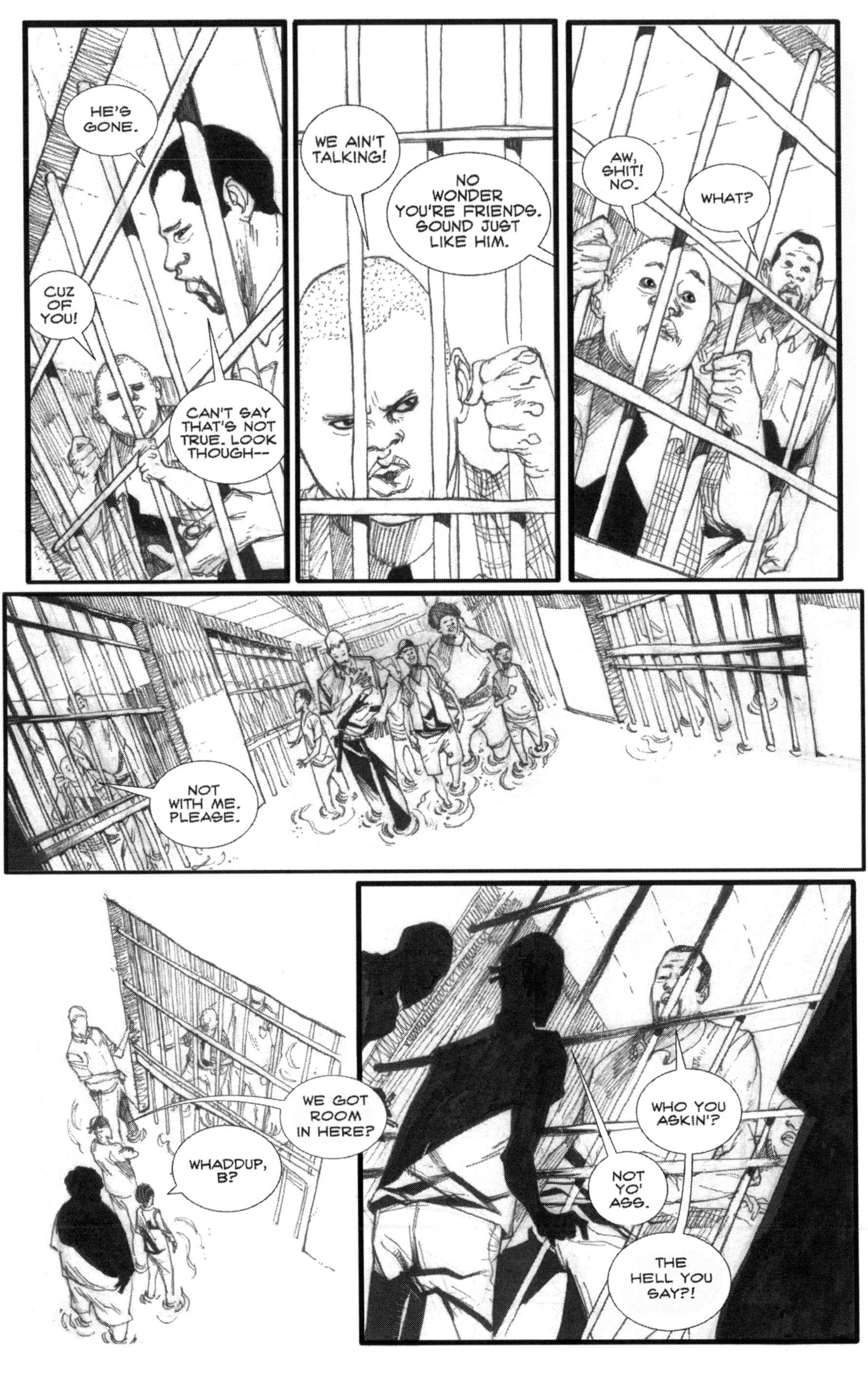
HE'S GONE.
CUZ OF YOU!
CAN'T SAY THAT'S NOT TRUE. LOOK THOUGH--
WE AIN'T TALKING!
NO WONDER YOU'RE FRIENDS. SOUND JUST LIKE HIM.
AW, SHIT! NO.
WHAT?
NOT WITH ME. PLEASE.
WHADDUP, B?
WE GOT ROOM IN HERE?
WHO YOU ASKIN'?
NOT YO' ASS.
THE HELL YOU SAY?!

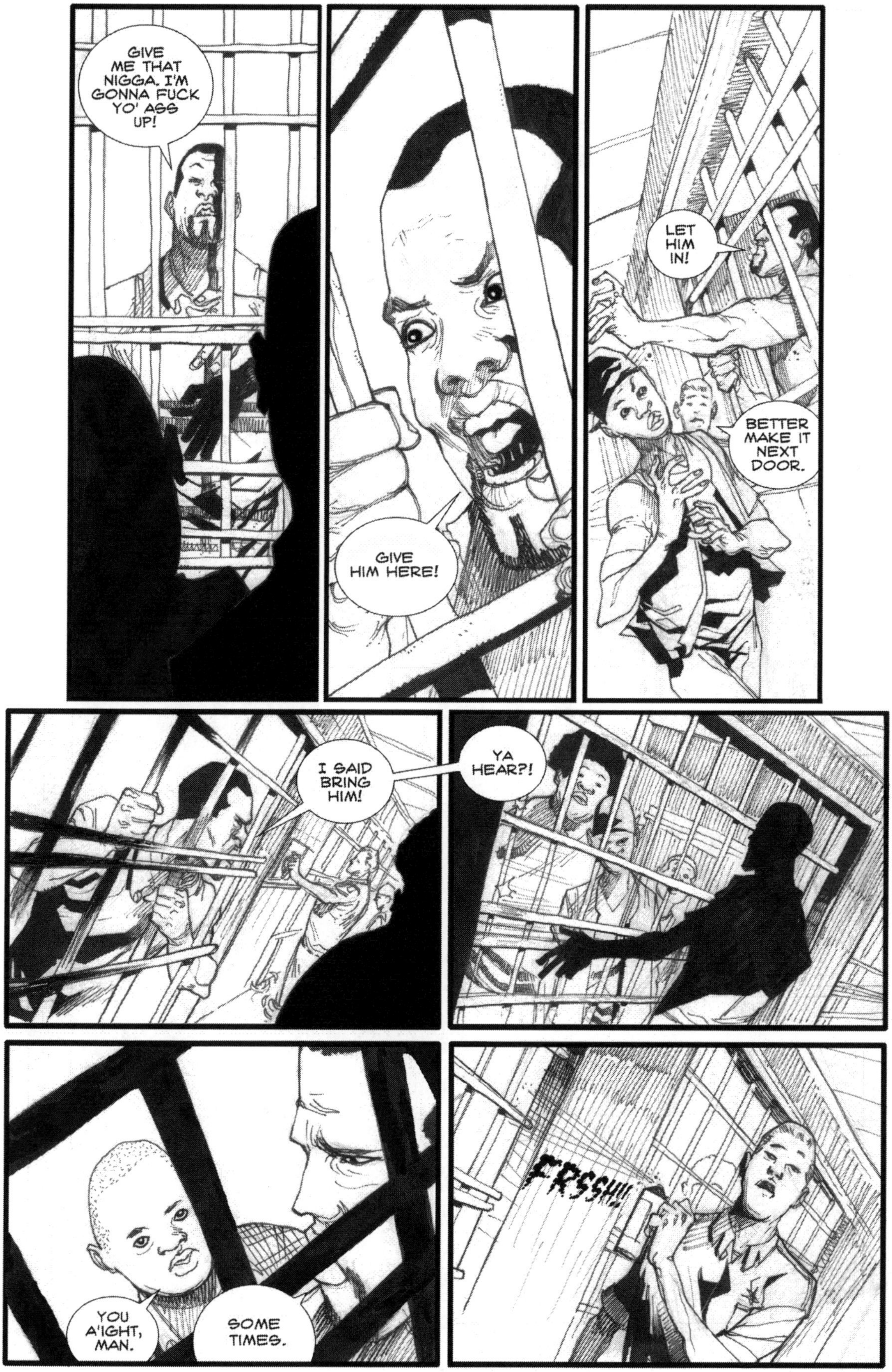
GIVE ME THAT NIGGA. I'M GONNA FUCK YO' ASS UP!
GIVE HIM HERE!
LET HIM IN!
BETTER MAKE IT NEXT DOOR.
I SAID BRING HIM!
YA HEAR?!
YOU A'IGHT, MAN.
SOME TIMES.
FRSSH!!

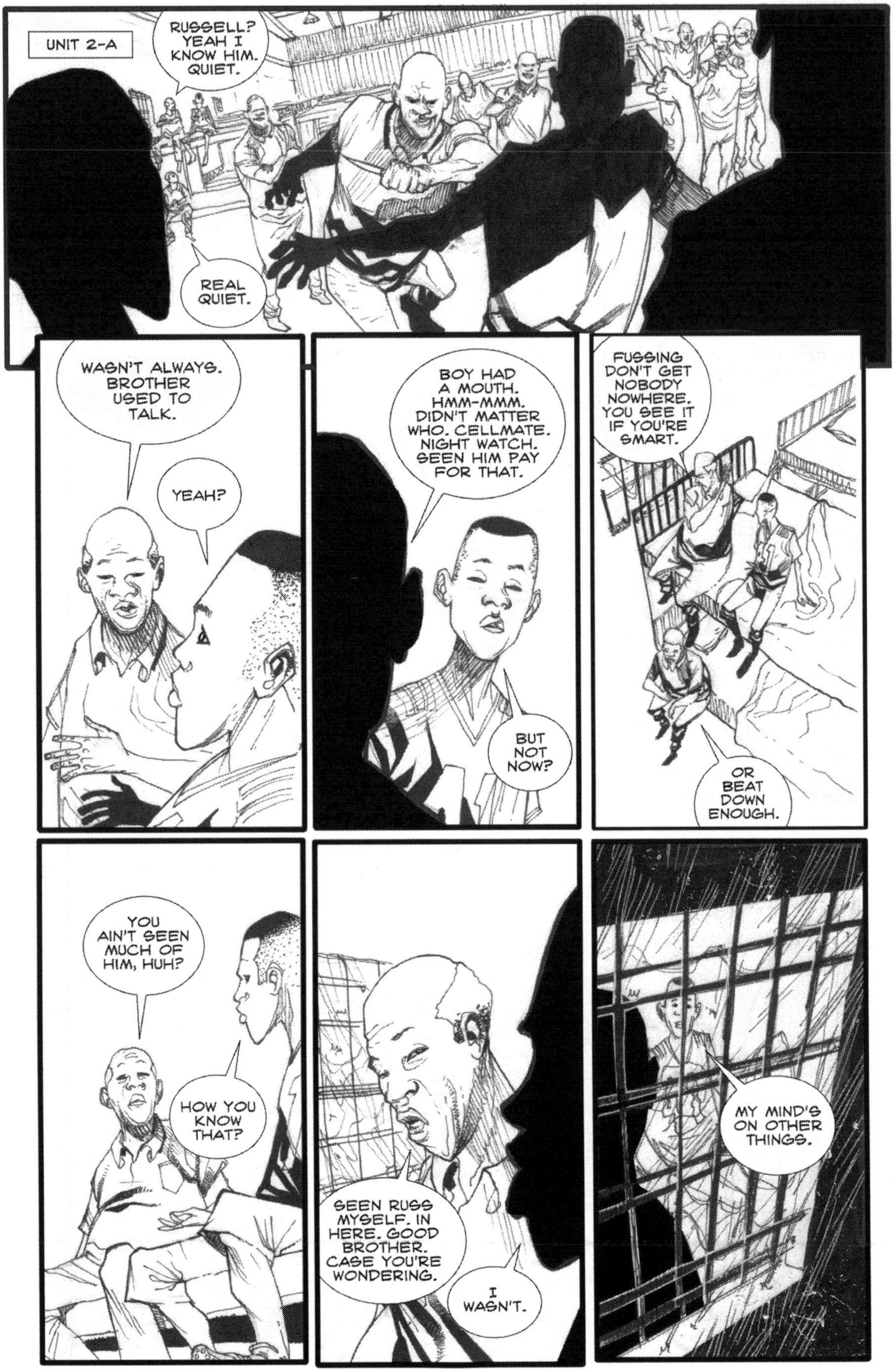
UNIT 2-A
RUSSELL? YEAH I KNOW HIM. QUIET.
REAL QUIET.
WASN'T ALWAYS. BROTHER USED TO TALK.
YEAH?
BOY HAD A MOUTH. HMM-MMM. DIDN'T MATTER WHO. CELLMATE. NIGHT WATCH. SEEN HIM PAY FOR THAT.
BUT NOT NOW?
FUSSING DON'T GET NOBODY NOWHERE. YOU SEE IT IF YOU'RE SMART.
OR BEAT DOWN ENOUGH.
YOU AIN'T SEEN MUCH OF HIM, HUH?
HOW YOU KNOW THAT?
SEEN RUSS MYSELF. IN HERE. GOOD BROTHER. CASE YOU'RE WONDERING.
I WASN'T.
MY MIND'S ON OTHER THINGS.

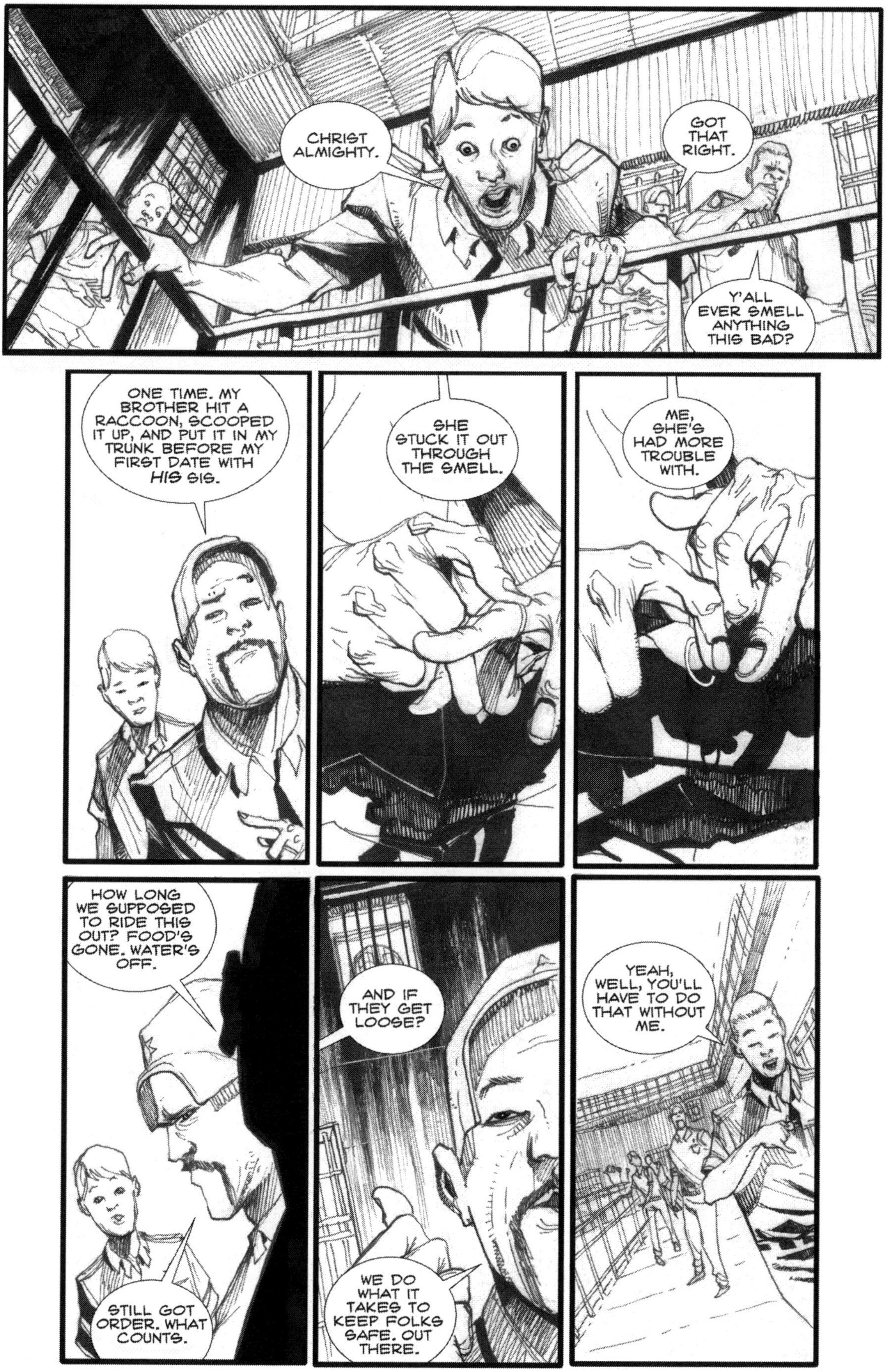
CHRIST ALMIGHTY.
GOT THAT RIGHT.
Y'ALL EVER SMELL ANYTHING THIS BAD?
ONE TIME. MY BROTHER HIT A RACCOON, SCOOPED IT UP, AND PUT IT IN MY TRUNK BEFORE MY FIRST DATE WITH HIS SIS.
SHE STUCK IT OUT THROUGH THE SMELL.
ME, SHE'S HAD MORE TROUBLE WITH.
HOW LONG WE SUPPOSED TO RIDE THIS OUT? FOOD'S GONE. WATER'S OFF.
STILL GOT ORDER. WHAT COUNTS.
AND IF THEY GET LOOSE?
WE DO WHAT IT TAKES TO KEEP FOLKS SAFE. OUT THERE.
YEAH, WELL, YOU'LL HAVE TO DO THAT WITHOUT ME.

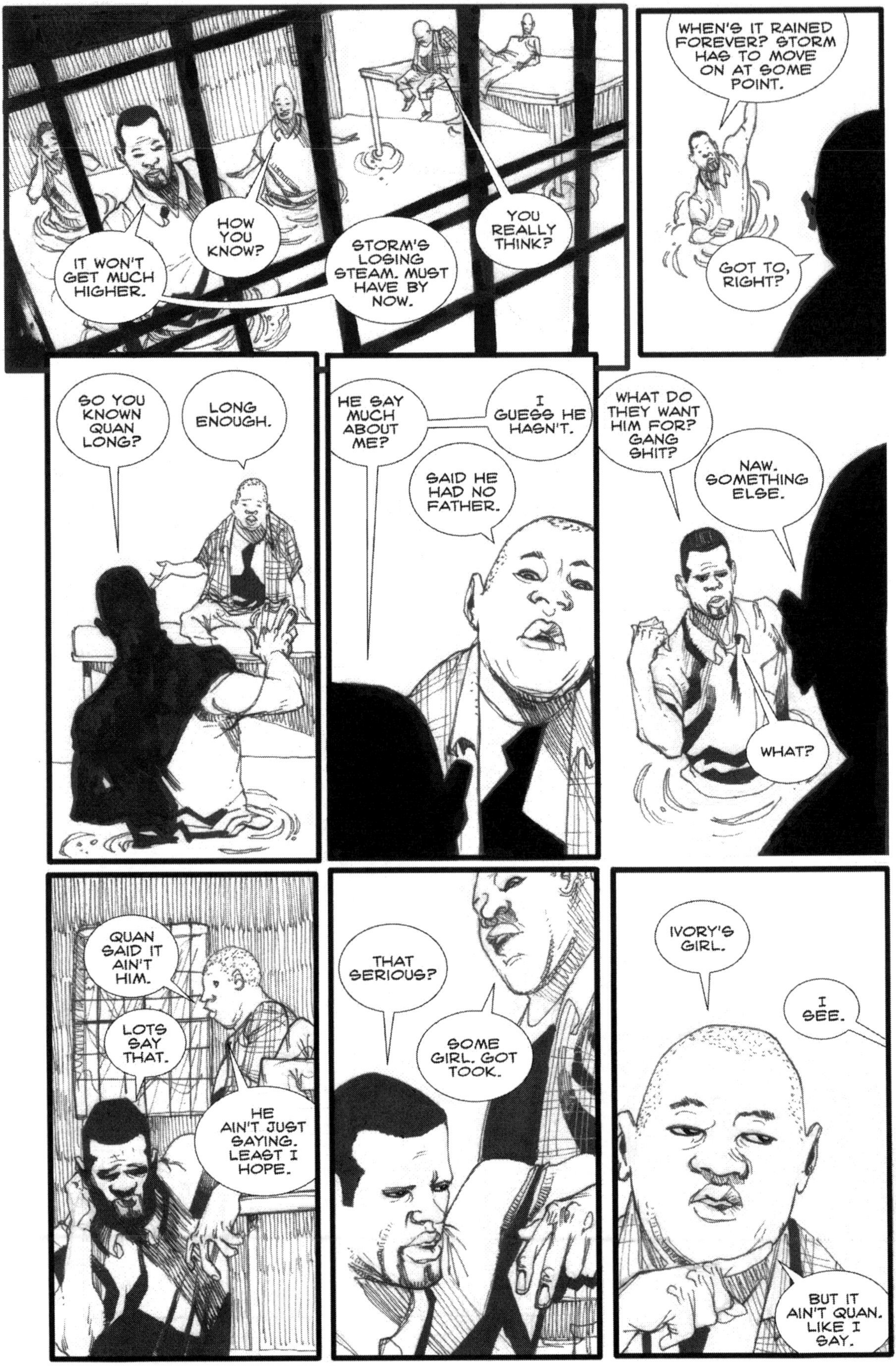
IT WON'T GET MUCH HIGHER.
HOW YOU KNOW?
STORM'S LOSING STEAM. MUST HAVE BY NOW.
YOU REALLY THINK?
WHEN'S IT RAINED FOREVER? STORM HAS TO MOVE ON AT SOME POINT.
GOT TO, RIGHT?
SO YOU KNOWN QUAN LONG?
LONG ENOUGH.
HE SAY MUCH ABOUT ME?
I GUESS HE HASN'T.
SAID HE HAD NO FATHER.
WHAT DO THEY WANT HIM FOR? GANG SHIT?
NAW. SOMETHING ELSE.
WHAT?
QUAN SAID IT AIN'T HIM.
LOTS SAY THAT.
HE AIN'T JUST SAYING. LEAST I HOPE.
THAT SERIOUS?
SOME GIRL. GOT TOOK.
IVORY'S GIRL.
I SEE.
BUT IT AIN'T QUAN. LIKE I SAY.

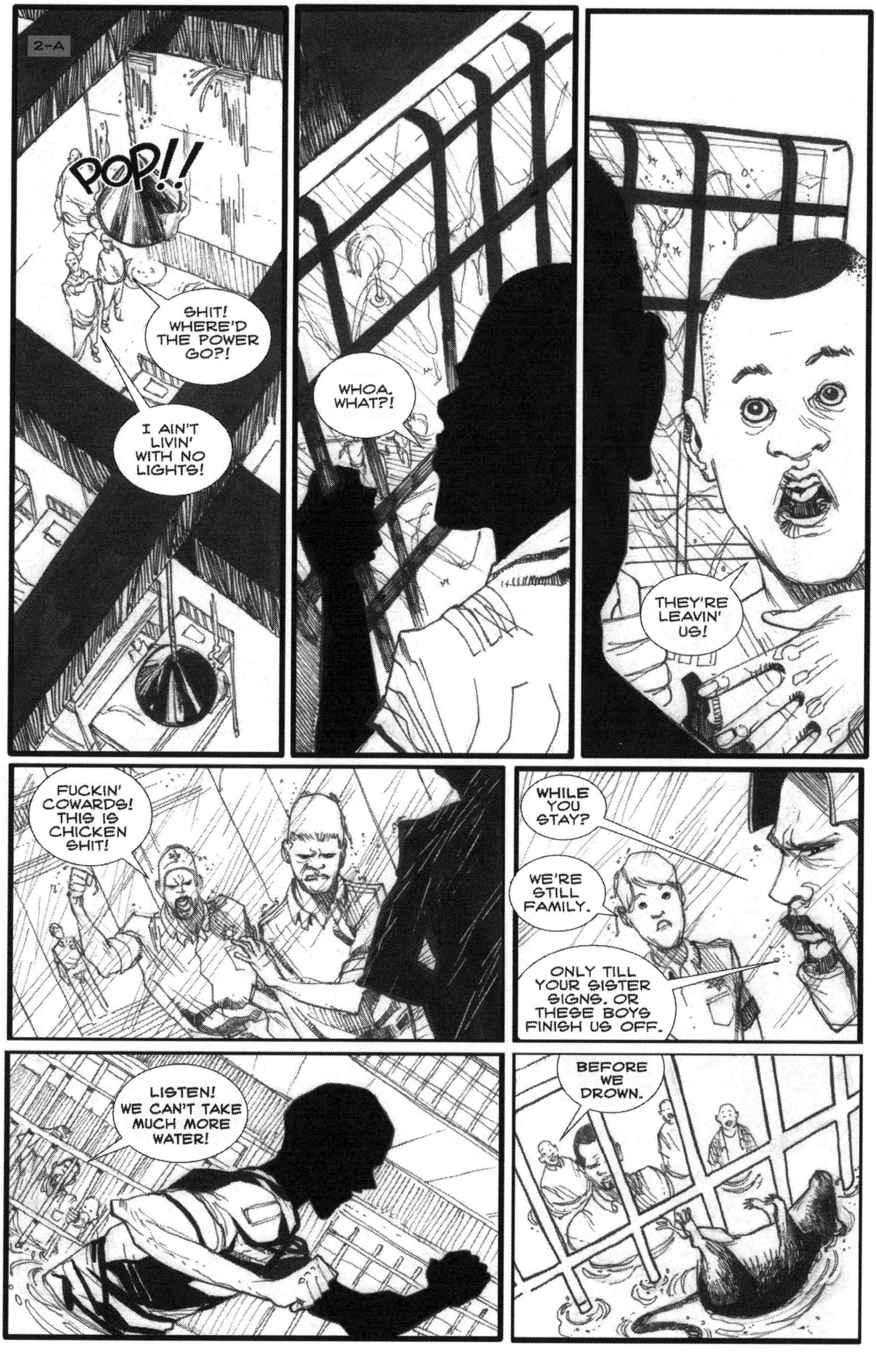
2-A
POP!!
SHIT! WHERE'D THE POWER GO?!
I AIN'T LIVIN' WITH NO LIGHTS!
WHOA. WHAT?!
THEY'RE LEAVIN' US!
FUCKIN' COWARDS! THIS IS CHICKEN SHIT!
WHILE YOU STAY?
WE'RE STILL FAMILY.
ONLY TILL YOUR SISTER SIGNS. OR THESE BOYS FINISH US OFF.
LISTEN! WE CAN'T TAKE MUCH MORE WATER!
BEFORE WE DROWN.

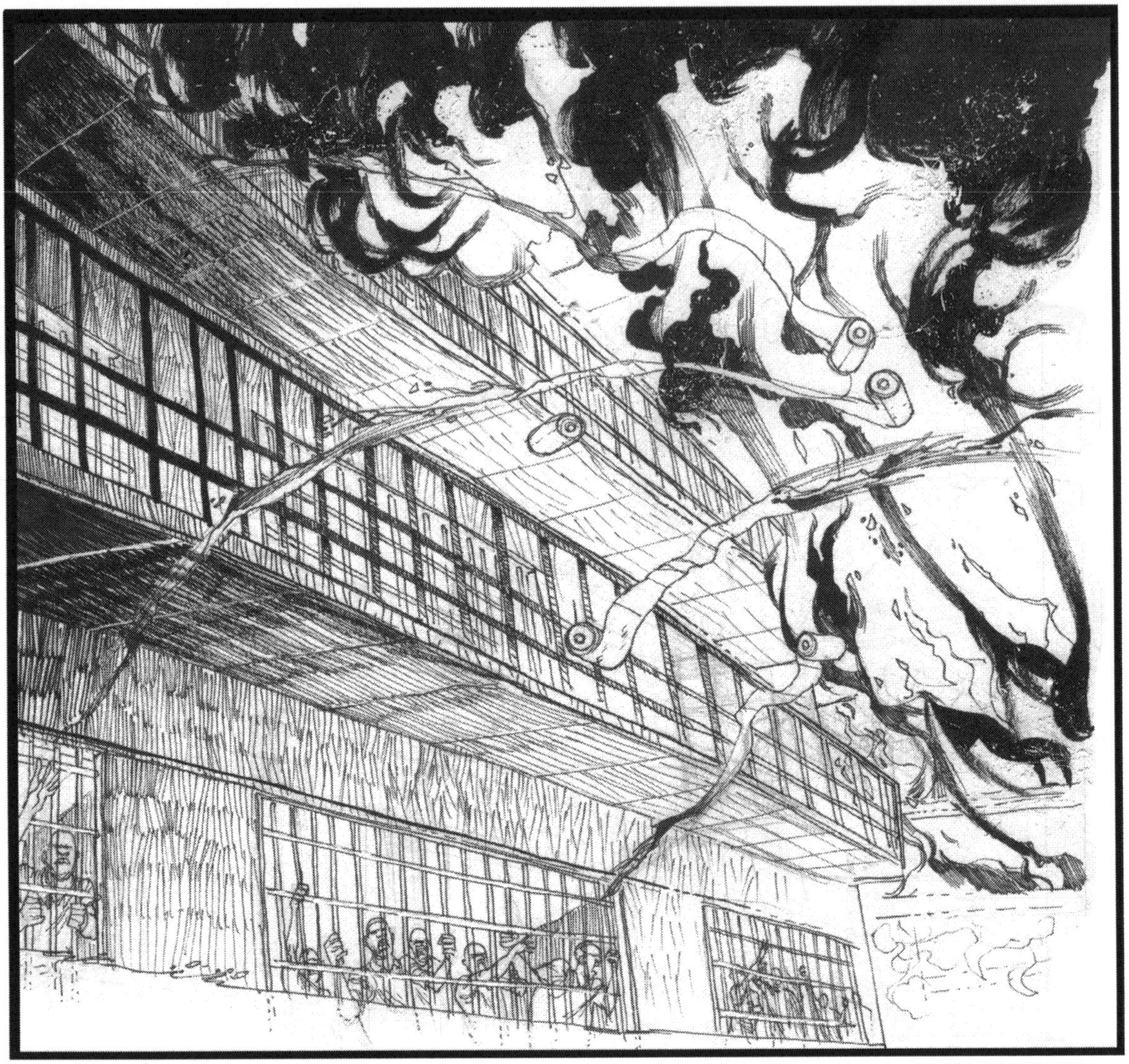

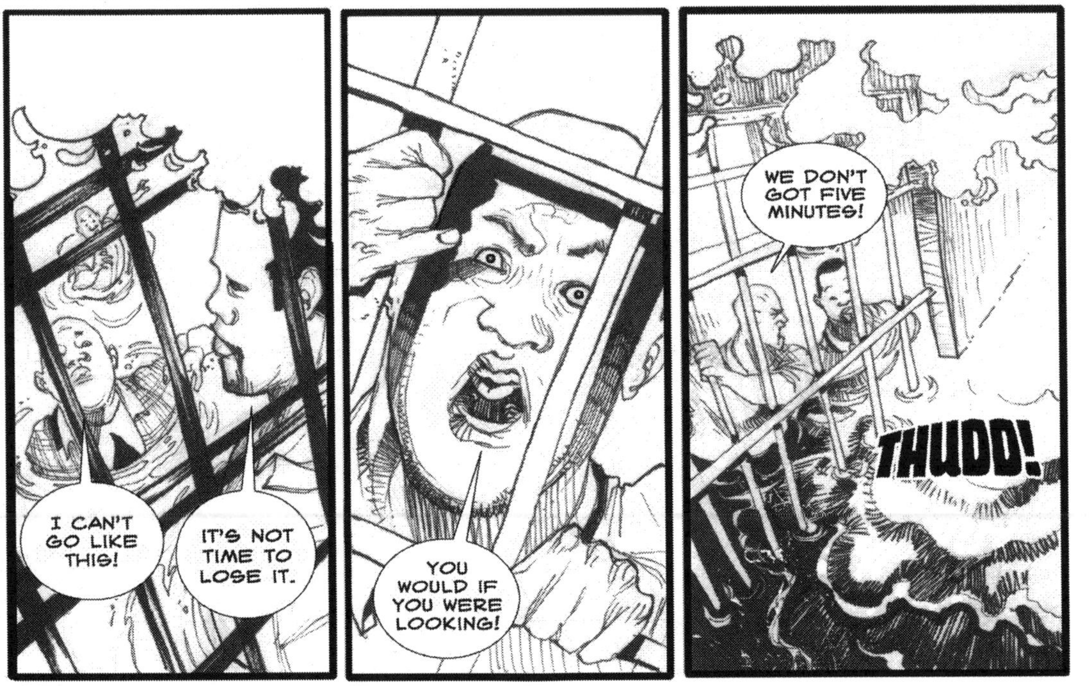
I CAN'T GO LIKE THIS!
IT'S NOT TIME TO LOSE IT.
YOU WOULD IF YOU WERE LOOKING!
WE DON'T GOT FIVE MINUTES!
THUDD!

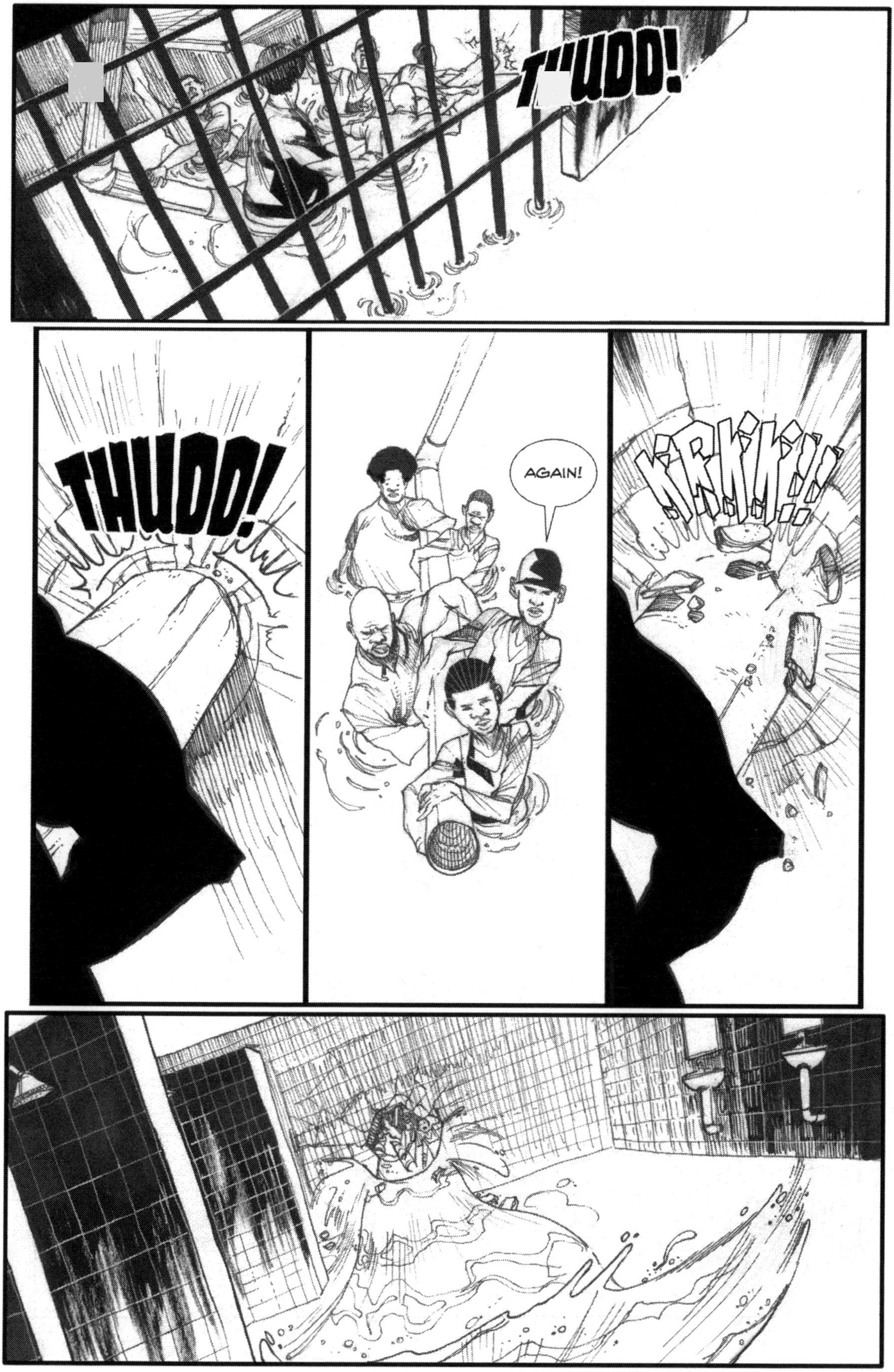
THUDD!
AGAIN!
KRKK!!

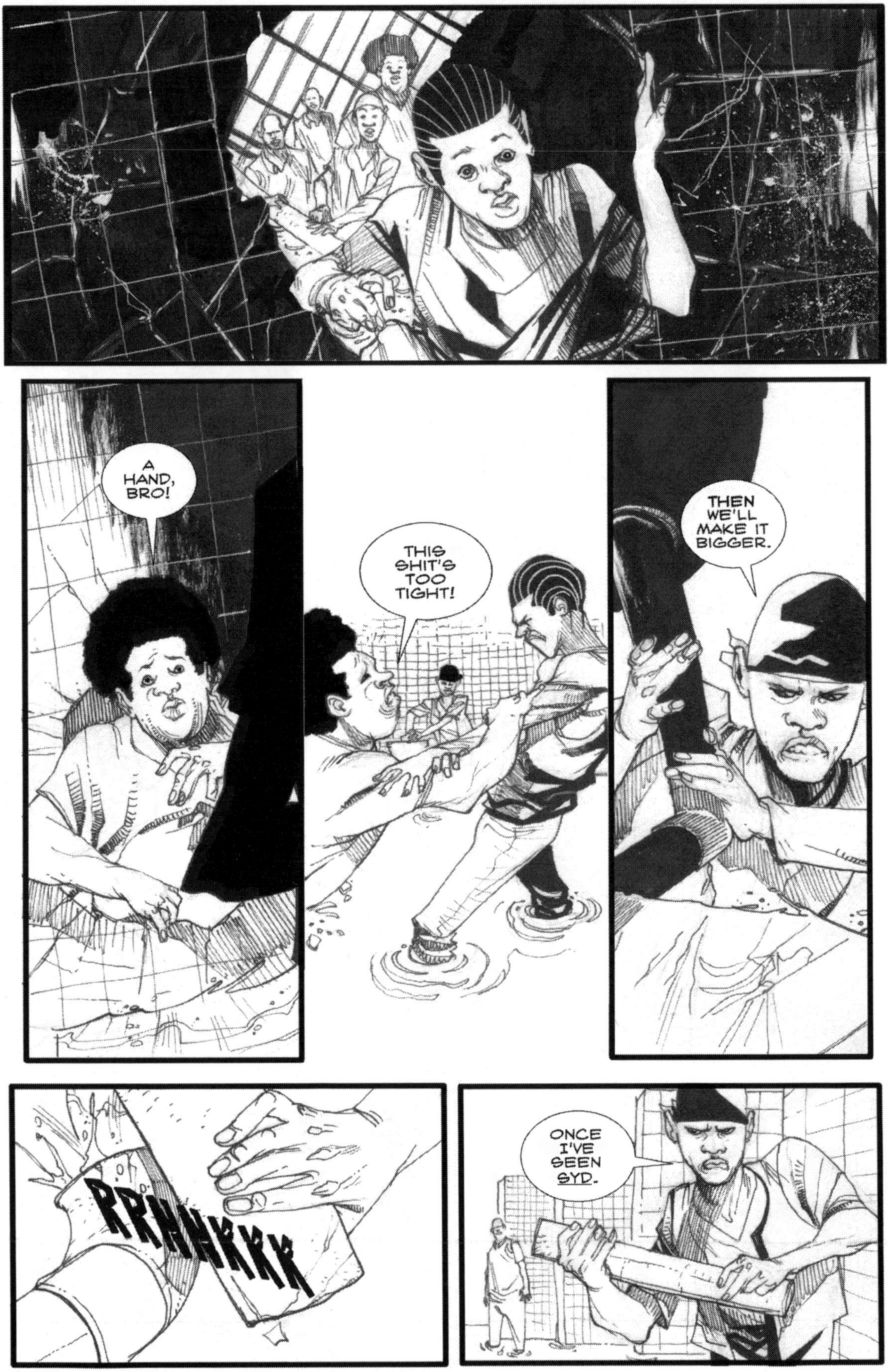
A HAND, BRO!
THIS SHIT'S TOO TIGHT!
THEN WE'LL MAKE IT BIGGER.
RRHHHRKKK
ONCE I'VE SEEN SYD.

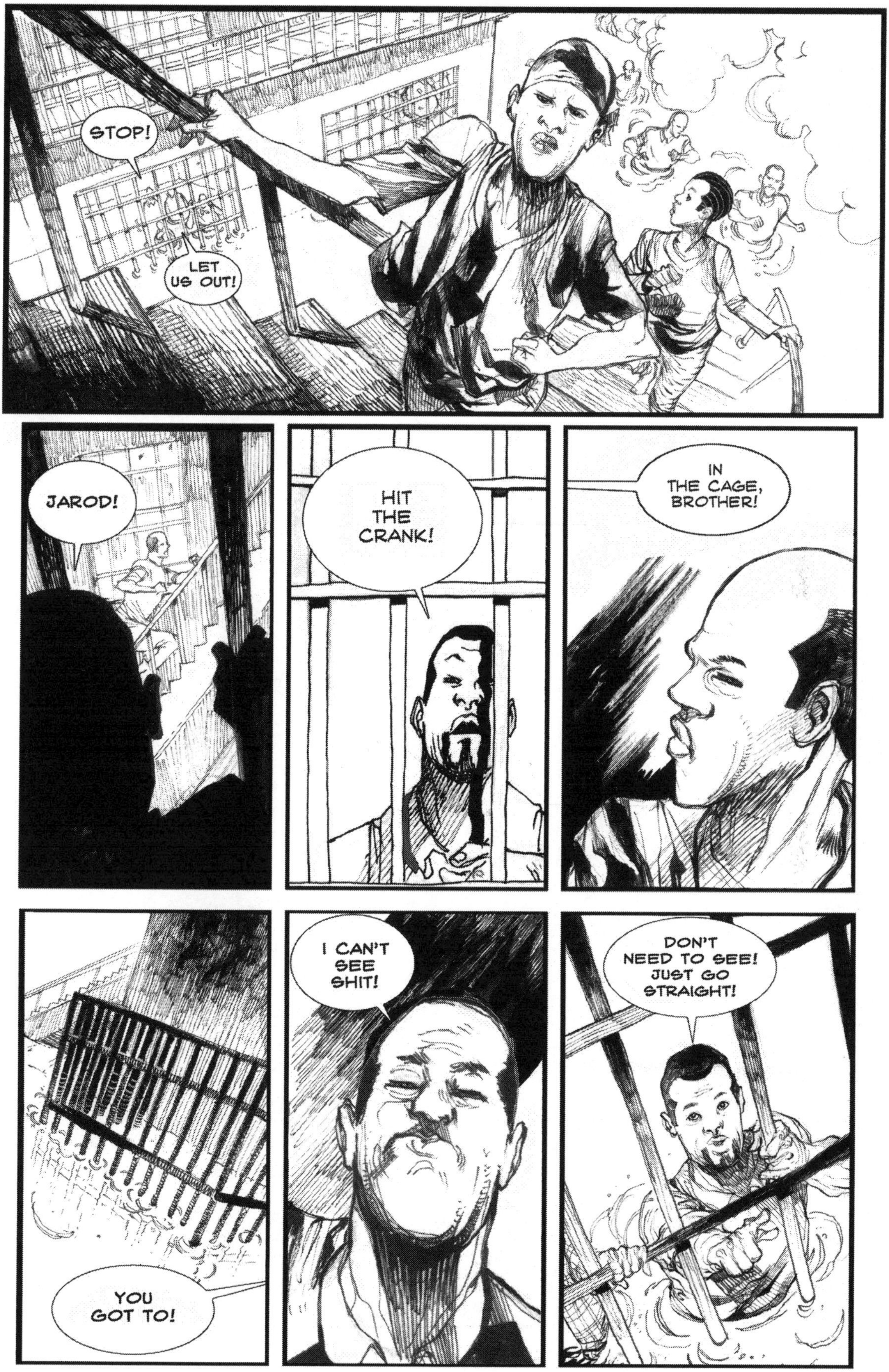
STOP!
LET US OUT!
JAROD!
HIT THE CRANK!
IN THE CAGE, BROTHER!
YOU GOT TO!
I CAN'T SEE SHIT!
DON'T NEED TO SEE! JUST GO STRAIGHT!

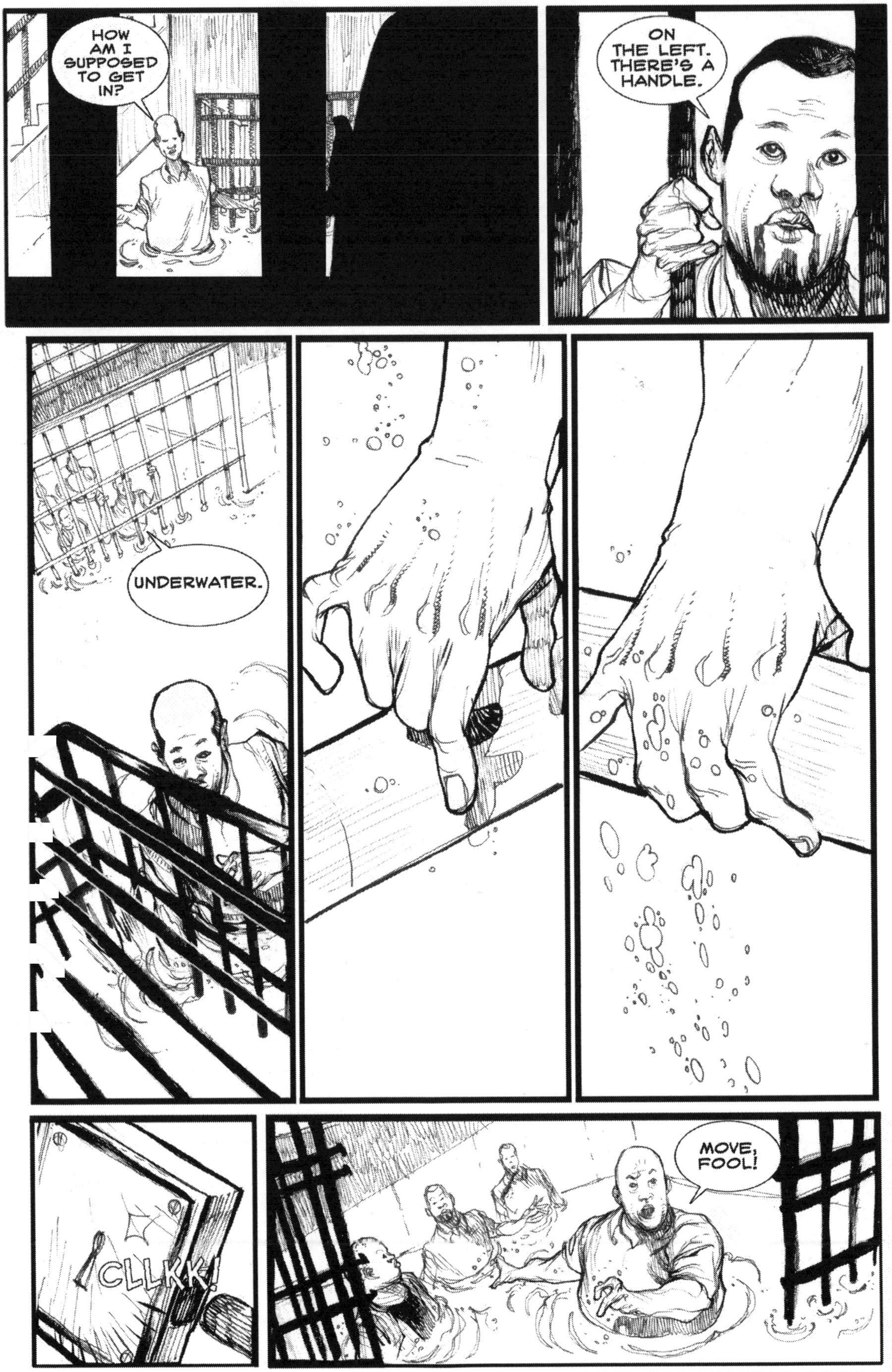
HOW AM I SUPPOSED TO GET IN?
ON THE LEFT. THERE'S A HANDLE.
UNDERWATER.
CLLKK!
MOVE, FOOL!

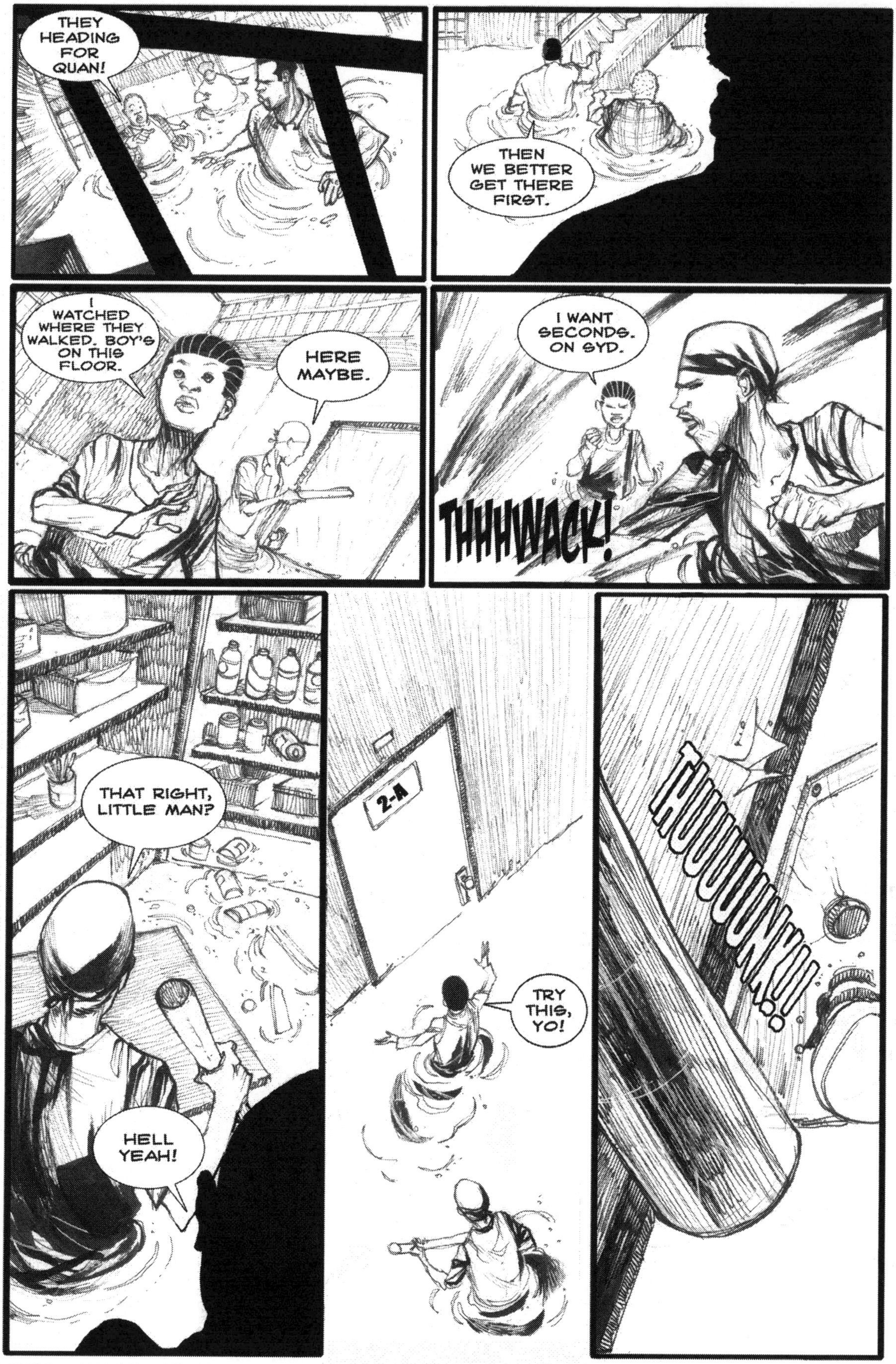
THEY HEADING FOR QUAN!
THEN WE BETTER GET THERE FIRST.
I WATCHED WHERE THEY WALKED. BOY'S ON THIS FLOOR.
HERE MAYBE.
I WANT SECONDS. ON SYD.
THHHWACK!
THAT RIGHT, LITTLE MAN?
HELL YEAH!
2-A
TRY THIS, YO!
THUUUUNK!!!

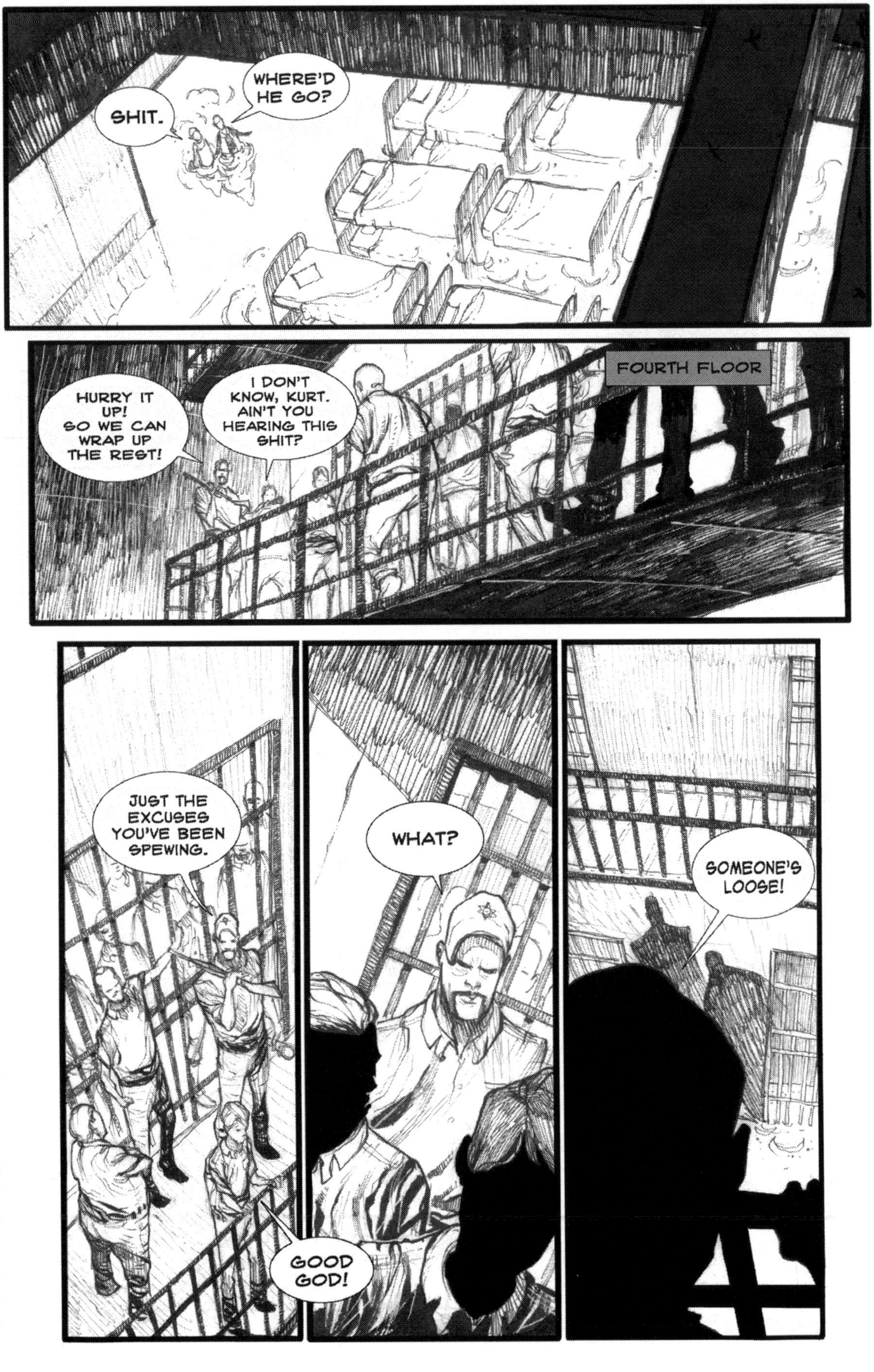
SHIT.
WHERE'D HE GO?
FOURTH FLOOR
HURRY IT UP! SO WE CAN WRAP UP THE REST!
I DON'T KNOW, KURT. AIN'T YOU HEARING THIS SHIT?
JUST THE EXCUSES YOU'VE BEEN SPEWING.
GOOD GOD!
WHAT?
SOMEONE'S LOOSE!

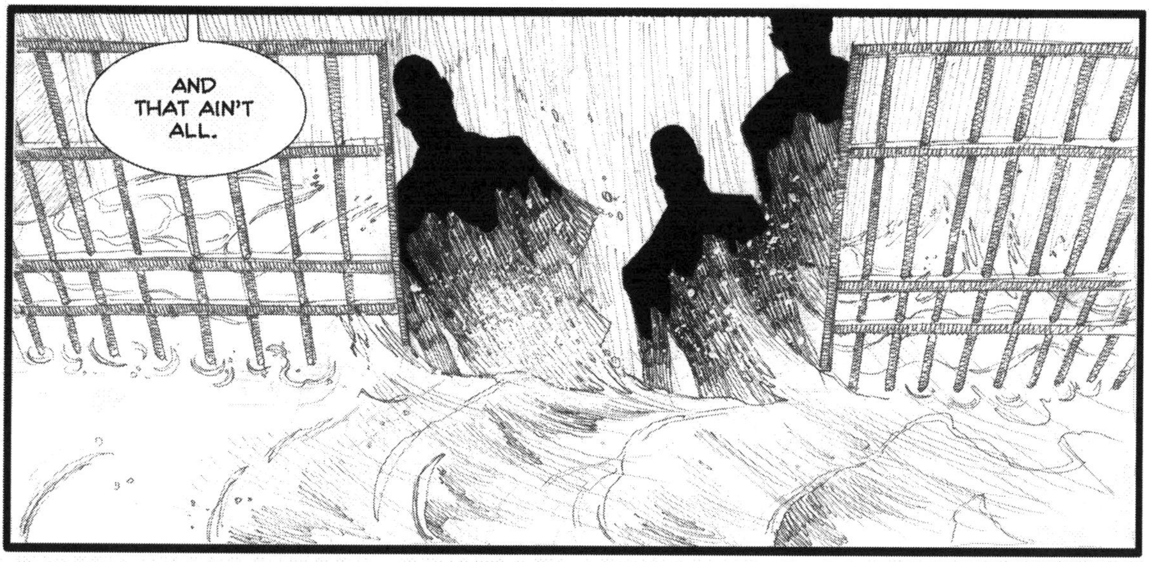
AND THAT AIN'T ALL.

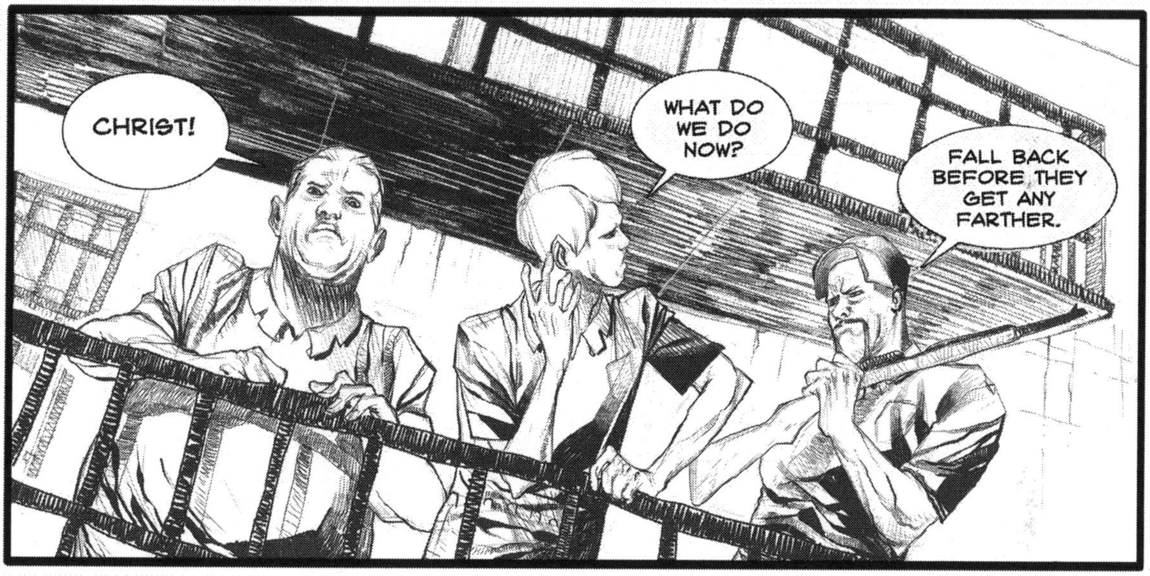
CHRIST!
WHAT DO WE DO NOW?
FALL BACK BEFORE THEY GET ANY FARTHER.

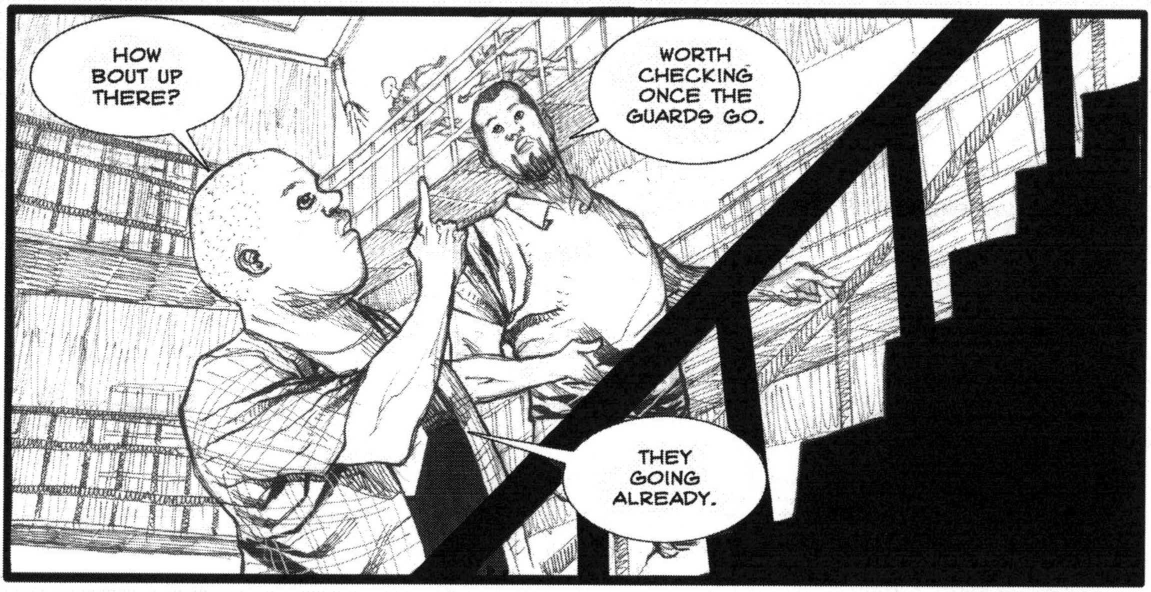
HOW BOUT UP THERE?
WORTH CHECKING ONCE THE GUARDS GO.
THEY GOING ALREADY.

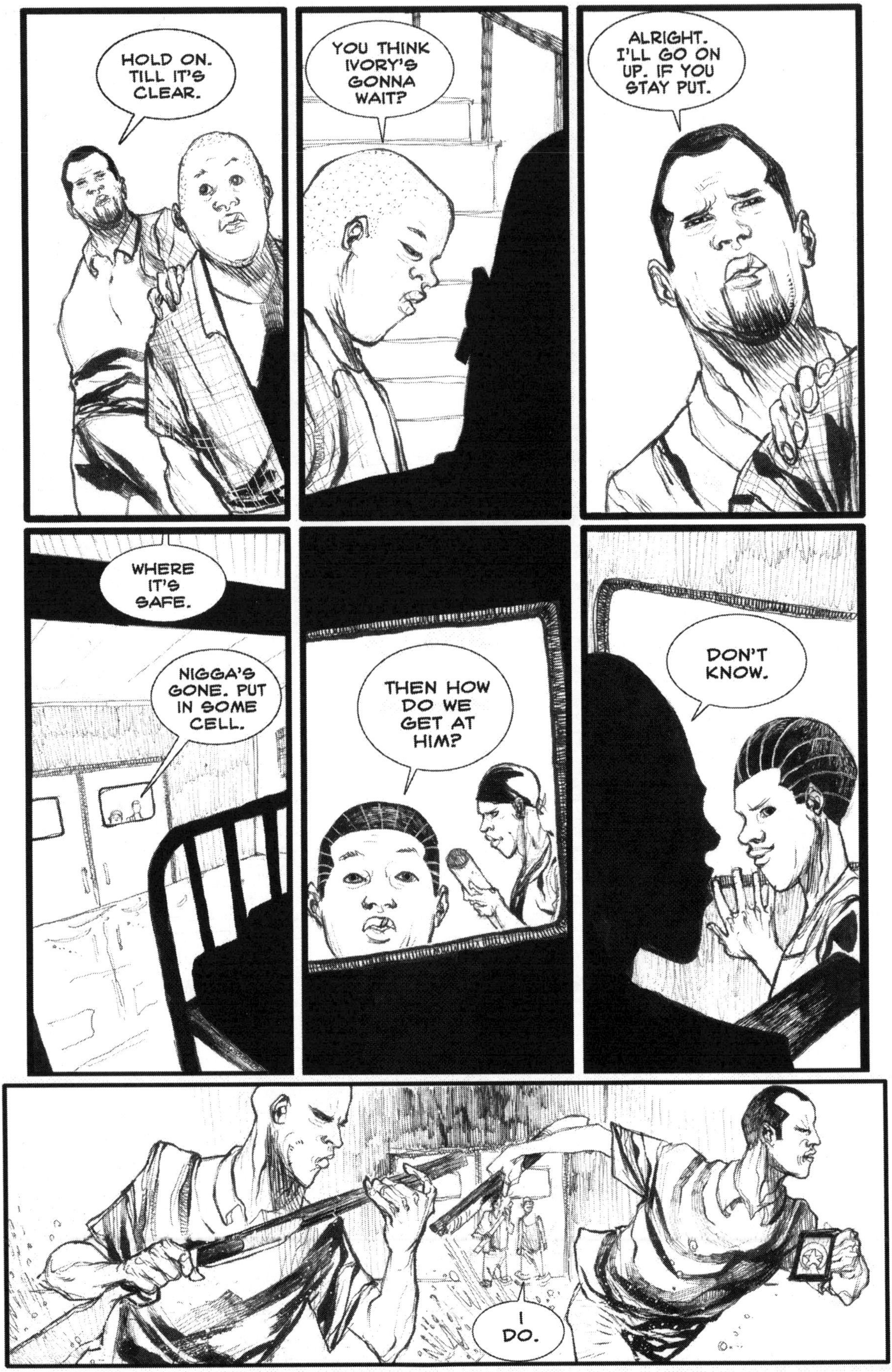
HOLD ON. TILL IT'S CLEAR.
YOU THINK IVORY'S GONNA WAIT?
ALRIGHT. I'LL GO ON UP. IF YOU STAY PUT.
WHERE IT'S SAFE.
NIGGA'S GONE. PUT IN SOME CELL.
THEN HOW DO WE GET AT HIM?
DON'T KNOW.
I DO.

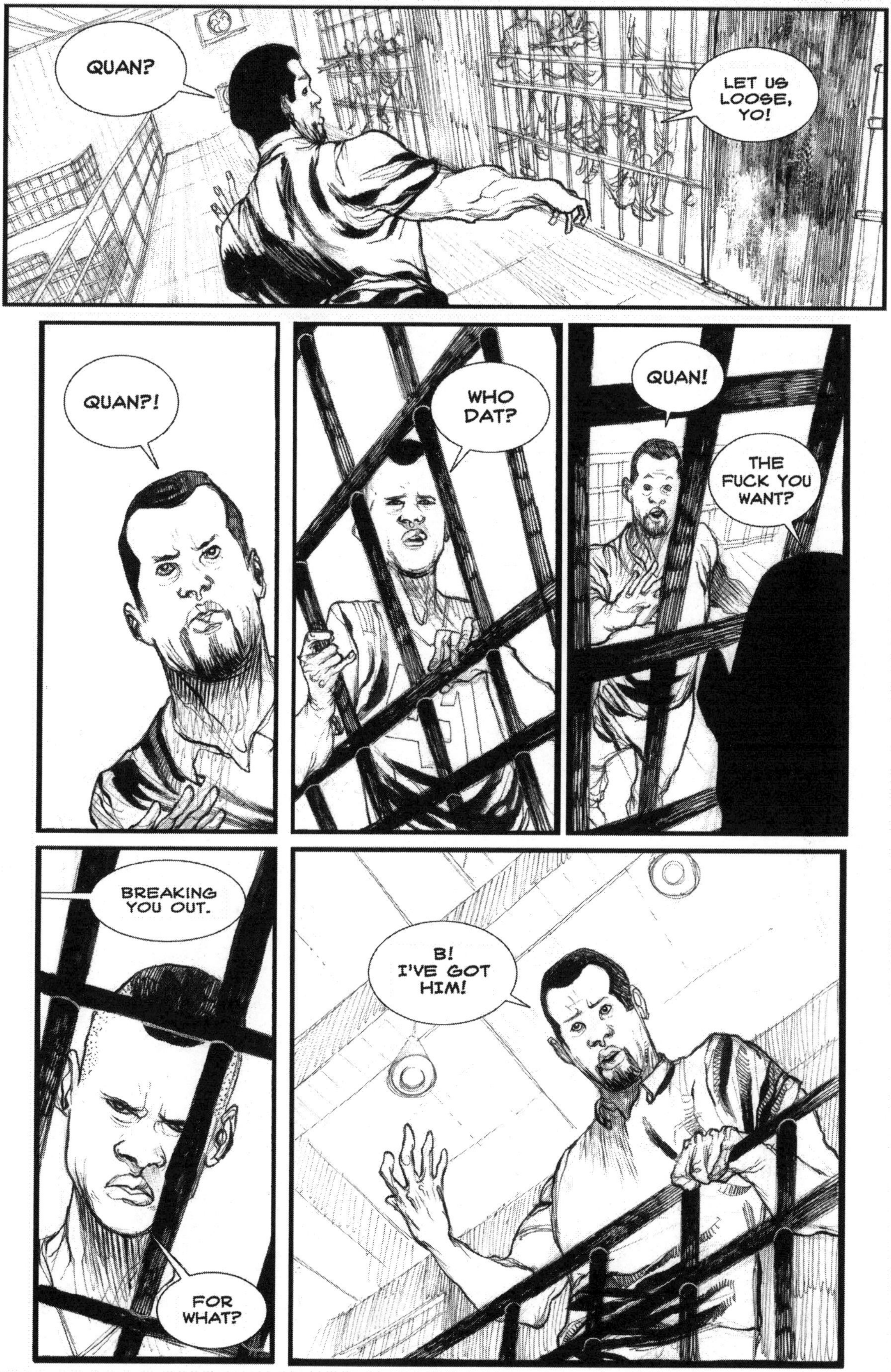
QUAN?
LET US LOOSE, YO!
QUAN?!
WHO DAT?
QUAN!
THE FUCK YOU WANT?
BREAKING YOU OUT.
FOR WHAT?
B! I'VE GOT HIM!

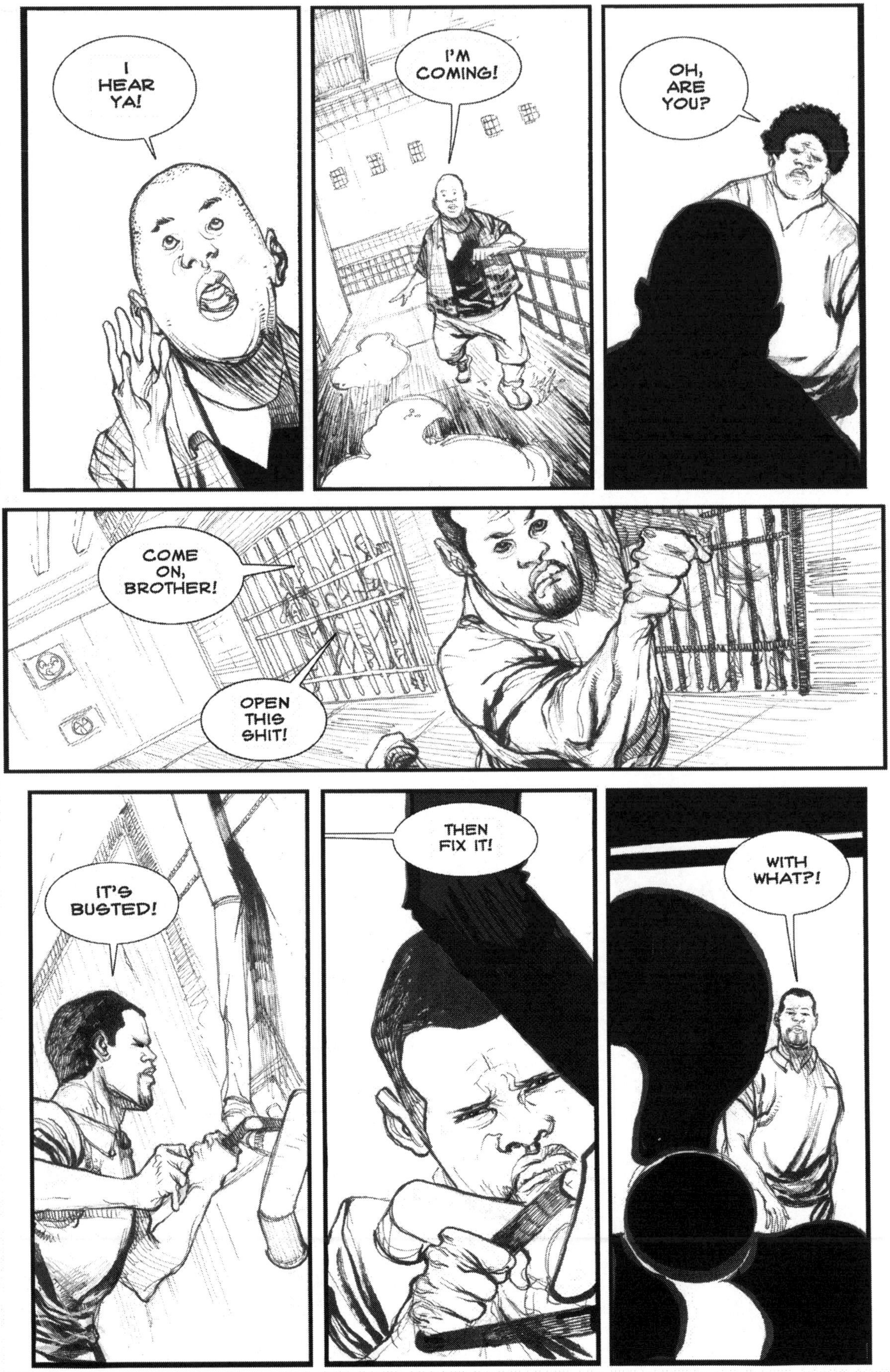
I HEAR YA!
I'M COMING!
OH, ARE YOU?
COME ON, BROTHER!
OPEN THIS SHIT!
IT'S BUSTED!
THEN FIX IT!
WITH WHAT?!

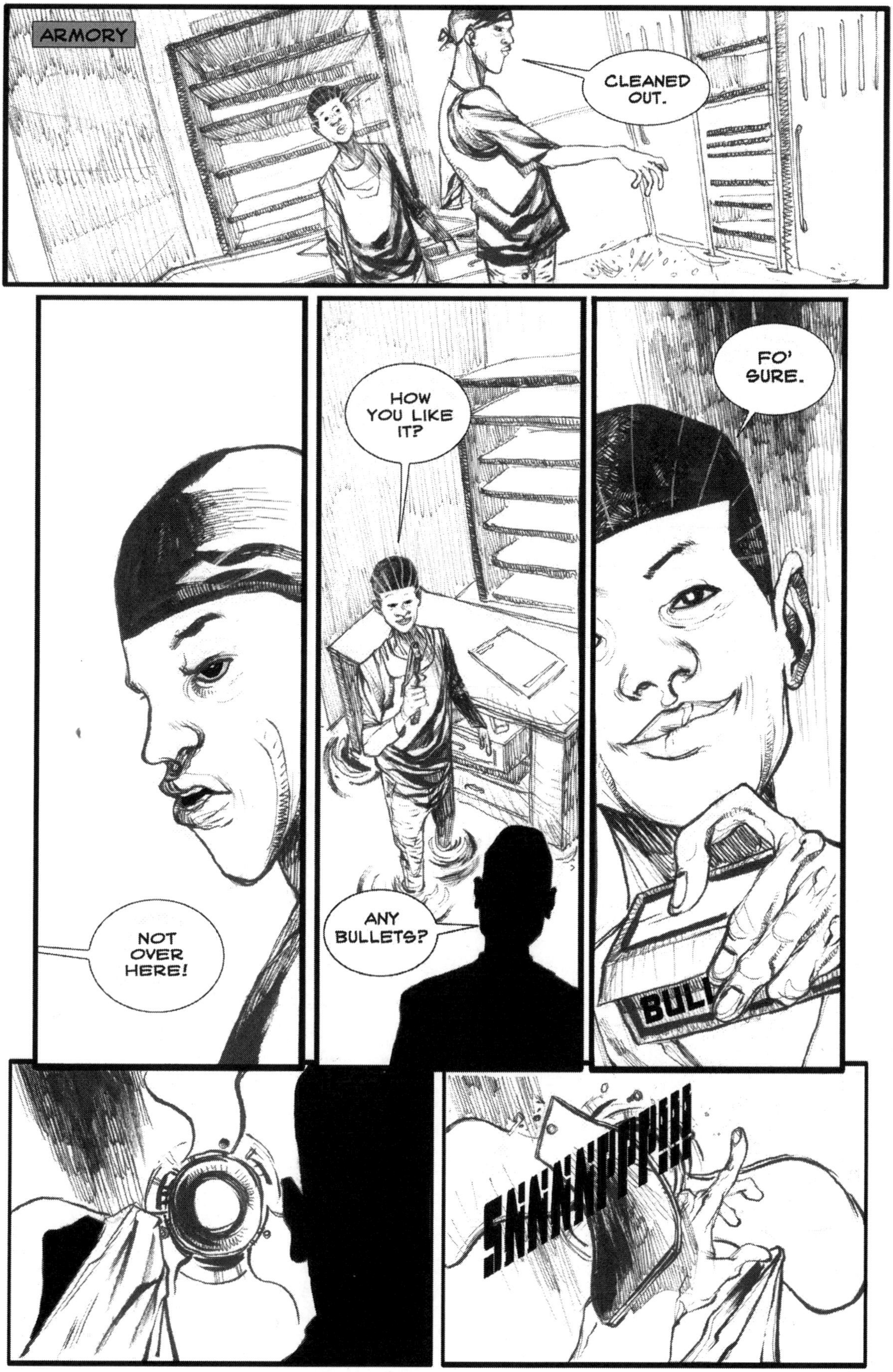
ARMORY
CLEANED OUT.
NOT OVER HERE!
HOW YOU LIKE IT?
ANY BULLETS?
FO' SURE.
BULL
SNNNNPPP!!!

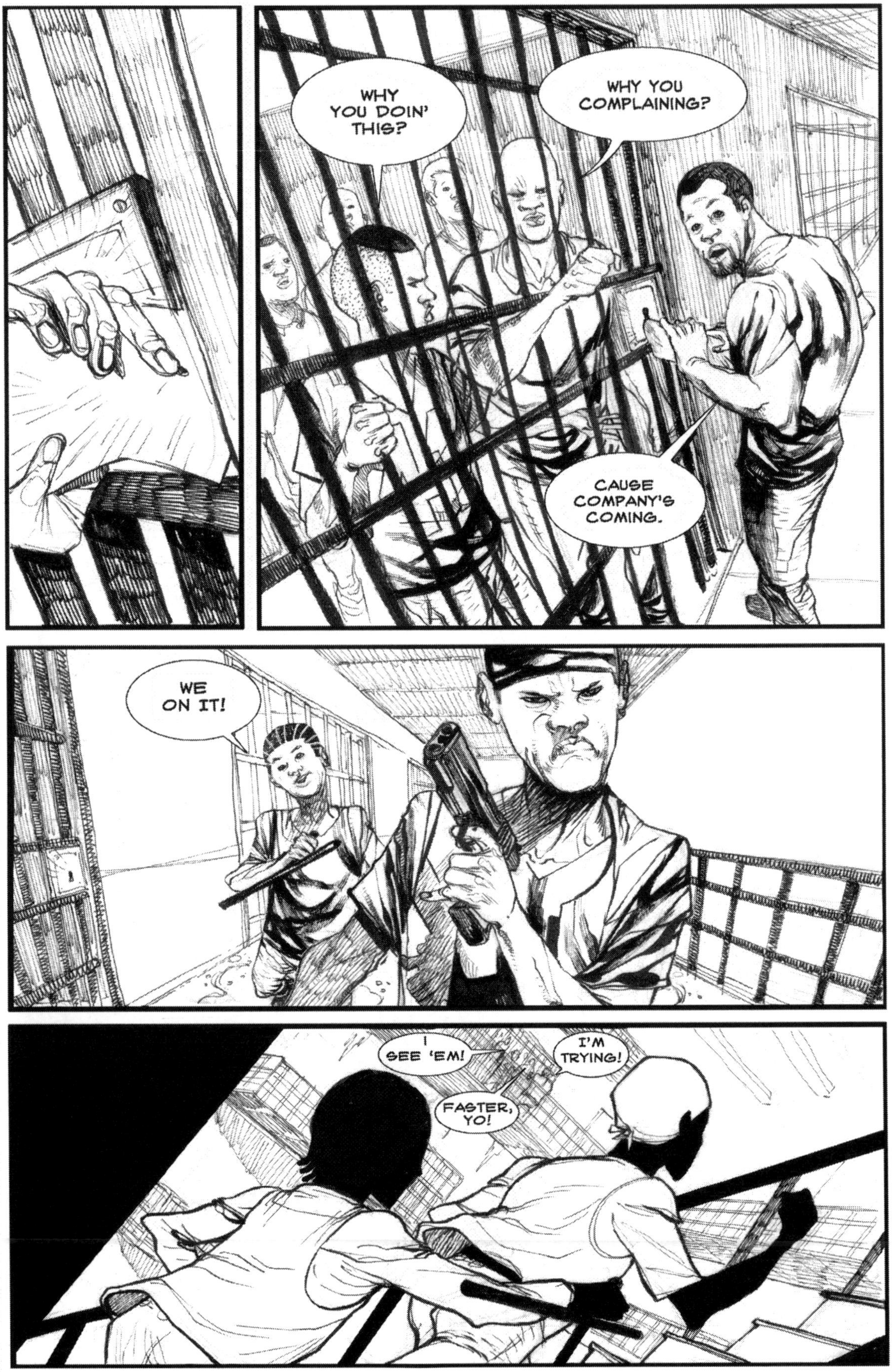
WHY YOU DOIN' THIS?
WHY YOU COMPLAINING?
CAUSE COMPANY'S COMING.
WE ON IT!
I SEE 'EM!
I'M TRYING!
FASTER, YO!

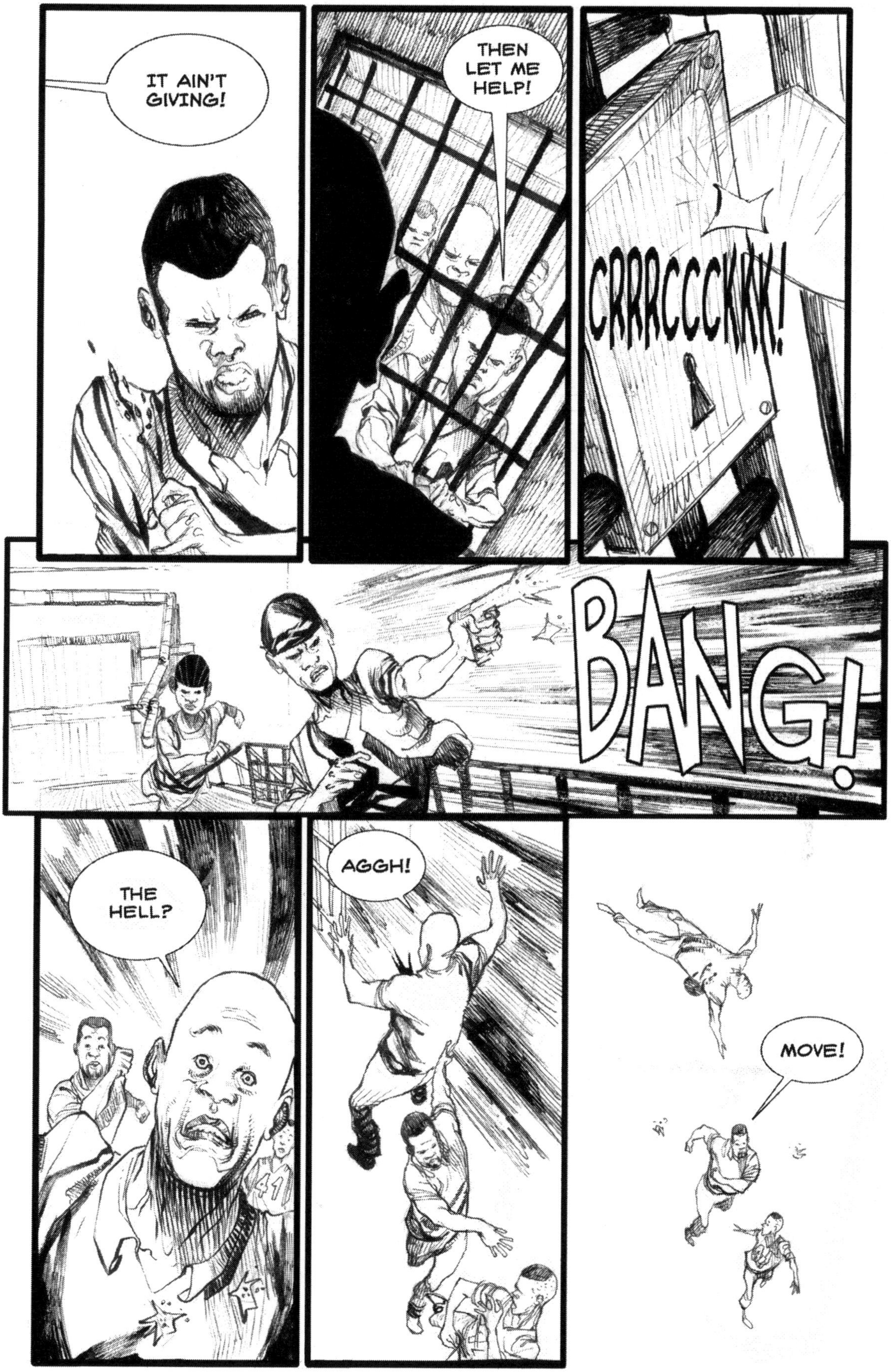
IT AIN'T GIVING!
THEN LET ME HELP!
CRRRCCCKKK!
BANG!
THE HELL?
AGGH!
MOVE!

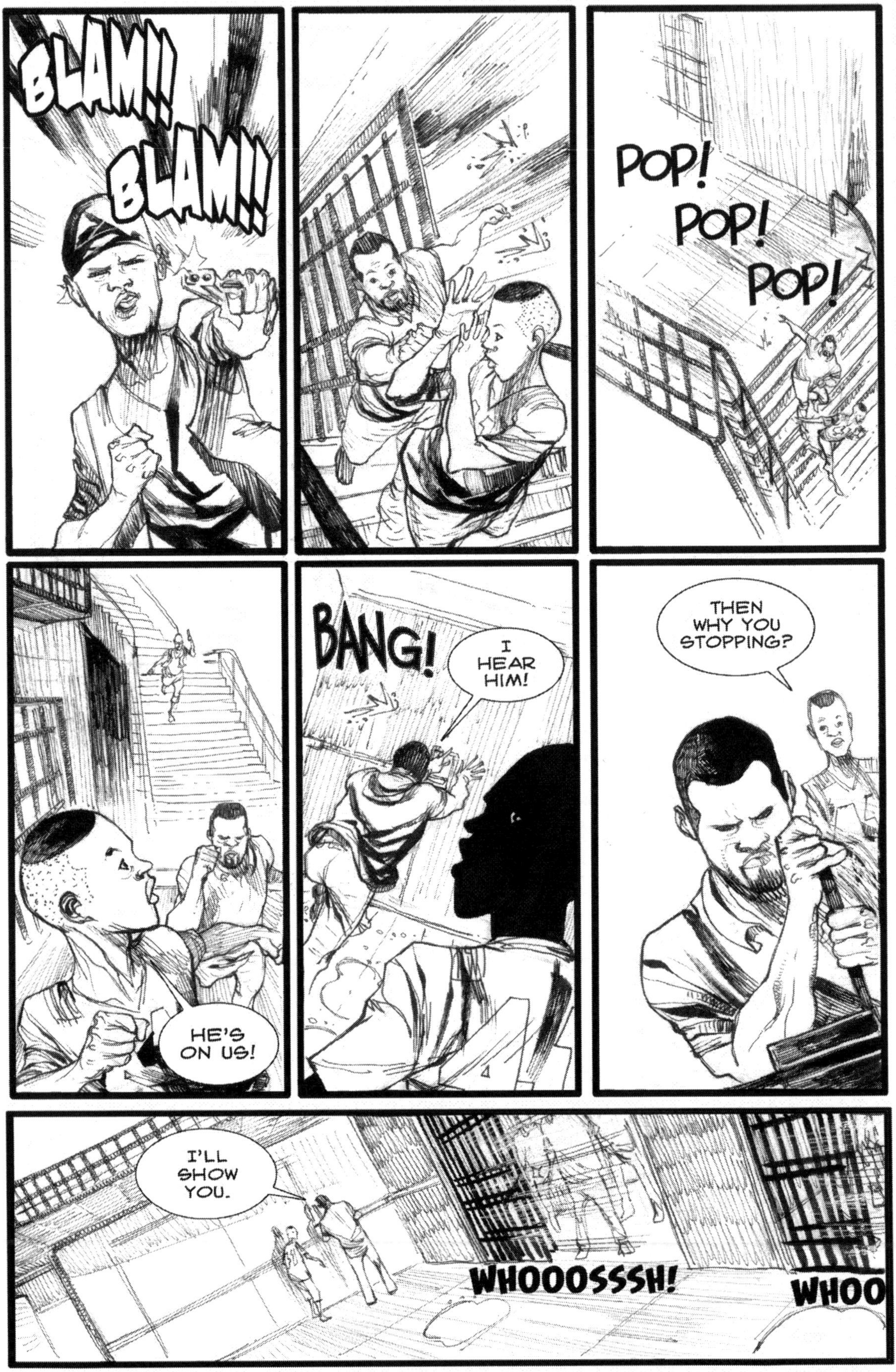
BLAM!!
BLAM!!
POP!
POP!
POP!
HE'S ON US!
BANG!
I HEAR HIM!
THEN WHY YOU STOPPING?
I'LL SHOW YOU.
WHOOOSSSH!
WHOO

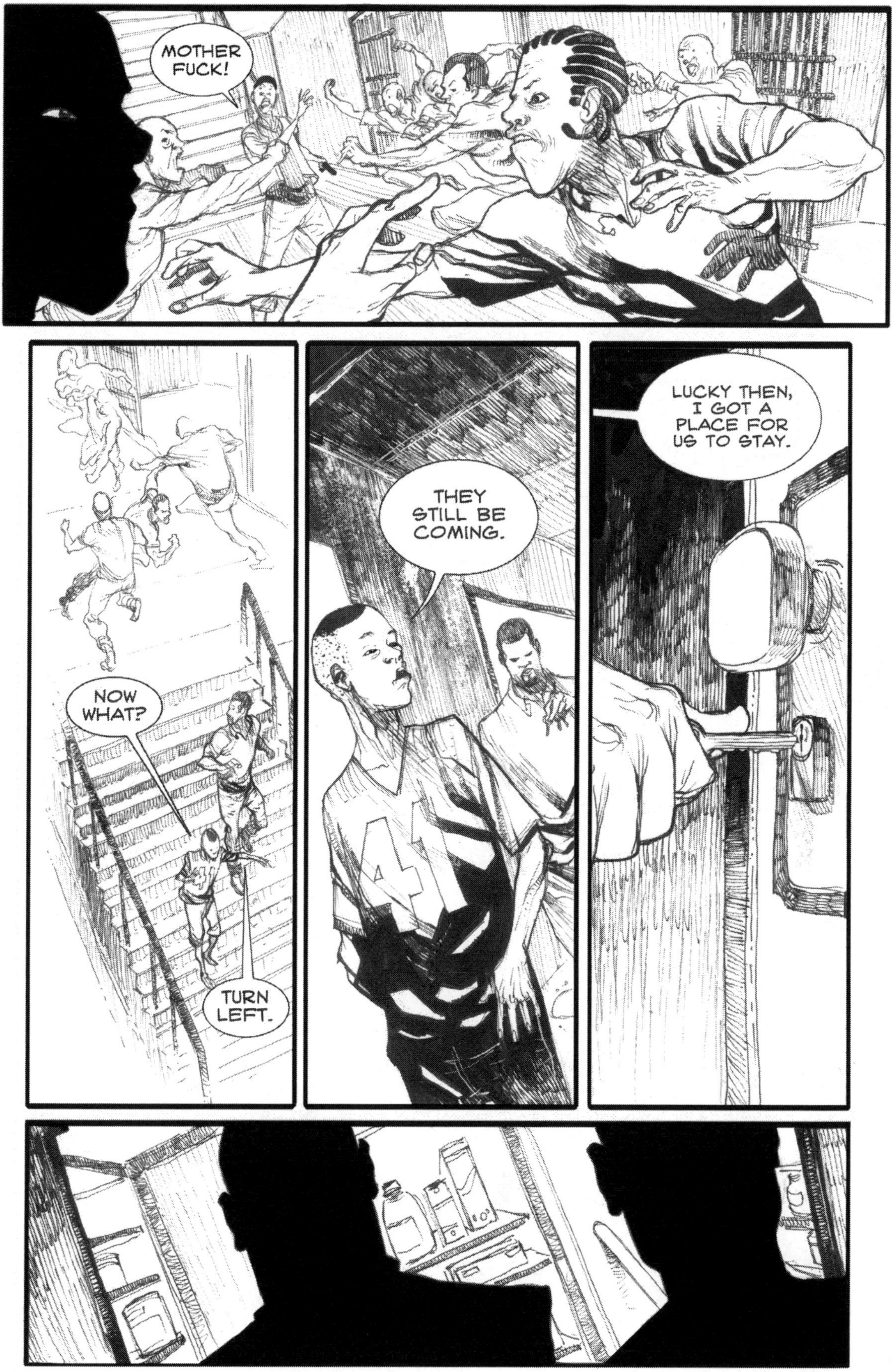
MOTHER FUCK!
NOW WHAT?
TURN LEFT.
THEY STILL BE COMING.
LUCKY THEN, I GOT A PLACE FOR US TO STAY.

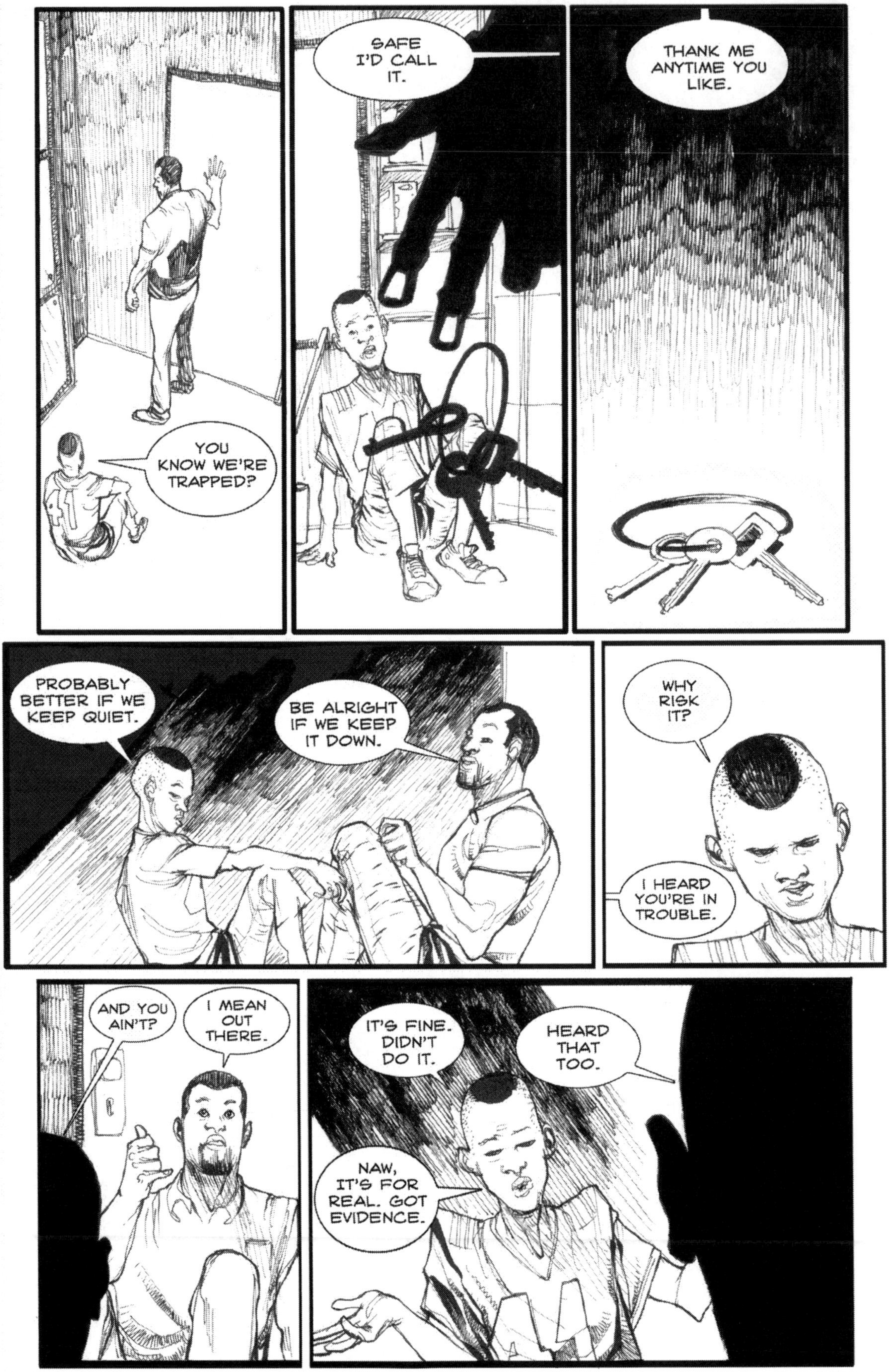
YOU KNOW WE'RE TRAPPED?
SAFE I'D CALL IT.
THANK ME ANYTIME YOU LIKE.
PROBABLY BETTER IF WE KEEP QUIET.
BE ALRIGHT IF WE KEEP IT DOWN.
WHY RISK IT?
I HEARD YOU'RE IN TROUBLE.
AND YOU AIN'T?
I MEAN OUT THERE.
IT'S FINE. DIDN'T DO IT.
HEARD THAT TOO.
NAW, IT'S FOR REAL. GOT EVIDENCE.

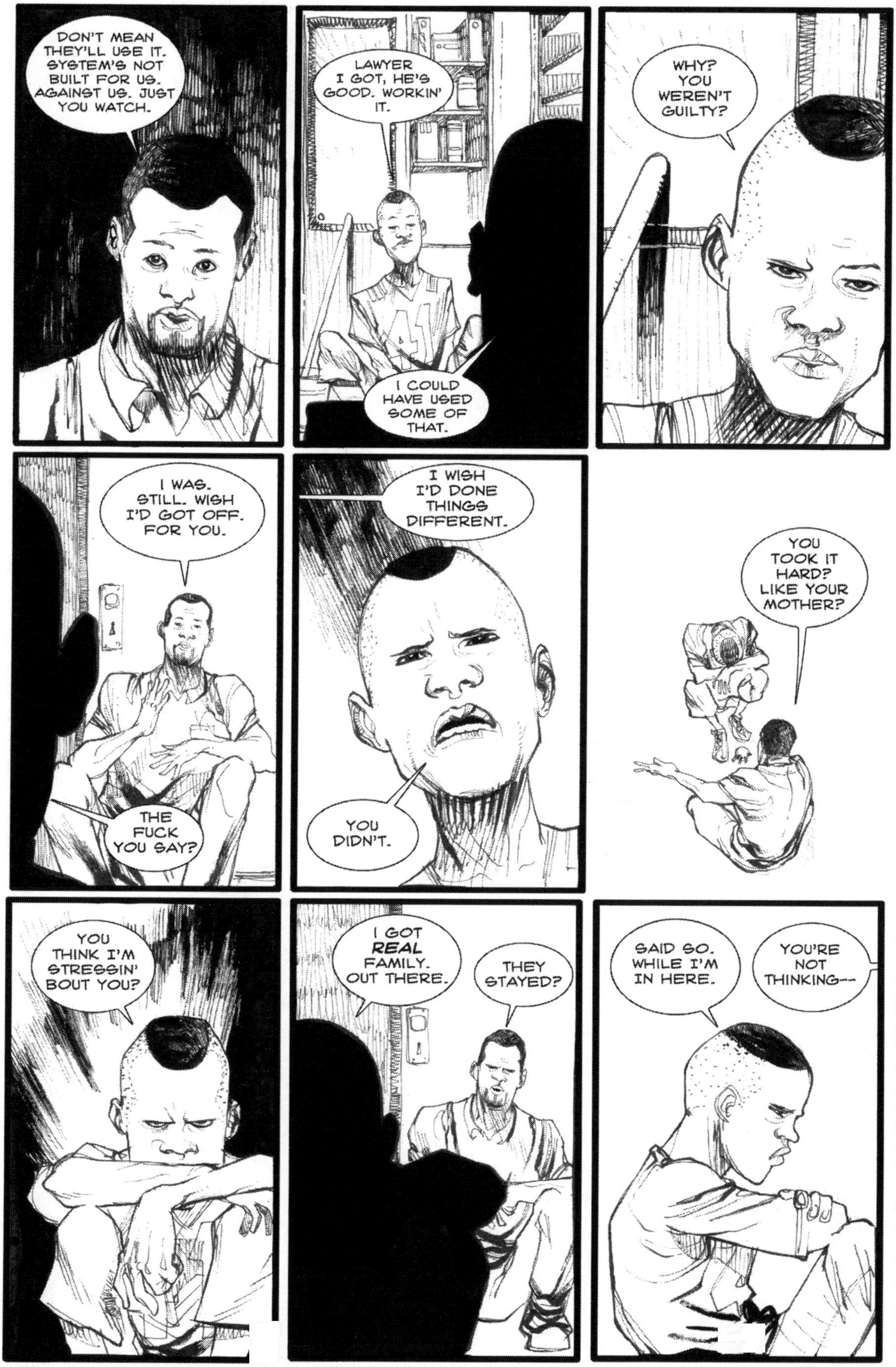
DON'T MEAN THEY'LL USE IT. SYSTEM'S NOT BUILT FOR US. AGAINST US. JUST YOU WATCH.
LAWYER I GOT, HE'S GOOD. WORKIN' IT.
I COULD HAVE USED SOME OF THAT.
WHY? YOU WEREN'T GUILTY?
I WAS. STILL. WISH I'D GOT OFF. FOR YOU.
THE FUCK YOU SAY?
I WISH I'D DONE THINGS DIFFERENT.
YOU DIDN'T.
YOU TOOK IT HARD? LIKE YOUR MOTHER?
YOU THINK I'M STRESSIN' BOUT YOU?
I GOT REAL FAMILY. OUT THERE.
THEY STAYED?
SAID SO. WHILE I'M IN HERE.
YOU'RE NOT THINKING--

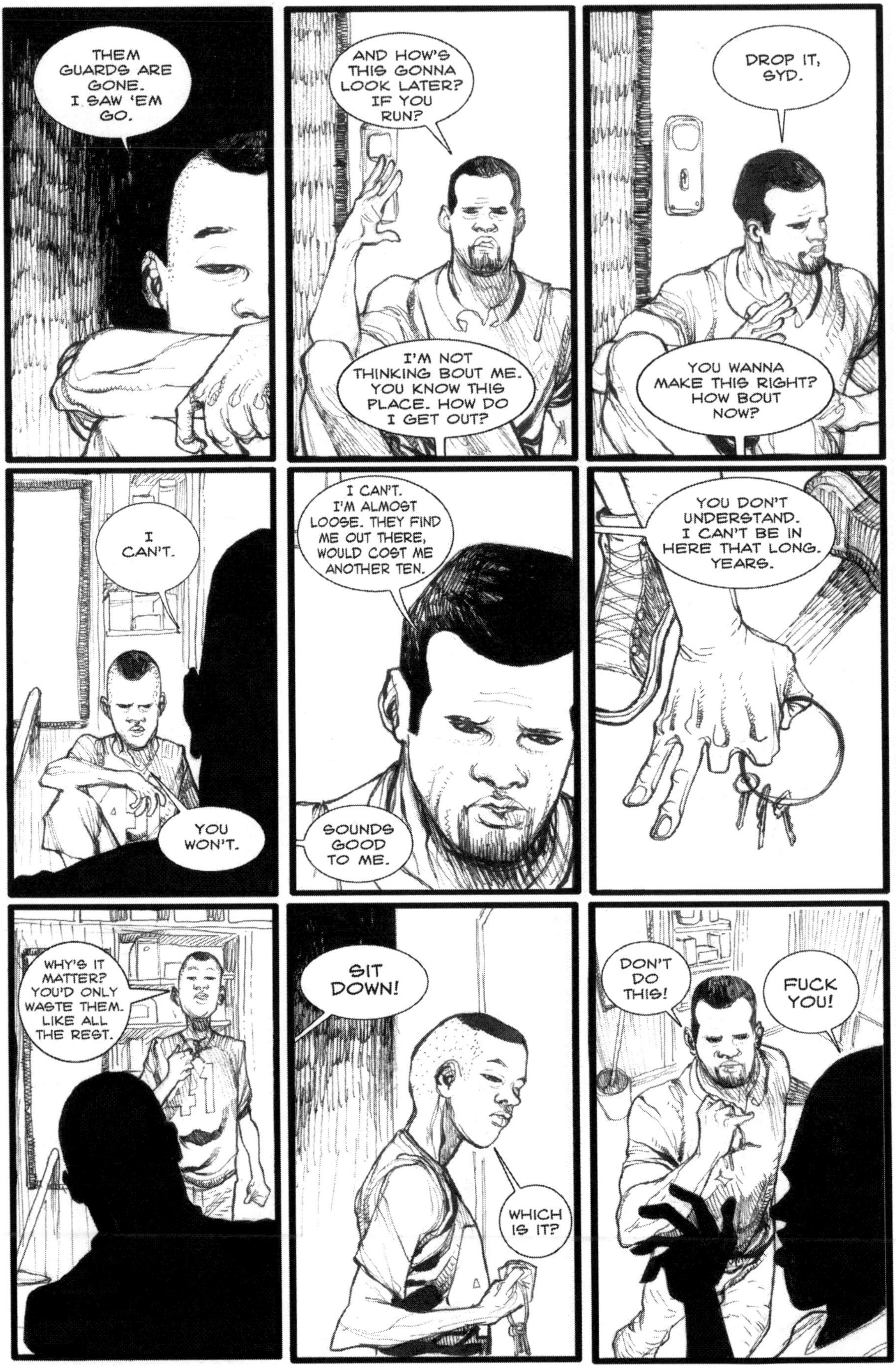
THEM GUARDS ARE GONE. I SAW 'EM GO.
AND HOW'S THIS GONNA LOOK LATER? IF YOU RUN?
I'M NOT THINKING BOUT ME. YOU KNOW THIS PLACE. HOW DO I GET OUT?
DROP IT, SYD.
YOU WANNA MAKE THIS RIGHT? HOW BOUT NOW?
I CAN'T.
YOU WON'T.
I CAN'T. I'M ALMOST LOOSE. THEY FIND ME OUT THERE, WOULD COST ME ANOTHER TEN.
SOUNDS GOOD TO ME.
YOU DON'T UNDERSTAND. I CAN'T BE IN HERE THAT LONG. YEARS.
WHY'S IT MATTER? YOU'D ONLY WASTE THEM. LIKE ALL THE REST.
SIT DOWN!
WHICH IS IT?
DON'T DO THIS!
FUCK YOU!

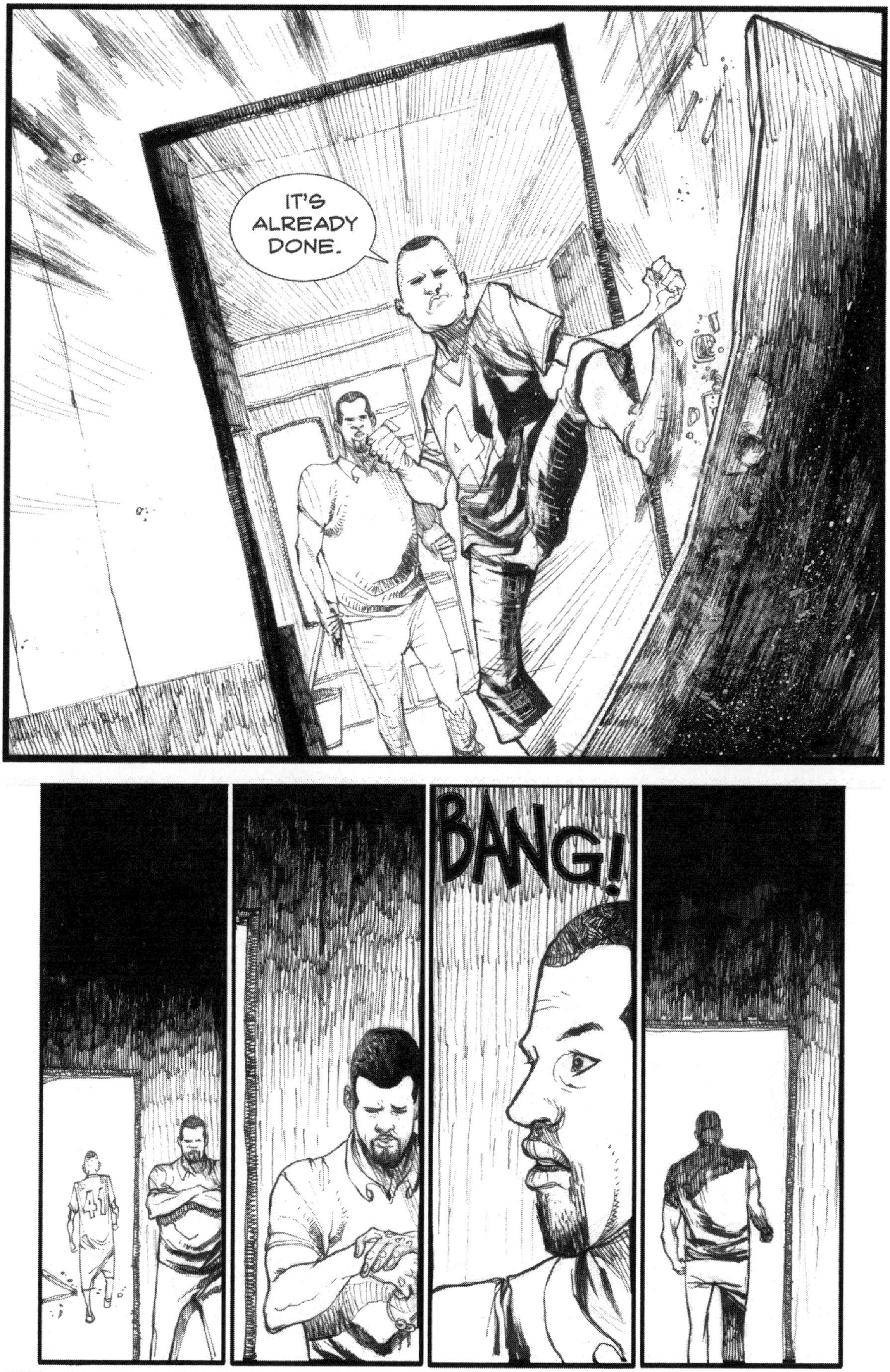
IT'S ALREADY DONE.
BANG!

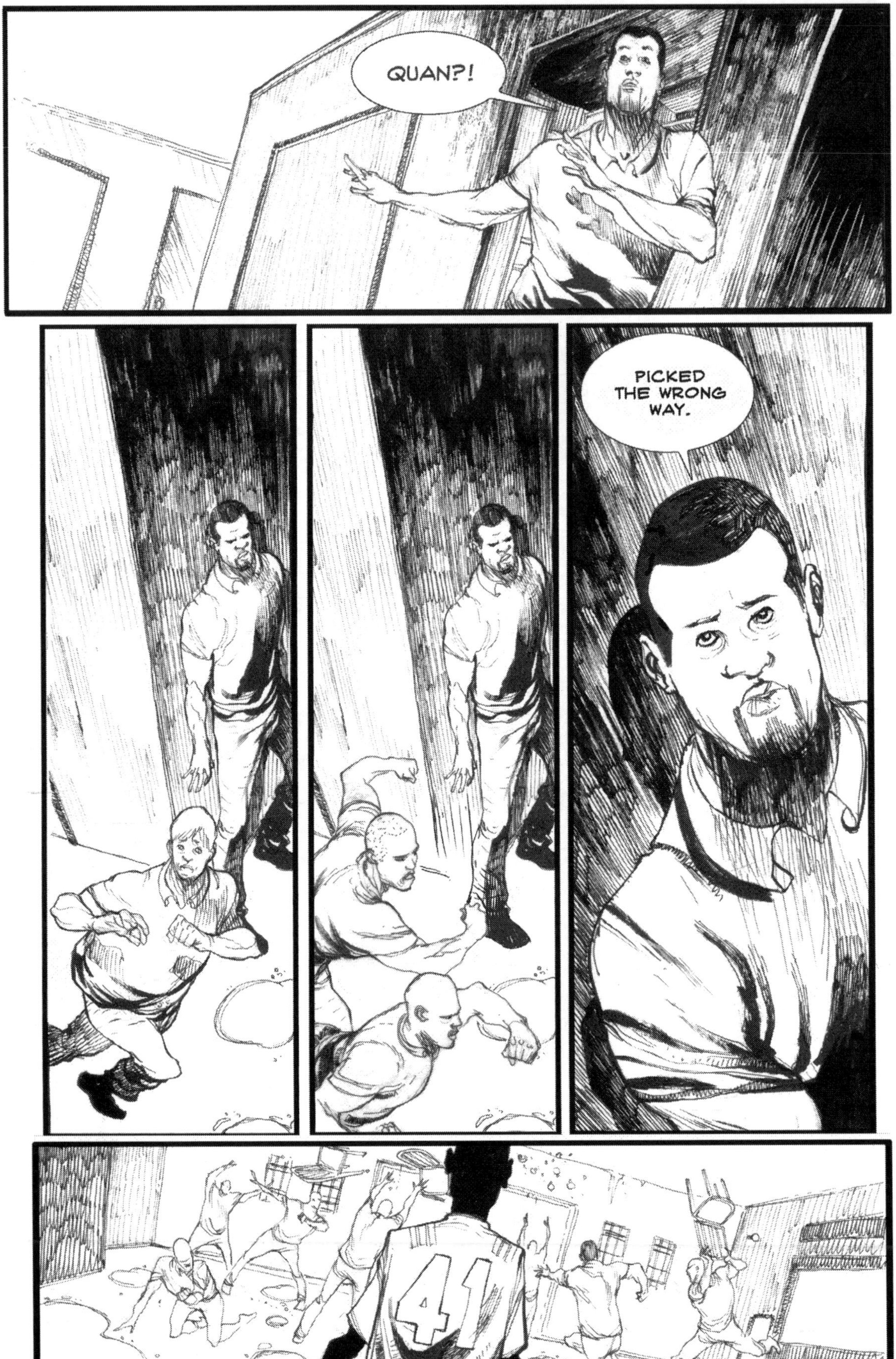
QUAN?!
PICKED THE WRONG WAY.

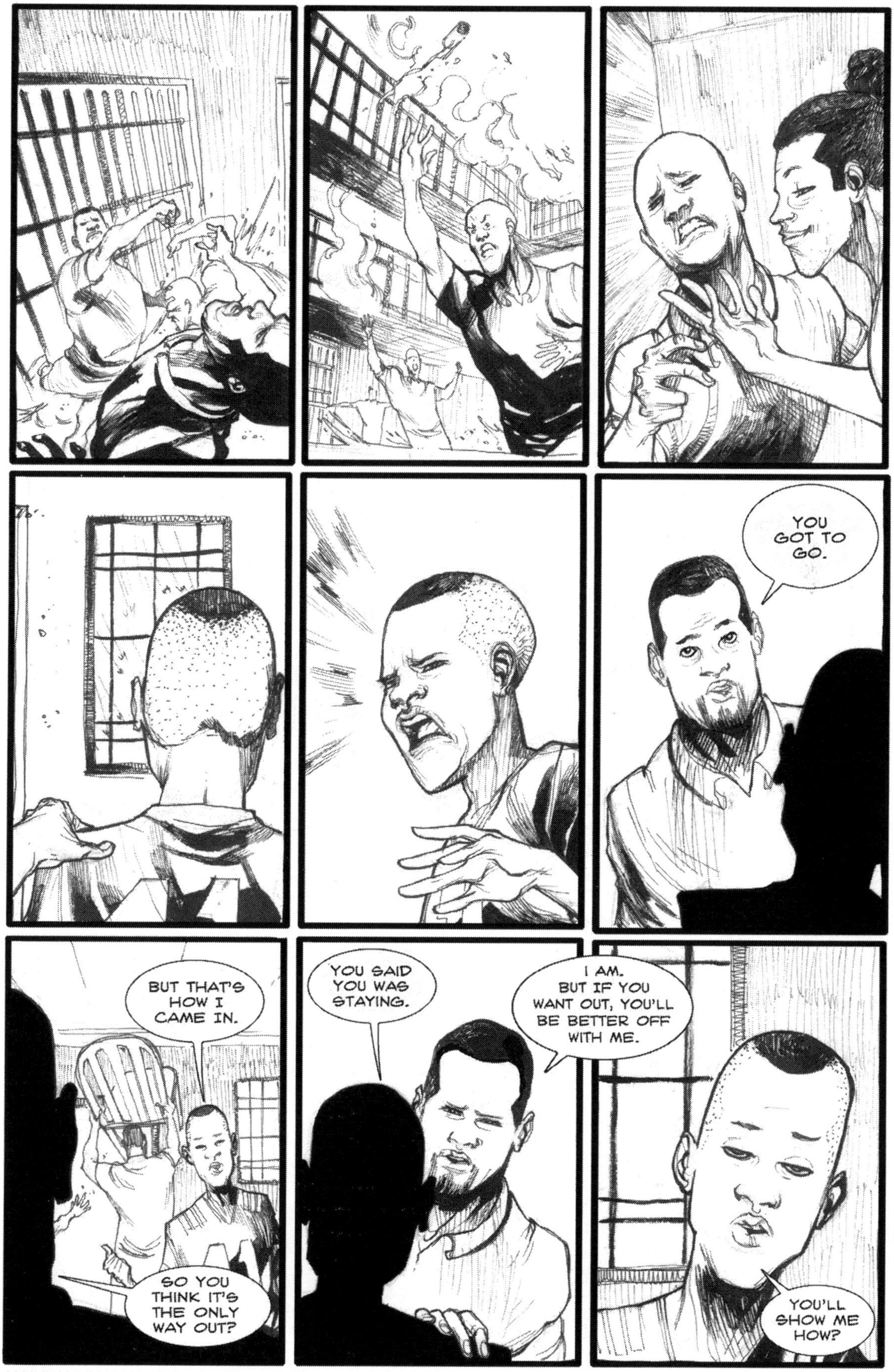
YOU GOT TO GO.
BUT THAT'S HOW I CAME IN.
SO YOU THINK IT'S THE ONLY WAY OUT?
YOU SAID YOU WAS STAYING.
I AM. BUT IF YOU WANT OUT, YOU'LL BE BETTER OFF WITH ME.
YOU'LL SHOW ME HOW?

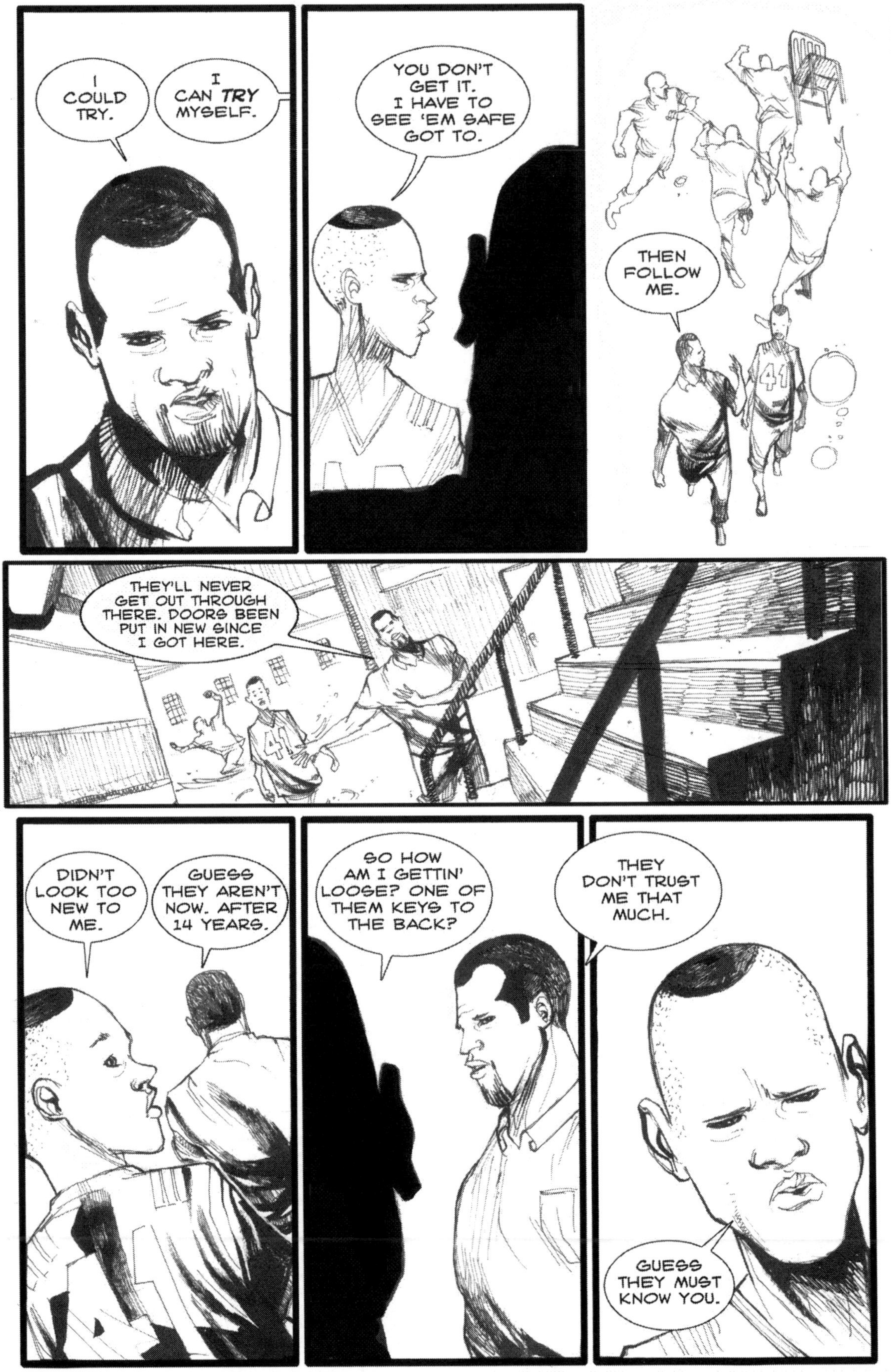
I COULD TRY.
I CAN TRY MYSELF.
YOU DON'T GET IT. I HAVE TO SEE 'EM SAFE GOT TO.
THEN FOLLOW ME.
41
THEY'LL NEVER GET OUT THROUGH THERE. DOORS BEEN PUT IN NEW SINCE I GOT HERE.
41
DIDN'T LOOK TOO NEW TO ME.
GUESS THEY AREN'T NOW. AFTER 14 YEARS.
SO HOW AM I GETTIN' LOOSE? ONE OF THEM KEYS TO THE BACK?
THEY DON'T TRUST ME THAT MUCH.
GUESS THEY MUST KNOW YOU.

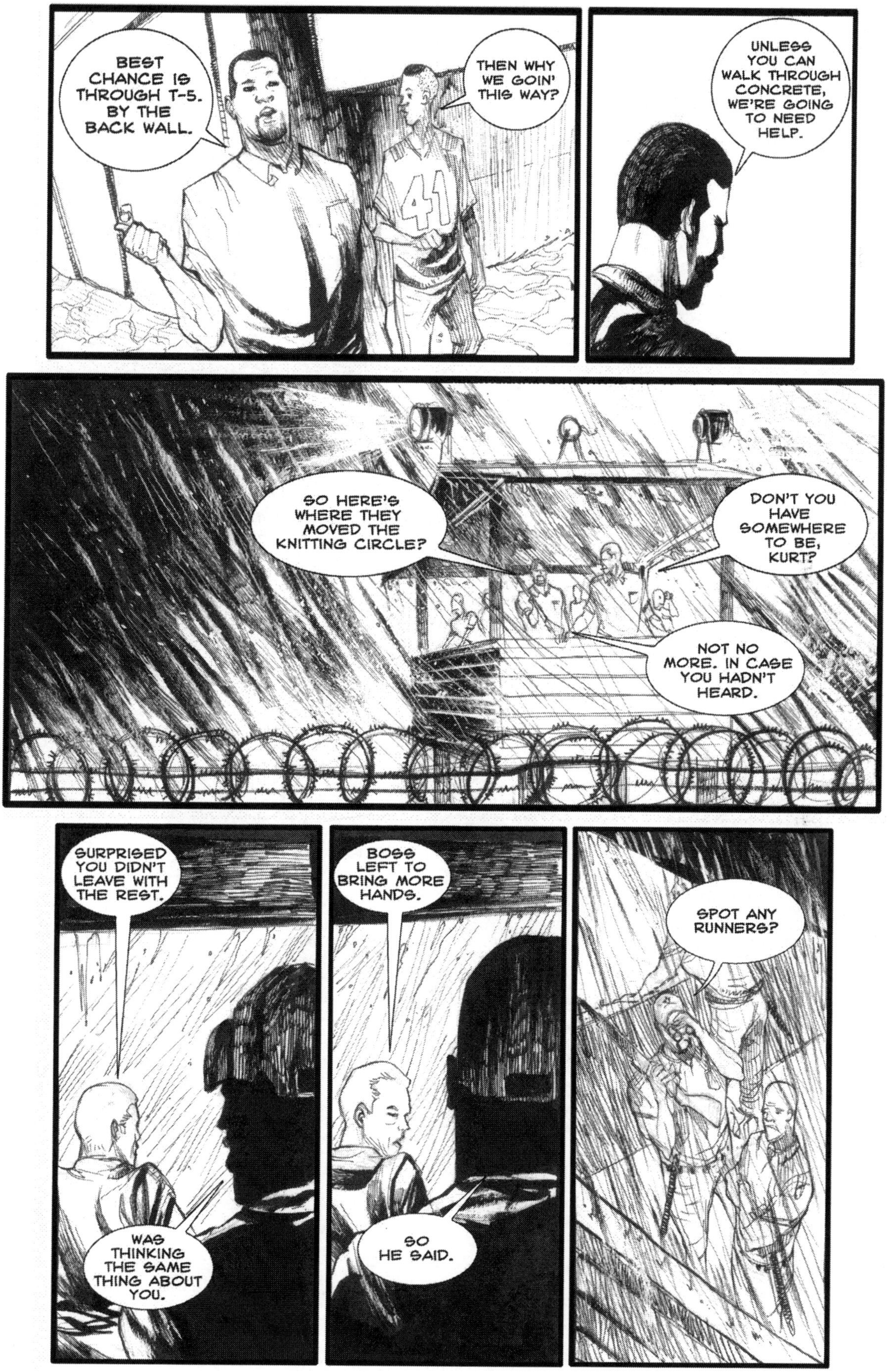
BEST CHANCE IS THROUGH T-5. BY THE BACK WALL.
THEN WHY WE GOIN' THIS WAY?
UNLESS YOU CAN WALK THROUGH CONCRETE, WE'RE GOING TO NEED HELP.
SO HERE'S WHERE THEY MOVED THE KNITTING CIRCLE?
DON'T YOU HAVE SOMEWHERE TO BE, KURT?
NOT NO MORE. IN CASE YOU HADN'T HEARD.
SURPRISED YOU DIDN'T LEAVE WITH THE REST.
WAS THINKING THE SAME THING ABOUT YOU.
BOSS LEFT TO BRING MORE HANDS.
SO HE SAID.
SPOT ANY RUNNERS?

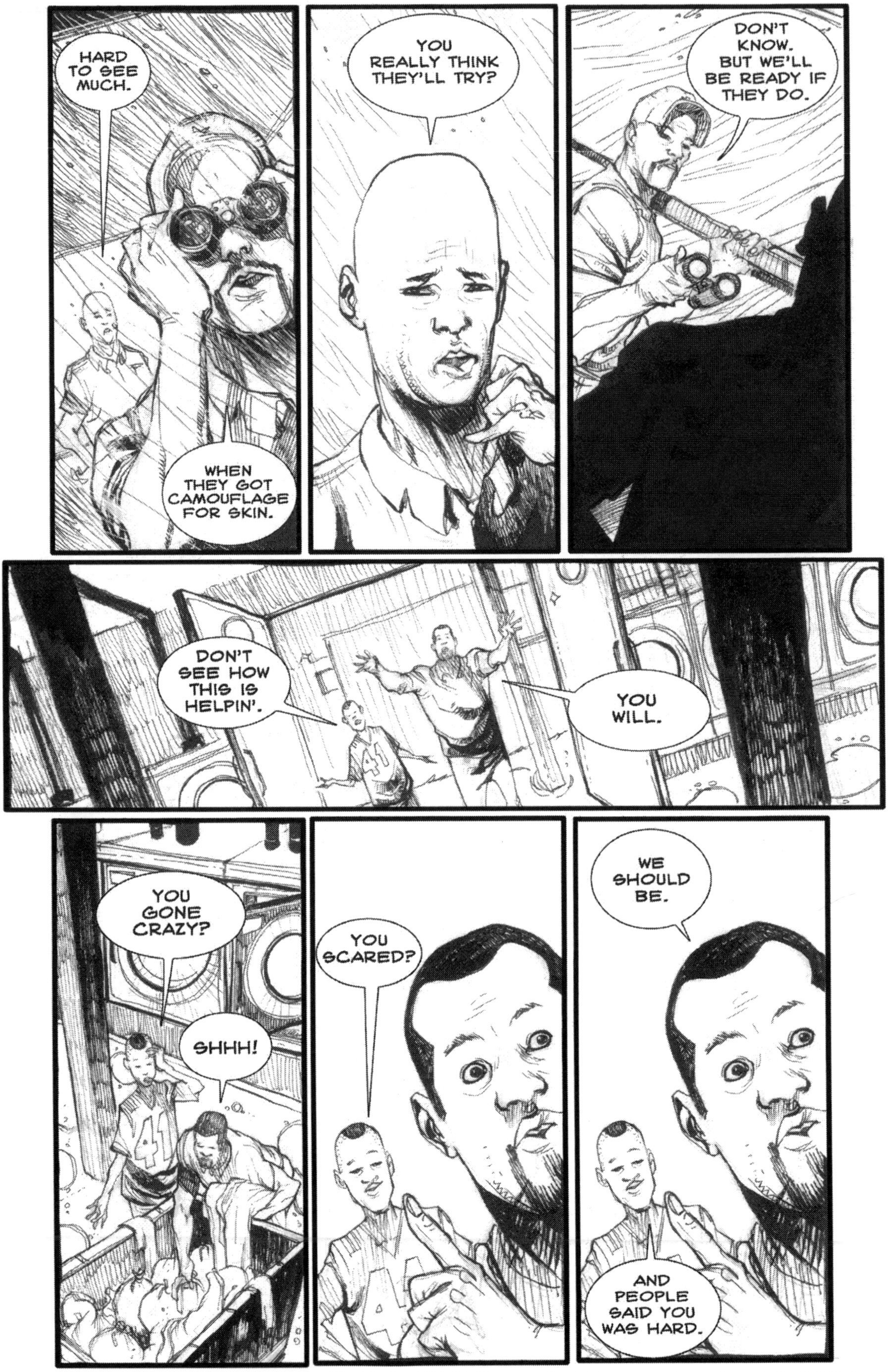
HARD TO SEE MUCH.
WHEN THEY GOT CAMOUFLAGE FOR SKIN.
YOU REALLY THINK THEY'LL TRY?
DON'T KNOW. BUT WE'LL BE READY IF THEY DO.
DON'T SEE HOW THIS IS HELPIN'.
YOU WILL.
YOU GONE CRAZY?
SHHH!
YOU SCARED?
WE SHOULD BE.
AND PEOPLE SAID YOU WAS HARD.

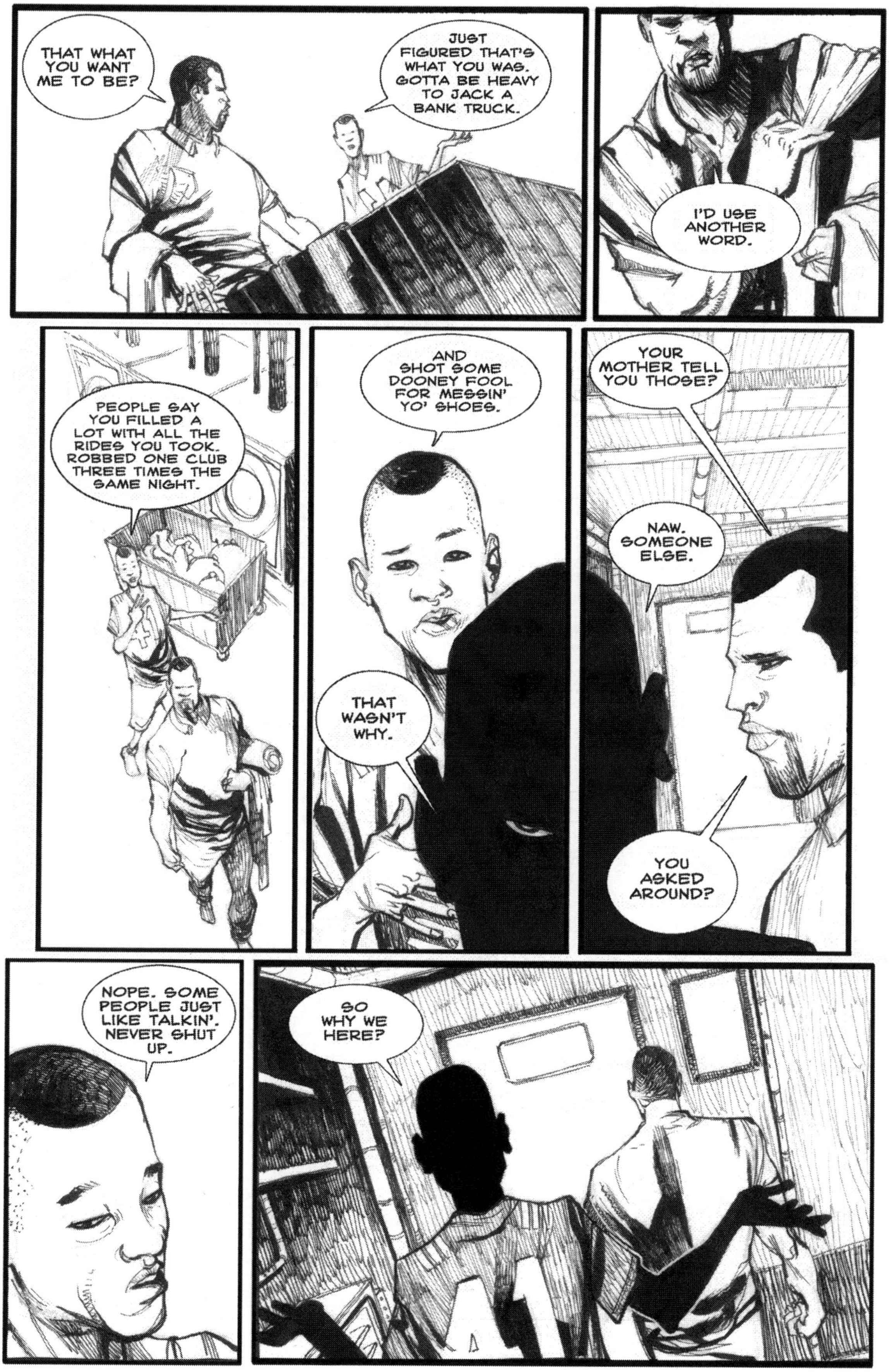

THAT WHAT YOU WANT ME TO BE?
JUST FIGURED THAT'S WHAT YOU WAS. GOTTA BE HEAVY TO JACK A BANK TRUCK.
I'D USE ANOTHER WORD.
PEOPLE SAY YOU FILLED A LOT WITH ALL THE RIDES YOU TOOK. ROBBED ONE CLUB THREE TIMES THE SAME NIGHT.
AND SHOT SOME DOONEY FOOL FOR MESSIN' YO' SHOES.
THAT WASN'T WHY.
YOUR MOTHER TELL YOU THOSE?
NAW. SOMEONE ELSE.
YOU ASKED AROUND?
NOPE. SOME PEOPLE JUST LIKE TALKIN'. NEVER SHUT UP.
SO WHY WE HERE?

KRRAAASH!!!
I DON'T SEE NO EXIT.
SO WE'LL MAKE ONE.
WITH THESE...
COME ON. THAT AIN'T WHO WE WANT.
SPEAK FOR YO'SELF!

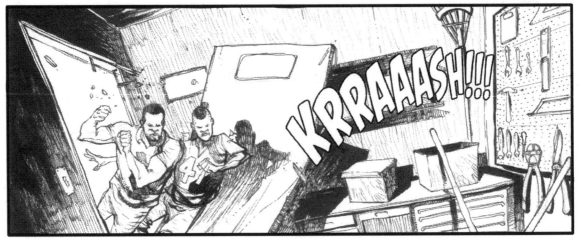

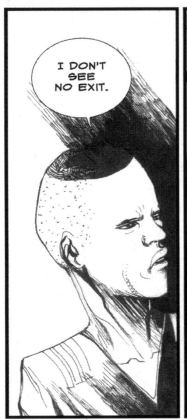

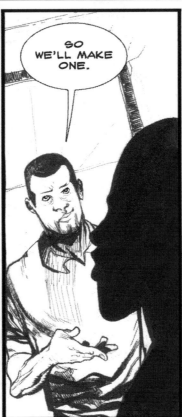

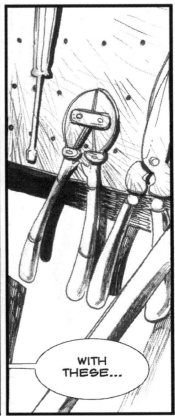

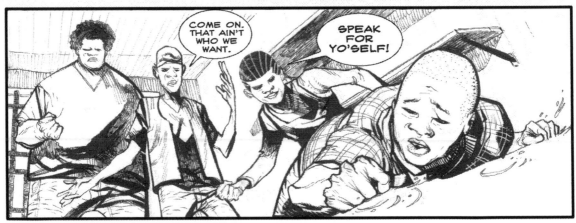

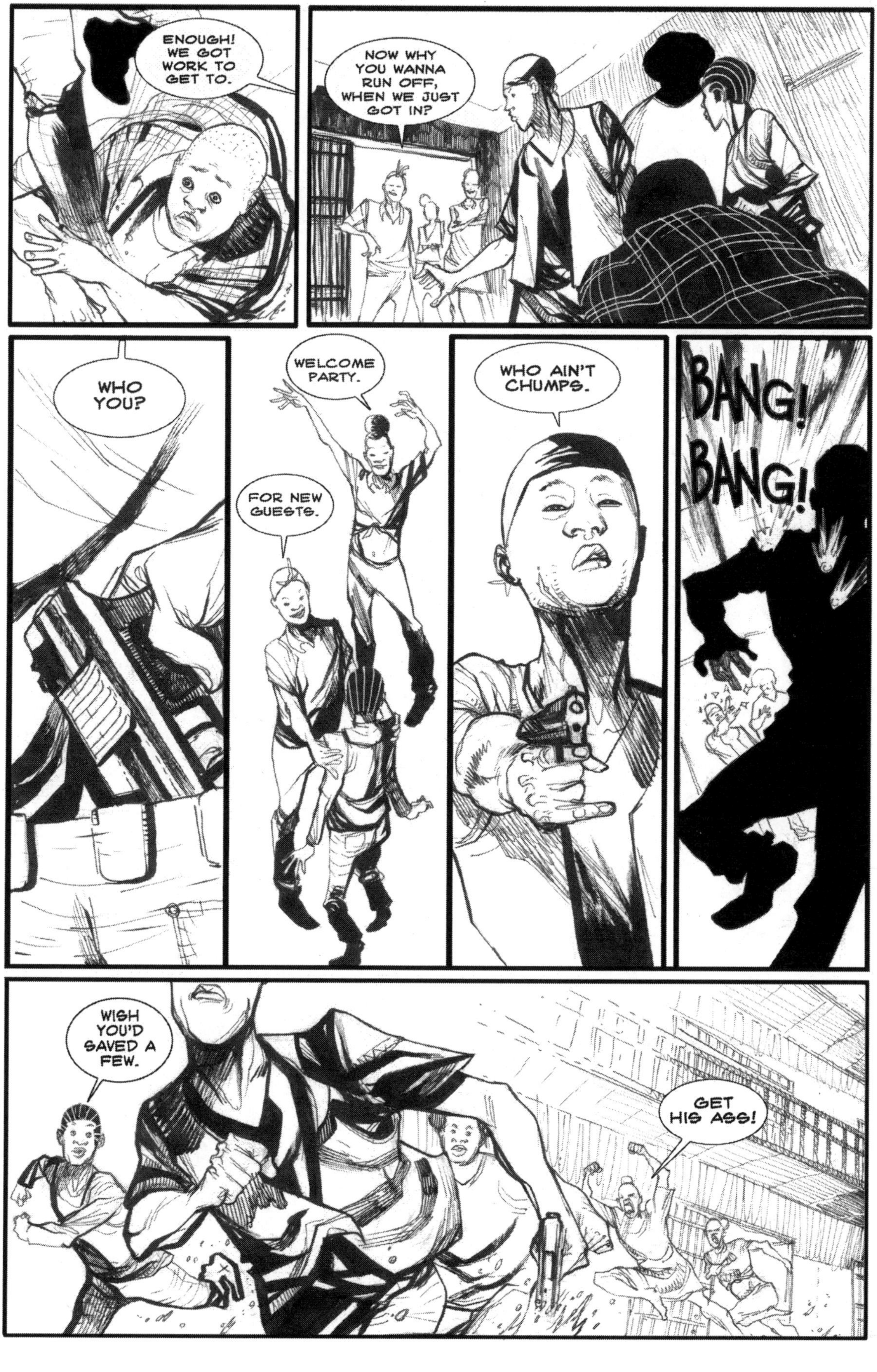
ENOUGH! WE GOT WORK TO GET TO.
NOW WHY YOU WANNA RUN OFF, WHEN WE JUST GOT IN?
WHO YOU?
WELCOME PARTY.
FOR NEW GUESTS.
WHO AIN'T CHUMPS.
BANG! BANG!
WISH YOU'D SAVED A FEW.
GET HIS ASS!

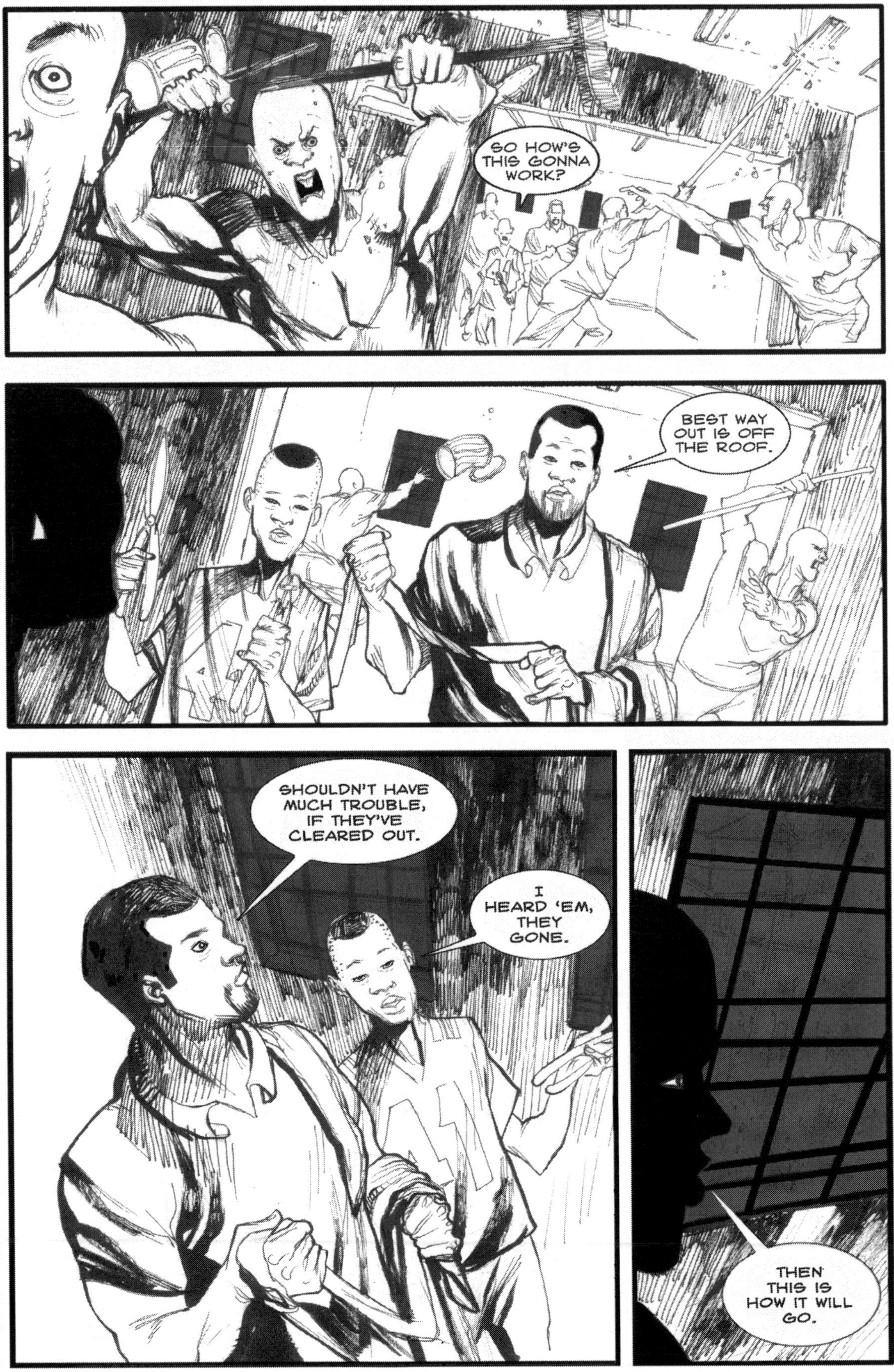
SO HOW'S THIS GONNA WORK?
BEST WAY OUT IS OFF THE ROOF.
SHOULDN'T HAVE MUCH TROUBLE, IF THEY'VE CLEARED OUT.
I HEARD 'EM, THEY GONE.
THEN THIS IS HOW IT WILL GO.

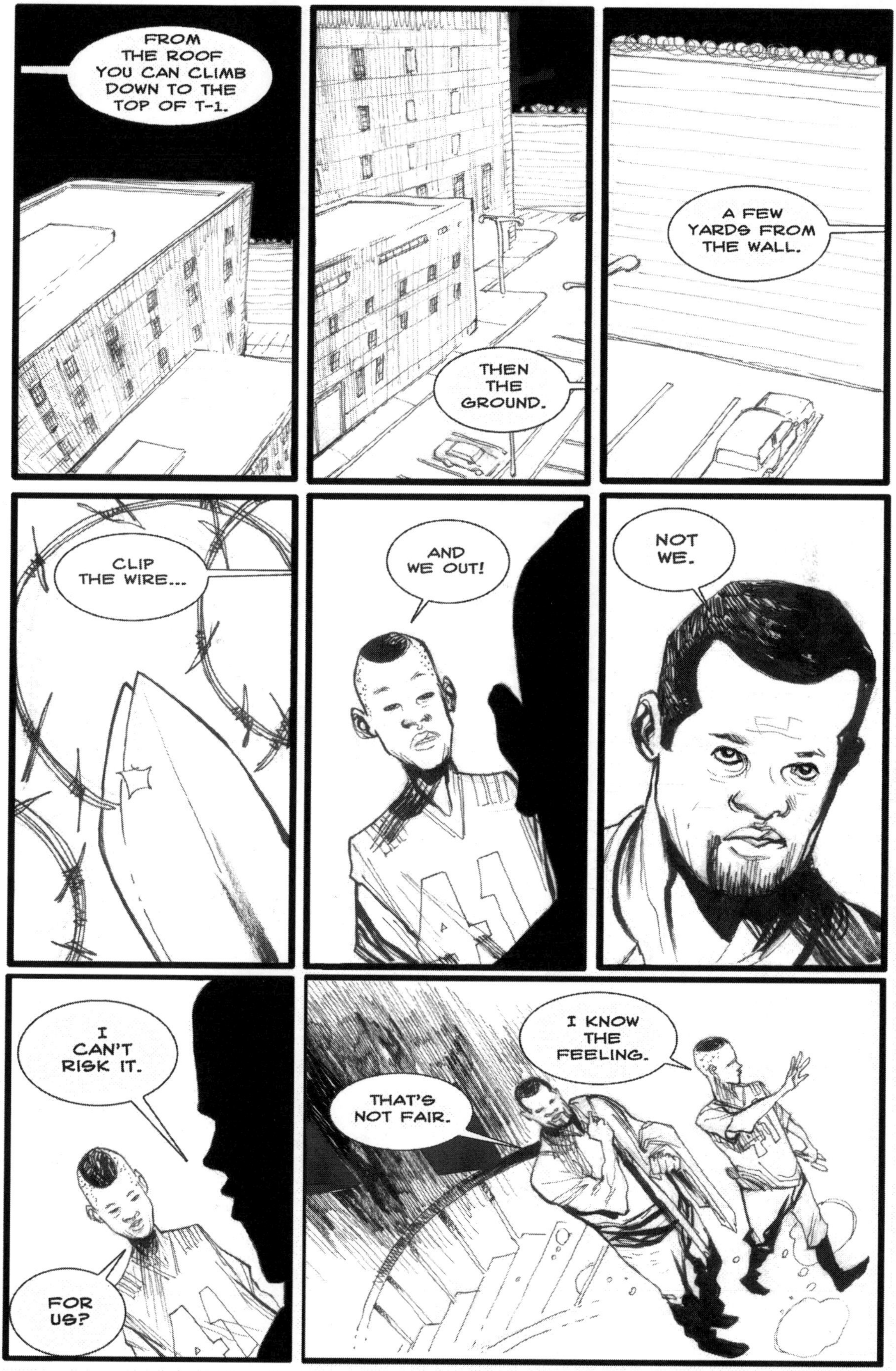

FROM THE ROOF YOU CAN CLIMB DOWN TO THE TOP OF T-1.
THEN THE GROUND.
A FEW YARDS FROM THE WALL.
CLIP THE WIRE...
AND WE OUT!
NOT WE.
I CAN'T RISK IT.
FOR US?
I KNOW THE FEELING.
THAT'S NOT FAIR.

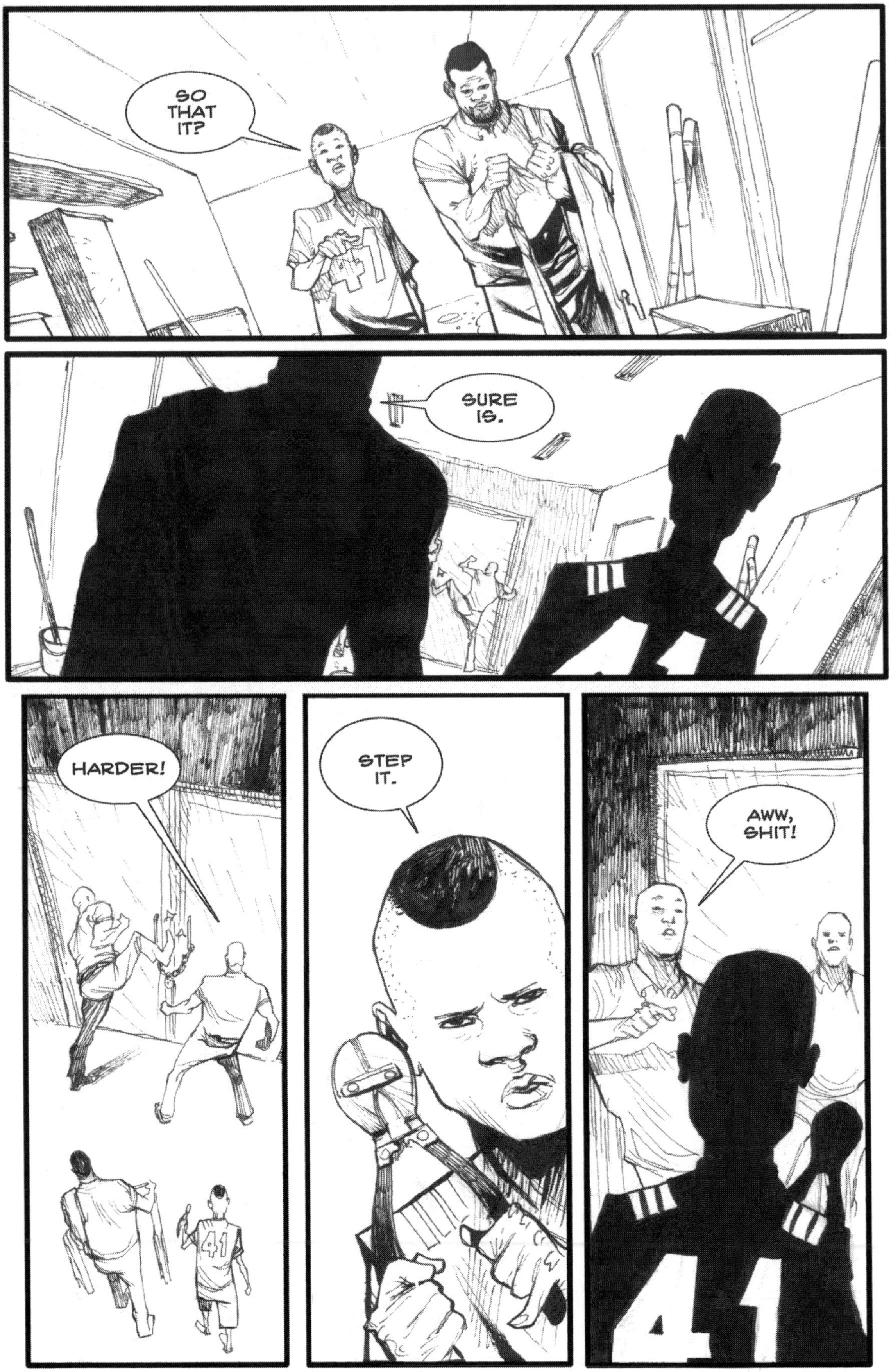
SO THAT IT?
SURE IS.
HARDER!
STEP IT.
AWW, SHIT!

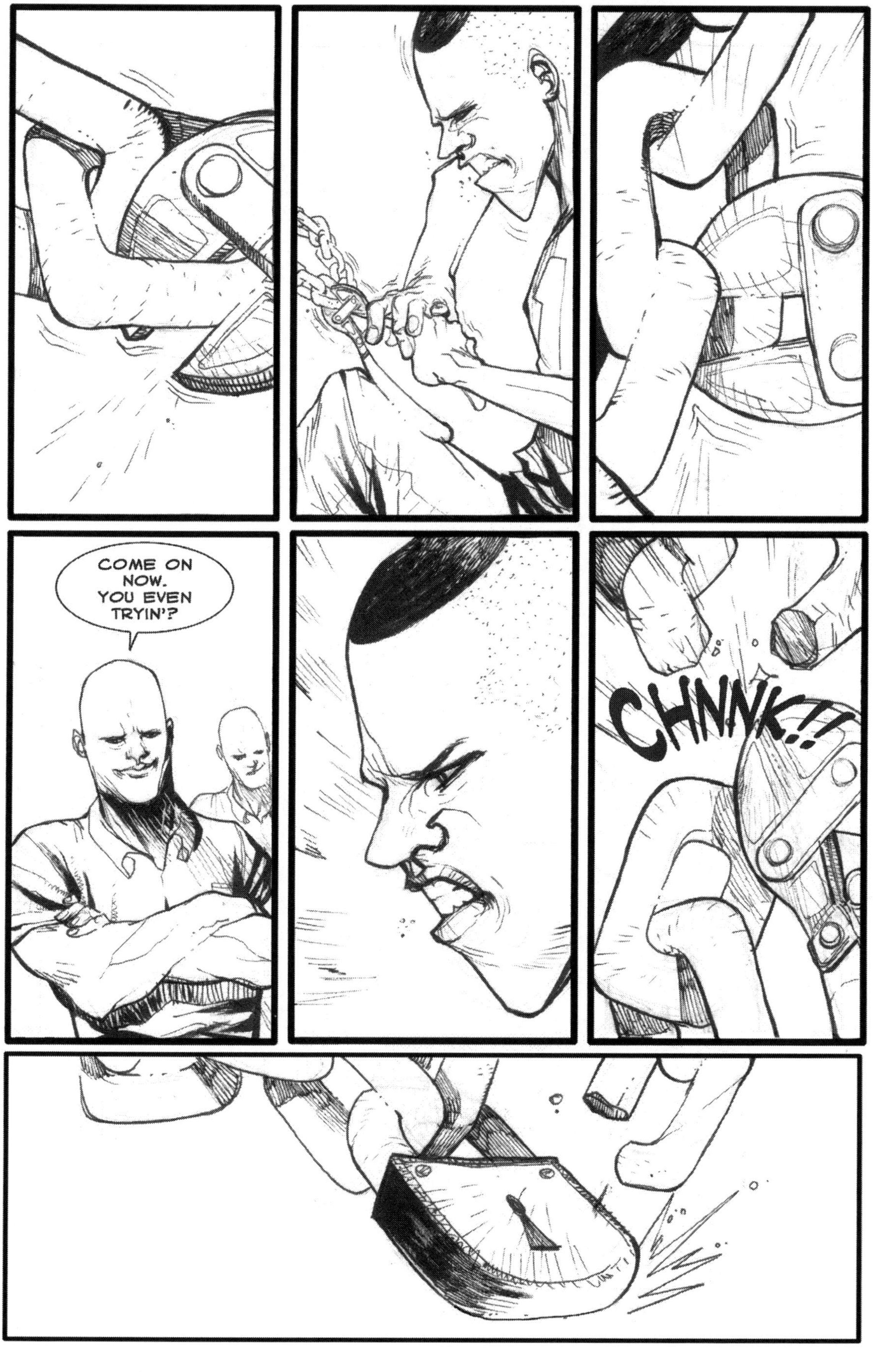
COME ON NOW. YOU EVEN TRYIN'?
CHNNK!!

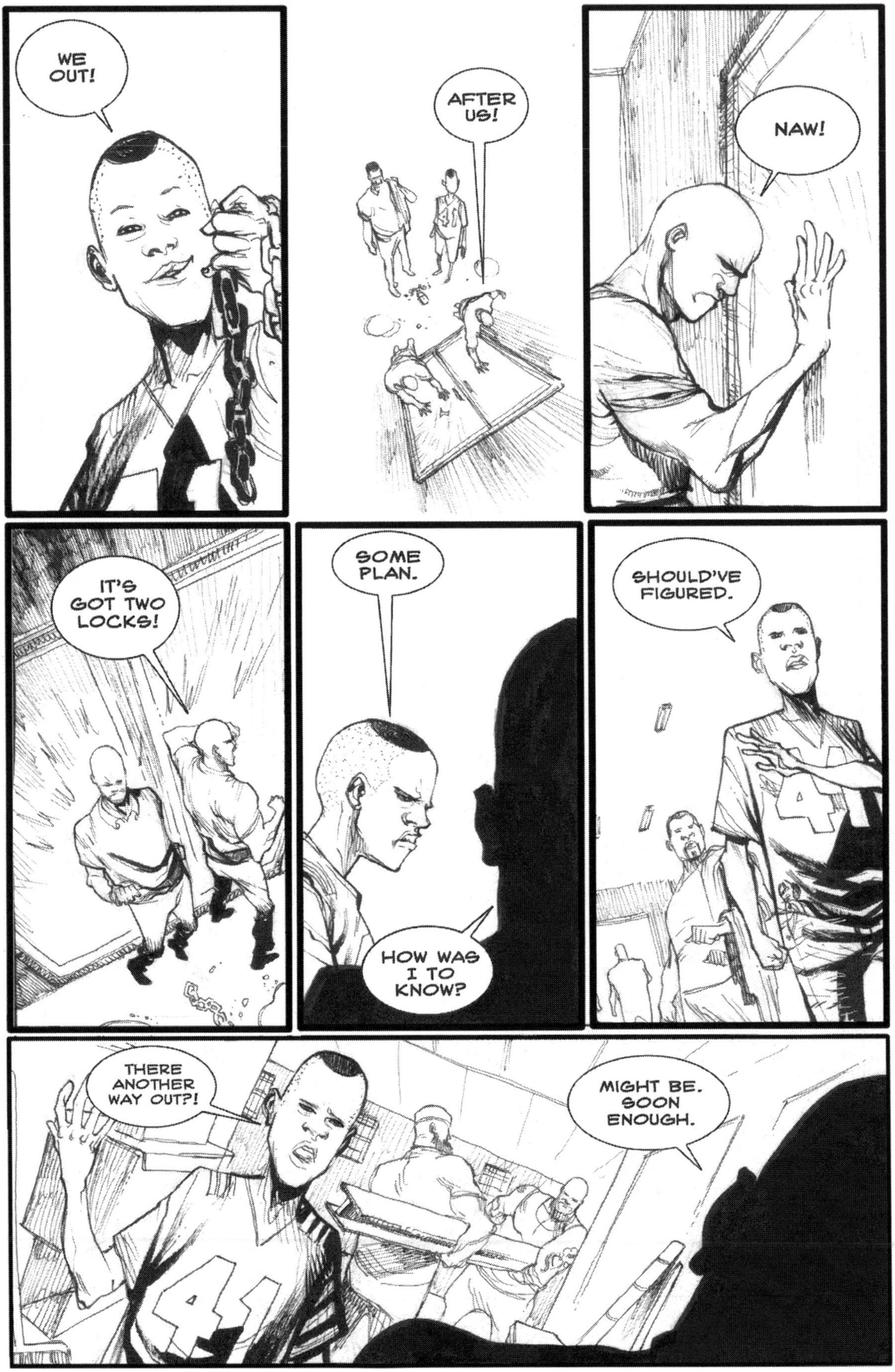
WE OUT!
AFTER US!
NAW!
IT'S GOT TWO LOCKS!
SOME PLAN.
HOW WAS I TO KNOW?
SHOULD'VE FIGURED.
THERE ANOTHER WAY OUT?!
MIGHT BE. SOON ENOUGH.

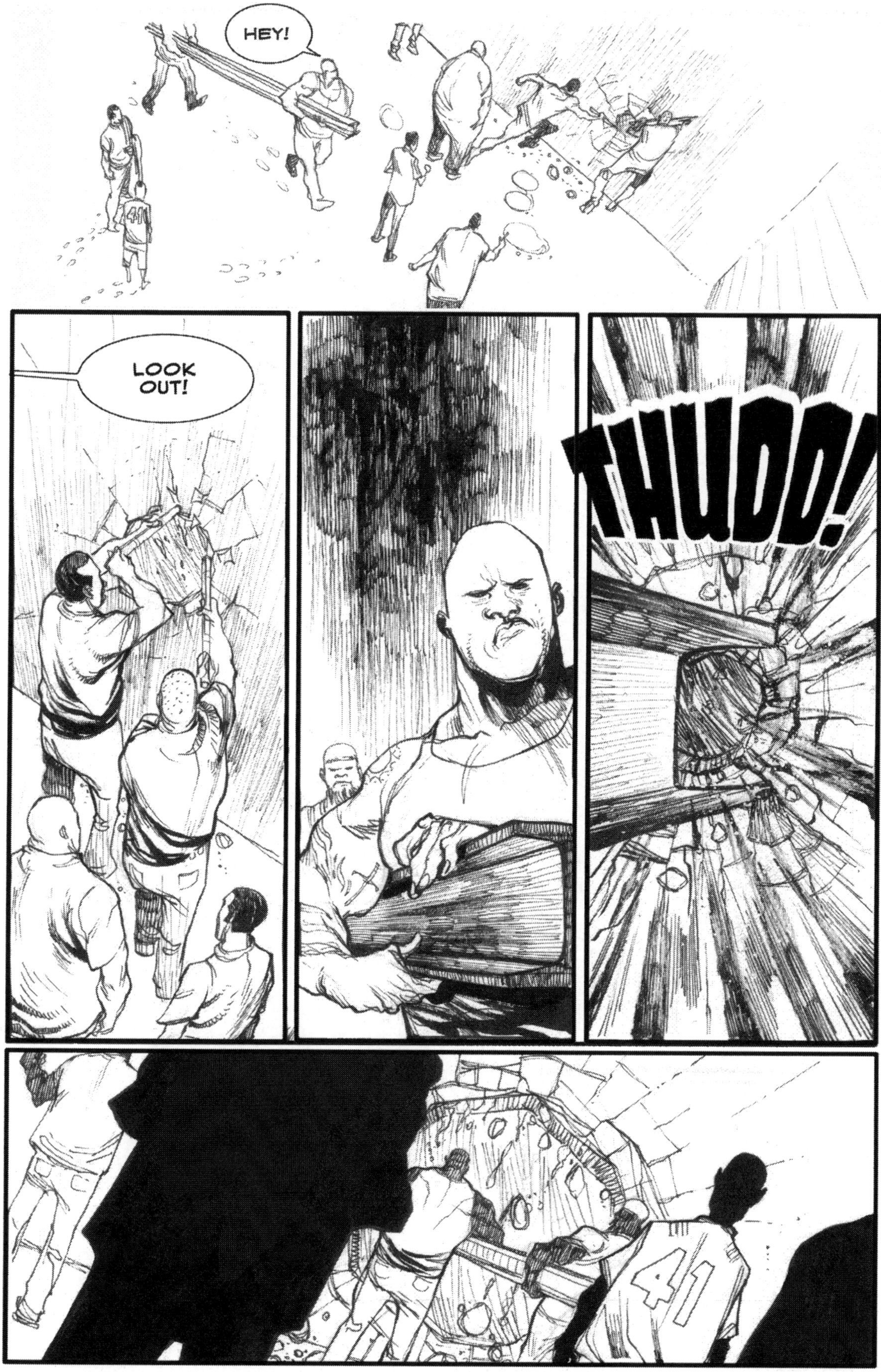
HEY!
LOOK OUT!
THUDD!

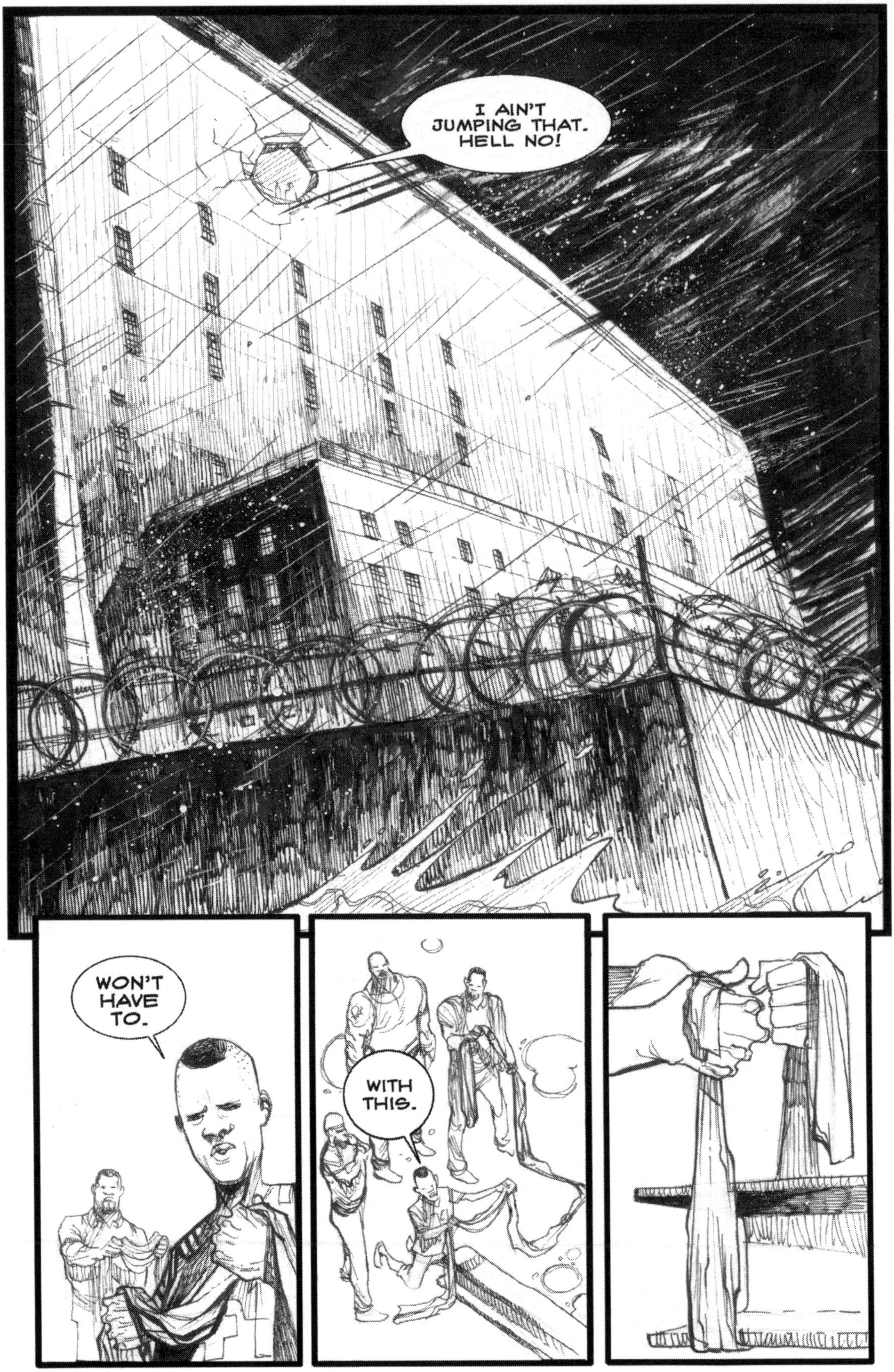
I AIN'T JUMPING THAT. HELL NO!
WON'T HAVE TO.
WITH THIS.

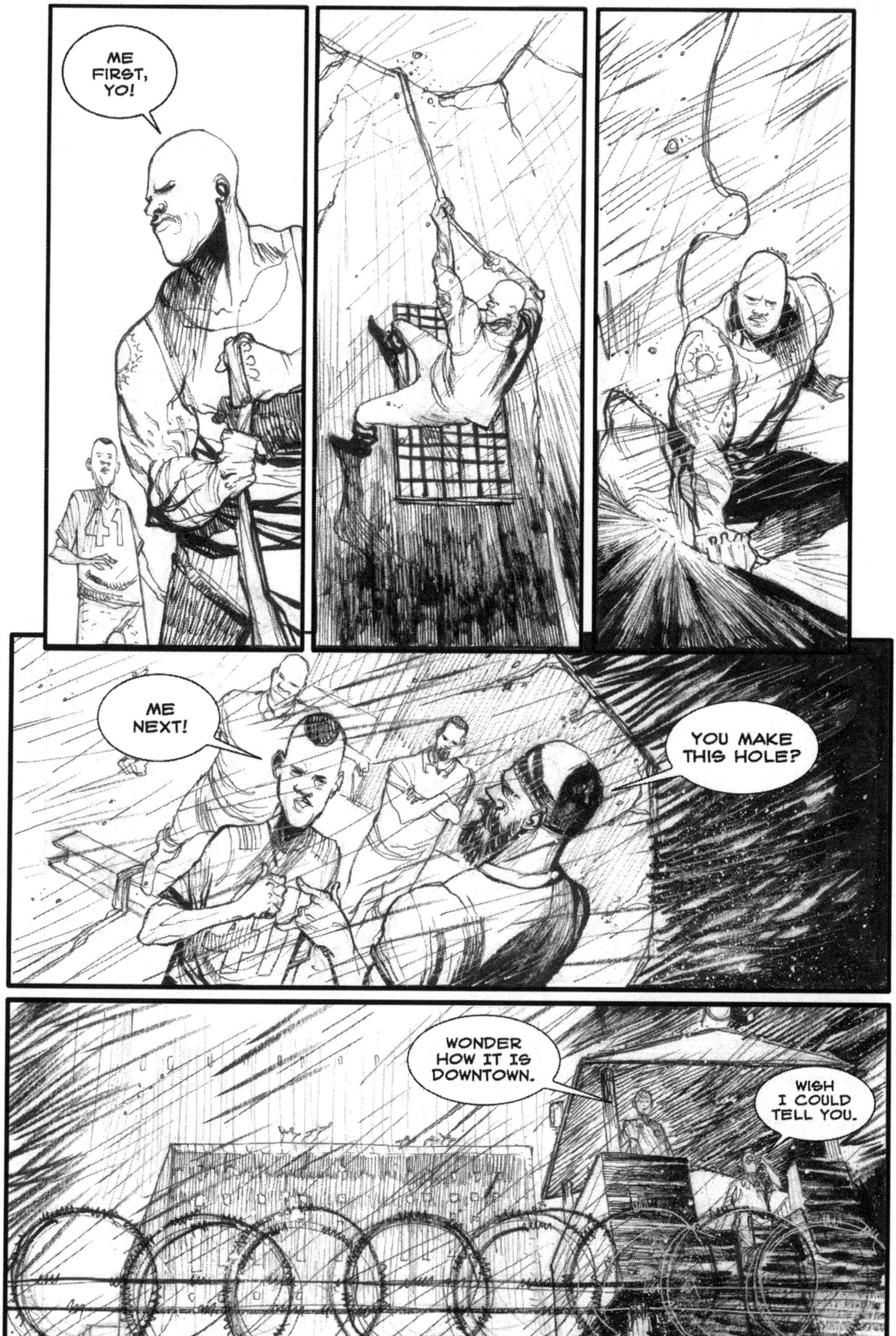
ME FIRST, YO!
ME NEXT!
YOU MAKE THIS HOLE?
WONDER HOW IT IS DOWNTOWN.
WISH I COULD TELL YOU.

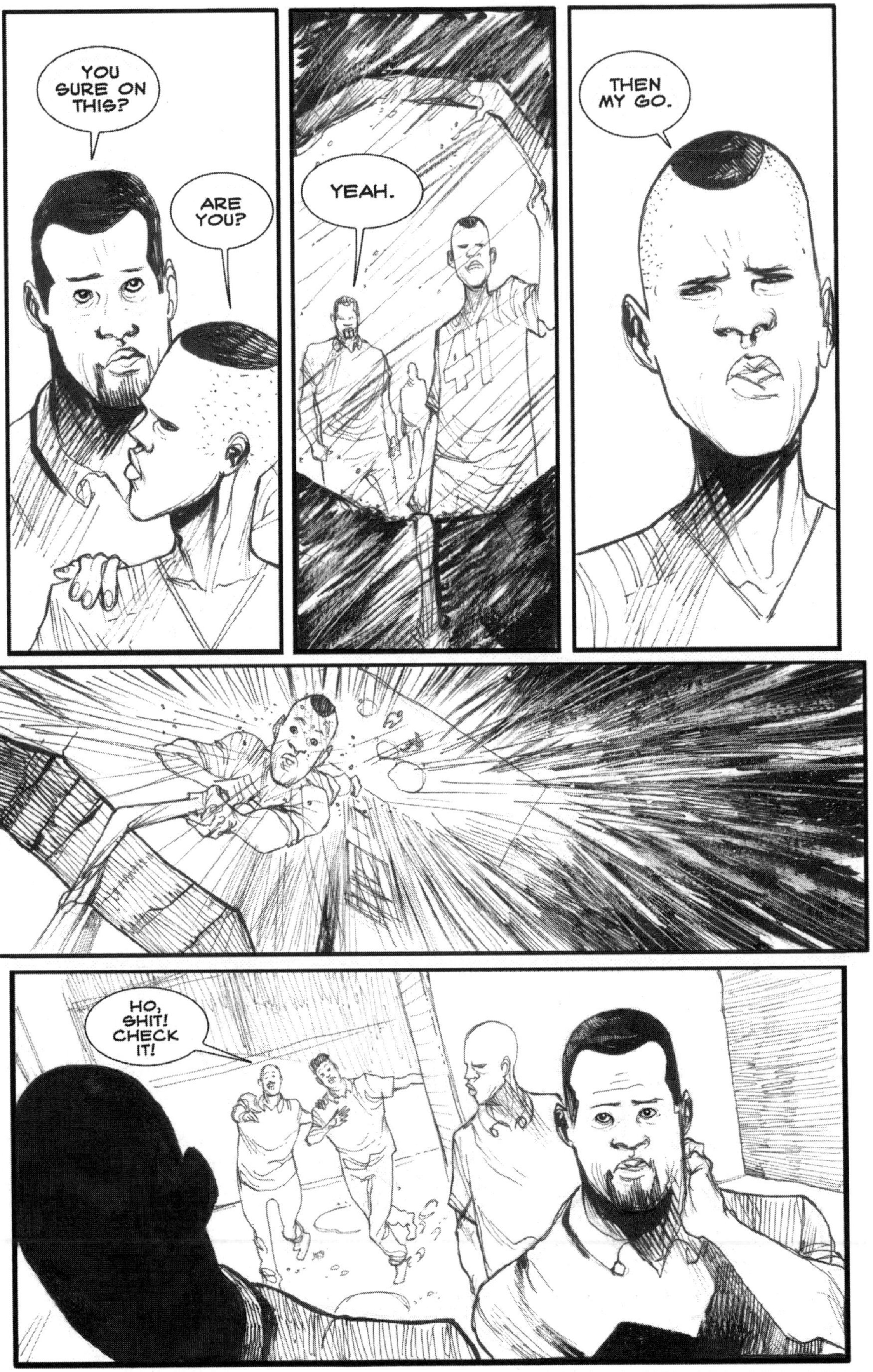
YOU SURE ON THIS?
ARE YOU?
YEAH.
THEN MY GO.
HO, SHIT! CHECK IT!

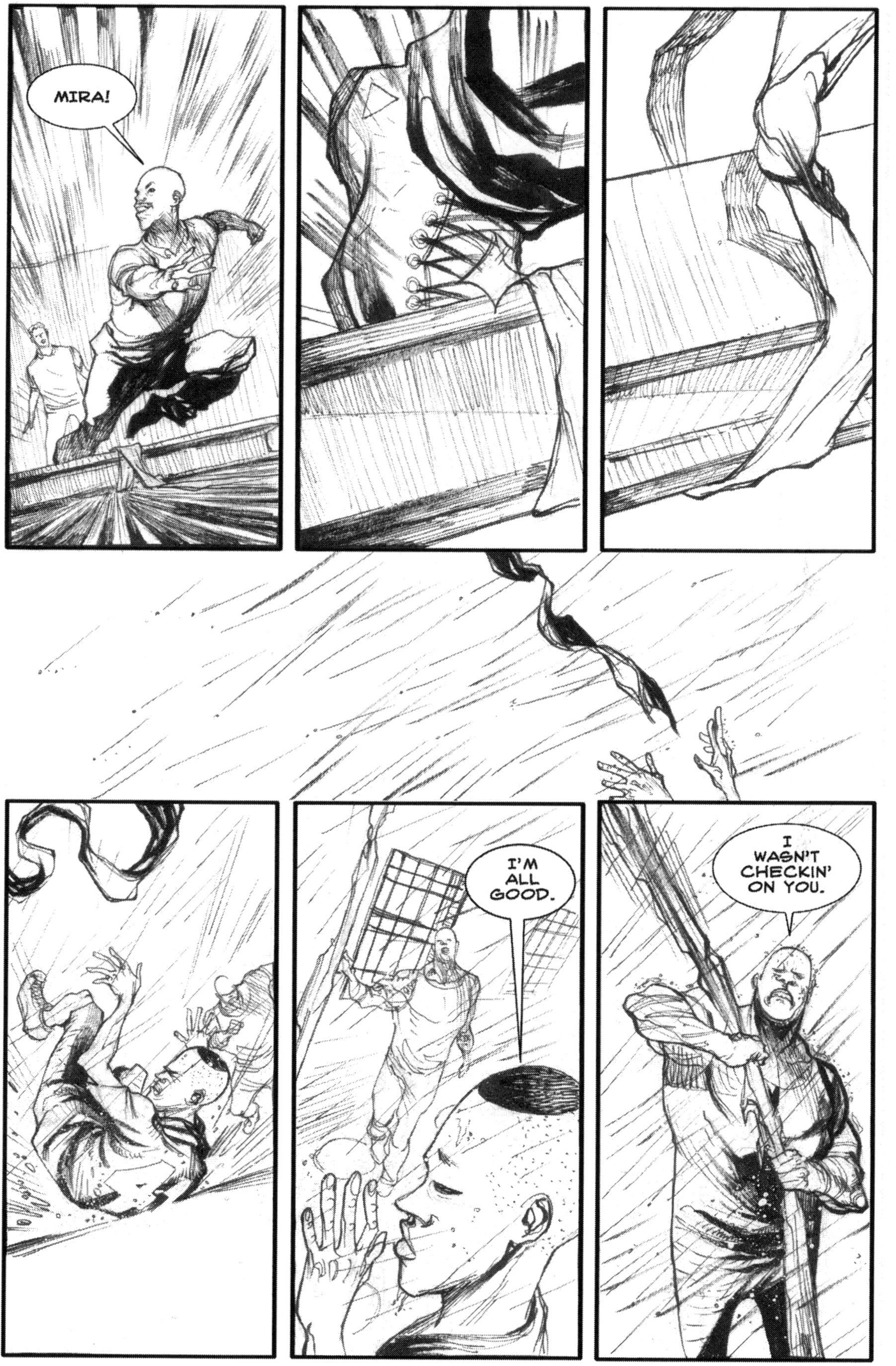
MIRA!
I'M ALL GOOD.
I WASN'T CHECKIN' ON YOU.

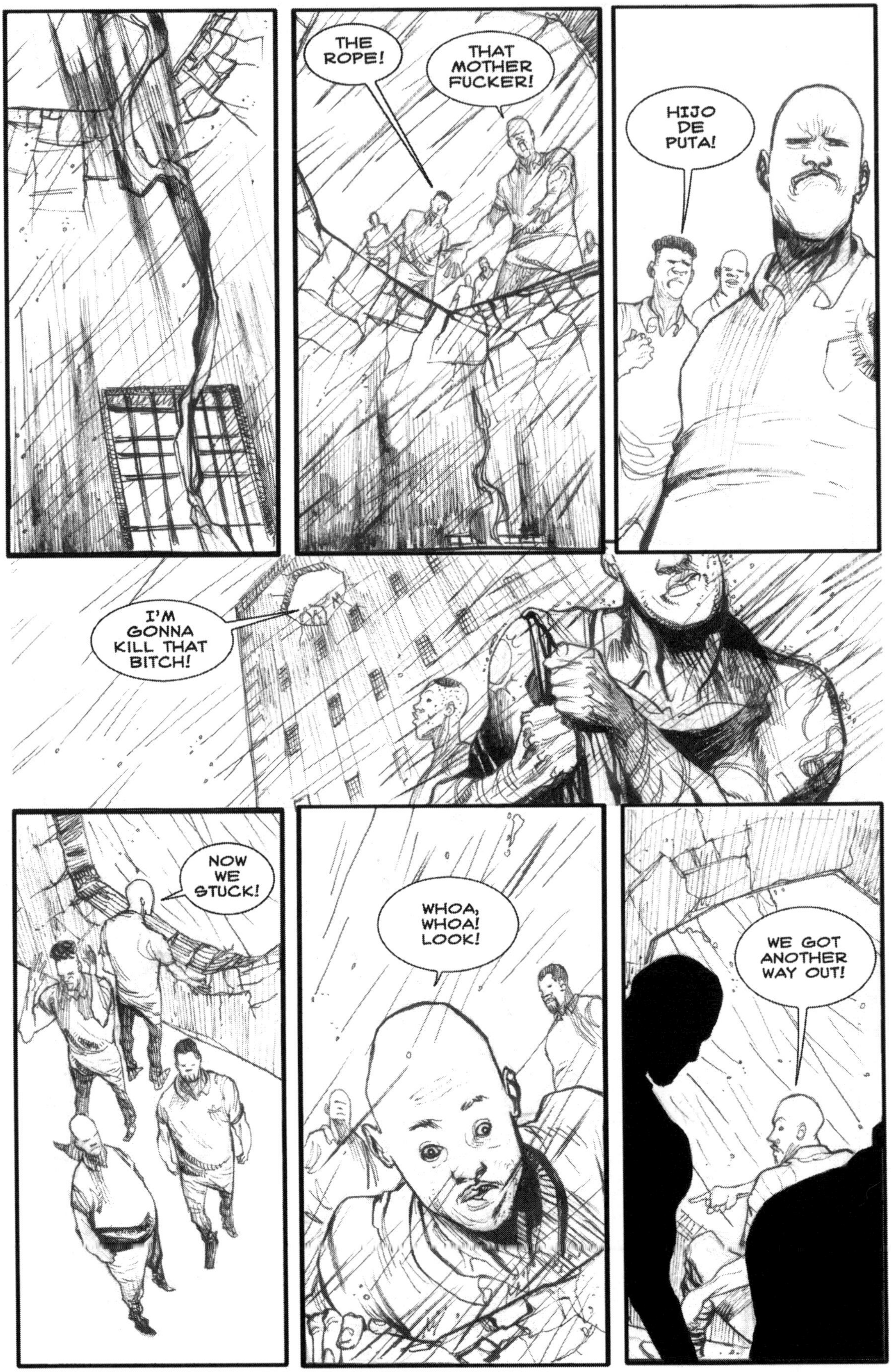
THE ROPE!
THAT MOTHER FUCKER!
HIJO DE PUTA!
I'M GONNA KILL THAT BITCH!
NOW WE STUCK!
WHOA, WHOA! LOOK!
WE GOT ANOTHER WAY OUT!

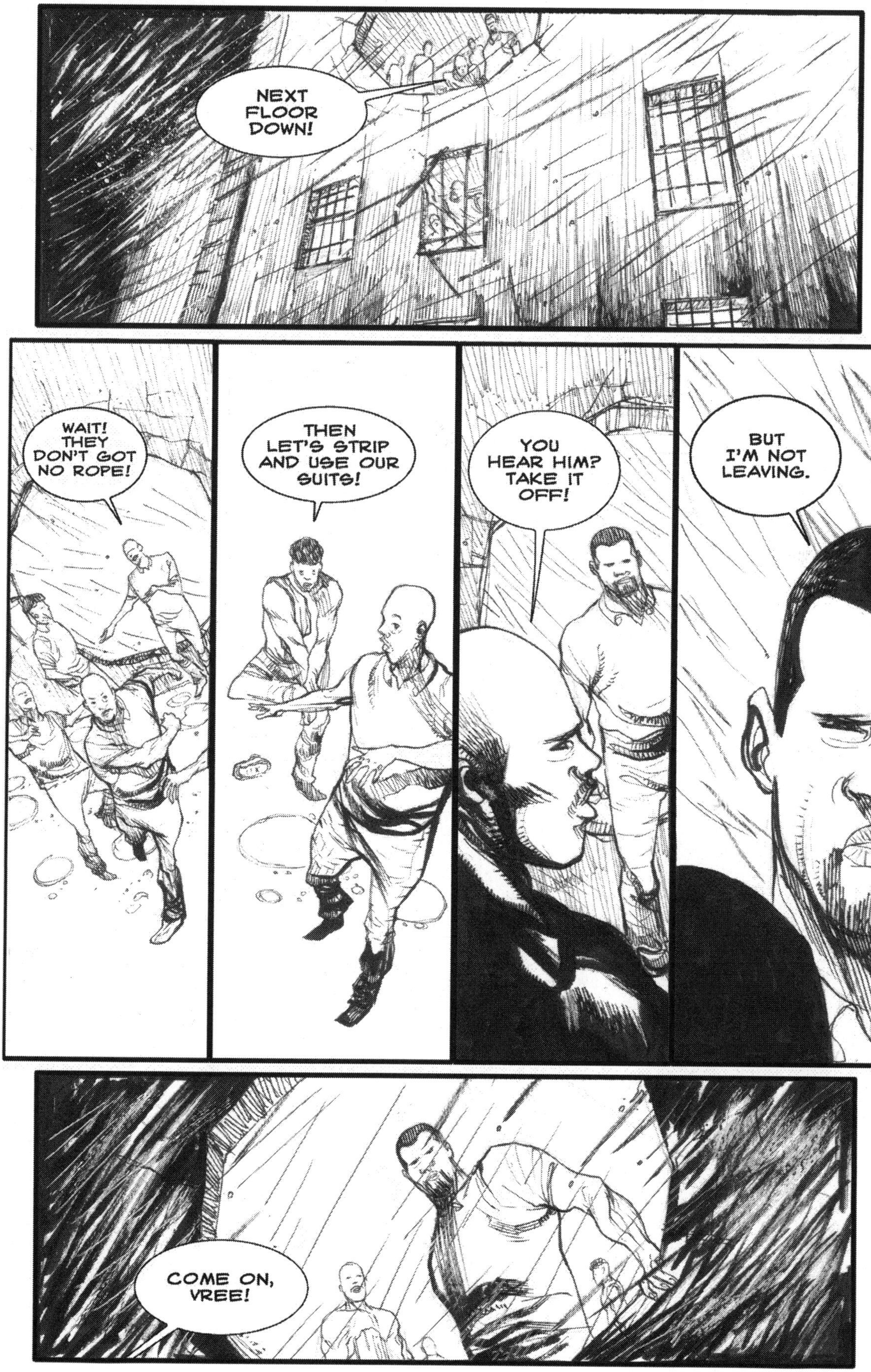
NEXT FLOOR DOWN!
WAIT! THEY DON'T GOT NO ROPE!
THEN LET'S STRIP AND USE OUR SUITS!
YOU HEAR HIM? TAKE IT OFF!
BUT I'M NOT LEAVING.
COME ON, VREE!

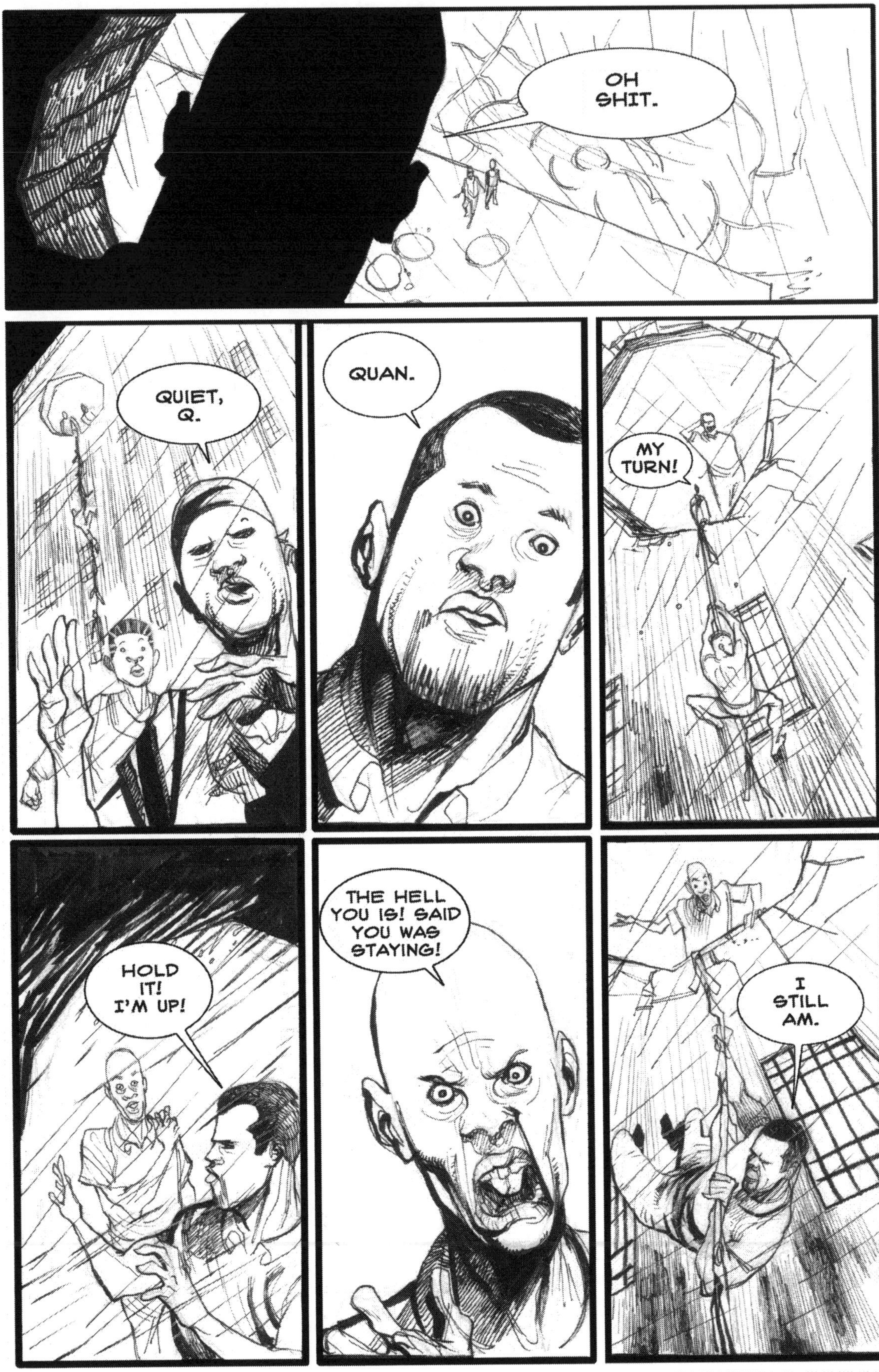
OH SHIT.
QUIET, Q.
QUAN.
MY TURN!
HOLD IT! I'M UP!
THE HELL YOU IS! SAID YOU WAS STAYING!
I STILL AM.

WAIT UP!

FUCK THIS! I'M GOING!

DON'T!

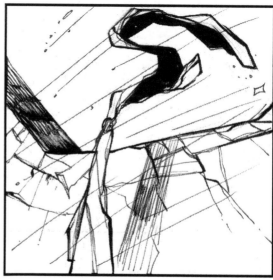

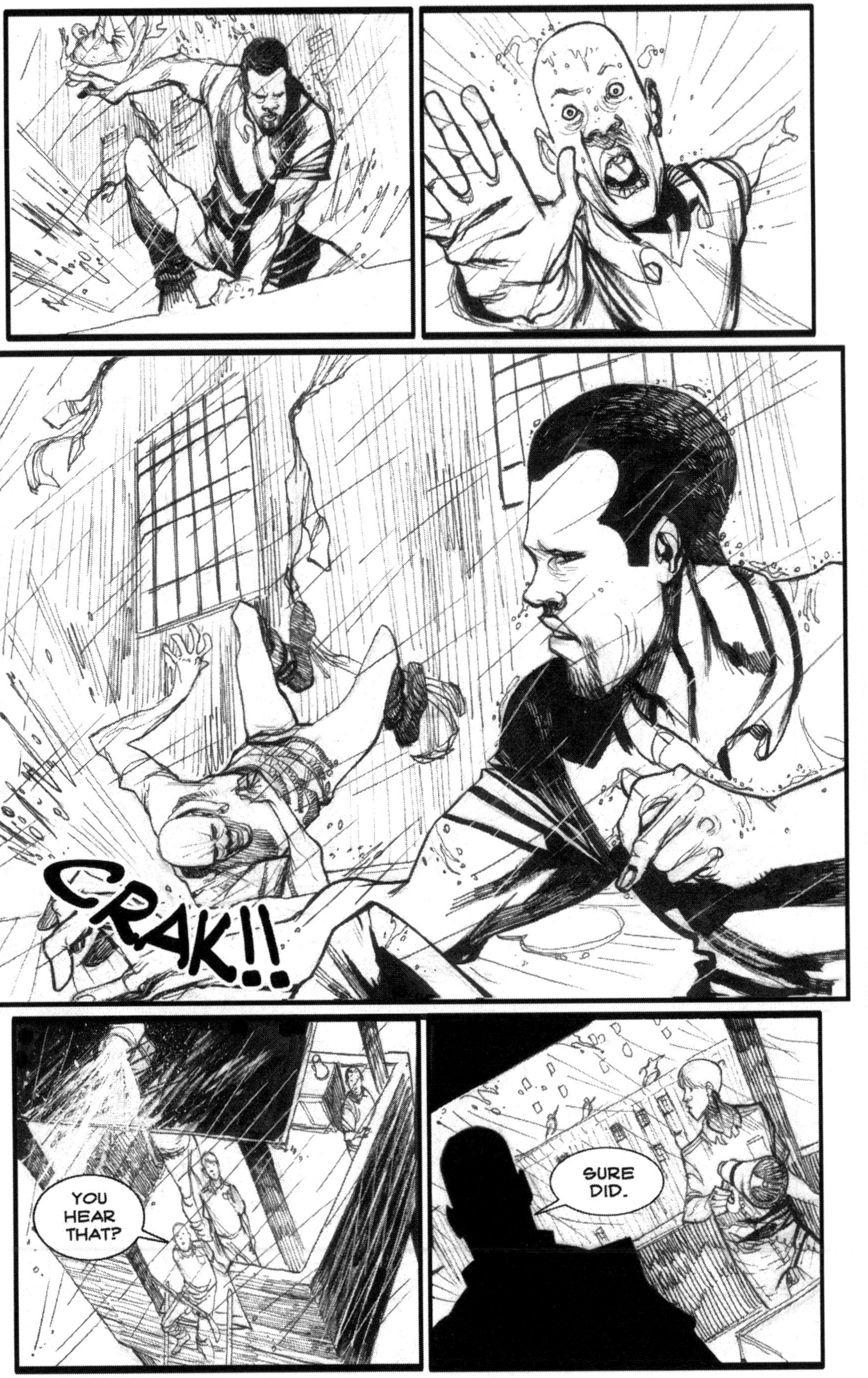
CRAK!!
YOU HEAR THAT?
SURE DID.

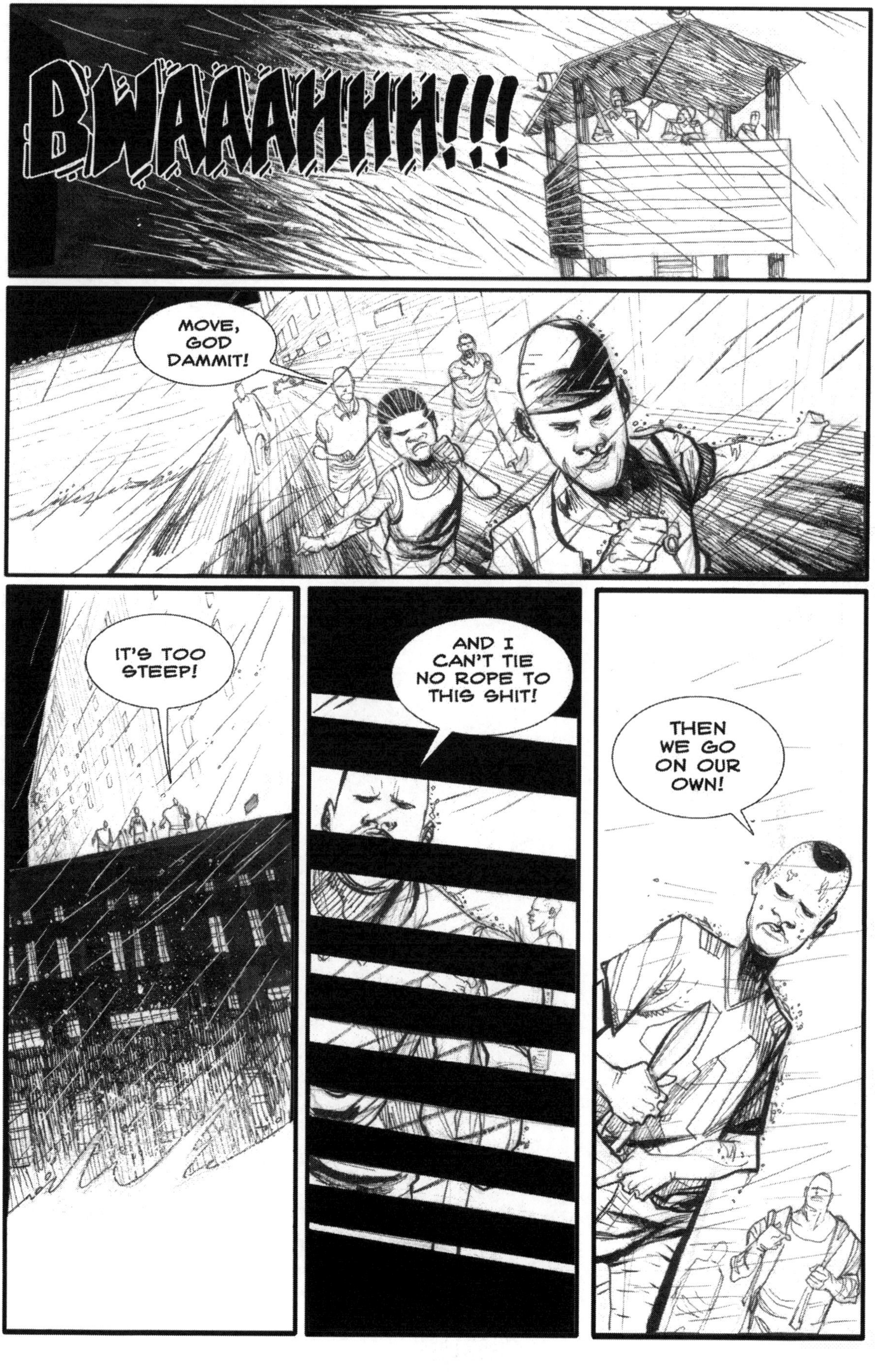
BWAAAHHH!!!
MOVE, GOD DAMMIT!
IT'S TOO STEEP!
AND I CAN'T TIE NO ROPE TO THIS SHIT!
THEN WE GO ON OUR OWN!

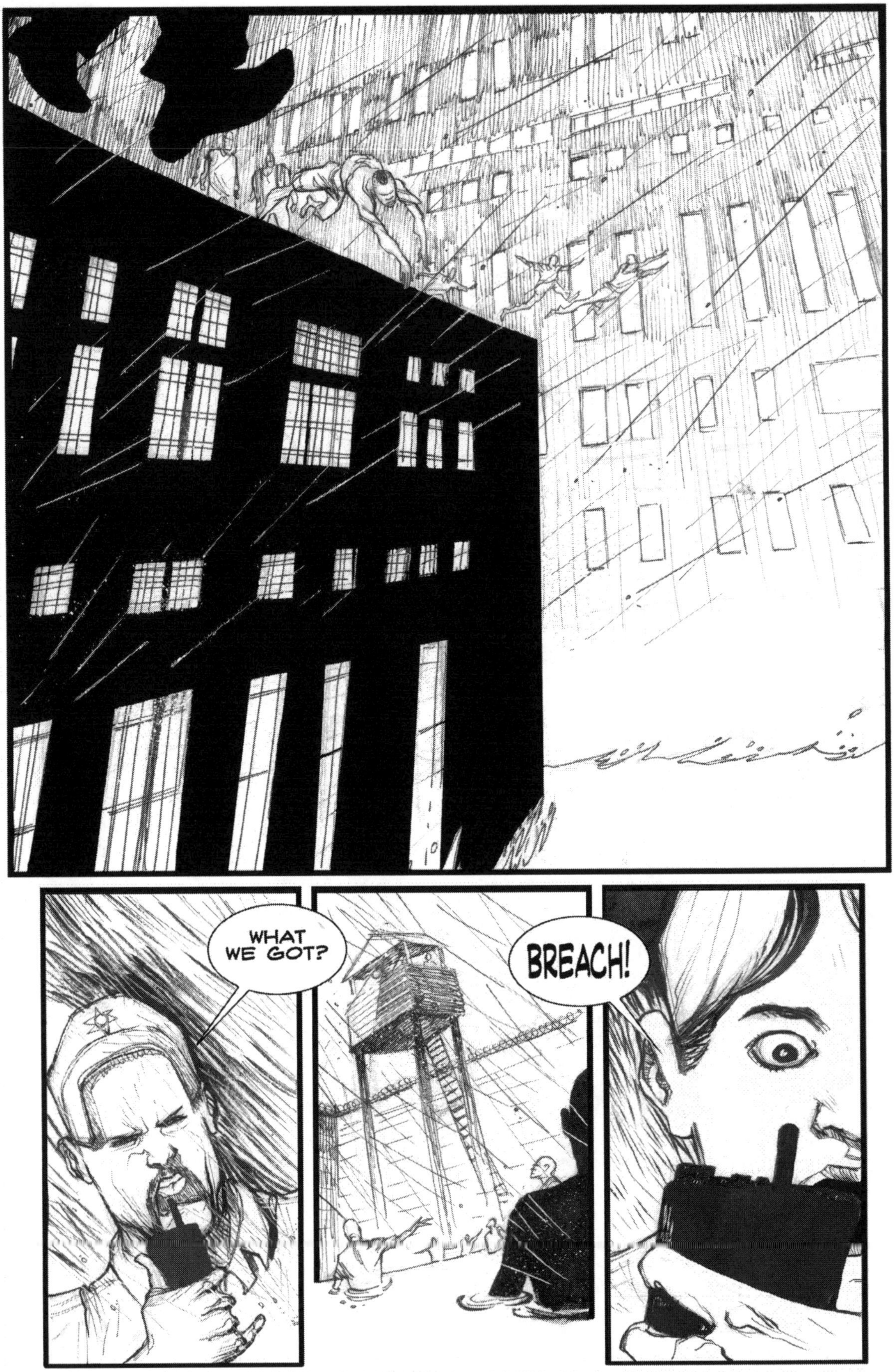
WHAT WE GOT?
BREACH!

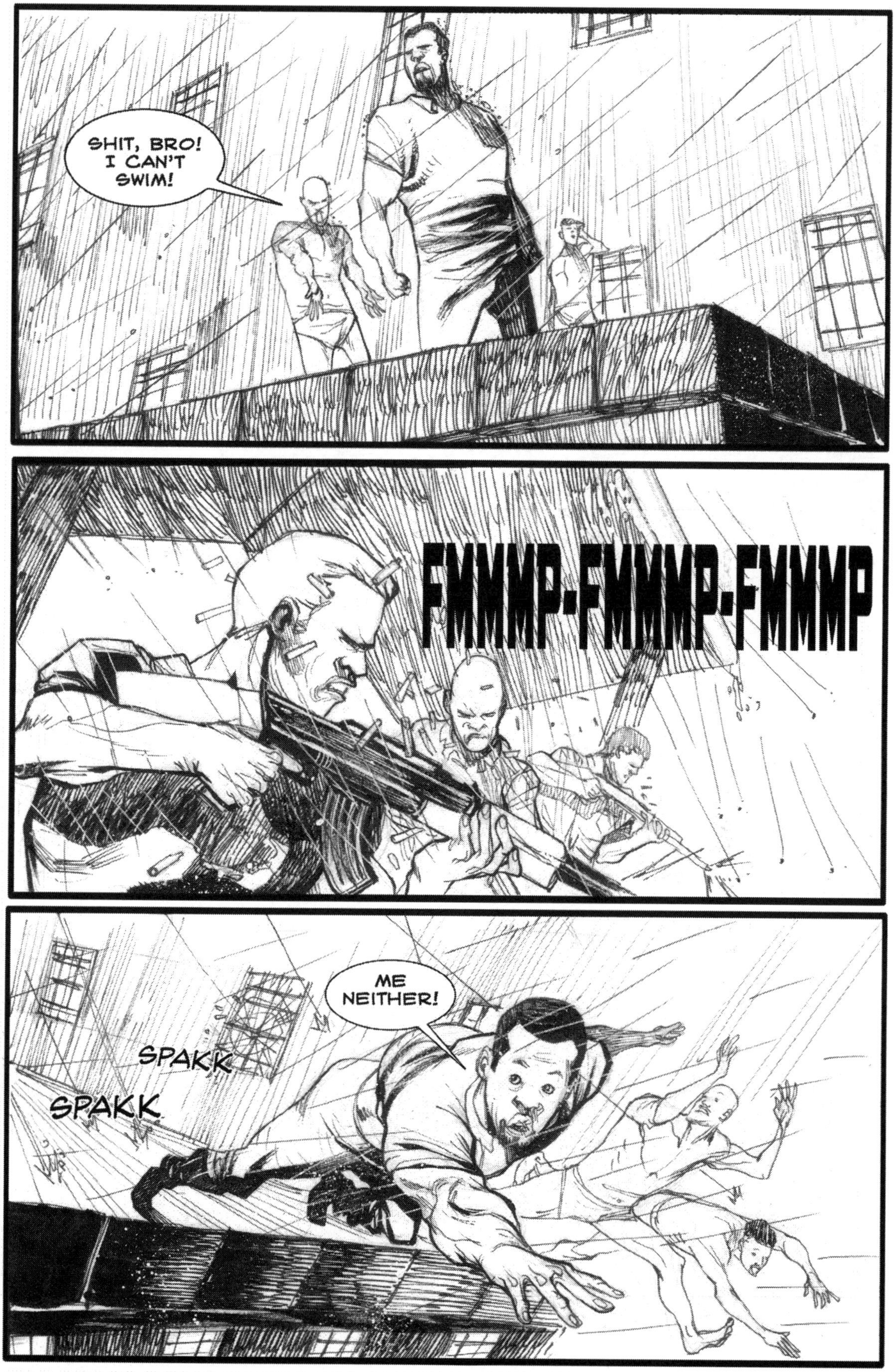
SHIT, BRO! I CAN'T SWIM!
FMMMP-FMMMP-FMMMP
ME NEITHER!
SPAKK
SPAKK

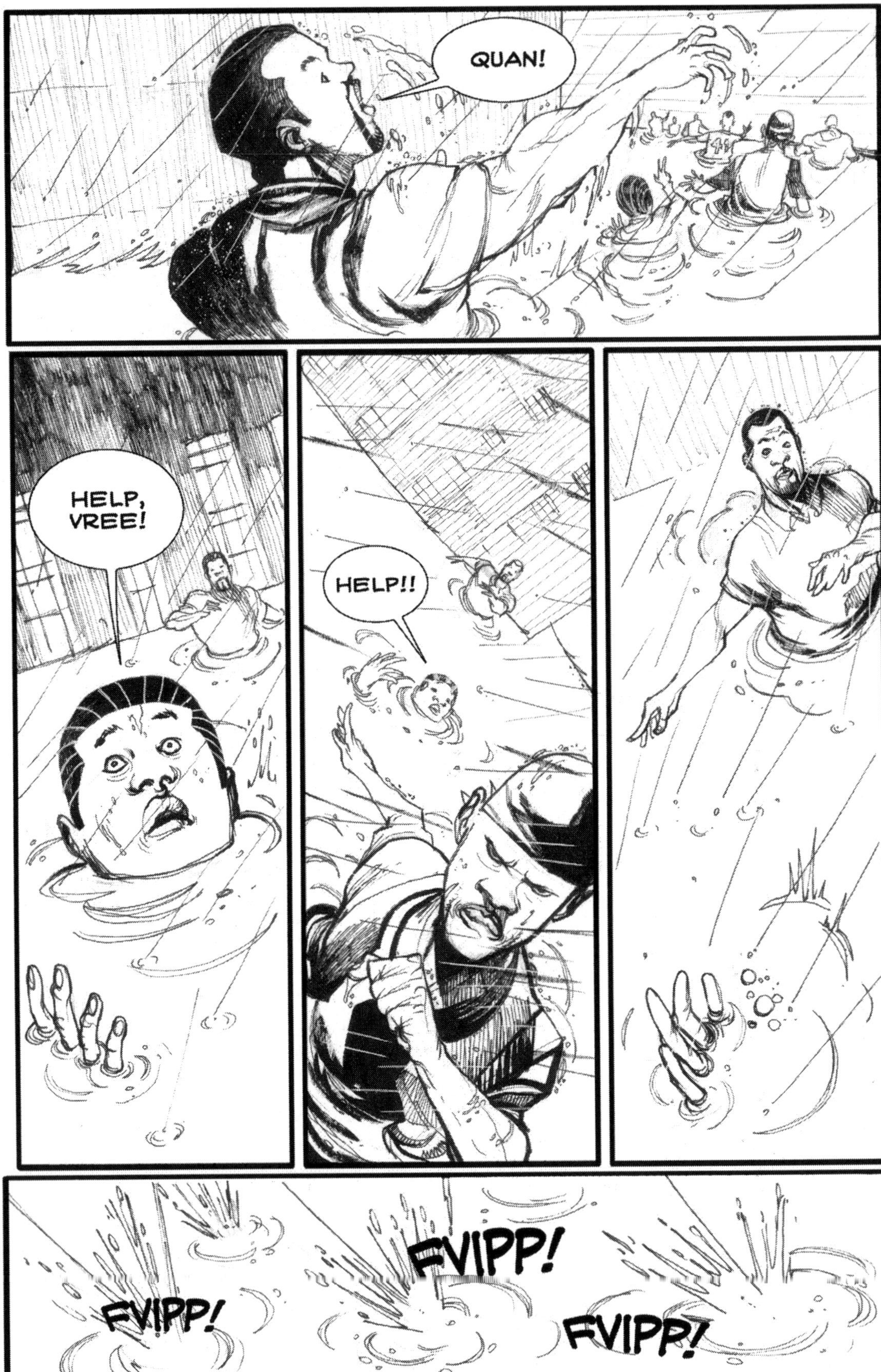
QUAN!
HELP, VREE!
HELP!!
FVIPP!
FVIPP!
FVIPP!

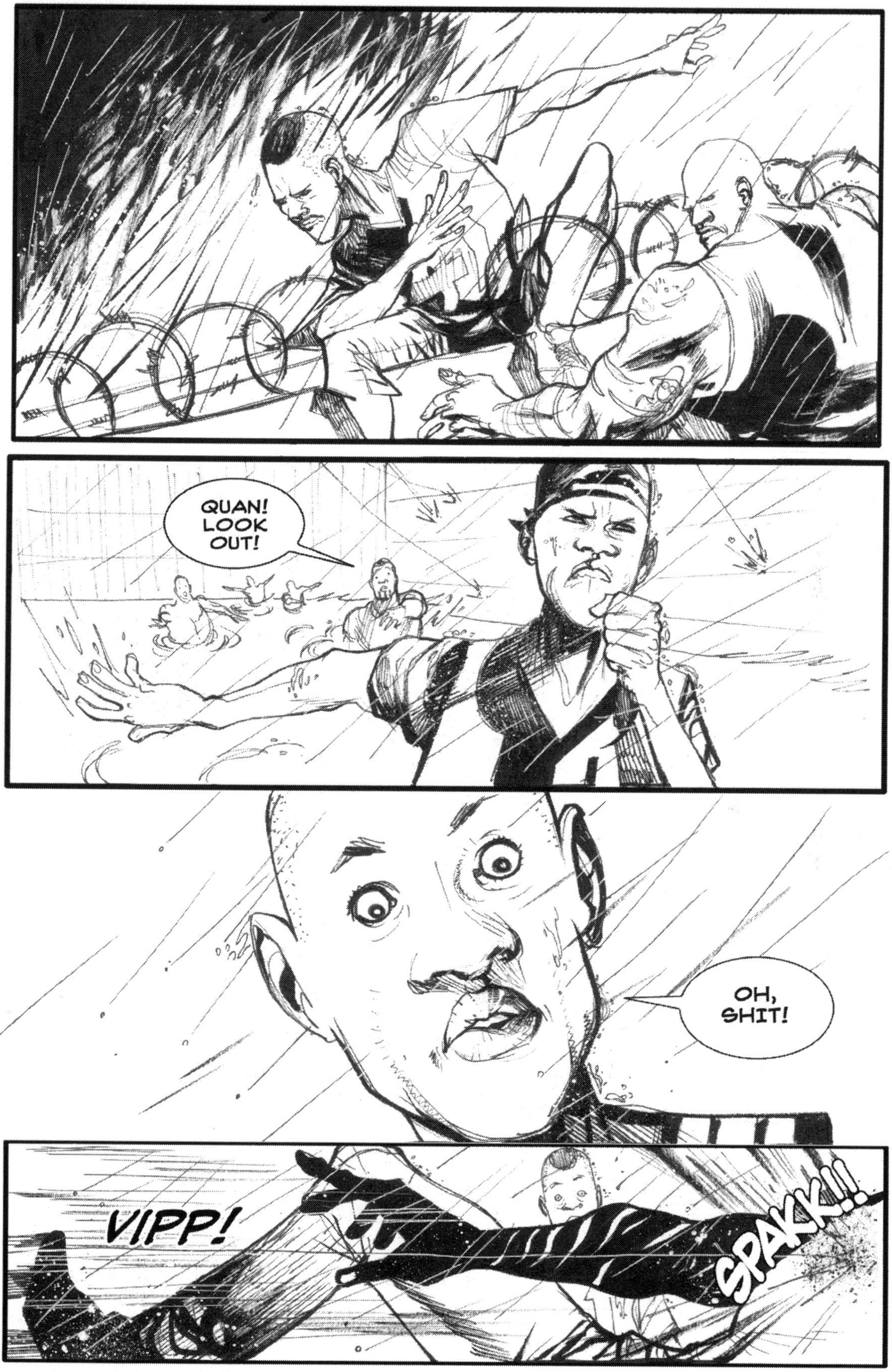
QUAN! LOOK OUT!
OH, SHIT!
VIPP!
SPAKK!!

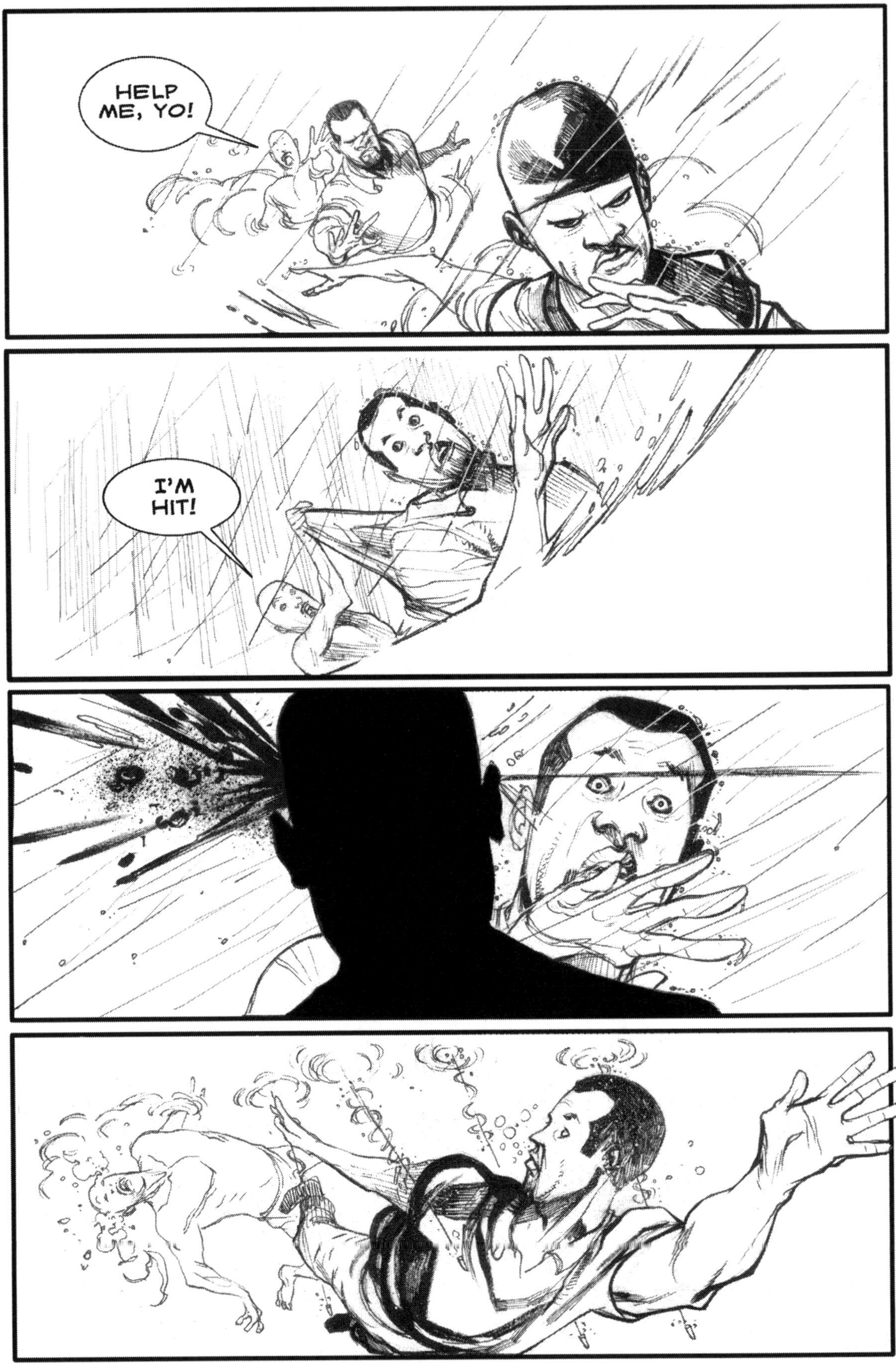
HELP ME, YO!
I'M HIT!

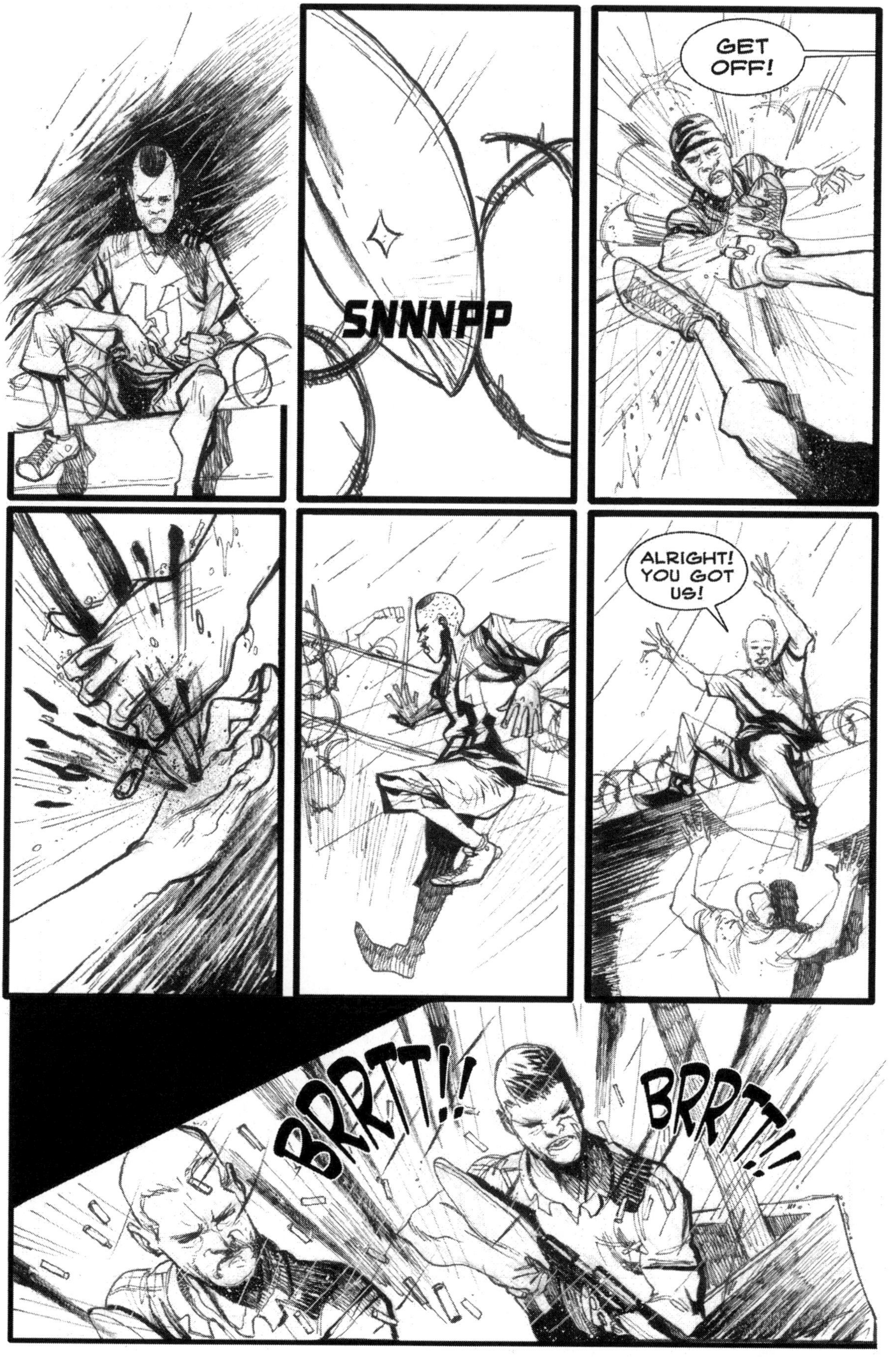
SNNNPP
GET OFF!
ALRIGHT! YOU GOT US!
BRRTT!!
BRRTT!!!

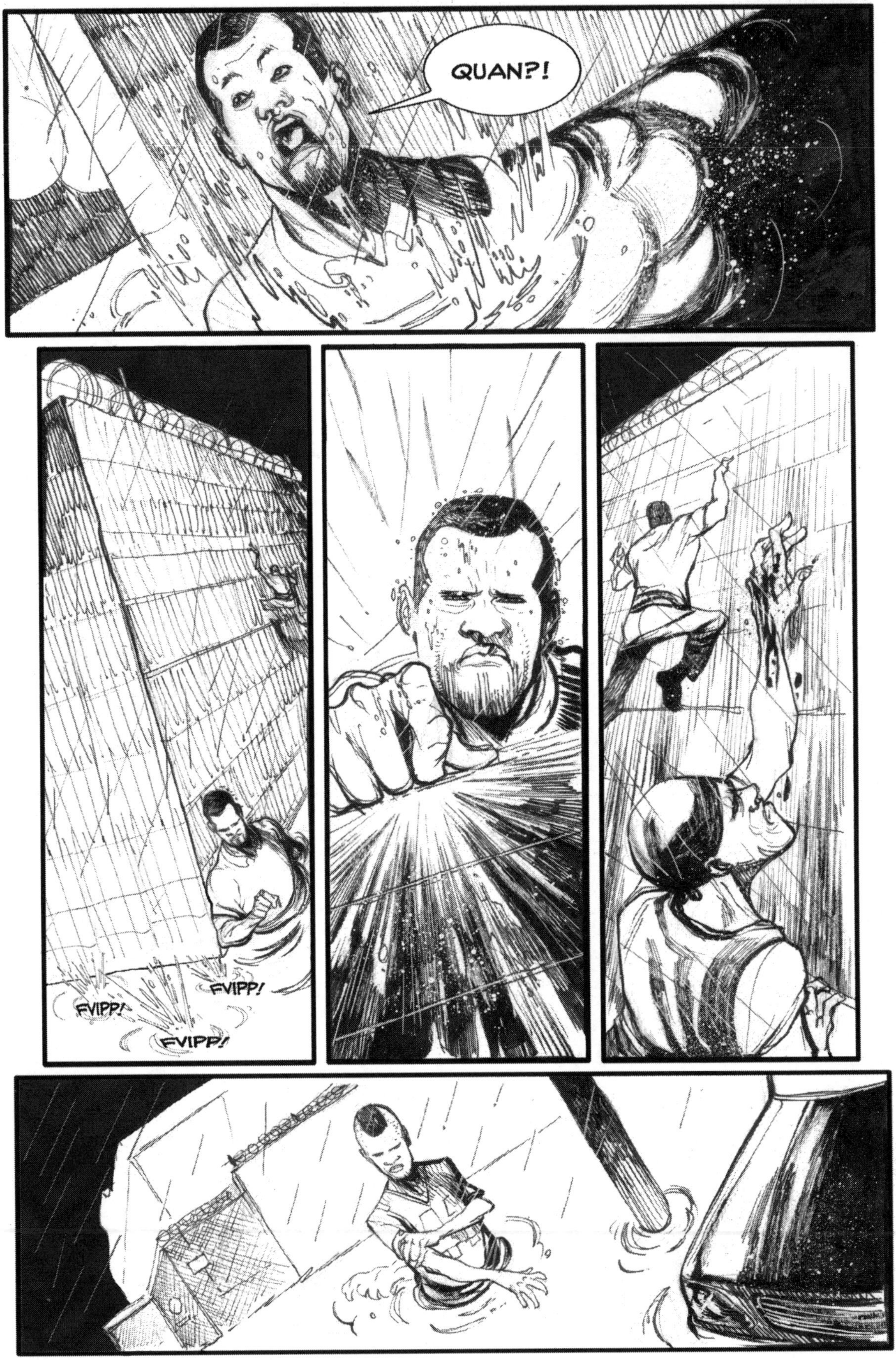
QUAN?!
FVIPP!
FVIPP!
FVIPP!

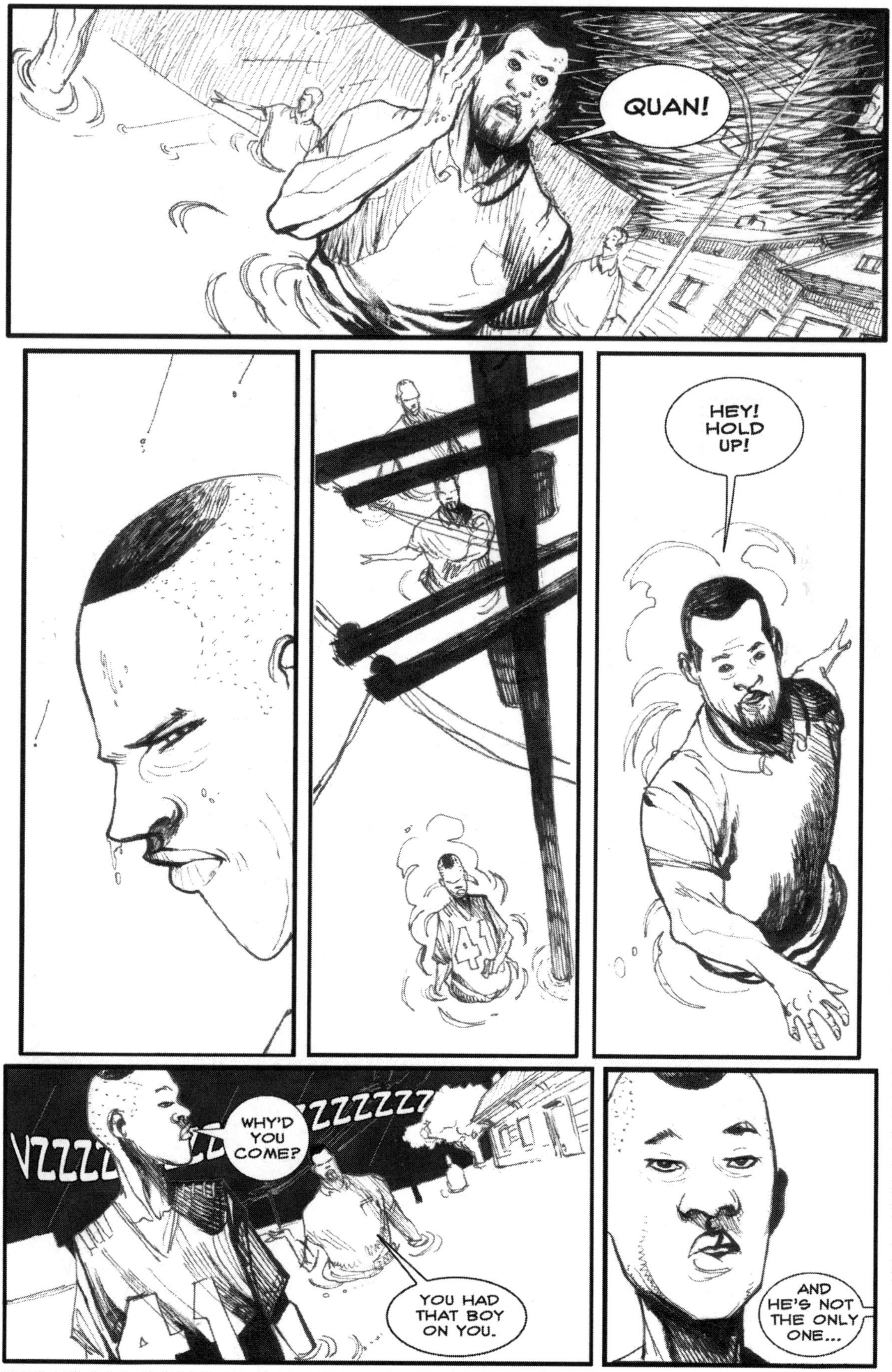
QUAN!
HEY! HOLD UP!
VZZZZZZZZZZZZZZ
WHY'D YOU COME?
YOU HAD THAT BOY ON YOU.
AND HE'S NOT THE ONLY ONE...

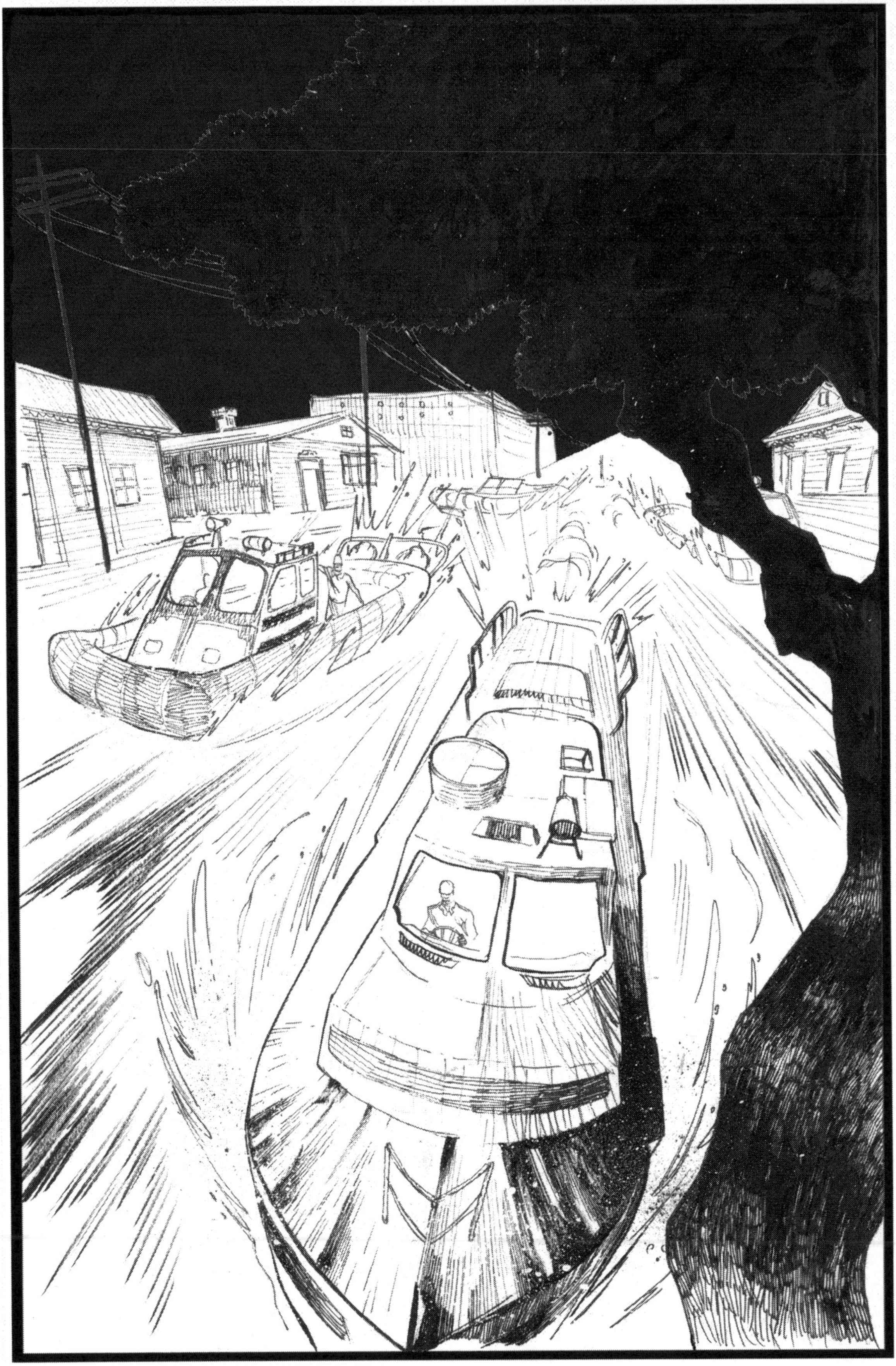

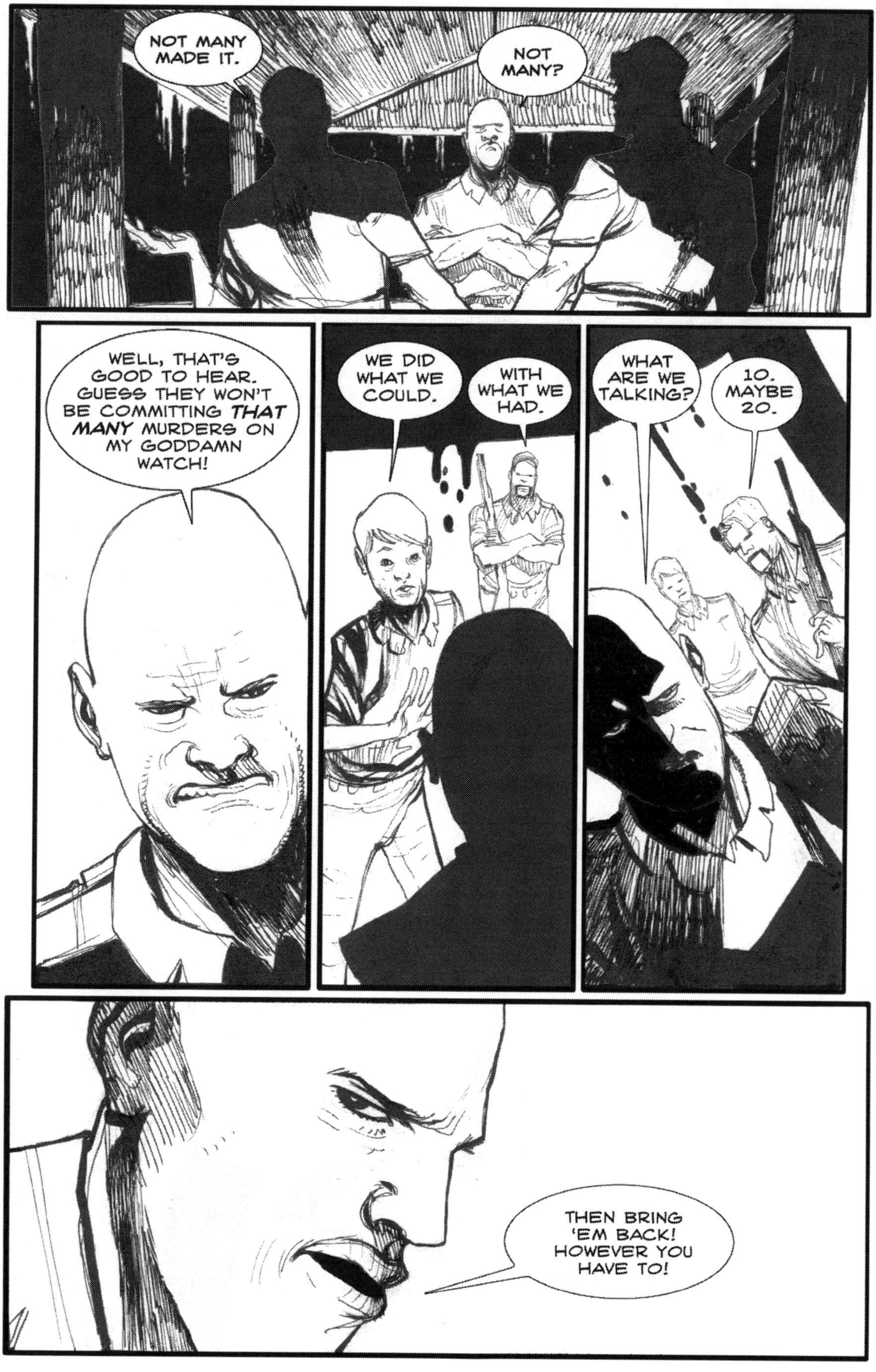
NOT MANY MADE IT.
NOT MANY?
WELL, THAT'S GOOD TO HEAR. GUESS THEY WON'T BE COMMITTING *THAT MANY* MURDERS ON MY GODDAMN WATCH!
WE DID WHAT WE COULD.
WITH WHAT WE HAD.
WHAT ARE WE TALKING?
10. MAYBE 20.
THEN BRING 'EM BACK! HOWEVER YOU HAVE TO!

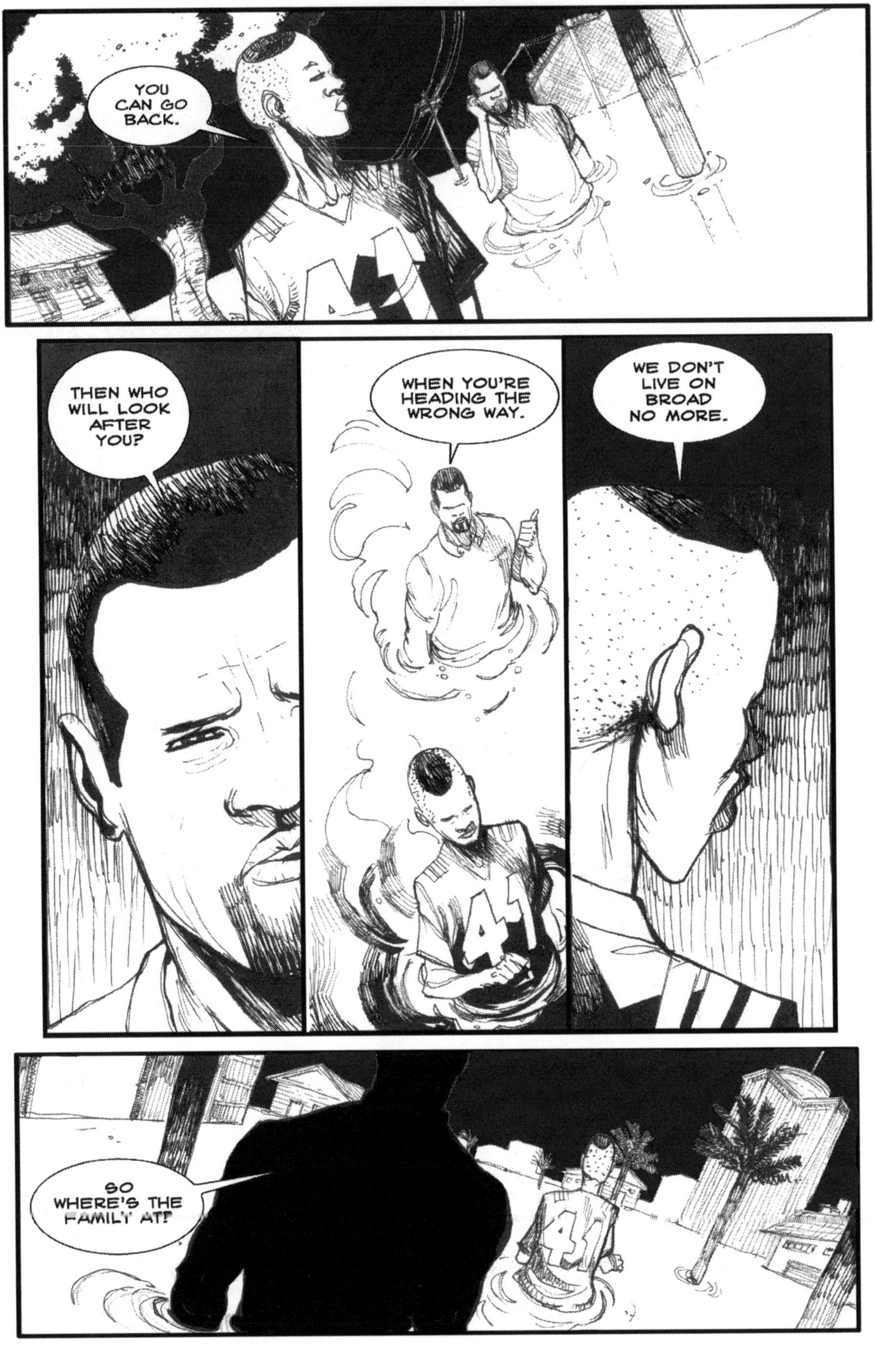
YOU CAN GO BACK.
THEN WHO WILL LOOK AFTER YOU?
WHEN YOU'RE HEADING THE WRONG WAY.
WE DON'T LIVE ON BROAD NO MORE.
SO WHERE'S THE FAMILY AT?

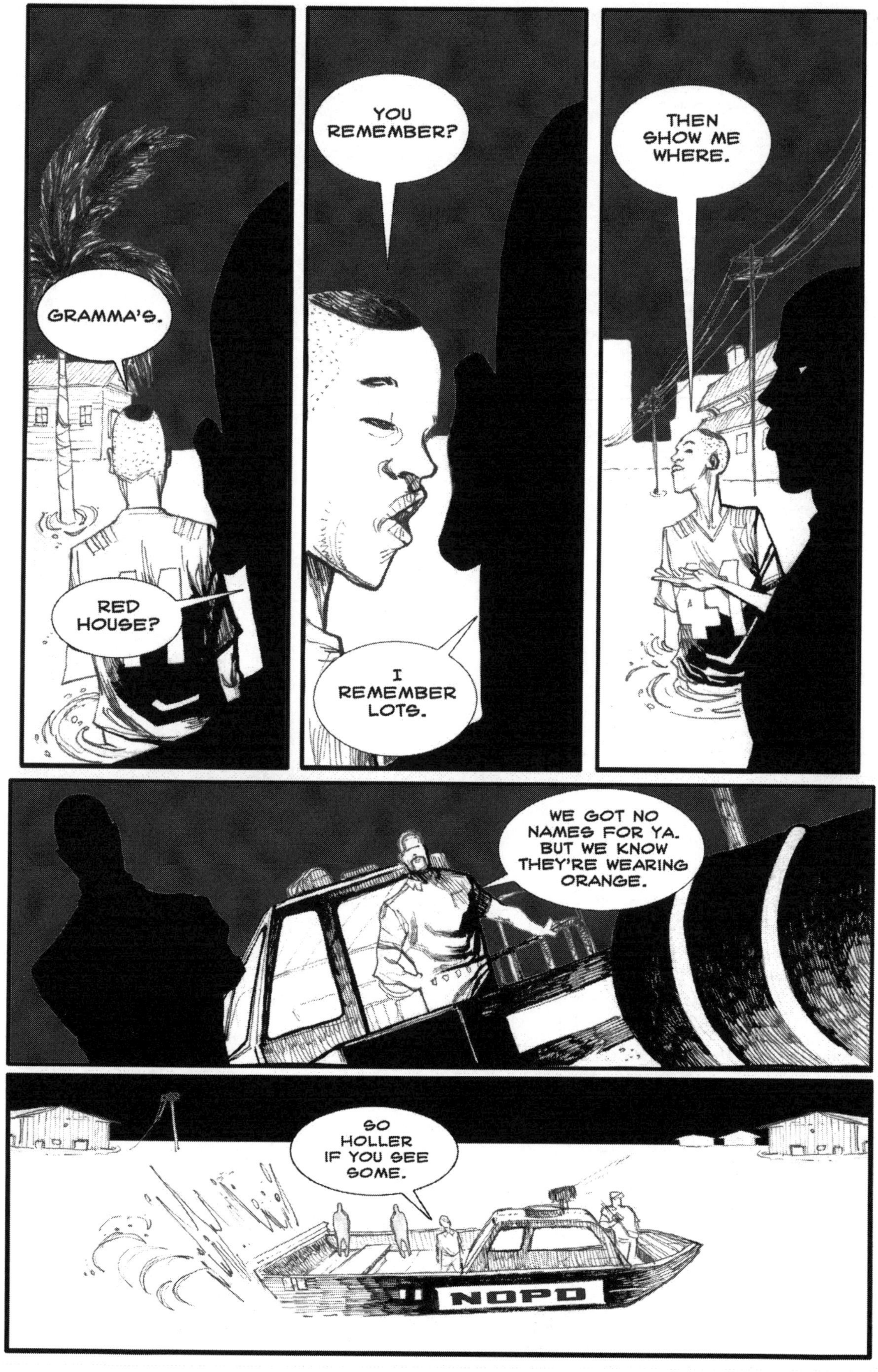
GRAMMA'S.
RED HOUSE?
YOU REMEMBER?
I REMEMBER LOTS.
THEN SHOW ME WHERE.
WE GOT NO NAMES FOR YA. BUT WE KNOW THEY'RE WEARING ORANGE.
SO HOLLER IF YOU SEE SOME.
NOPD

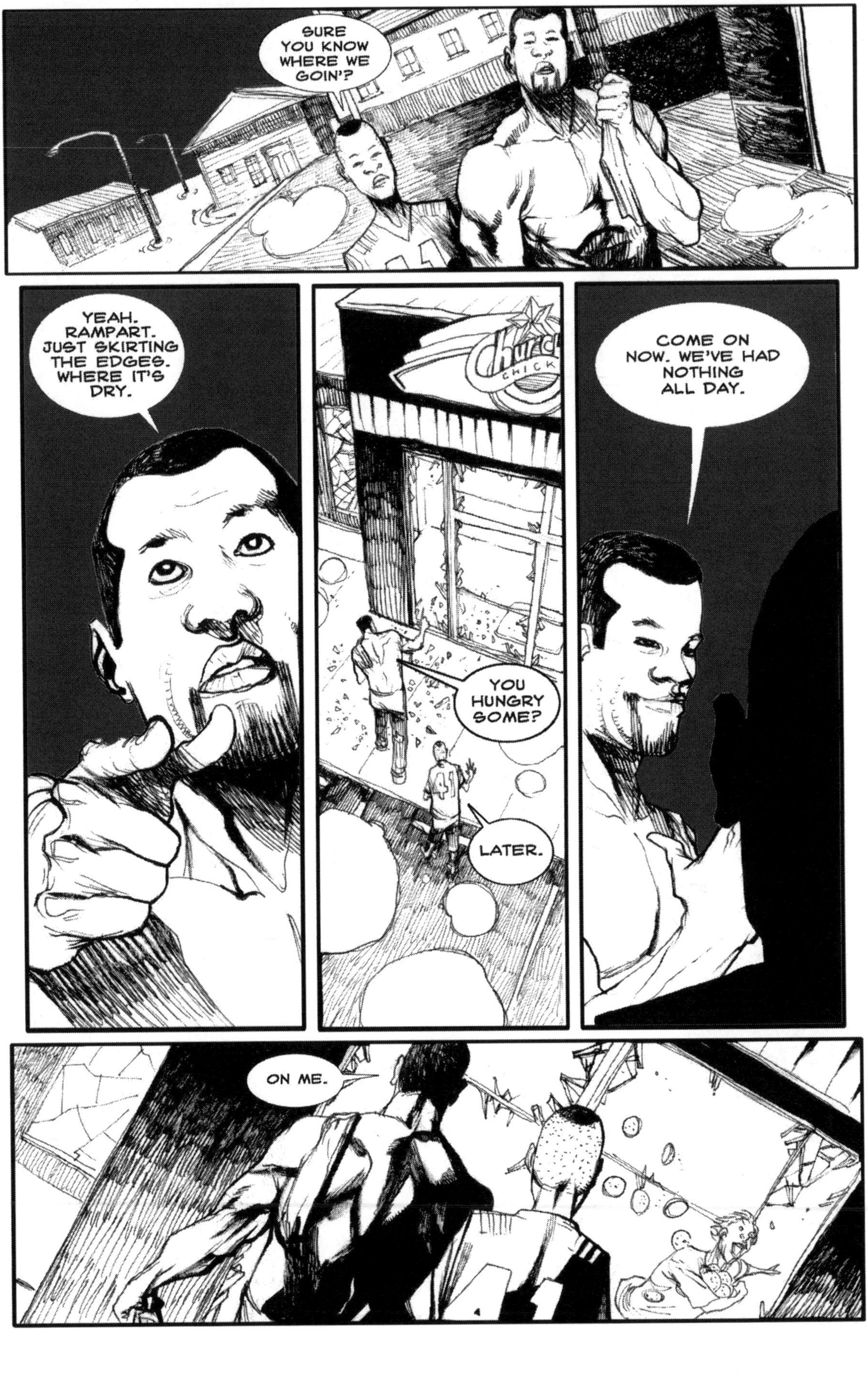
SURE YOU KNOW WHERE WE GOIN'?
YEAH. RAMPART. JUST SKIRTING THE EDGES. WHERE IT'S DRY.
YOU HUNGRY SOME?
LATER.
COME ON NOW. WE'VE HAD NOTHING ALL DAY.
ON ME.

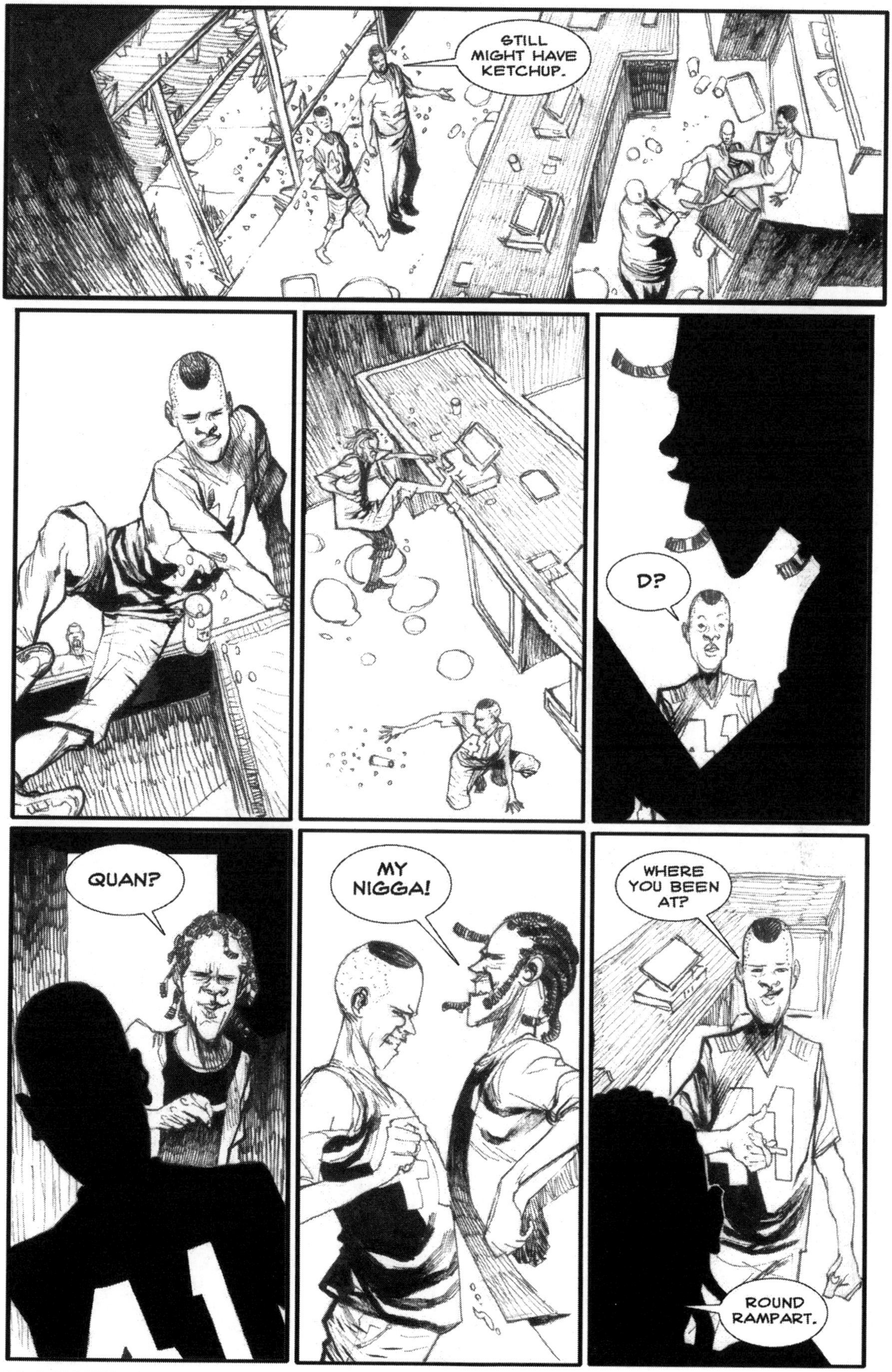
STILL MIGHT HAVE KETCHUP.
D?
QUAN?
MY NIGGA!
WHERE YOU BEEN AT?
ROUND RAMPART.

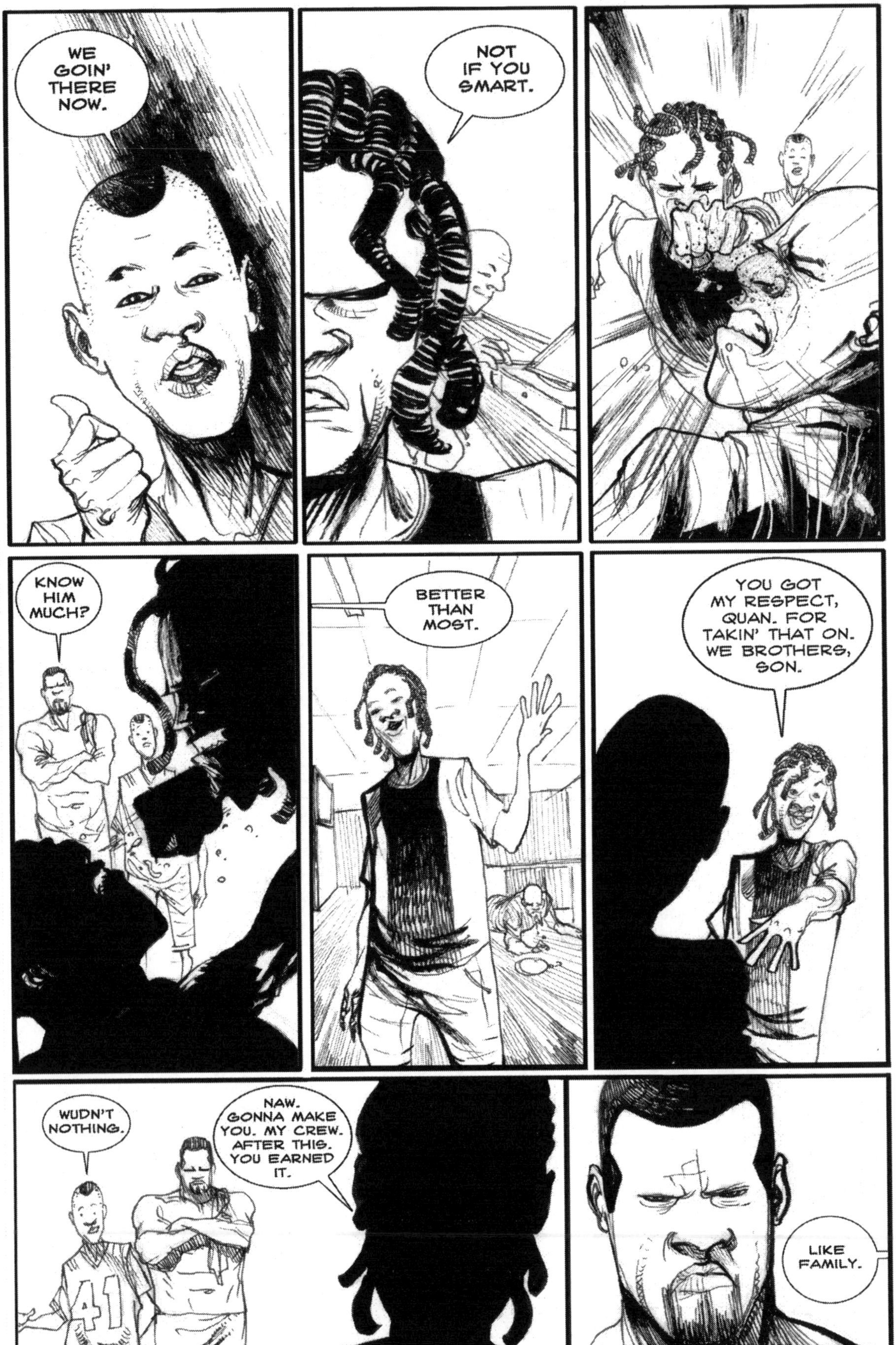
WE GOIN' THERE NOW.
NOT IF YOU SMART.
KNOW HIM MUCH?
BETTER THAN MOST.
YOU GOT MY RESPECT, QUAN. FOR TAKIN' THAT ON. WE BROTHERS, SON.
WUDN'T NOTHING.
NAW. GONNA MAKE YOU. MY CREW. AFTER THIS. YOU EARNED IT.
41
LIKE FAMILY.

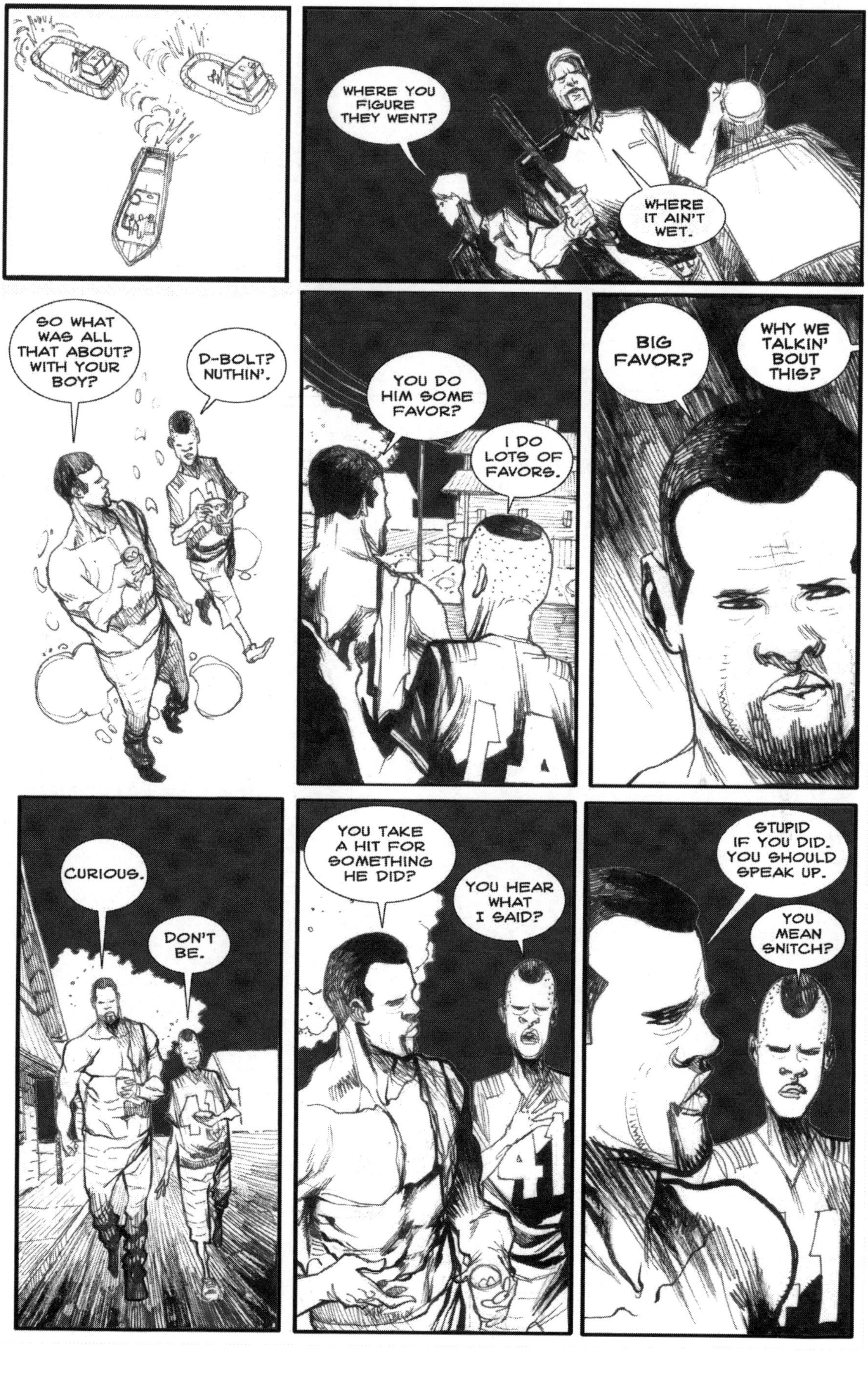
WHERE YOU FIGURE THEY WENT?
WHERE IT AIN'T WET.
SO WHAT WAS ALL THAT ABOUT? WITH YOUR BOY?
D-BOLT? NUTHIN'.
YOU DO HIM SOME FAVOR?
I DO LOTS OF FAVORS.
BIG FAVOR?
WHY WE TALKIN' BOUT THIS?
CURIOUS.
DON'T BE.
YOU TAKE A HIT FOR SOMETHING HE DID?
YOU HEAR WHAT I SAID?
STUPID IF YOU DID. YOU SHOULD SPEAK UP.
YOU MEAN SNITCH?

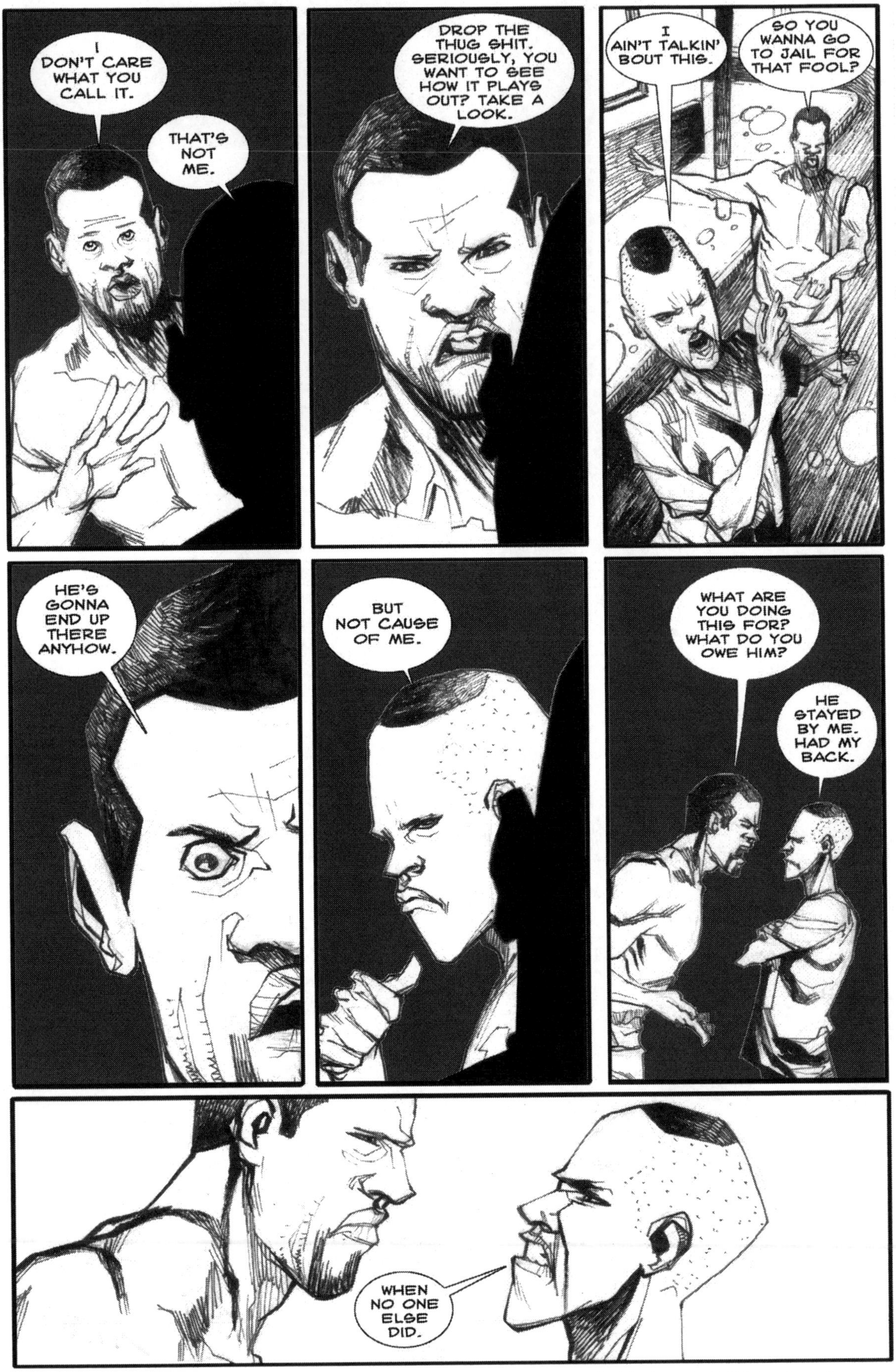
I DON'T CARE WHAT YOU CALL IT.
THAT'S NOT ME.
DROP THE THUG SHIT. SERIOUSLY, YOU WANT TO SEE HOW IT PLAYS OUT? TAKE A LOOK.
SO YOU WANNA GO TO JAIL FOR THAT FOOL?
I AIN'T TALKIN' BOUT THIS.
HE'S GONNA END UP THERE ANYHOW.
BUT NOT CAUSE OF ME.
WHAT ARE YOU DOING THIS FOR? WHAT DO YOU OWE HIM?
HE STAYED BY ME. HAD MY BACK.
WHEN NO ONE ELSE DID.

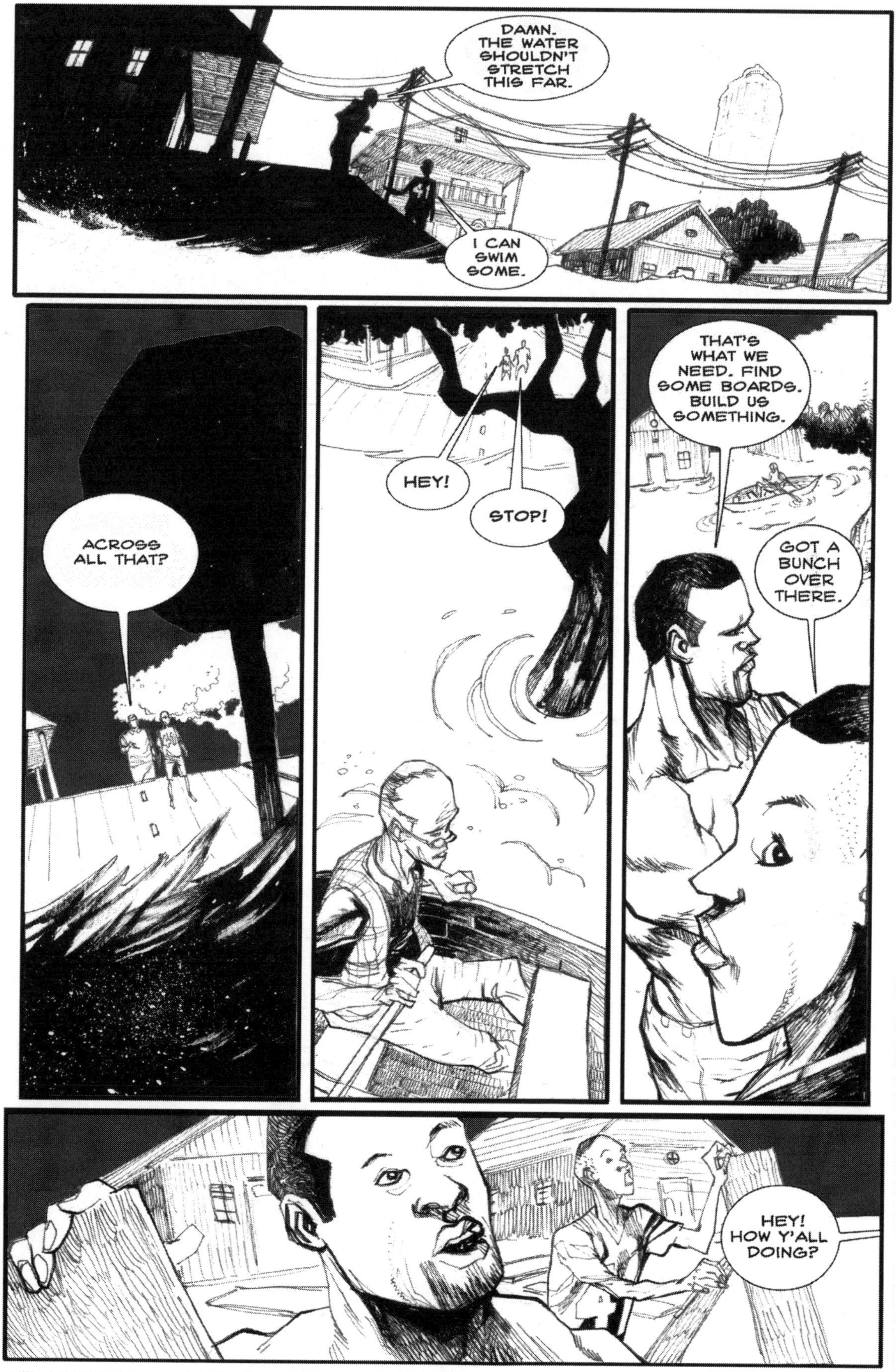
DAMN. THE WATER SHOULDN'T STRETCH THIS FAR.
I CAN SWIM SOME.
ACROSS ALL THAT?
HEY!
STOP!
THAT'S WHAT WE NEED. FIND SOME BOARDS. BUILD US SOMETHING.
GOT A BUNCH OVER THERE.
HEY! HOW Y'ALL DOING?

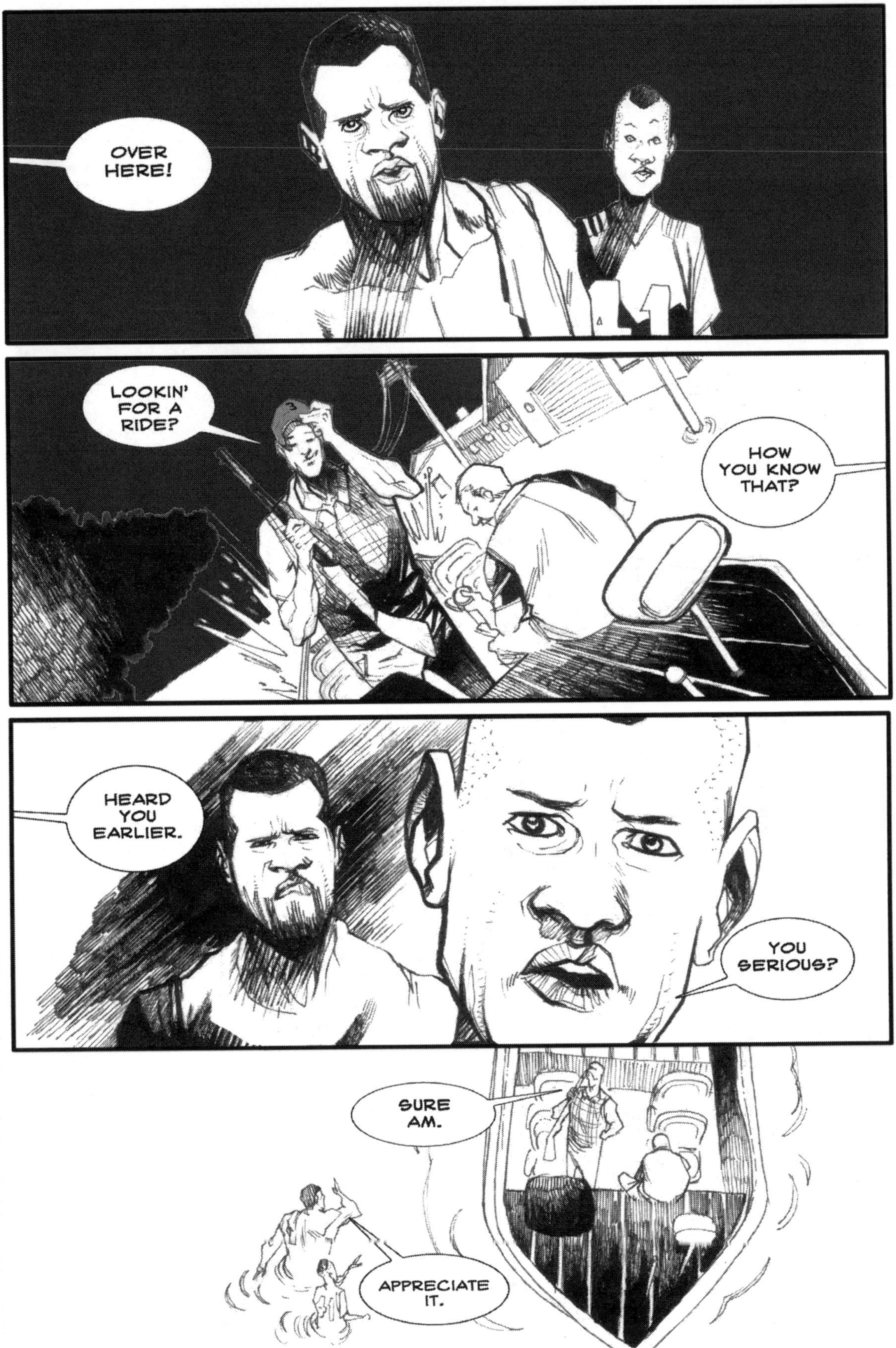
OVER HERE!
LOOKIN' FOR A RIDE?
HOW YOU KNOW THAT?
HEARD YOU EARLIER.
YOU SERIOUS?
SURE AM.
APPRECIATE IT.

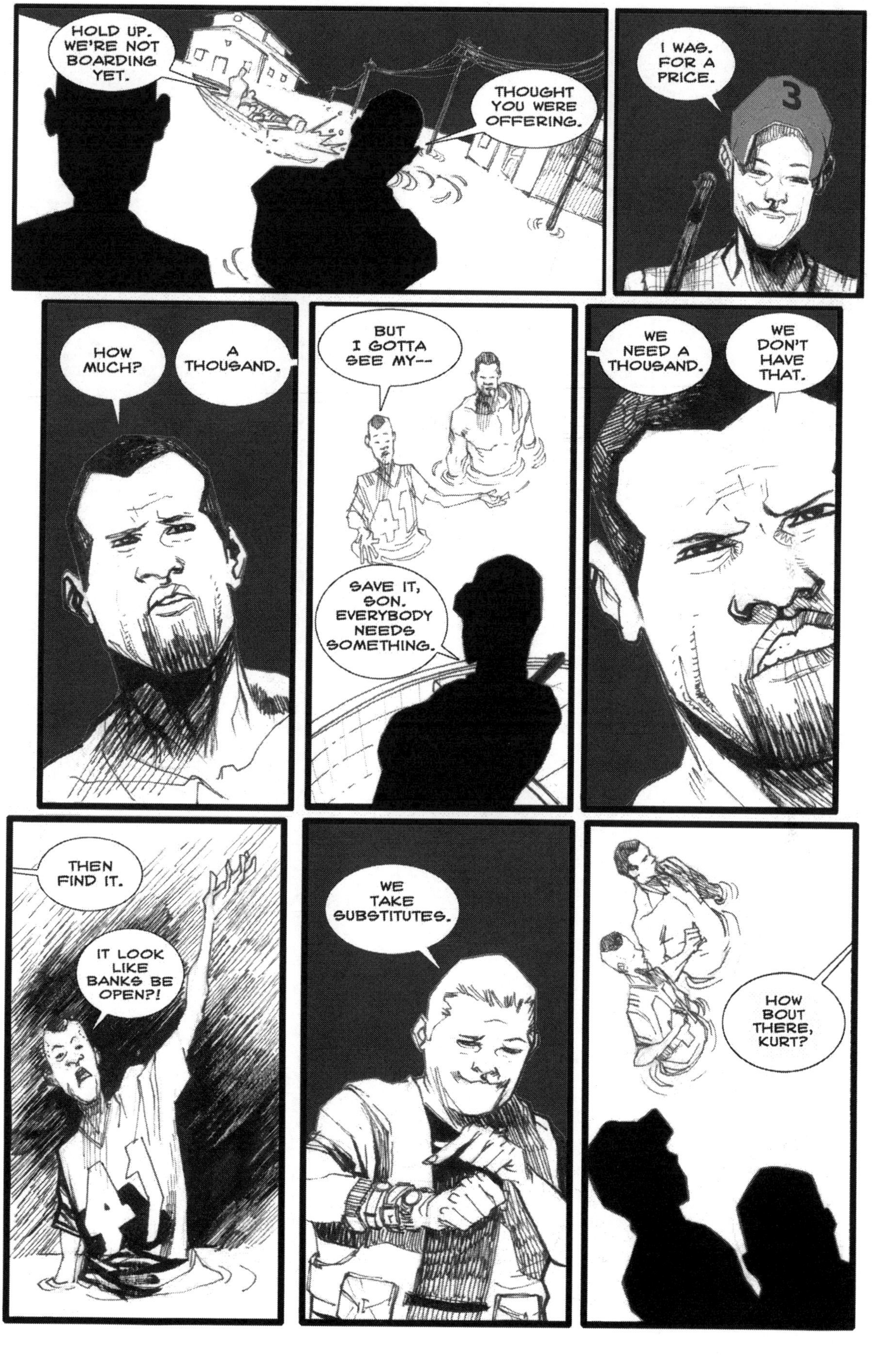
HOLD UP. WE'RE NOT BOARDING YET.
THOUGHT YOU WERE OFFERING.
I WAS. FOR A PRICE.
HOW MUCH?
A THOUSAND.
BUT I GOTTA SEE MY--
SAVE IT, SON. EVERYBODY NEEDS SOMETHING.
WE NEED A THOUSAND.
WE DON'T HAVE THAT.
THEN FIND IT.
IT LOOK LIKE BANKS BE OPEN?!
WE TAKE SUBSTITUTES.
HOW BOUT THERE, KURT?

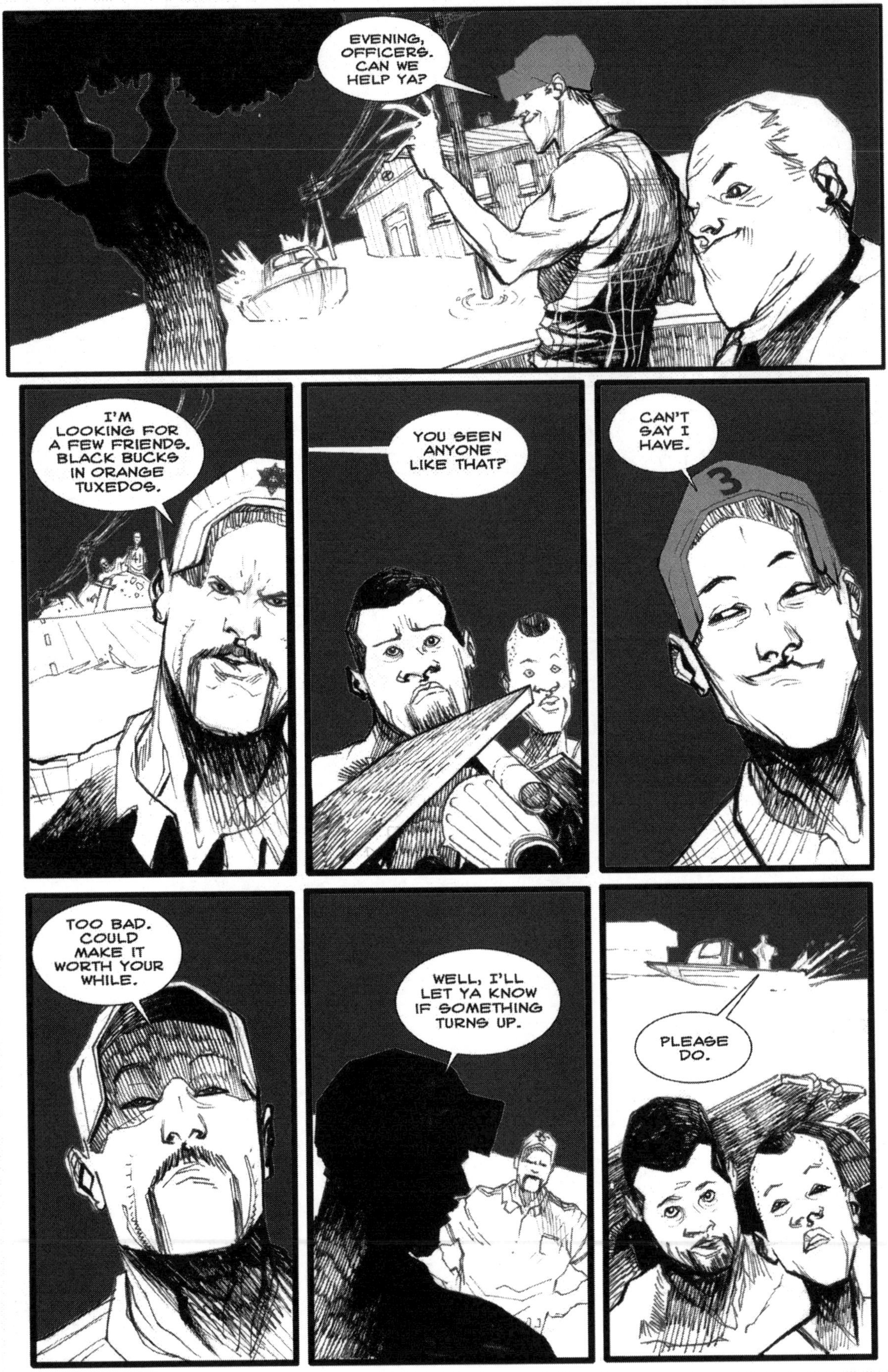
EVENING, OFFICERS. CAN WE HELP YA?
I'M LOOKING FOR A FEW FRIENDS. BLACK BUCKS IN ORANGE TUXEDOS.
YOU SEEN ANYONE LIKE THAT?
CAN'T SAY I HAVE.
TOO BAD. COULD MAKE IT WORTH YOUR WHILE.
WELL, I'LL LET YA KNOW IF SOMETHING TURNS UP.
PLEASE DO.

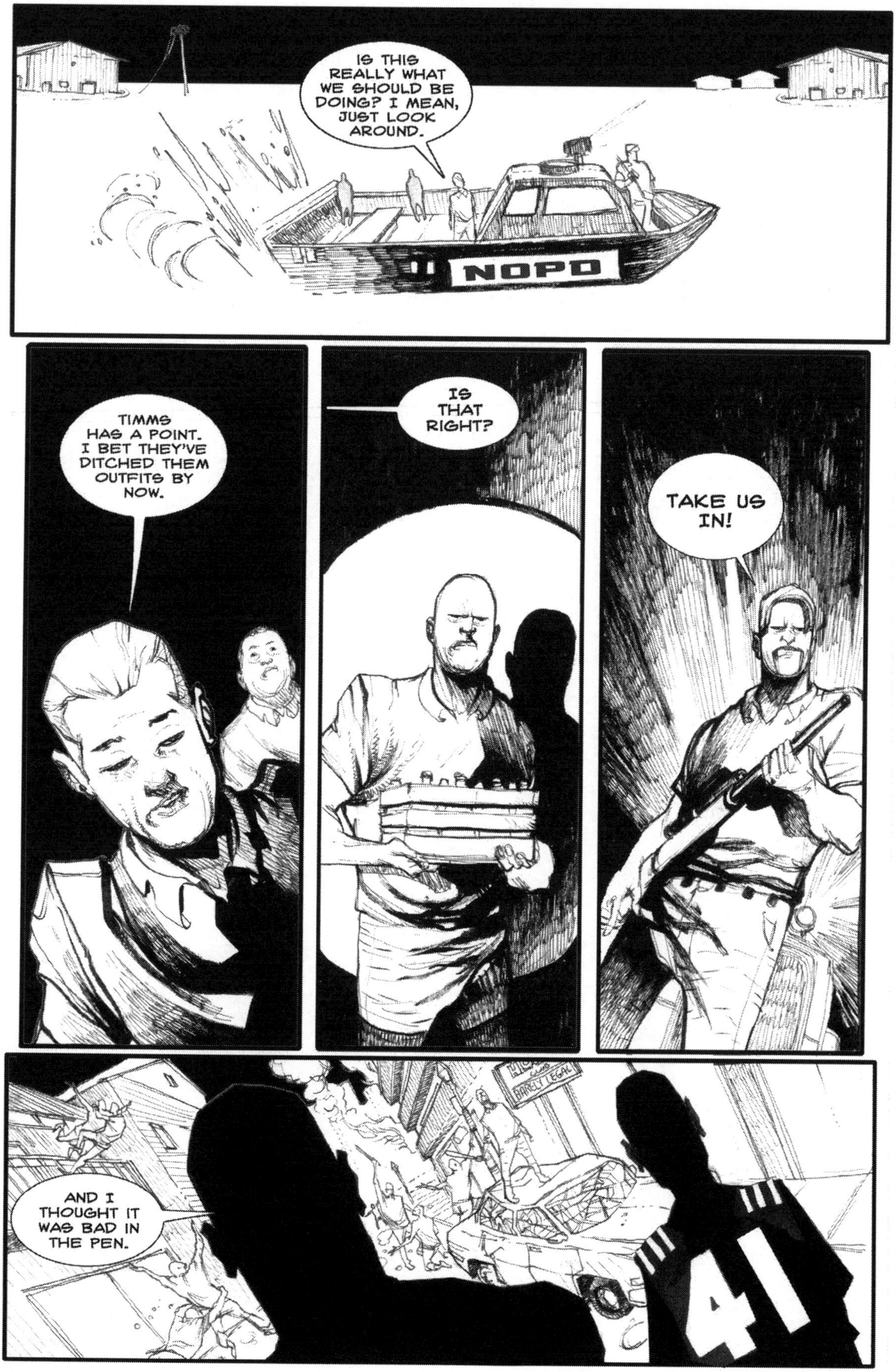
IS THIS REALLY WHAT WE SHOULD BE DOING? I MEAN, JUST LOOK AROUND.
NOPD
TIMMS HAS A POINT. I BET THEY'VE DITCHED THEM OUTFITS BY NOW.
IS THAT RIGHT?
TAKE US IN!
AND I THOUGHT IT WAS BAD IN THE PEN.
BARELY LEGAL
41

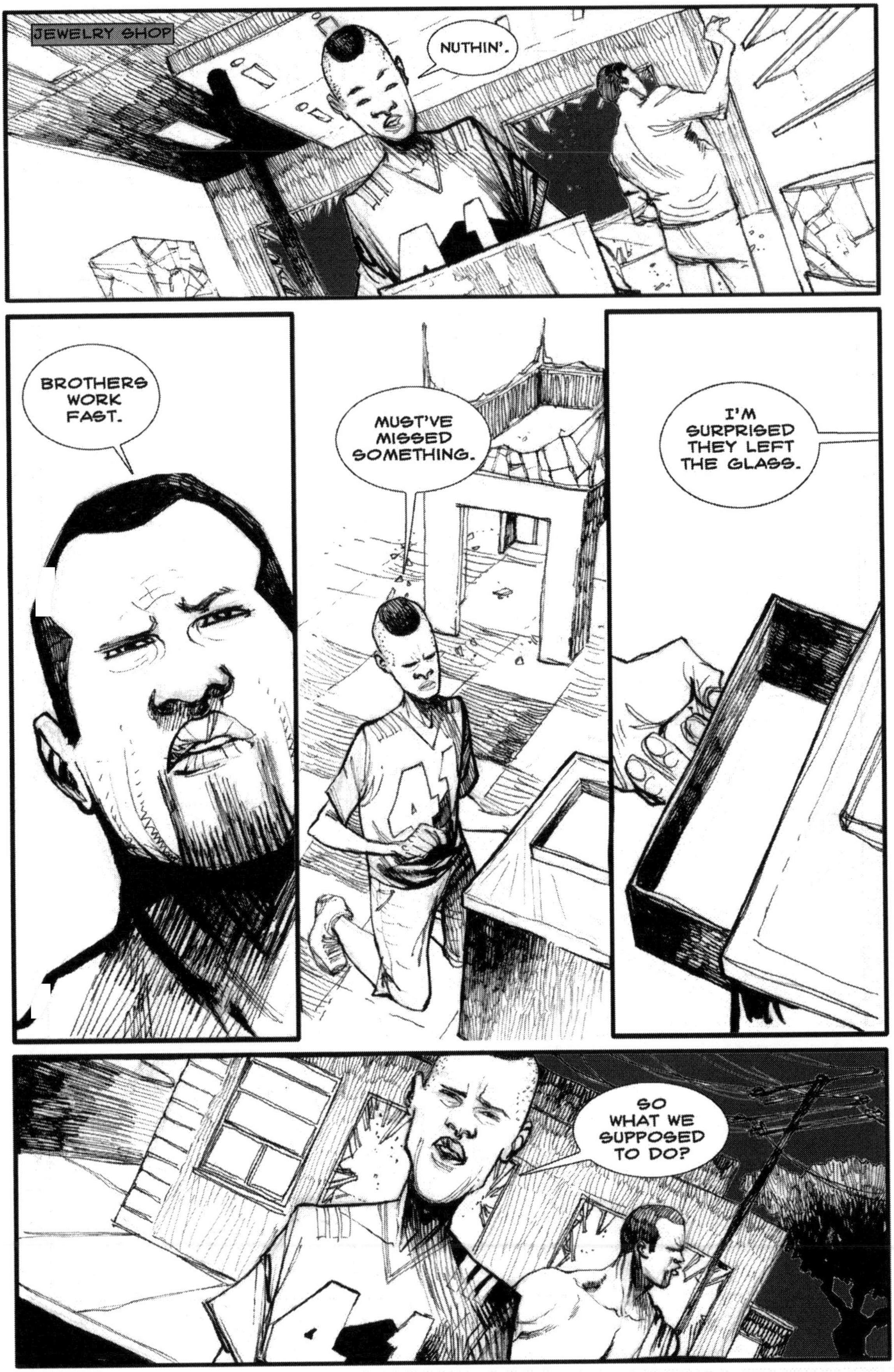
JEWELRY SHOP
NUTHIN'.
BROTHERS WORK FAST.
MUST'VE MISSED SOMETHING.
I'M SURPRISED THEY LEFT THE GLASS.
SO WHAT WE SUPPOSED TO DO?

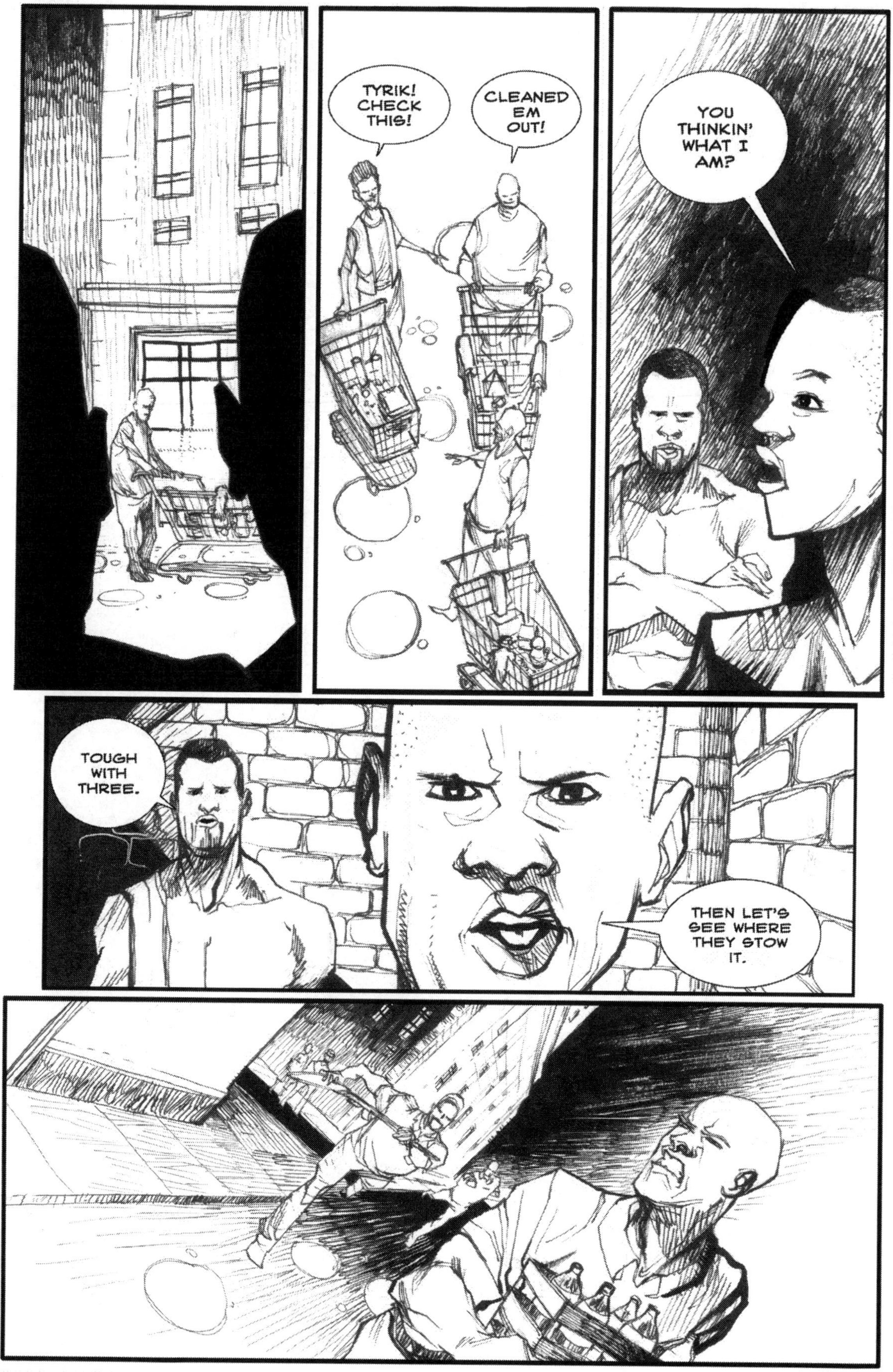
TYRIK! CHECK THIS!
CLEANED EM OUT!
YOU THINKIN' WHAT I AM?
TOUGH WITH THREE.
THEN LET'S SEE WHERE THEY STOW IT.

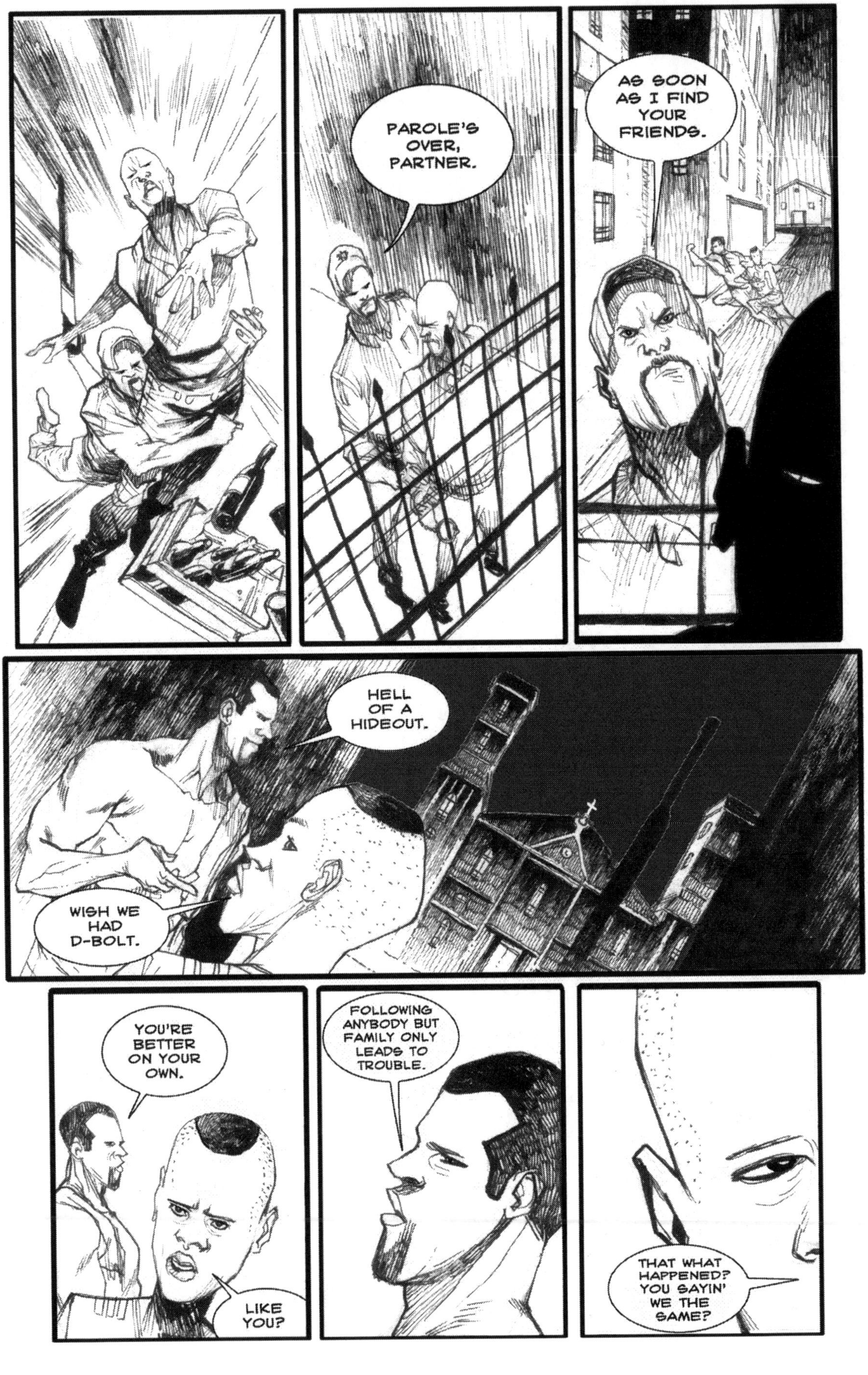
PAROLE'S OVER, PARTNER.
AS SOON AS I FIND YOUR FRIENDS.
HELL OF A HIDEOUT.
WISH WE HAD D-BOLT.
YOU'RE BETTER ON YOUR OWN.
LIKE YOU?
FOLLOWING ANYBODY BUT FAMILY ONLY LEADS TO TROUBLE.
THAT WHAT HAPPENED? YOU SAYIN' WE THE SAME?

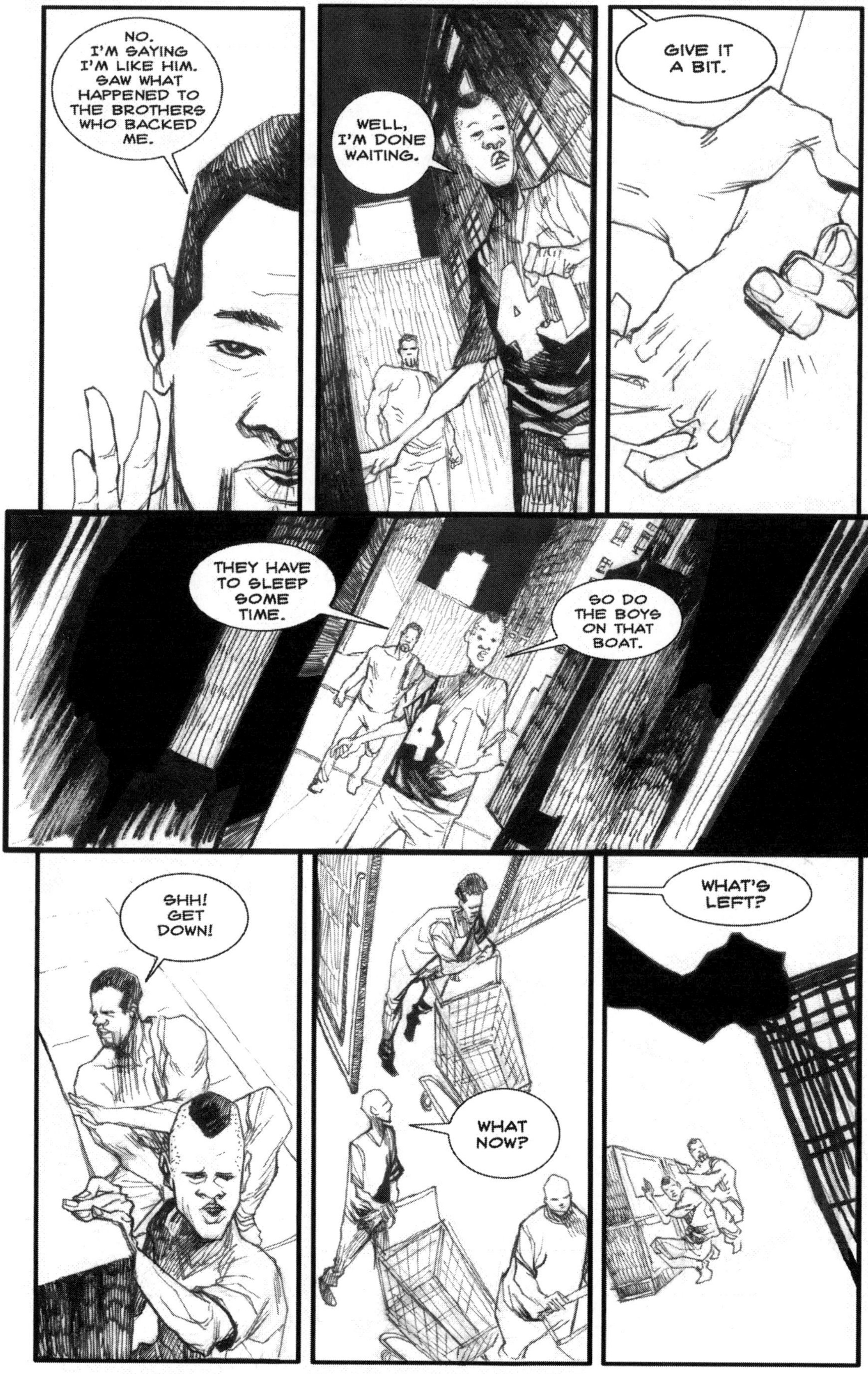
NO. I'M SAYING I'M LIKE HIM. SAW WHAT HAPPENED TO THE BROTHERS WHO BACKED ME.
WELL, I'M DONE WAITING.
GIVE IT A BIT.
THEY HAVE TO SLEEP SOME TIME.
SO DO THE BOYS ON THAT BOAT.
SHH! GET DOWN!
WHAT NOW?
WHAT'S LEFT?

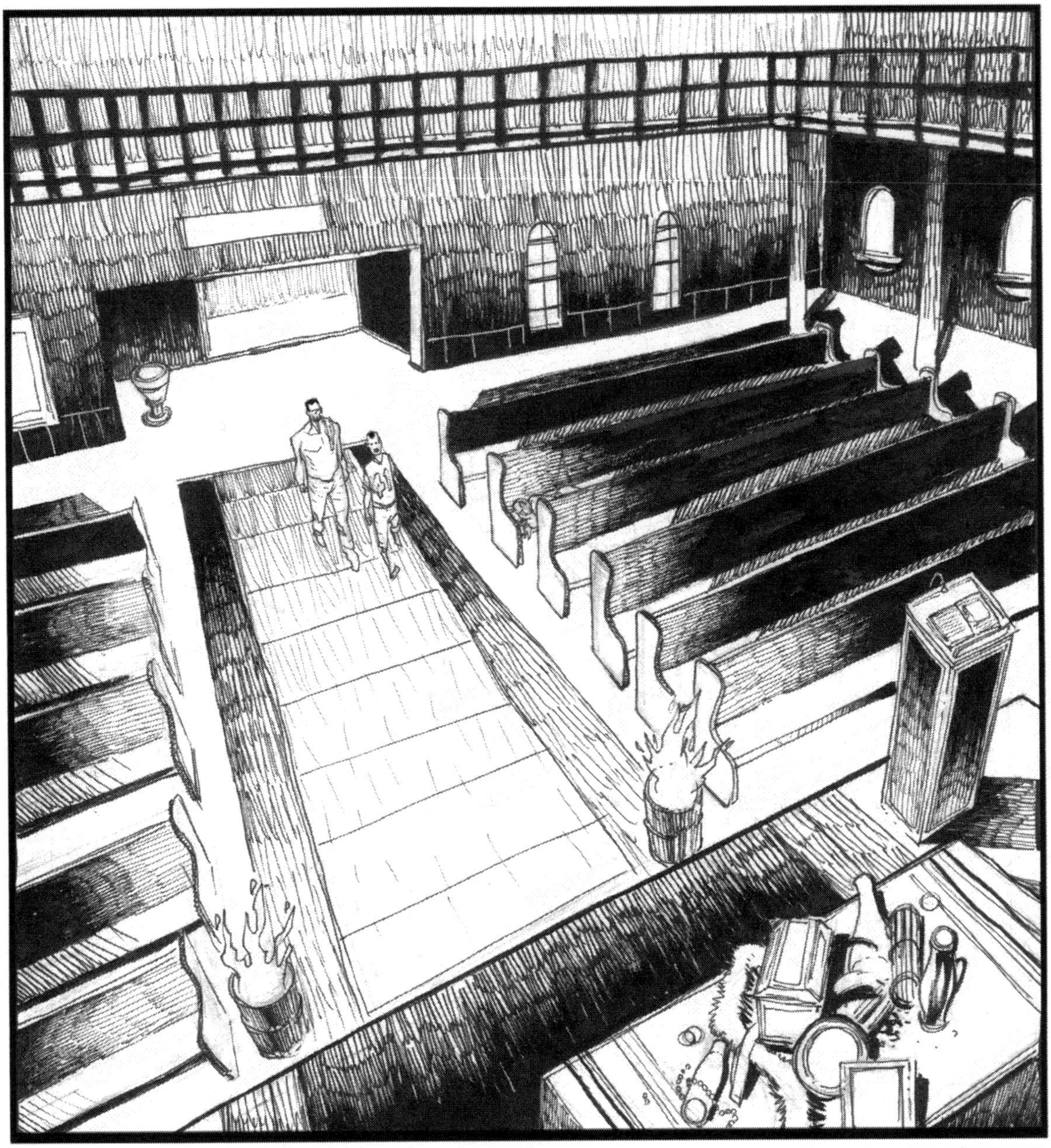

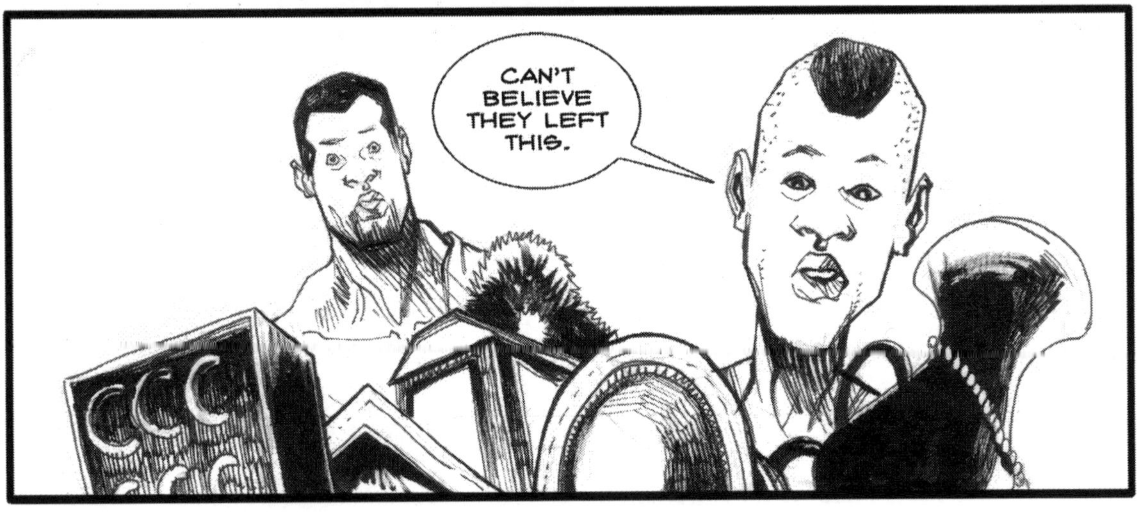
CAN'T BELIEVE THEY LEFT THIS.

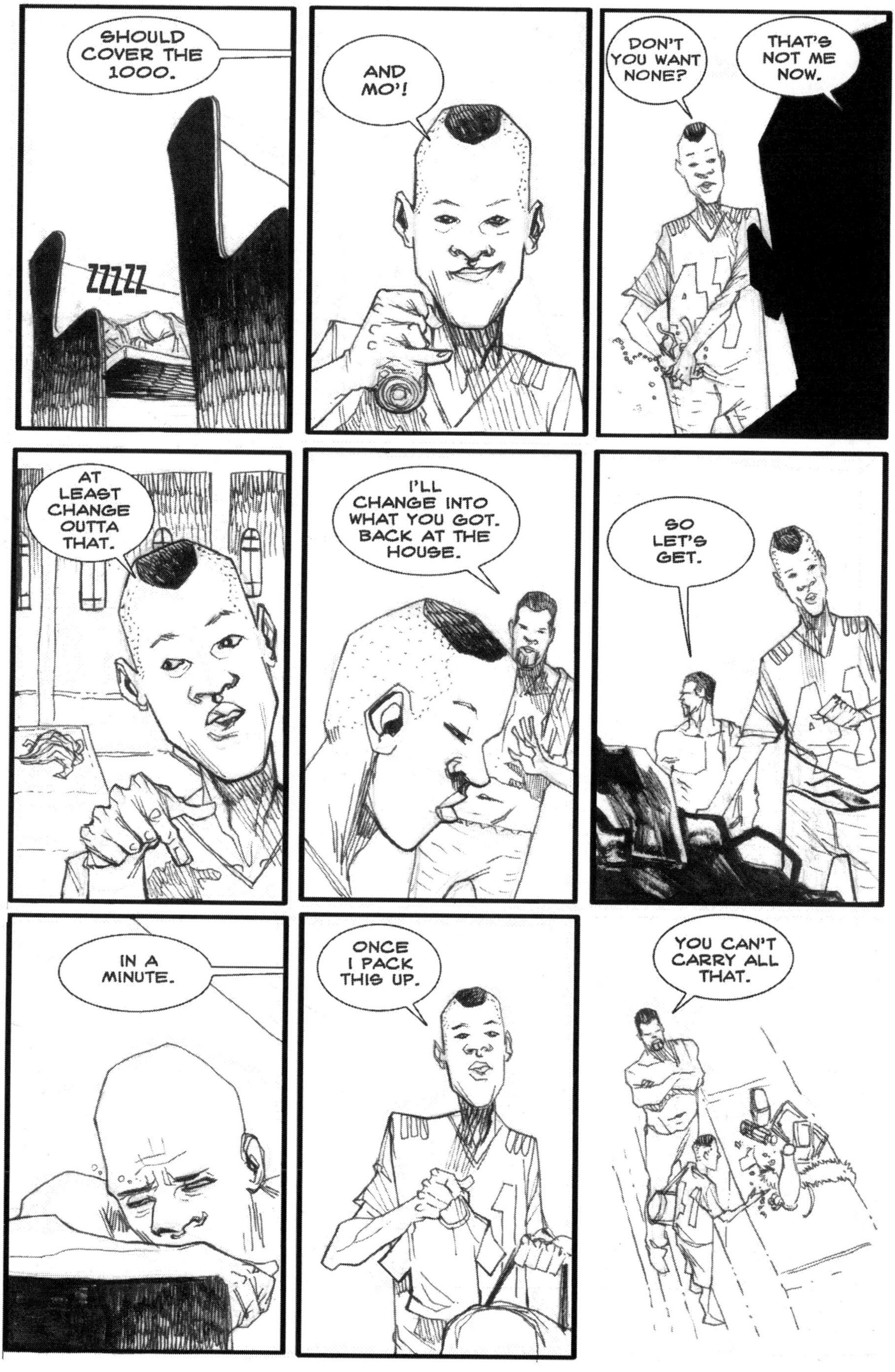
SHOULD COVER THE 1000.
ZZZZZ
AND MO'!
DON'T YOU WANT NONE?
THAT'S NOT ME NOW.
AT LEAST CHANGE OUTTA THAT.
I'LL CHANGE INTO WHAT YOU GOT. BACK AT THE HOUSE.
SO LET'S GET.
IN A MINUTE.
ONCE I PACK THIS UP.
YOU CAN'T CARRY ALL THAT.

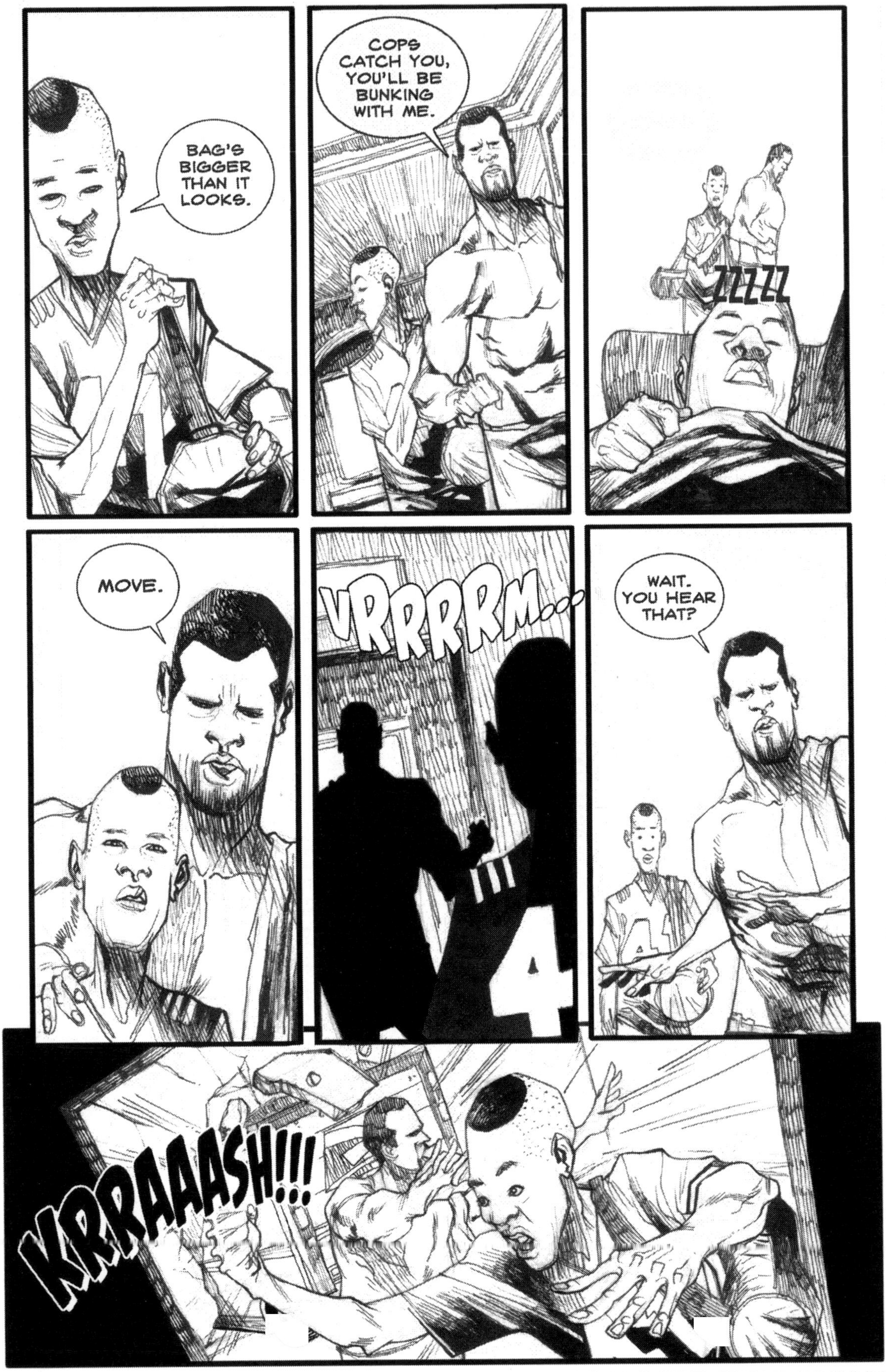
BAG'S BIGGER THAN IT LOOKS.
COPS CATCH YOU, YOU'LL BE BUNKING WITH ME.
ZZZZZ
MOVE.
VRRRRM...
WAIT. YOU HEAR THAT?
KRRAAASH!!!

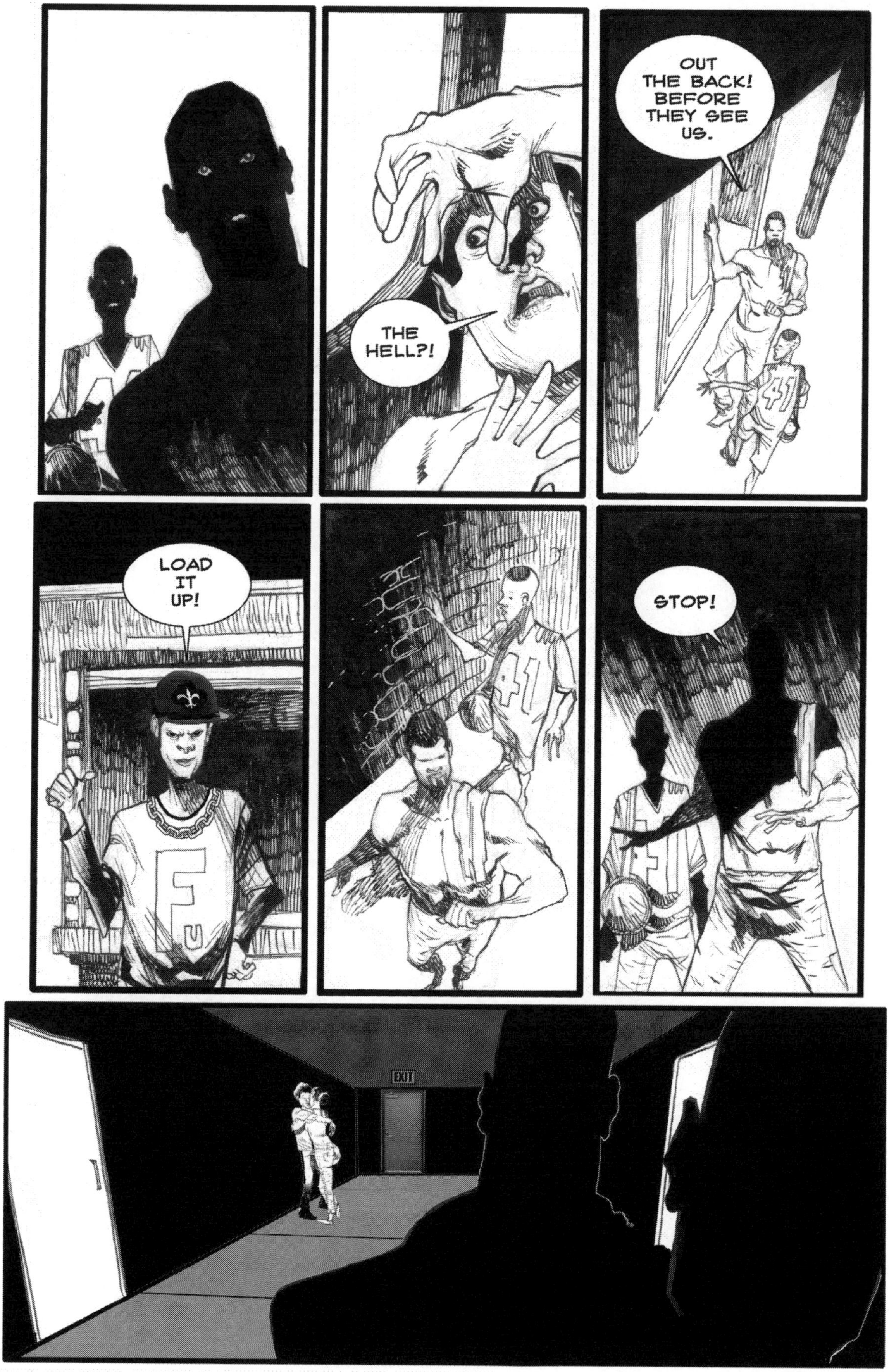
THE HELL?!
OUT THE BACK! BEFORE THEY SEE US.
LOAD IT UP!
STOP!
EXIT

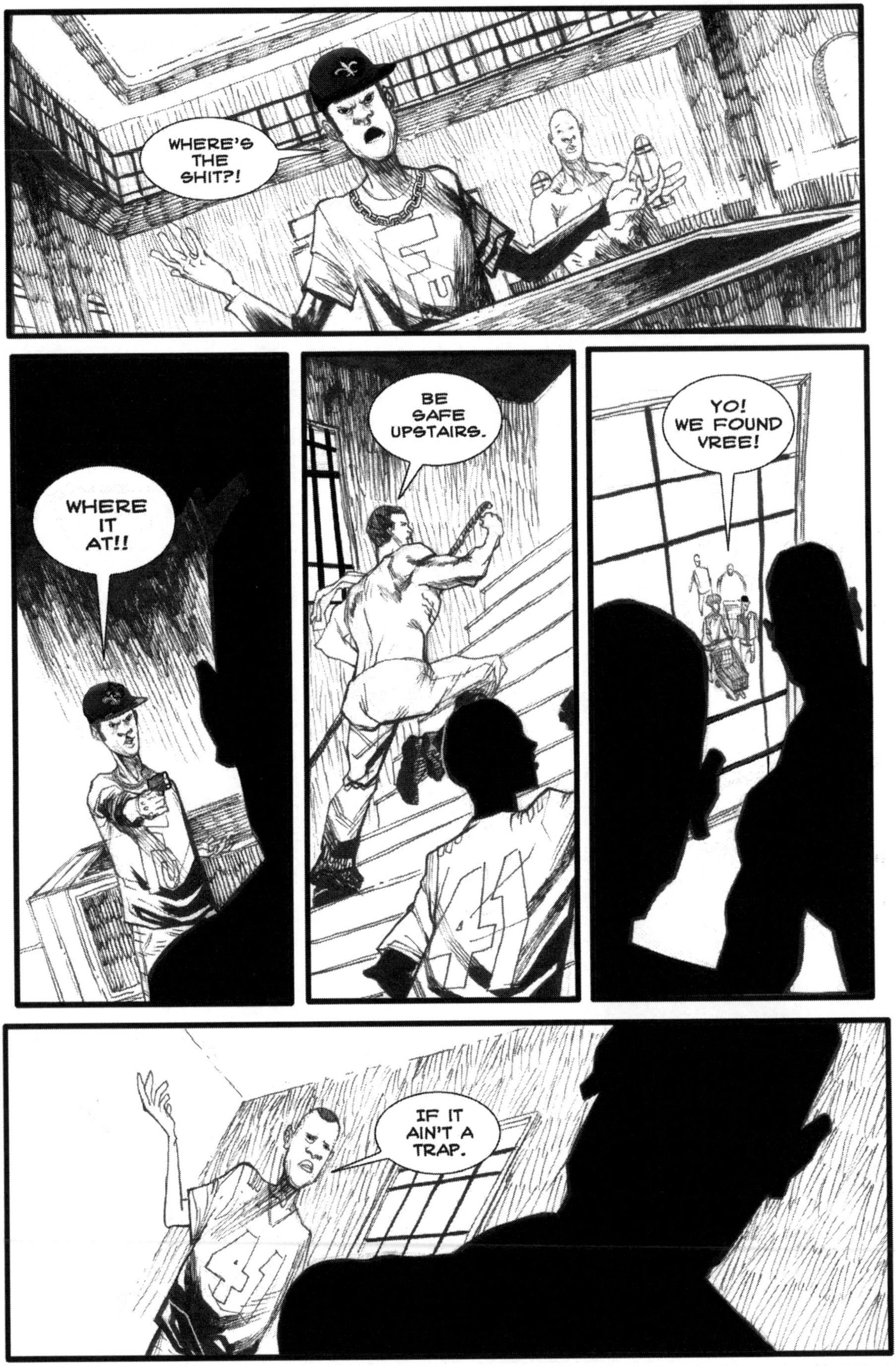
WHERE'S THE SHIT?!
WHERE IT AT!!
BE SAFE UPSTAIRS.
YO! WE FOUND VREE!
IF IT AIN'T A TRAP.

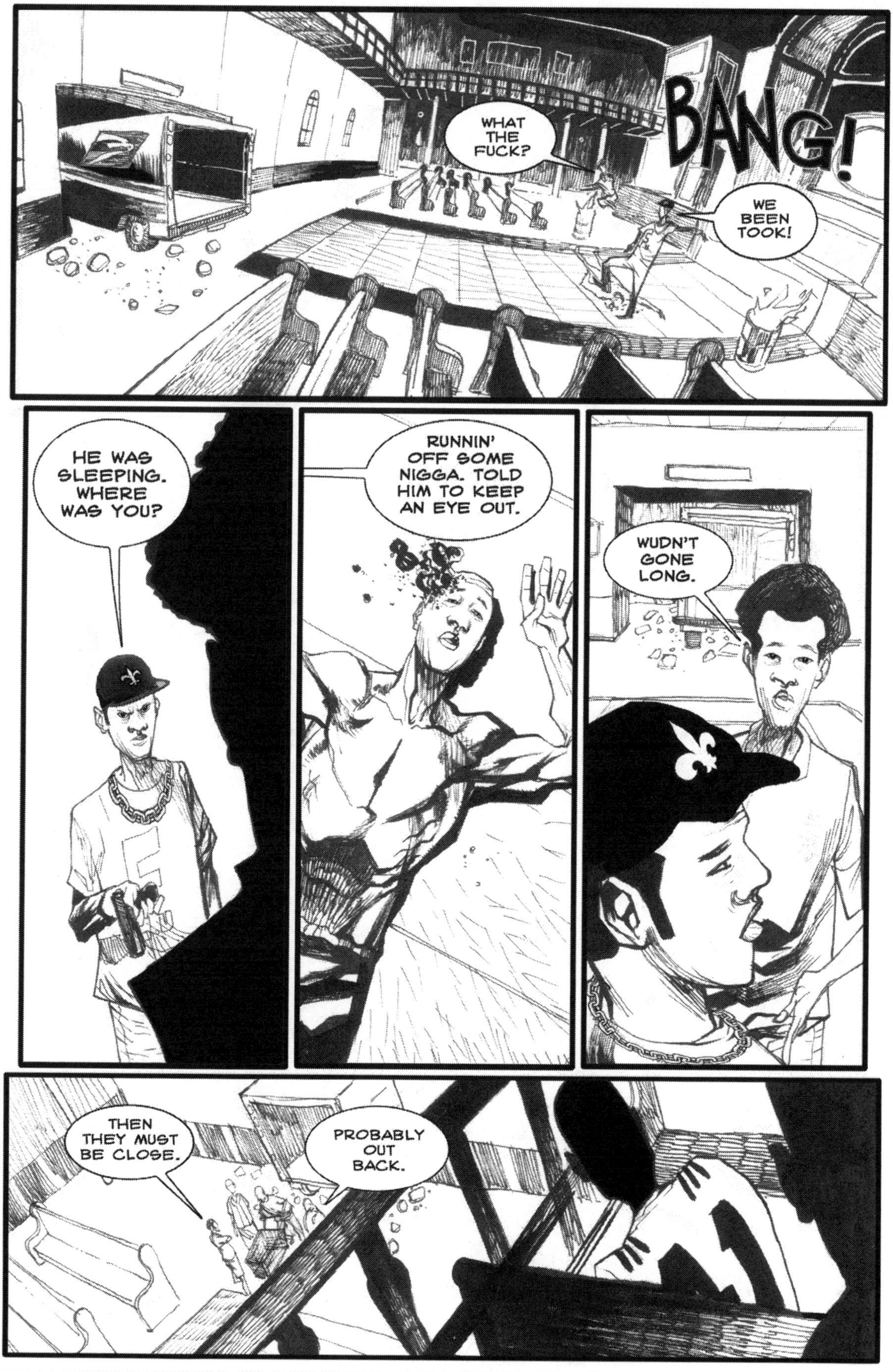
WHAT THE FUCK?
BANG!
WE BEEN TOOK!
HE WAS SLEEPING. WHERE WAS YOU?
RUNNIN' OFF SOME NIGGA. TOLD HIM TO KEEP AN EYE OUT.
WUDN'T GONE LONG.
THEN THEY MUST BE CLOSE.
PROBABLY OUT BACK.

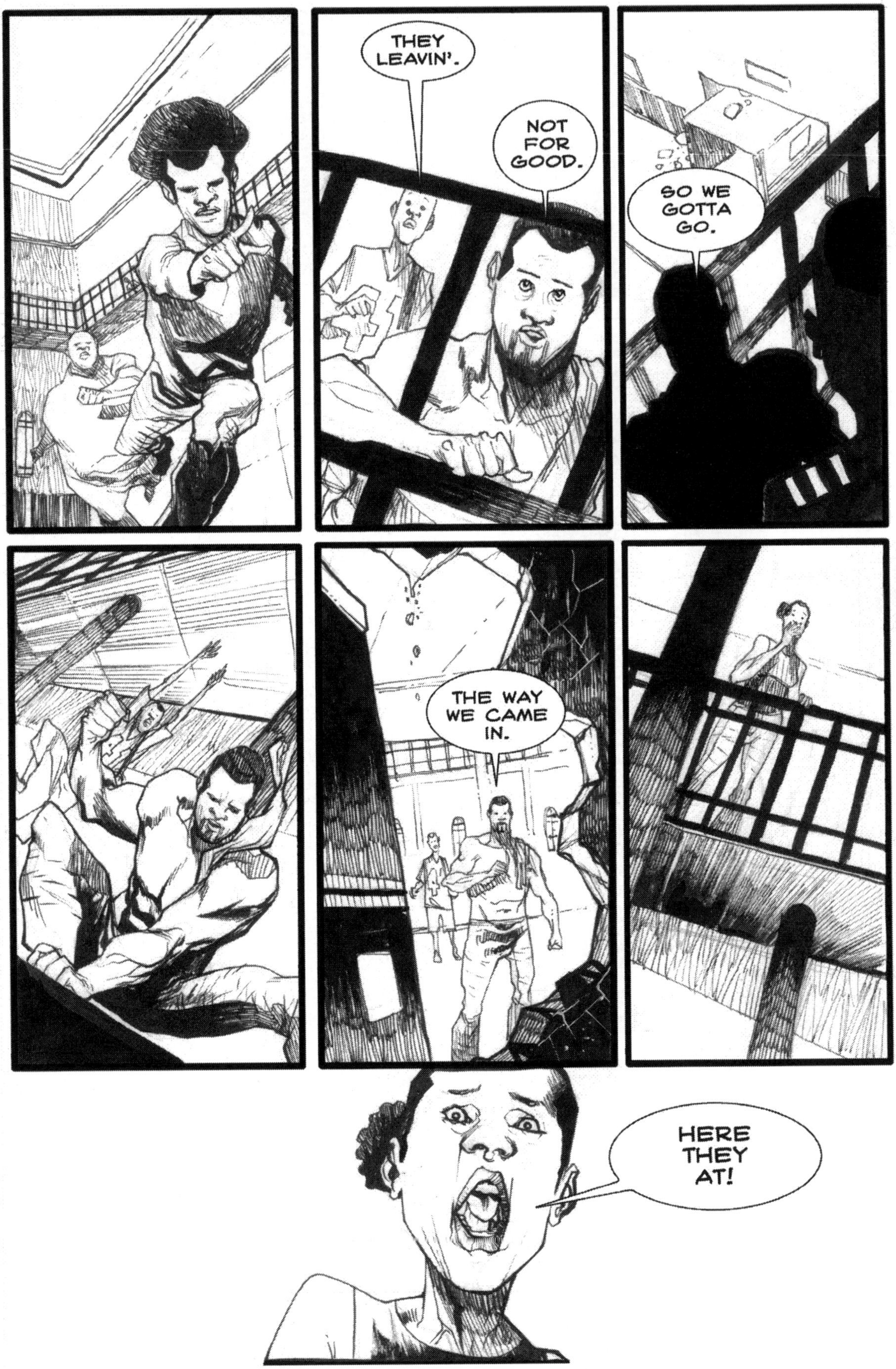
THEY LEAVIN'.
NOT FOR GOOD.
SO WE GOTTA GO.
THE WAY WE CAME IN.
HERE THEY AT!

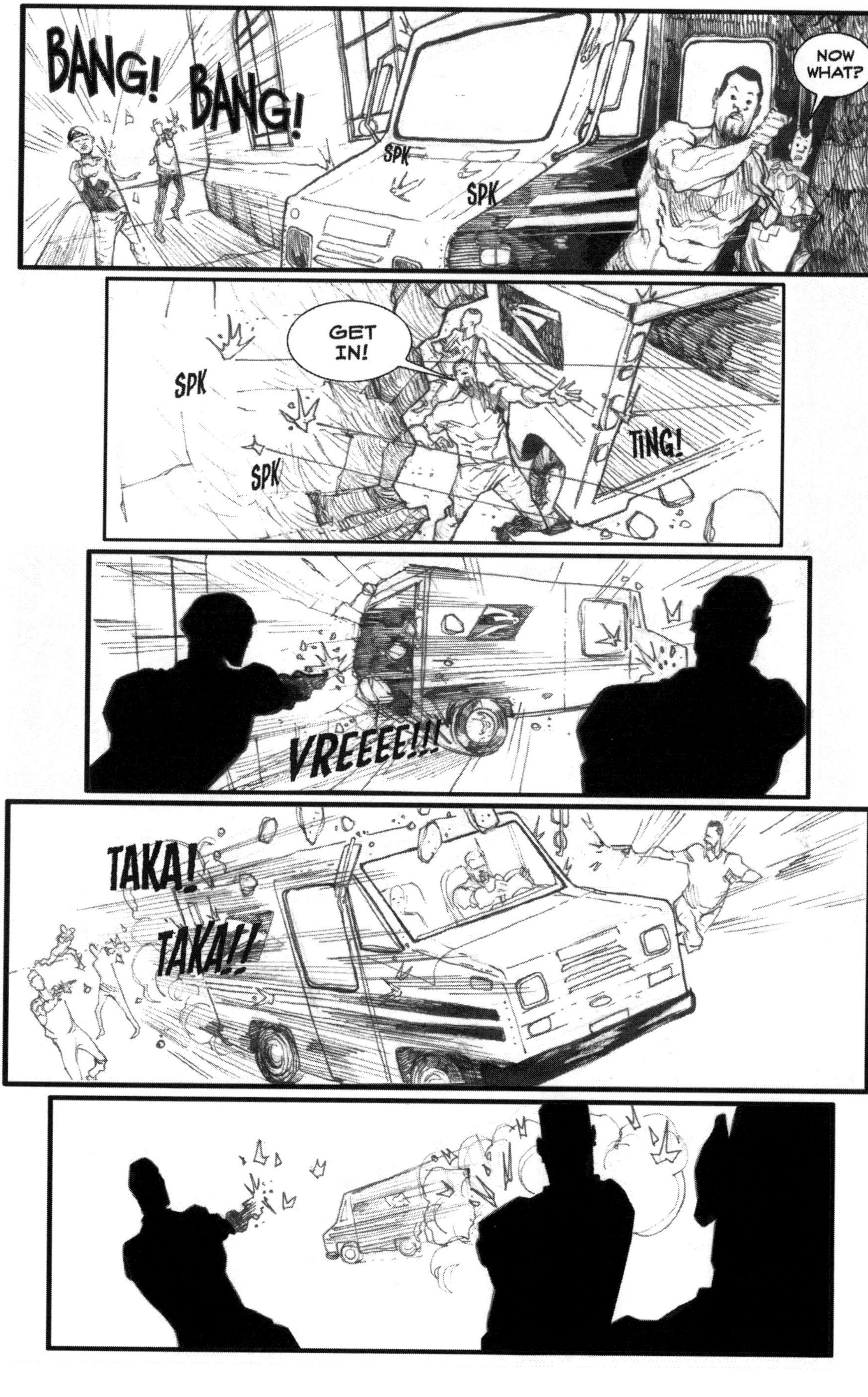
BANG!
BANG!
NOW WHAT?
SPK
SPK
GET IN!
SPK
SPK
TING!
VREEEE!!!
TAKA!
TAKA!!

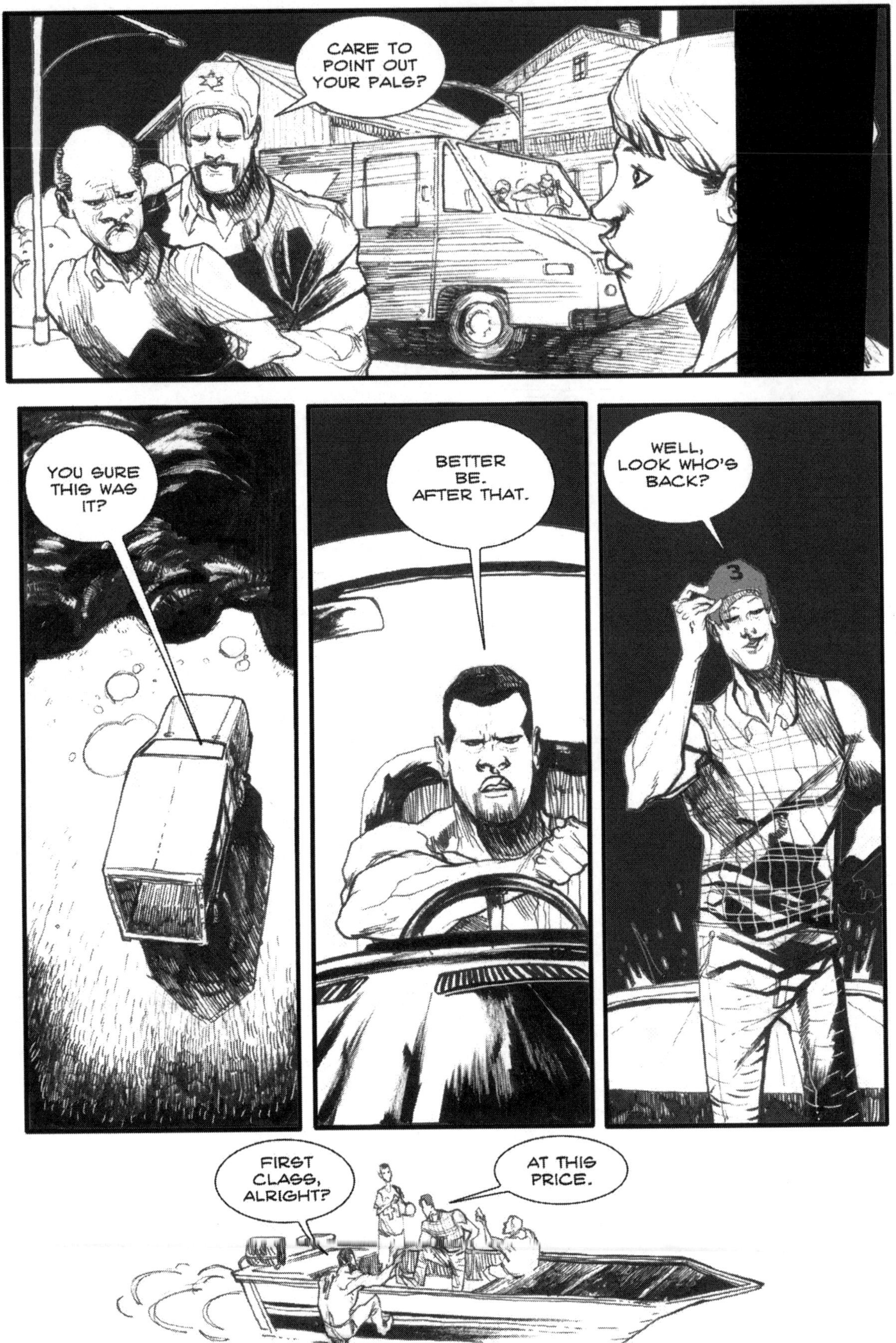
CARE TO POINT OUT YOUR PALS?
YOU SURE THIS WAS IT?
BETTER BE. AFTER THAT.
WELL, LOOK WHO'S BACK?
3
FIRST CLASS, ALRIGHT?
AT THIS PRICE.

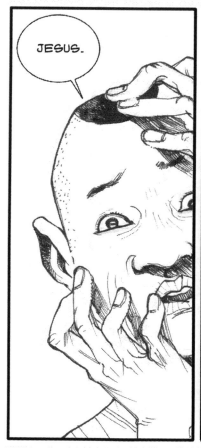

JESUS.

I'M SURE THEY'RE ALRIGHT.

DON'T KNOW. I'M WORRIED.

YOU'RE WORRIED? HOW ABOUT ME?

YOU?

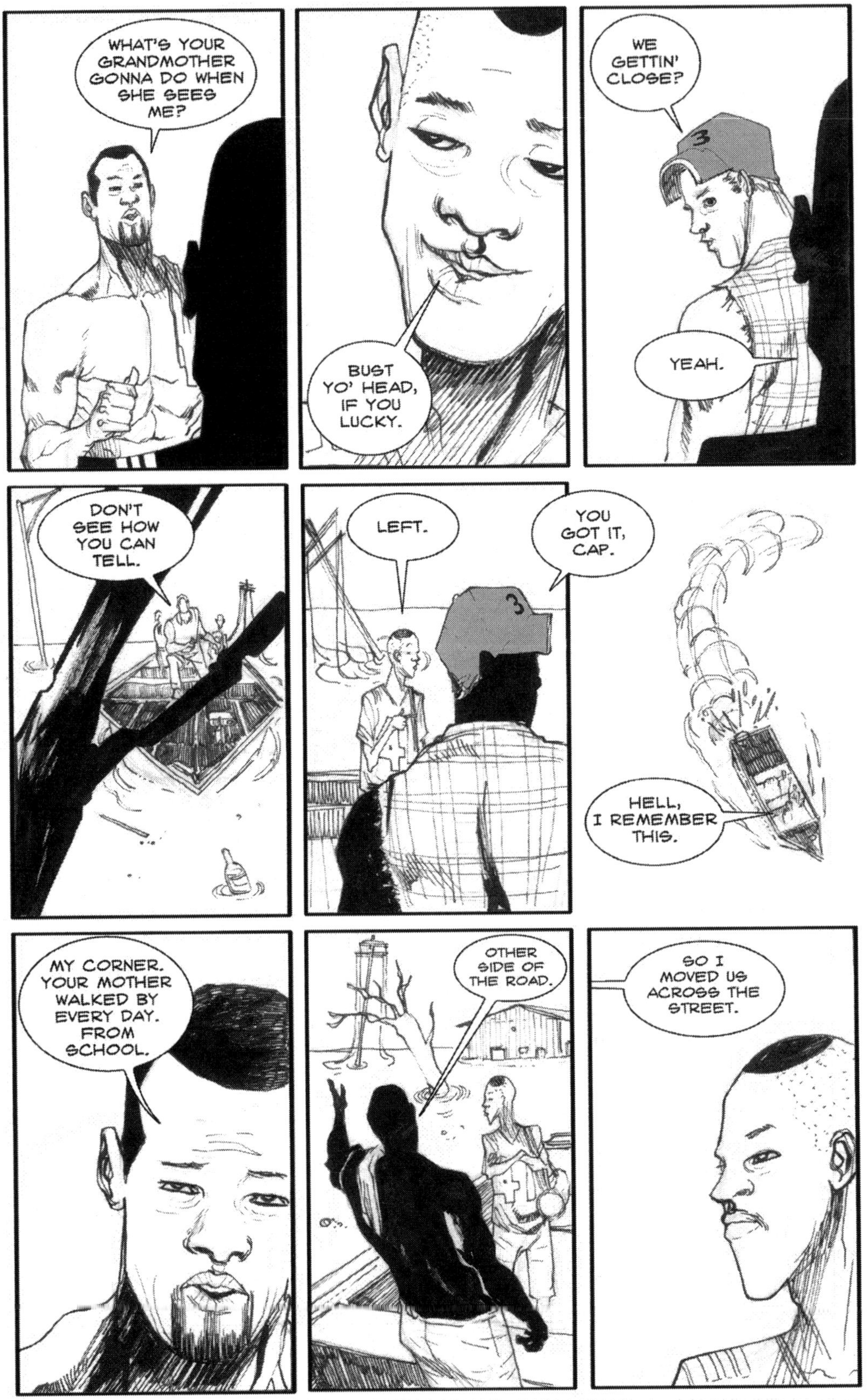
WHAT'S YOUR GRANDMOTHER GONNA DO WHEN SHE SEES ME?
BUST YO' HEAD, IF YOU LUCKY.
WE GETTIN' CLOSE?
YEAH.
DON'T SEE HOW YOU CAN TELL.
LEFT.
YOU GOT IT, CAP.
HELL, I REMEMBER THIS.
MY CORNER. YOUR MOTHER WALKED BY EVERY DAY. FROM SCHOOL.
OTHER SIDE OF THE ROAD.
SO I MOVED US ACROSS THE STREET.

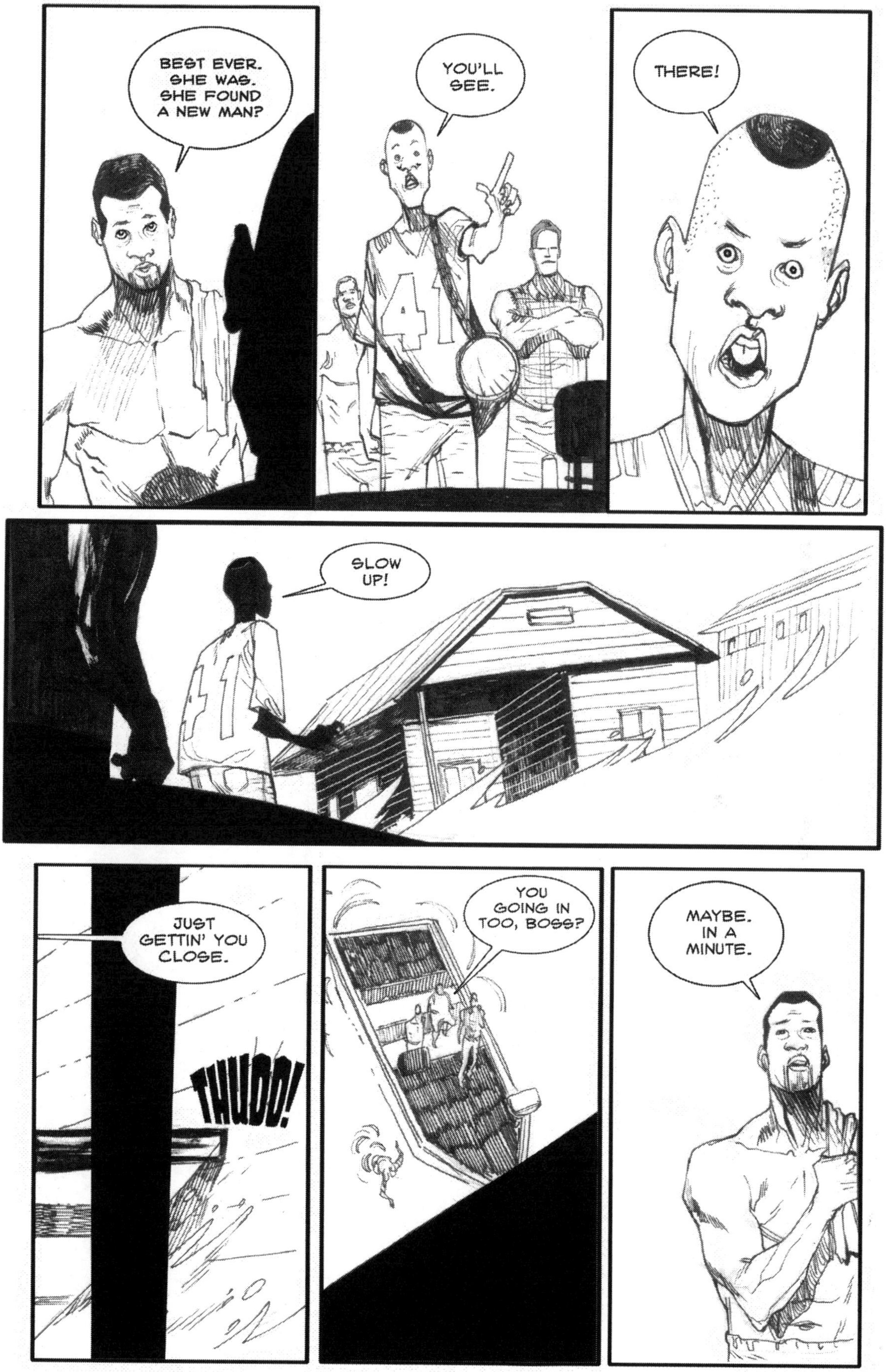
BEST EVER. SHE WAS. SHE FOUND A NEW MAN?
YOU'LL SEE.
THERE!
SLOW UP!
JUST GETTIN' YOU CLOSE.
THUDD!
YOU GOING IN TOO, BOSS?
MAYBE. IN A MINUTE.

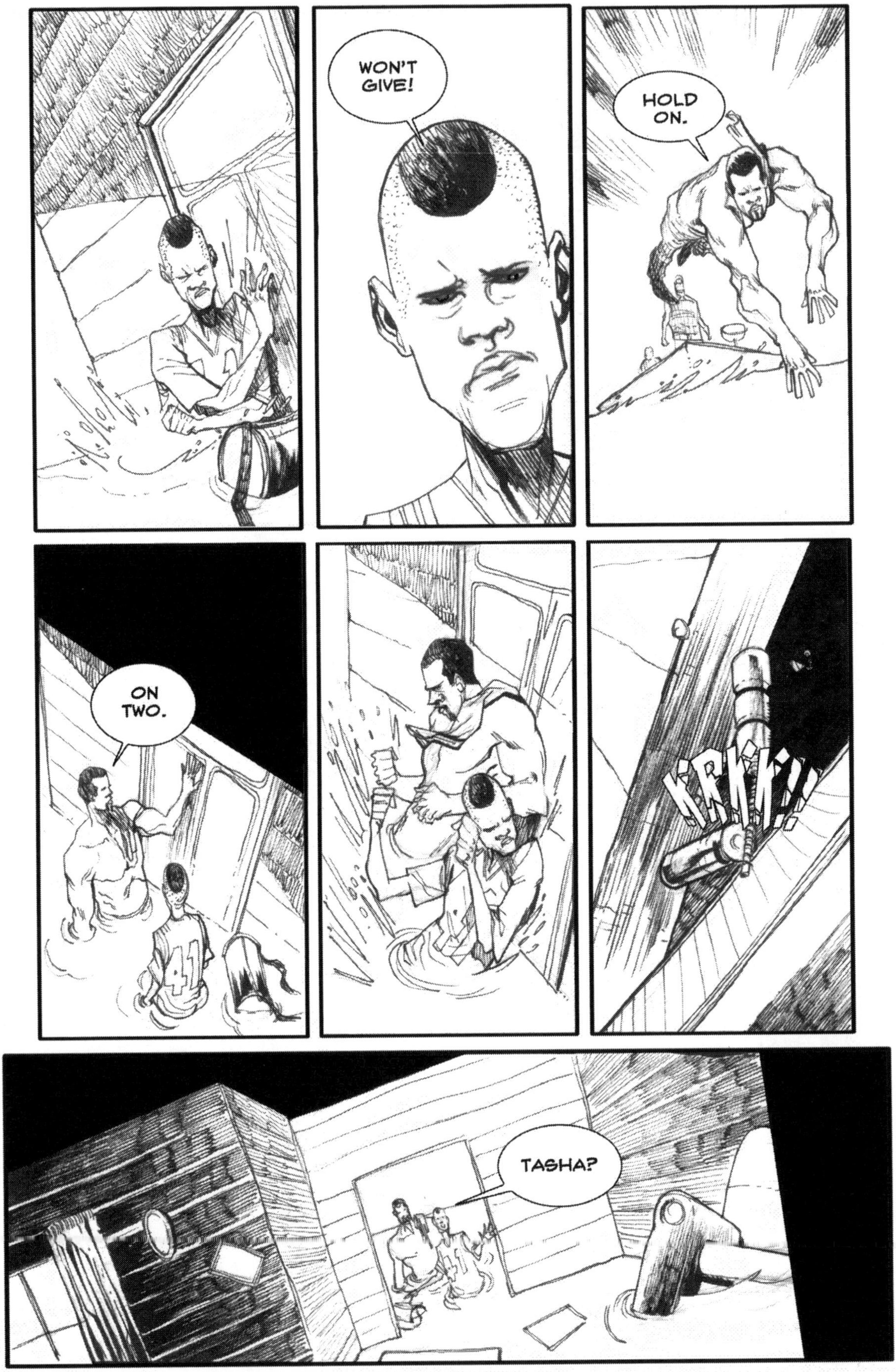
WON'T GIVE!
HOLD ON.
ON TWO.
KRKKK
TASHA?

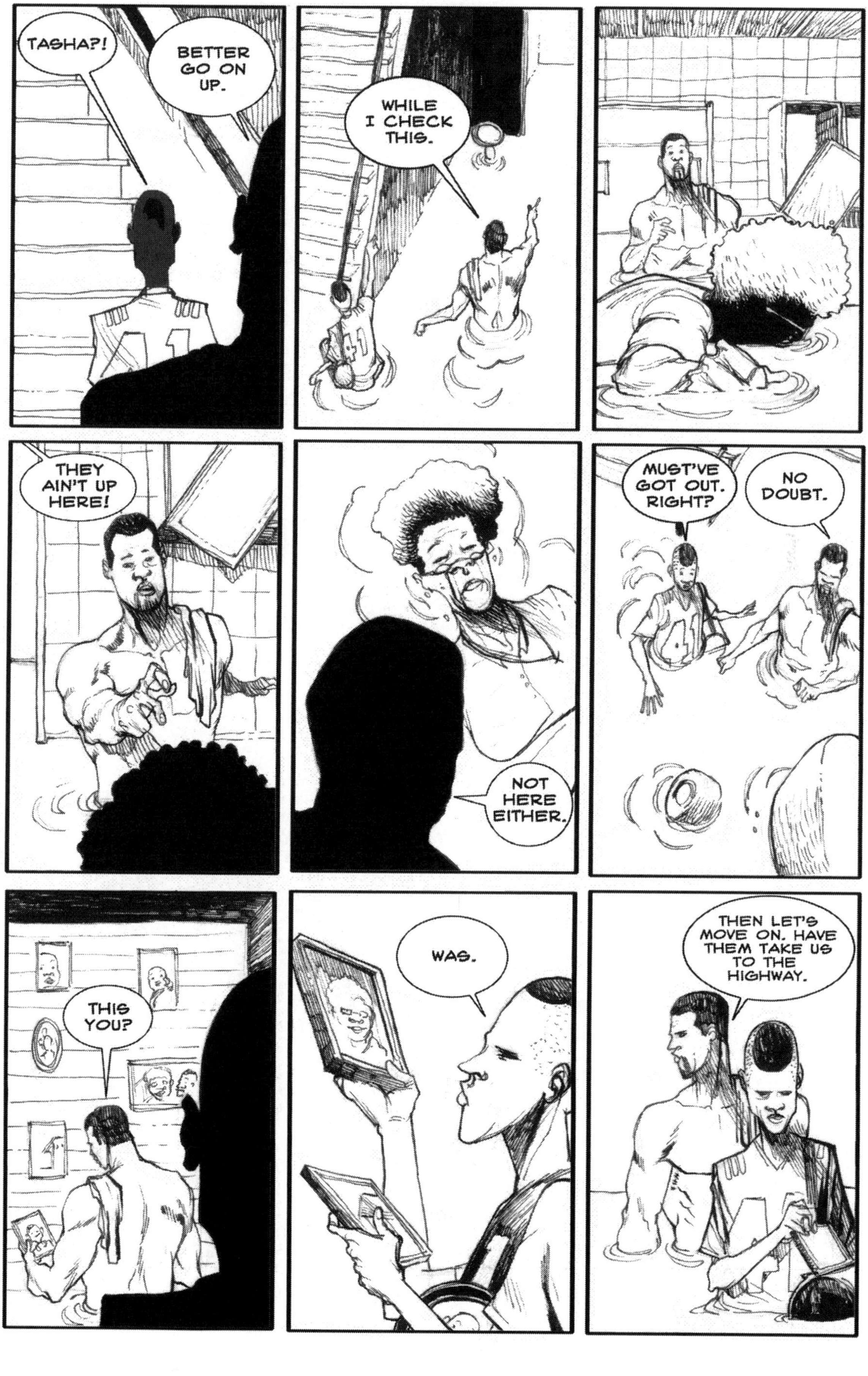
TASHA?!
BETTER GO ON UP.
WHILE I CHECK THIS.
THEY AIN'T UP HERE!
NOT HERE EITHER.
MUST'VE GOT OUT. RIGHT?
NO DOUBT.
THIS YOU?
WAS.
THEN LET'S MOVE ON. HAVE THEM TAKE US TO THE HIGHWAY.

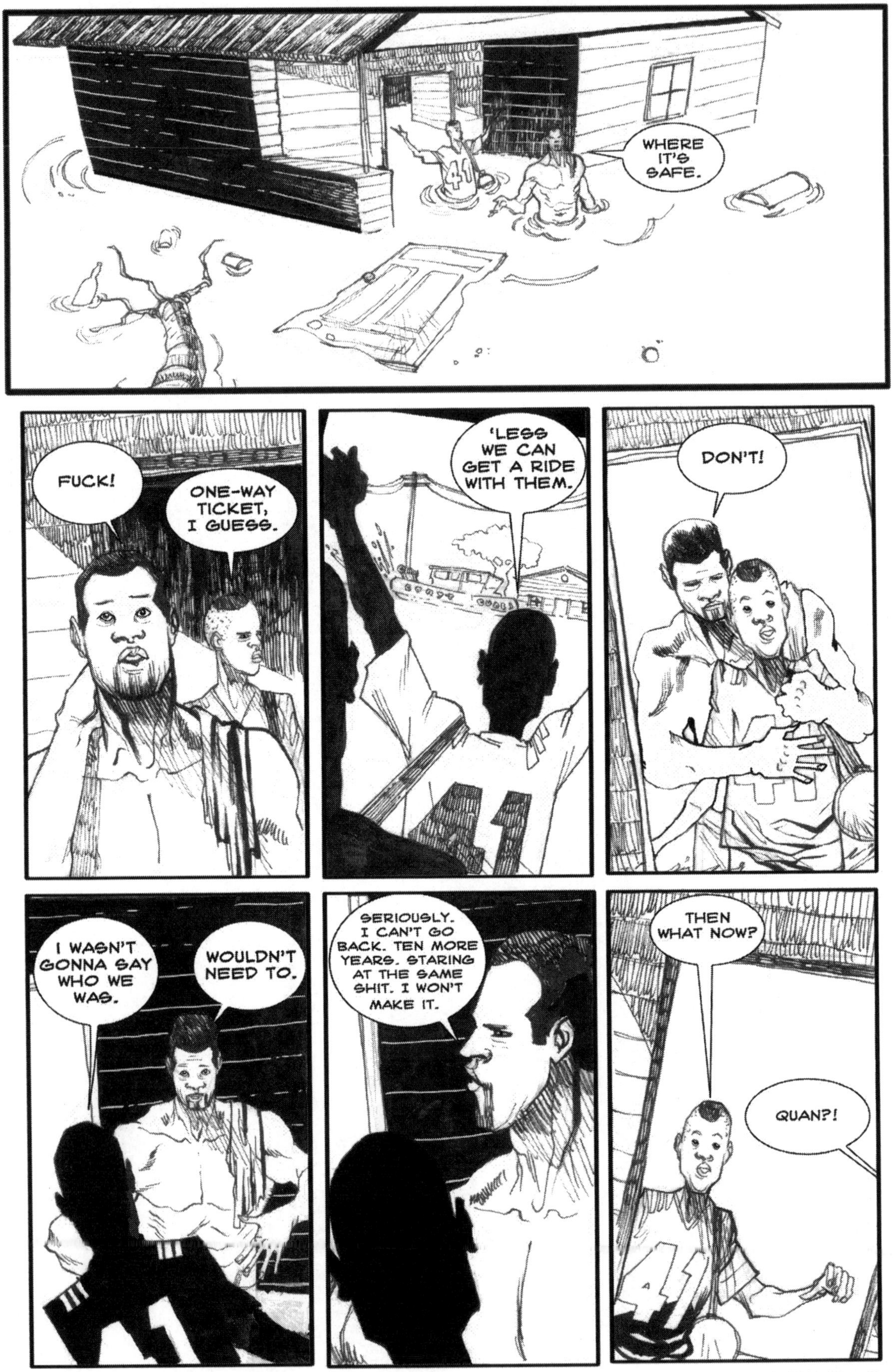
WHERE IT'S SAFE.
FUCK!
ONE-WAY TICKET, I GUESS.
'LESS WE CAN GET A RIDE WITH THEM.
DON'T!
I WASN'T GONNA SAY WHO WE WAS.
WOULDN'T NEED TO.
SERIOUSLY. I CAN'T GO BACK. TEN MORE YEARS. STARING AT THE SAME SHIT. I WON'T MAKE IT.
THEN WHAT NOW?
QUAN?!

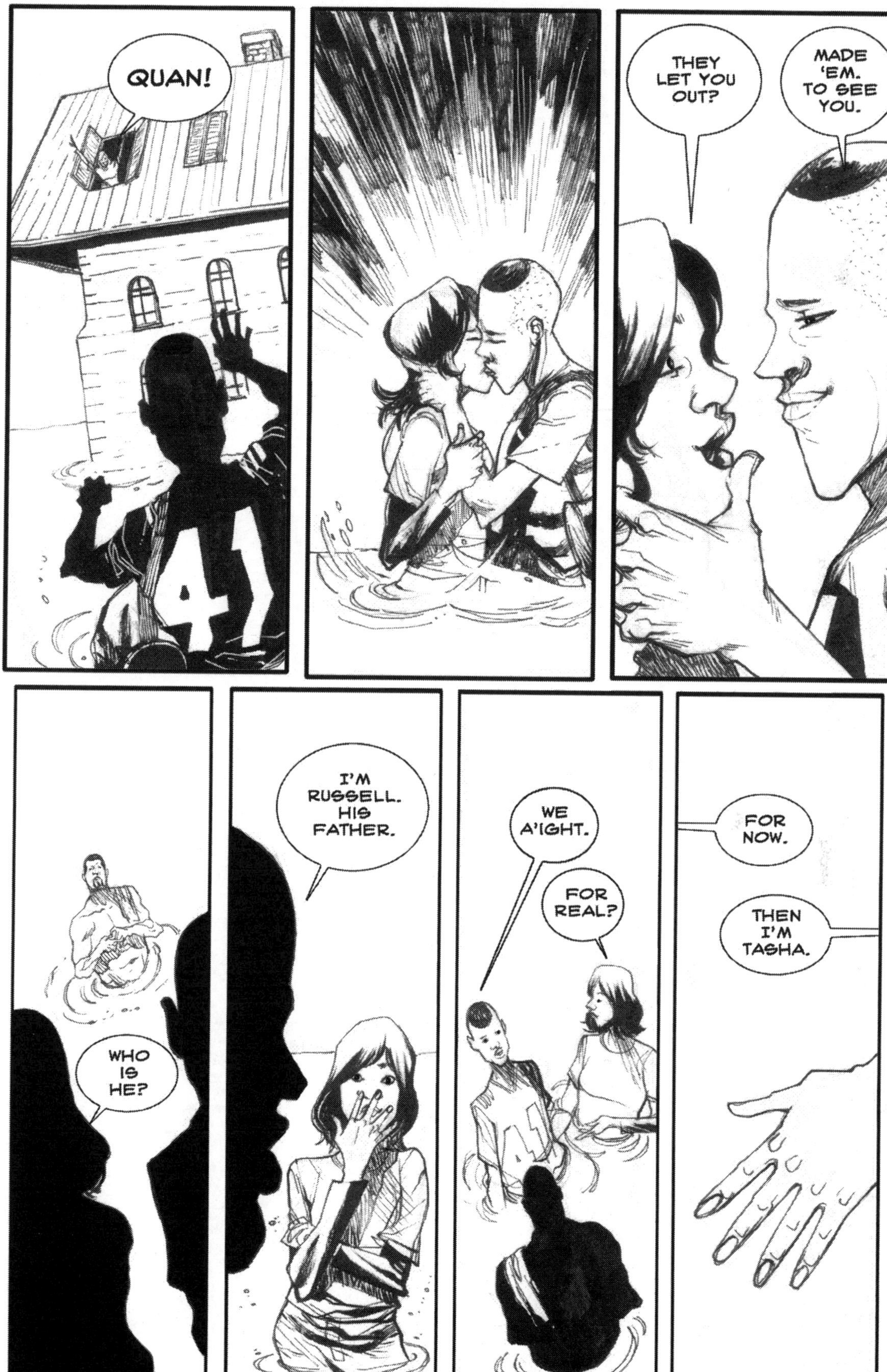
QUAN!
THEY LET YOU OUT?
MADE 'EM. TO SEE YOU.
WHO IS HE?
I'M RUSSELL. HIS FATHER.
WE A'IGHT.
FOR REAL?
FOR NOW.
THEN I'M TASHA.

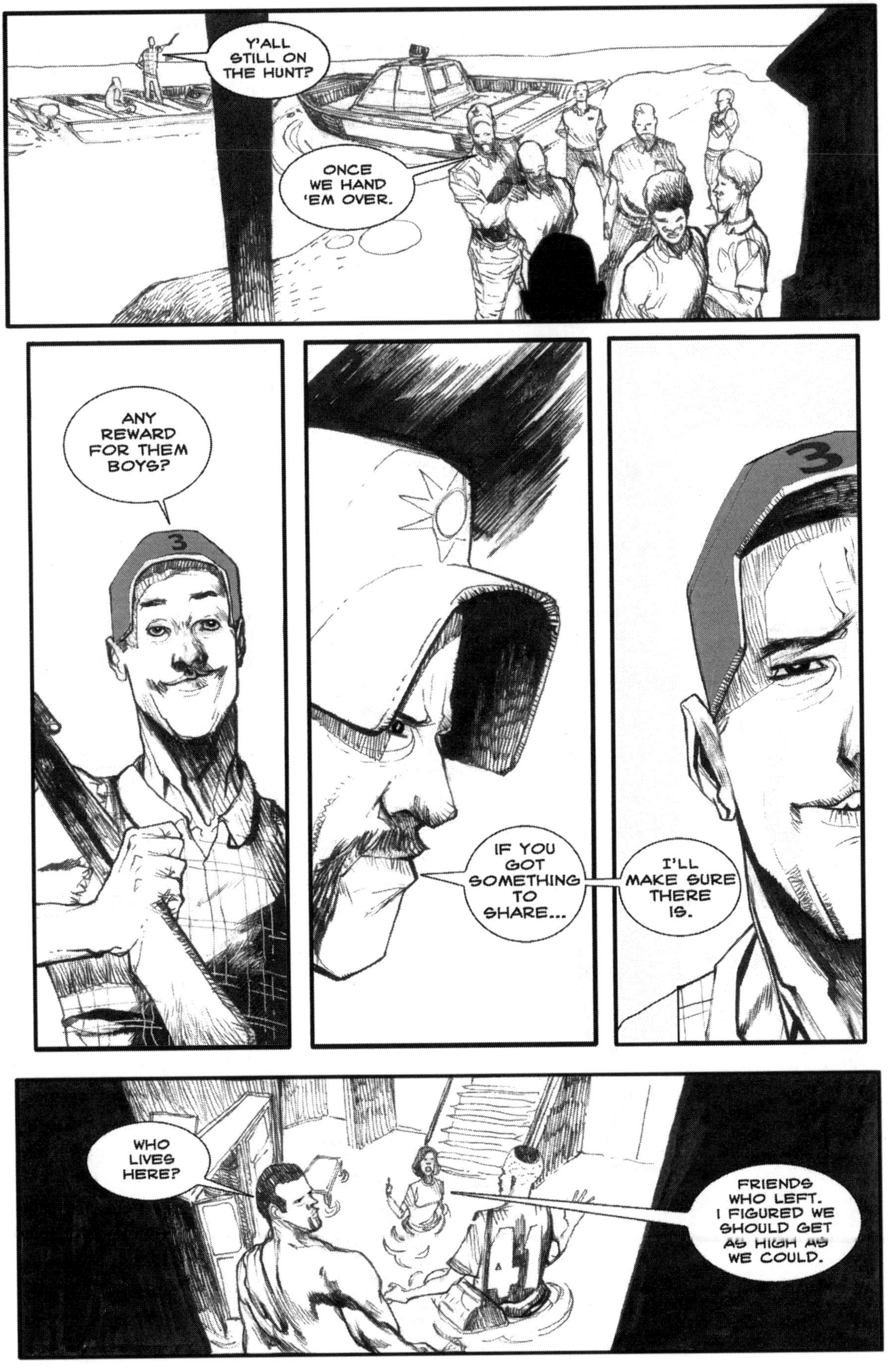
Y'ALL STILL ON THE HUNT?
ONCE WE HAND 'EM OVER.
ANY REWARD FOR THEM BOYS?
IF YOU GOT SOMETHING TO SHARE...
I'LL MAKE SURE THERE IS.
WHO LIVES HERE?
FRIENDS WHO LEFT. I FIGURED WE SHOULD GET AS HIGH AS WE COULD.

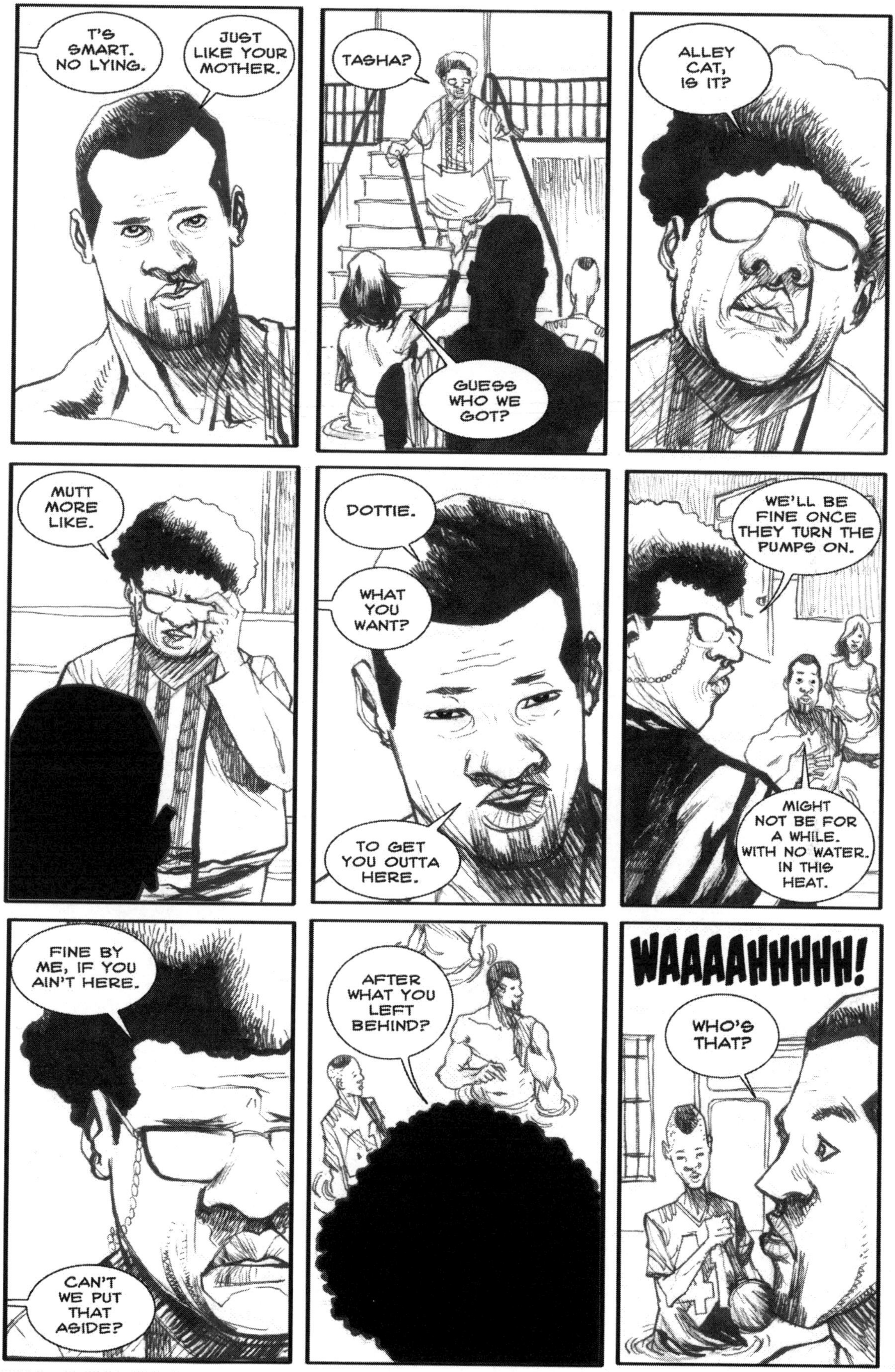
T'S SMART. NO LYING.
JUST LIKE YOUR MOTHER.
TASHA?
GUESS WHO WE GOT?
ALLEY CAT, IS IT?
MUTT MORE LIKE.
DOTTIE.
WHAT YOU WANT?
TO GET YOU OUTTA HERE.
WE'LL BE FINE ONCE THEY TURN THE PUMPS ON.
MIGHT NOT BE FOR A WHILE. WITH NO WATER. IN THIS HEAT.
FINE BY ME, IF YOU AIN'T HERE.
CAN'T WE PUT THAT ASIDE?
AFTER WHAT YOU LEFT BEHIND?
WAAAAHHHH!
WHO'S THAT?

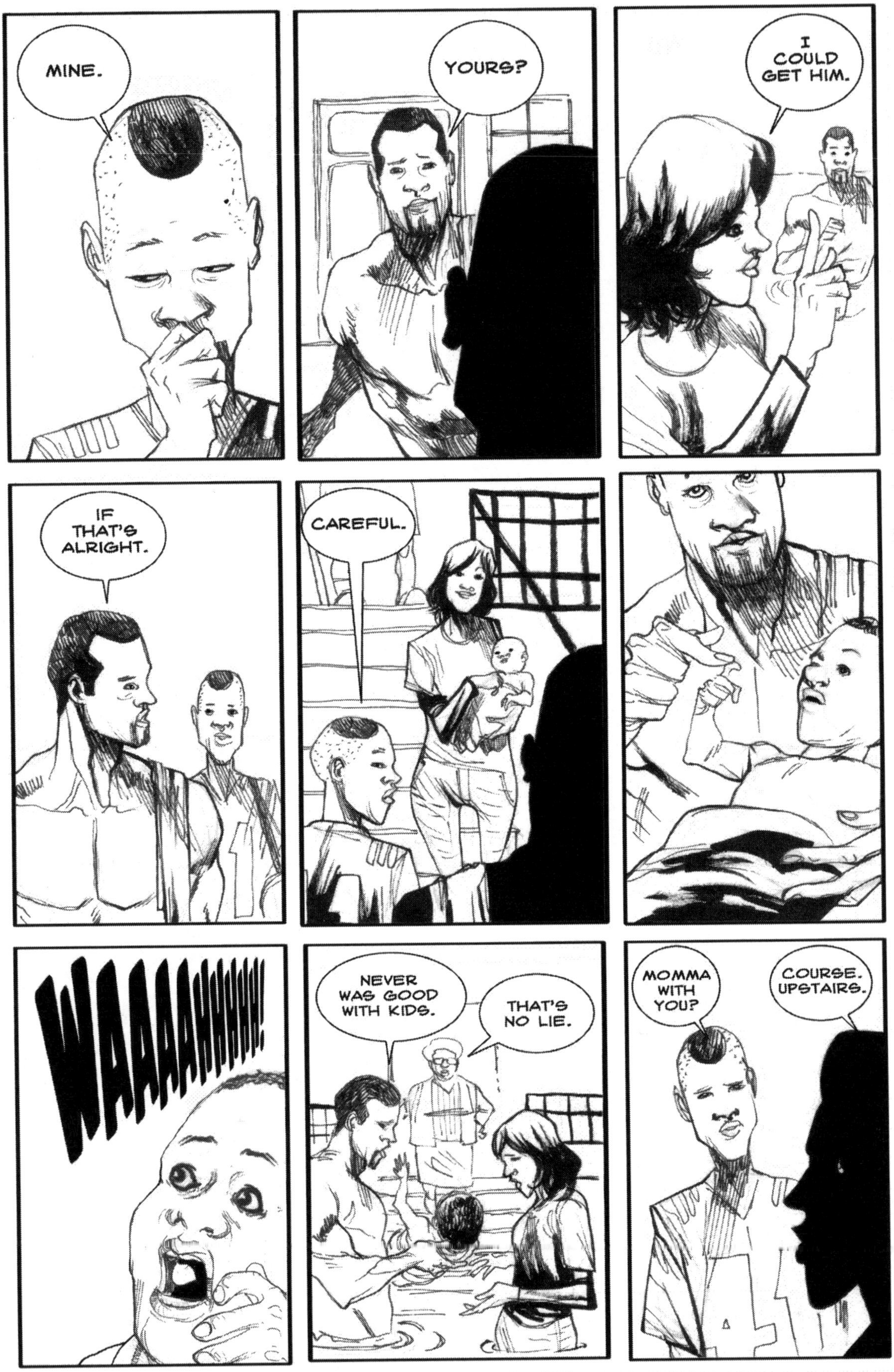
MINE.
YOURS?
I COULD GET HIM.
IF THAT'S ALRIGHT.
CAREFUL.
WAAAAHHHHH!
NEVER WAS GOOD WITH KIDS.
THAT'S NO LIE.
MOMMA WITH YOU?
COURSE. UPSTAIRS.

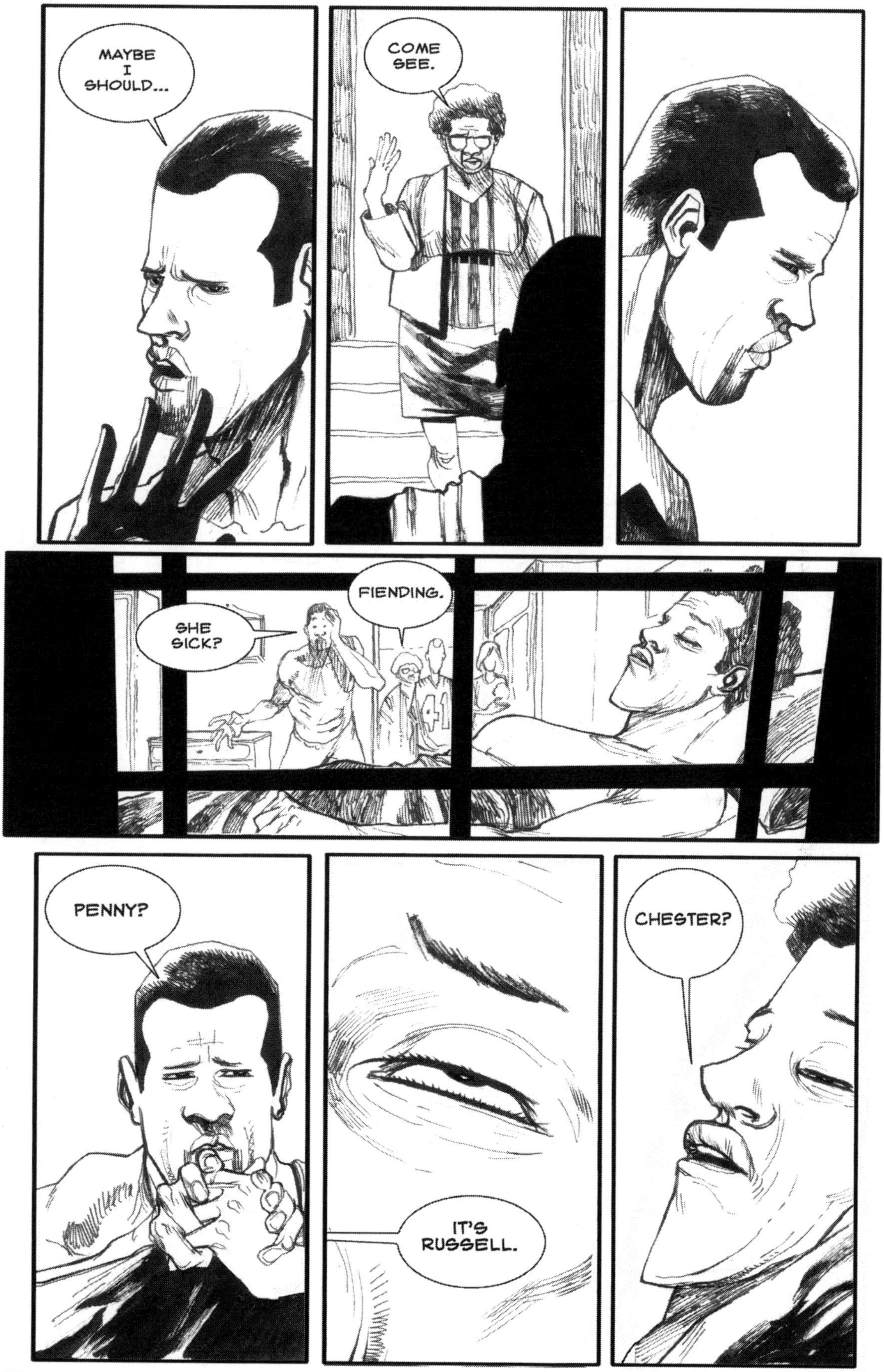
MAYBE I SHOULD...
COME SEE.
SHE SICK?
FIENDING.
PENNY?
IT'S RUSSELL.
CHESTER?

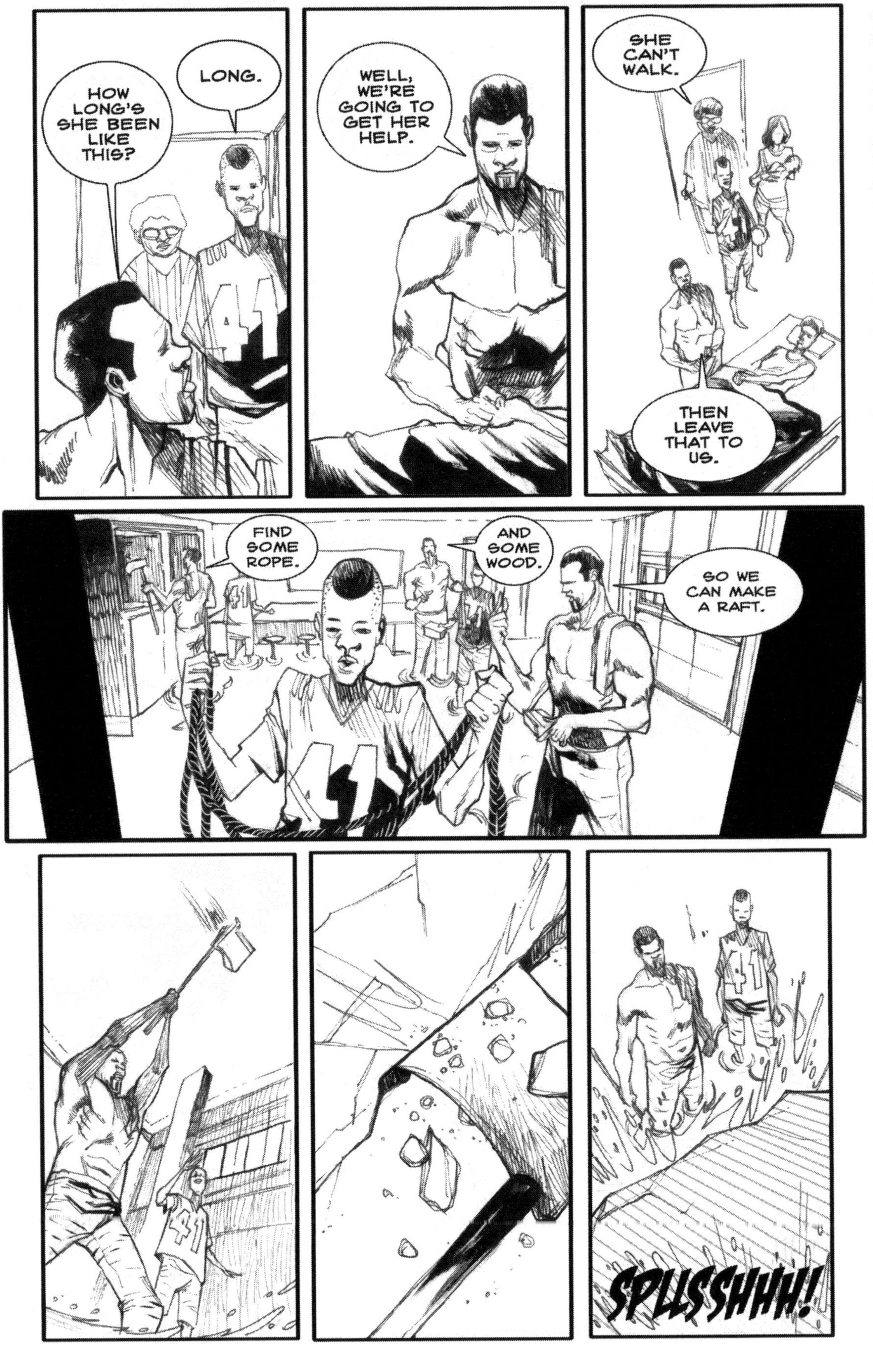
HOW LONG'S SHE BEEN LIKE THIS?
LONG.
WELL, WE'RE GOING TO GET HER HELP.
SHE CAN'T WALK.
THEN LEAVE THAT TO US.
FIND SOME ROPE.
AND SOME WOOD.
SO WE CAN MAKE A RAFT.
SPLISSHHH!

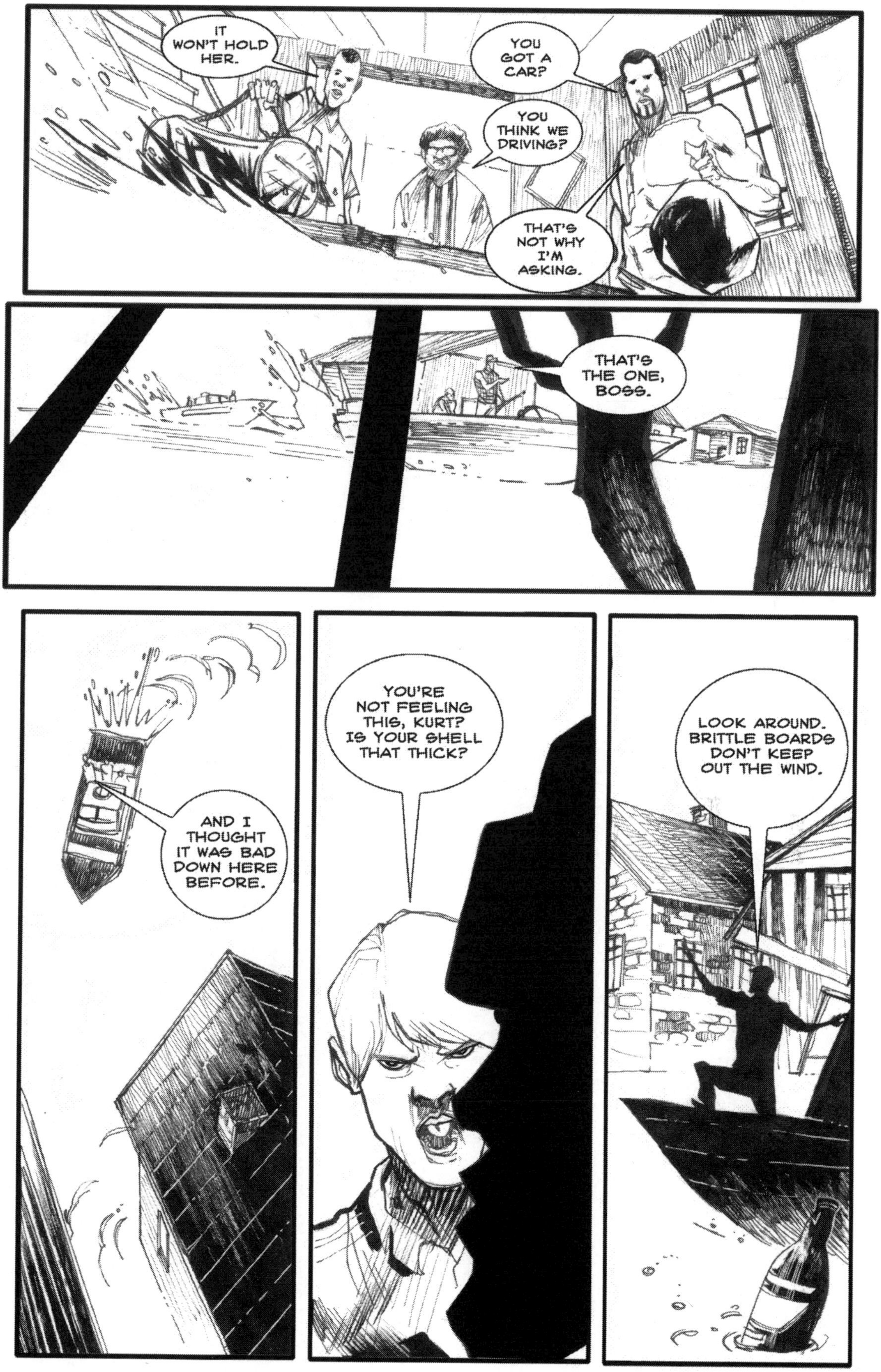
IT WON'T HOLD HER.
YOU GOT A CAR?
YOU THINK WE DRIVING?
THAT'S NOT WHY I'M ASKING.
THAT'S THE ONE, BOSS.
AND I THOUGHT IT WAS BAD DOWN HERE BEFORE.
YOU'RE NOT FEELING THIS, KURT? IS YOUR SHELL THAT THICK?
LOOK AROUND. BRITTLE BOARDS DON'T KEEP OUT THE WIND.

WHILE BRICK NEVER LETS ANYTHING IN.

INCLUDING PEOPLE, FROM WHAT MY SISTER SAYS.

YOU HEAR THAT?

YUP. IN THE GARAGE.

WFFF! WFFF!

SHOULD WE LOCK HER UP TOO?

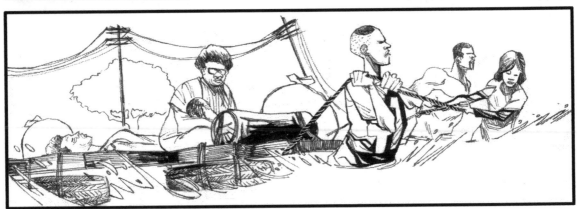

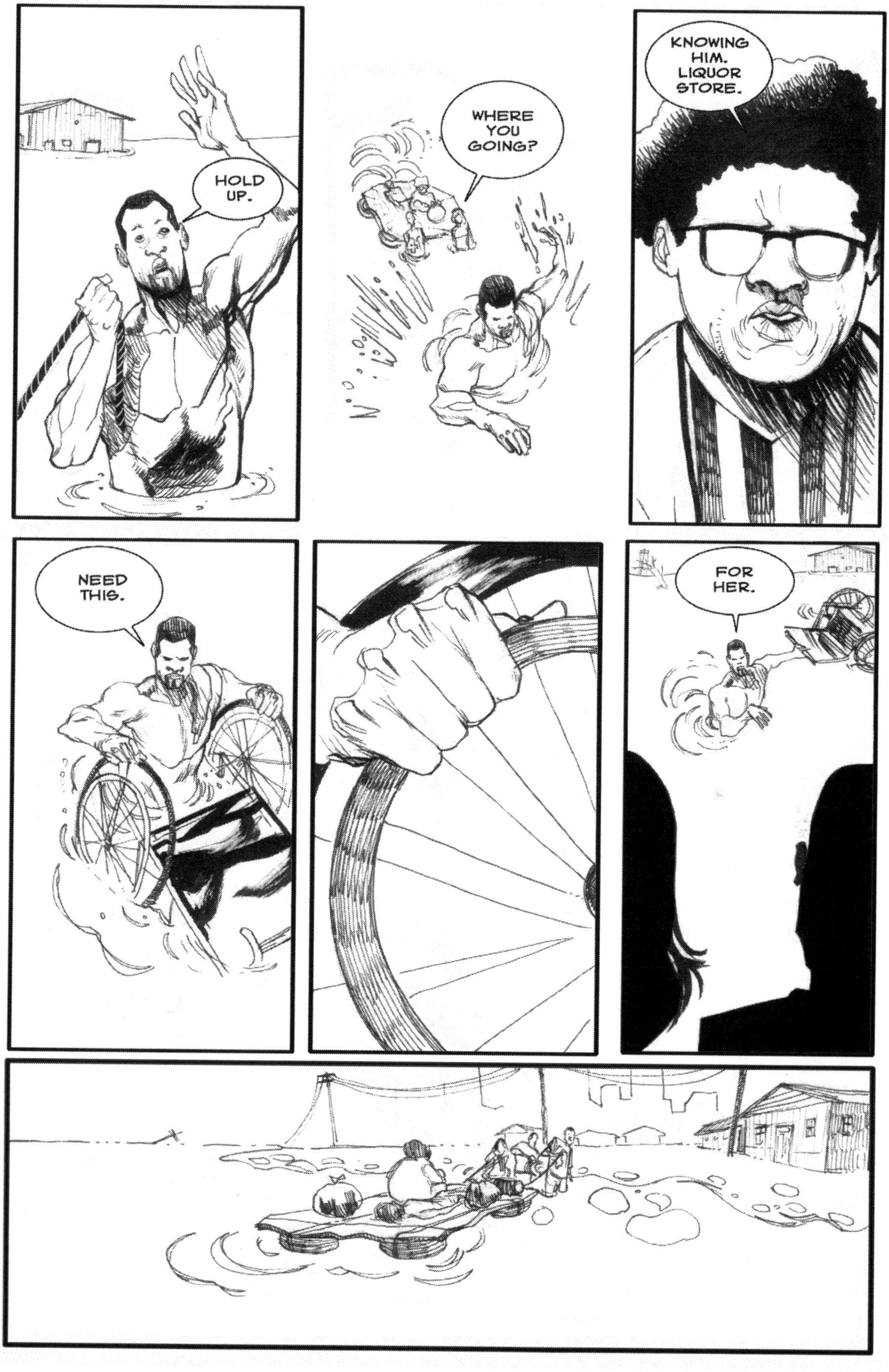
HOLD UP.
WHERE YOU GOING?
KNOWING HIM. LIQUOR STORE.
NEED THIS.
FOR HER.

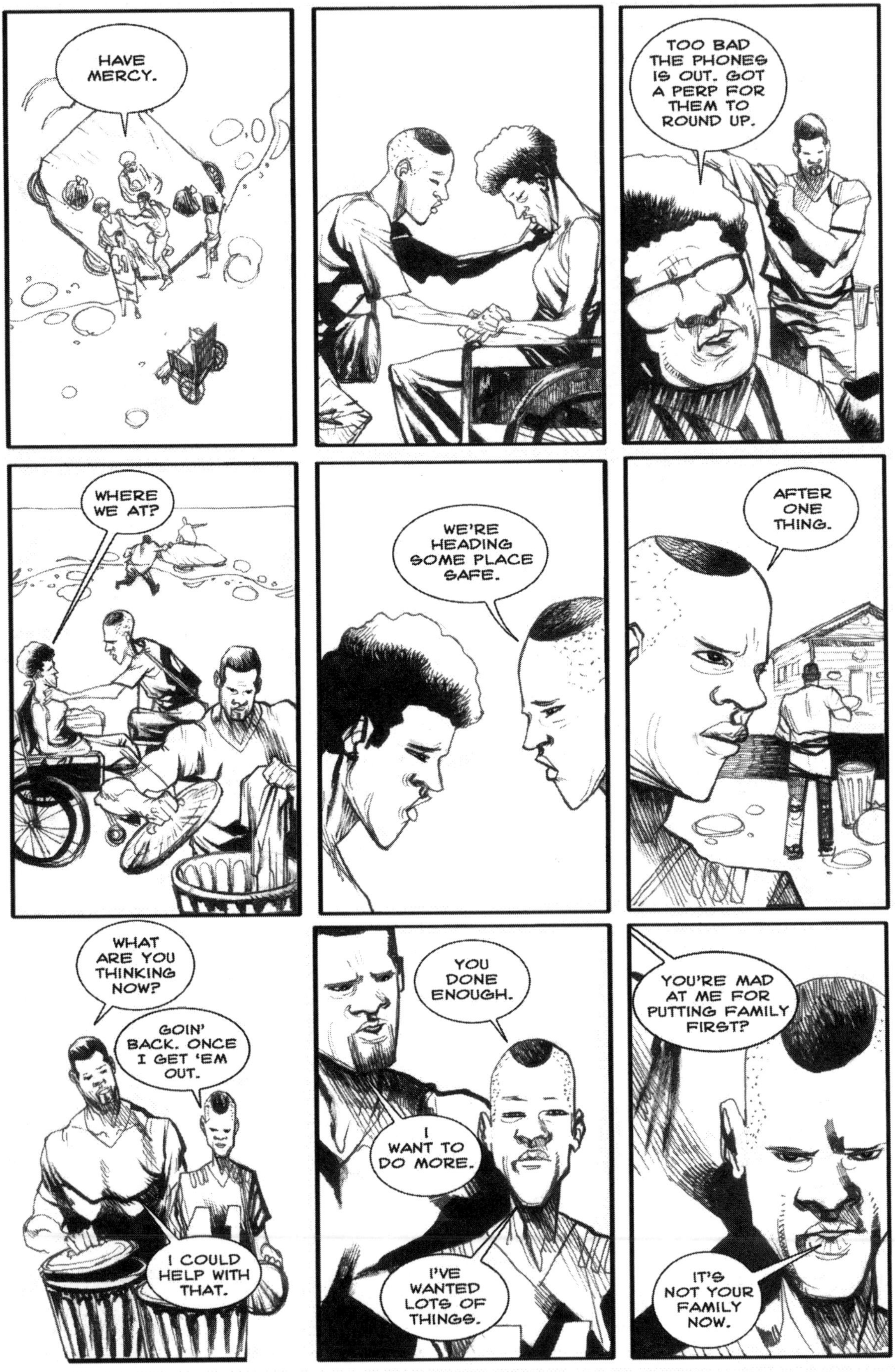
HAVE MERCY.
TOO BAD THE PHONES IS OUT. GOT A PERP FOR THEM TO ROUND UP.
WHERE WE AT?
WE'RE HEADING SOME PLACE SAFE.
AFTER ONE THING.
WHAT ARE YOU THINKING NOW?
GOIN' BACK. ONCE I GET 'EM OUT.
I COULD HELP WITH THAT.
YOU DONE ENOUGH.
I WANT TO DO MORE.
I'VE WANTED LOTS OF THINGS.
YOU'RE MAD AT ME FOR PUTTING FAMILY FIRST?
IT'S NOT YOUR FAMILY NOW.

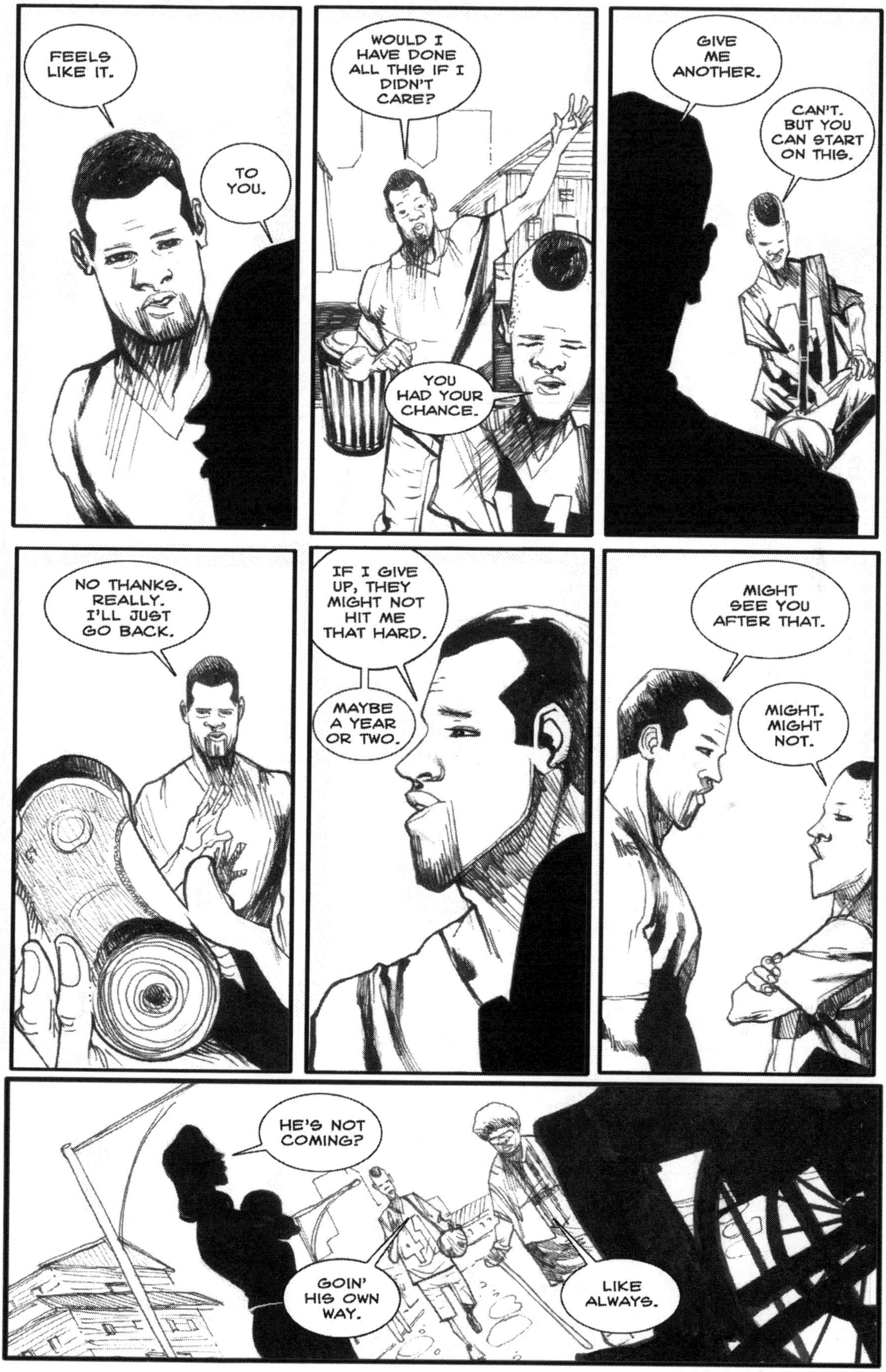
FEELS LIKE IT.
TO YOU.
WOULD I HAVE DONE ALL THIS IF I DIDN'T CARE?
YOU HAD YOUR CHANCE.
GIVE ME ANOTHER.
CAN'T. BUT YOU CAN START ON THIS.
NO THANKS. REALLY. I'LL JUST GO BACK.
IF I GIVE UP, THEY MIGHT NOT HIT ME THAT HARD.
MAYBE A YEAR OR TWO.
MIGHT SEE YOU AFTER THAT.
MIGHT. MIGHT NOT.
HE'S NOT COMING?
GOIN' HIS OWN WAY.
LIKE ALWAYS.

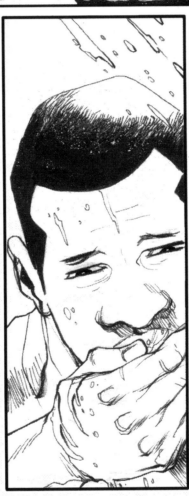

YO!

I SEEN HIM!

WHO?!

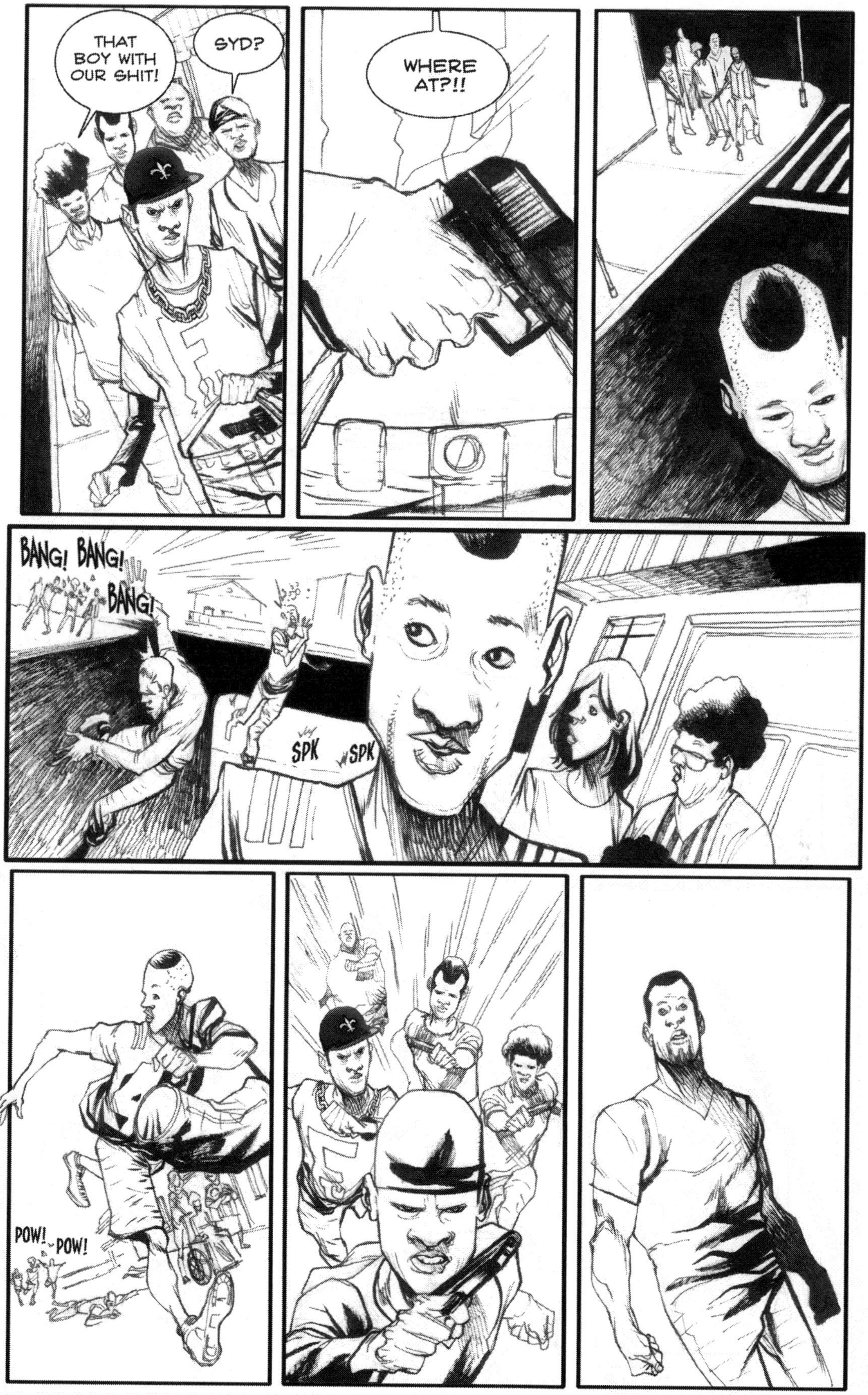
THAT BOY WITH OUR SHIT!
SYD?
WHERE AT?!!
BANG! BANG!
BANG!
SPK
SPK
POW!
POW!

OFFICER!

YOU HEAR THOSE SHOTS?!

HEARD 'EM ALL DAY.

YOU GOT TO STOP IT!

I WOULDN'T STAND A CHANCE.

WITHOUT BACK UP.

SPREAD IT OUT, TIMMS!

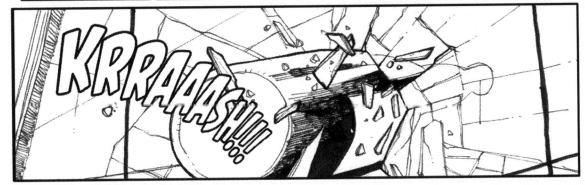

KRRAAASH!!!

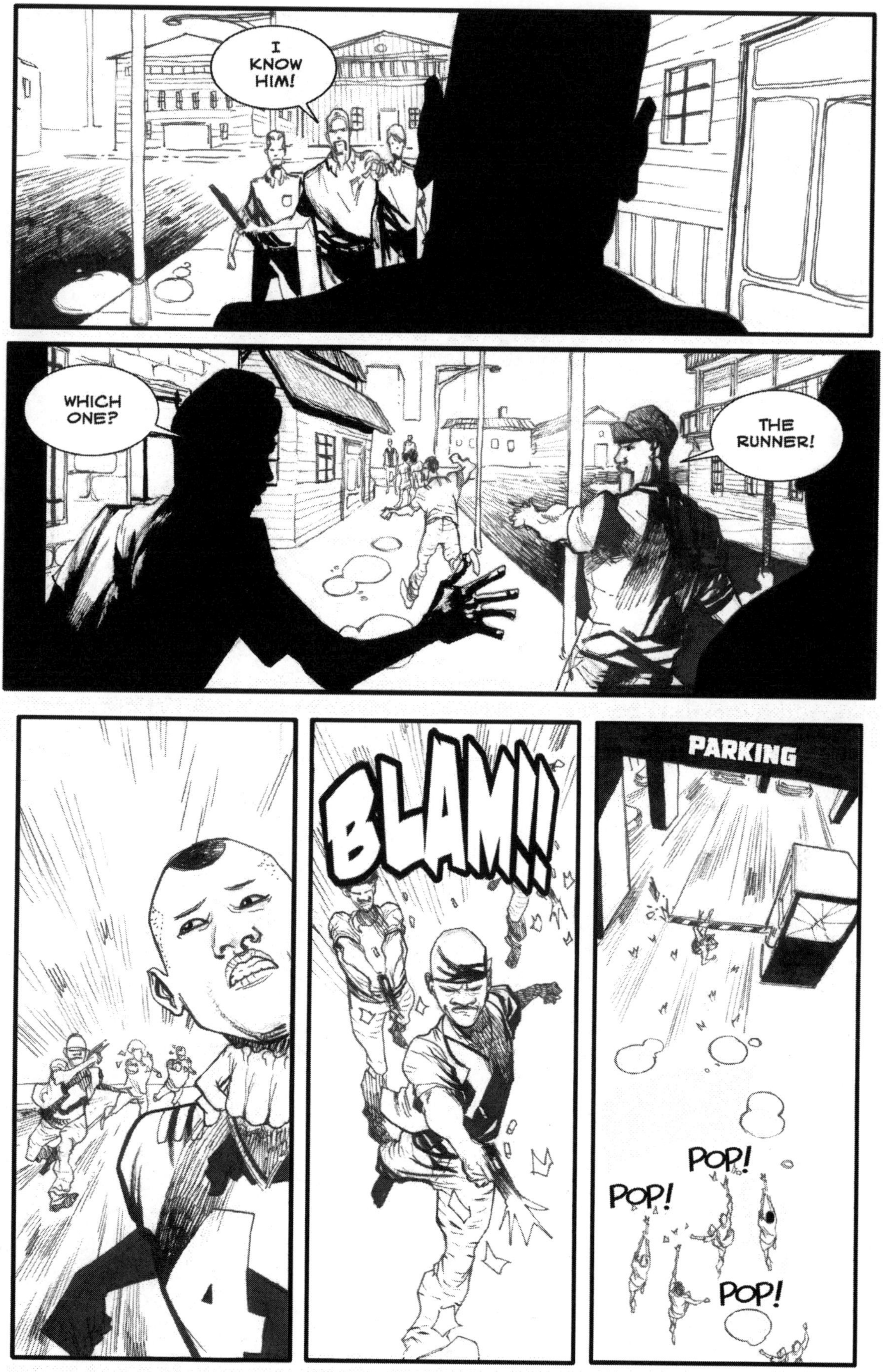
I KNOW HIM!
WHICH ONE?
THE RUNNER!
BLAM!!
PARKING
POP!
POP!
POP!

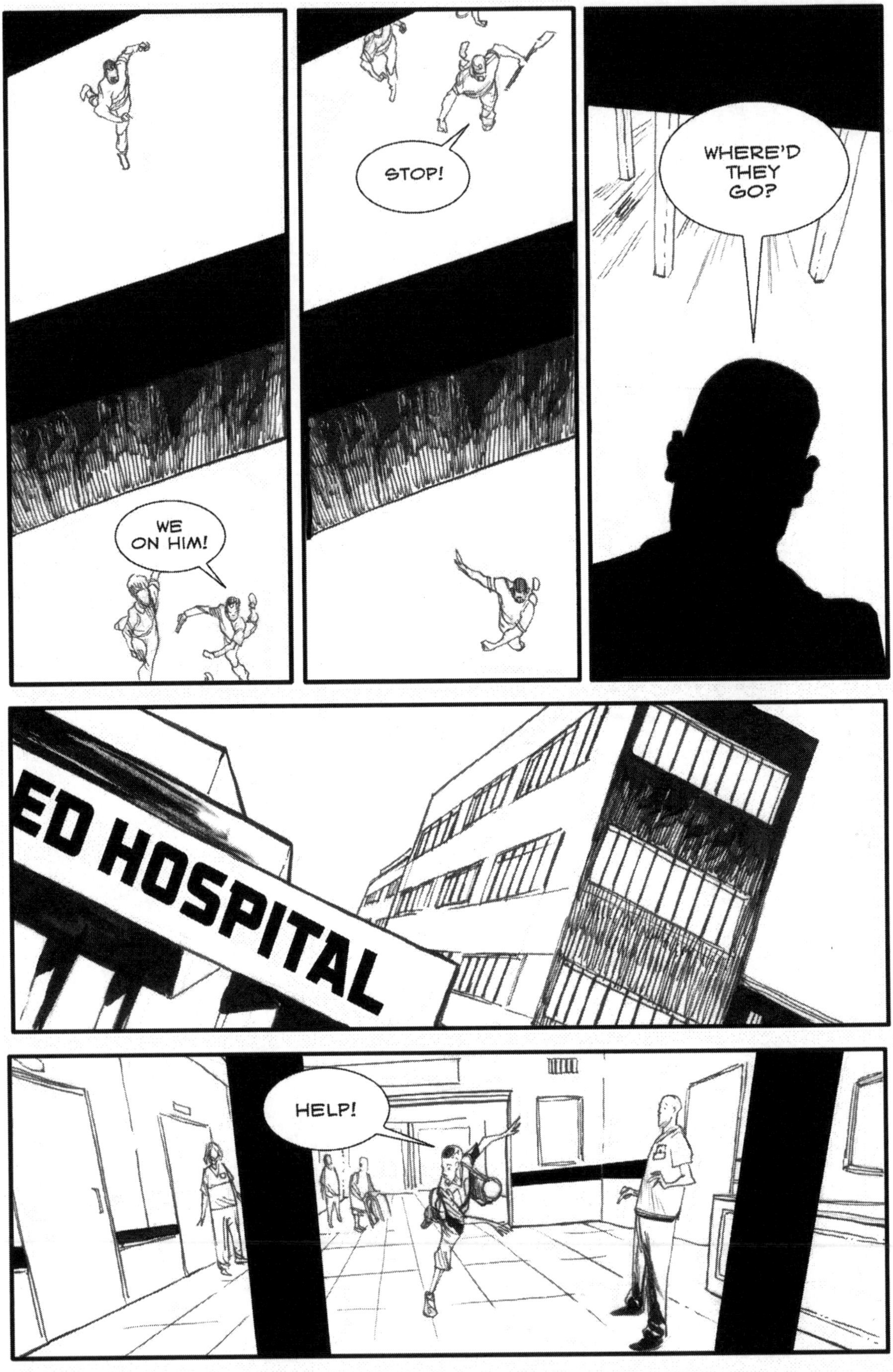
WE ON HIM!
STOP!
WHERE'D THEY GO?
ED HOSPITAL
HELP!

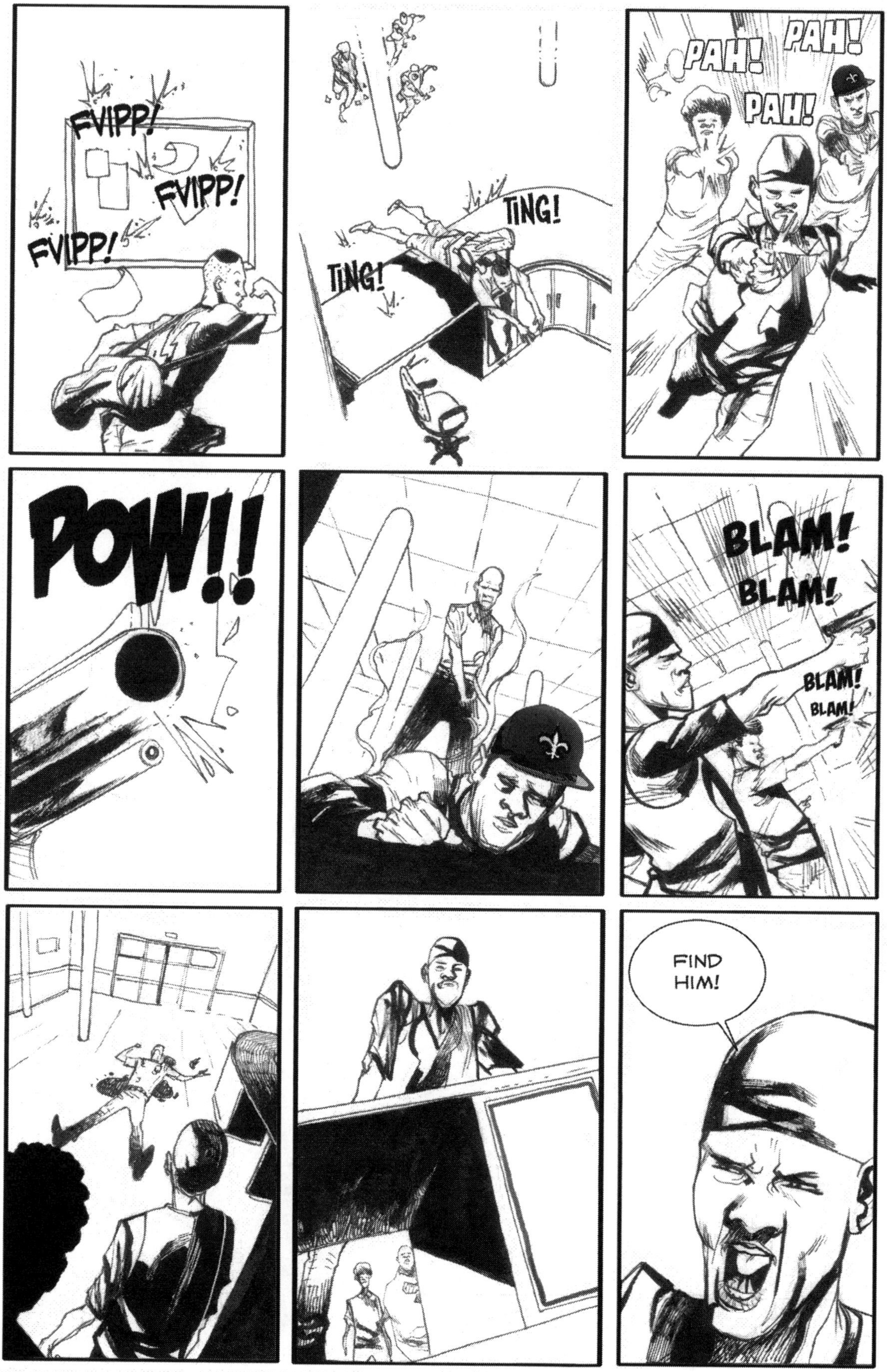
FVIPP!
FVIPP!
FVIPP!
TING!
TING!
PAH!
PAH!
PAH!
POW!!
BLAM!
BLAM!
BLAM!
BLAM!
FIND HIM!

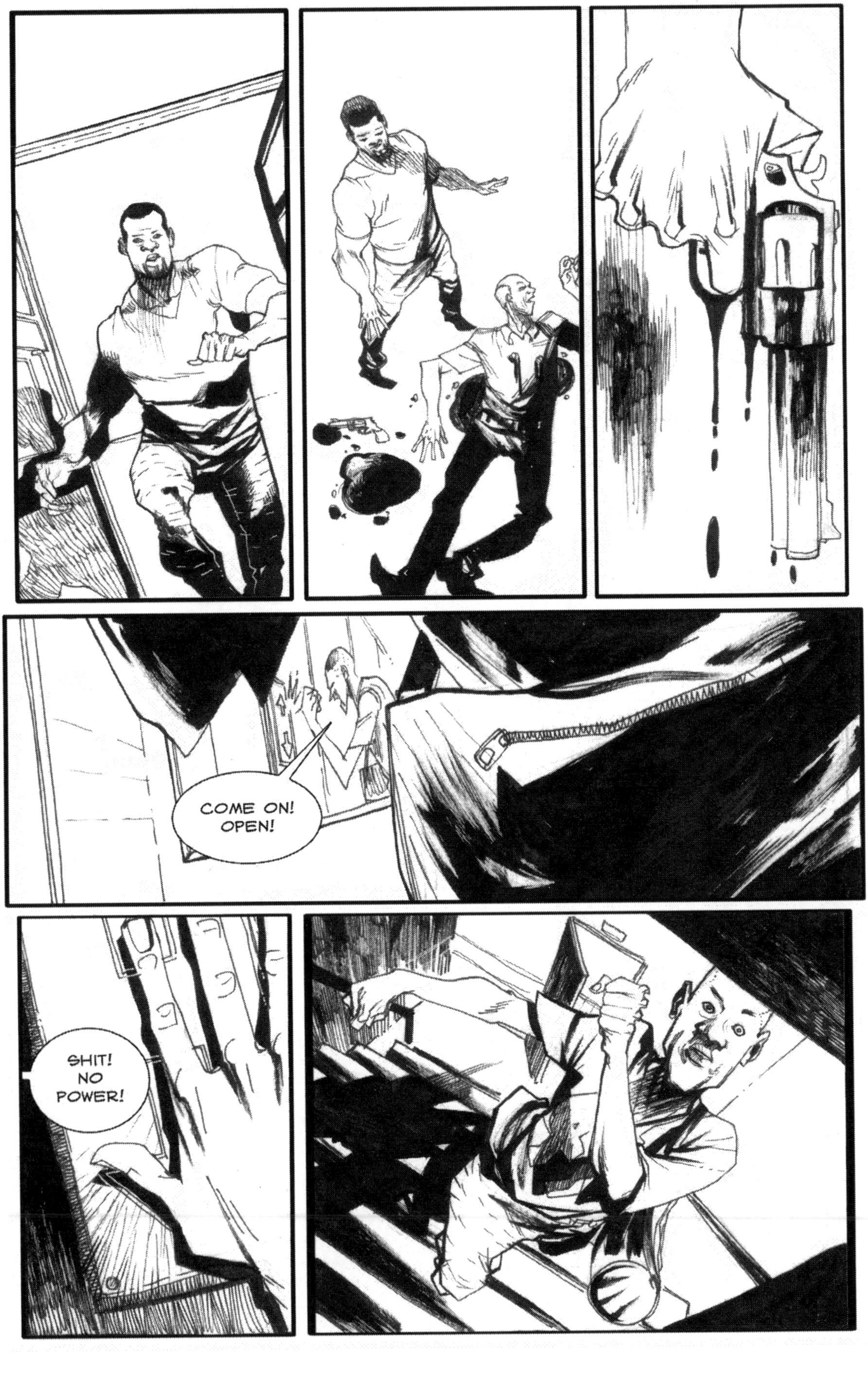
COME ON! OPEN!
SHIT! NO POWER!

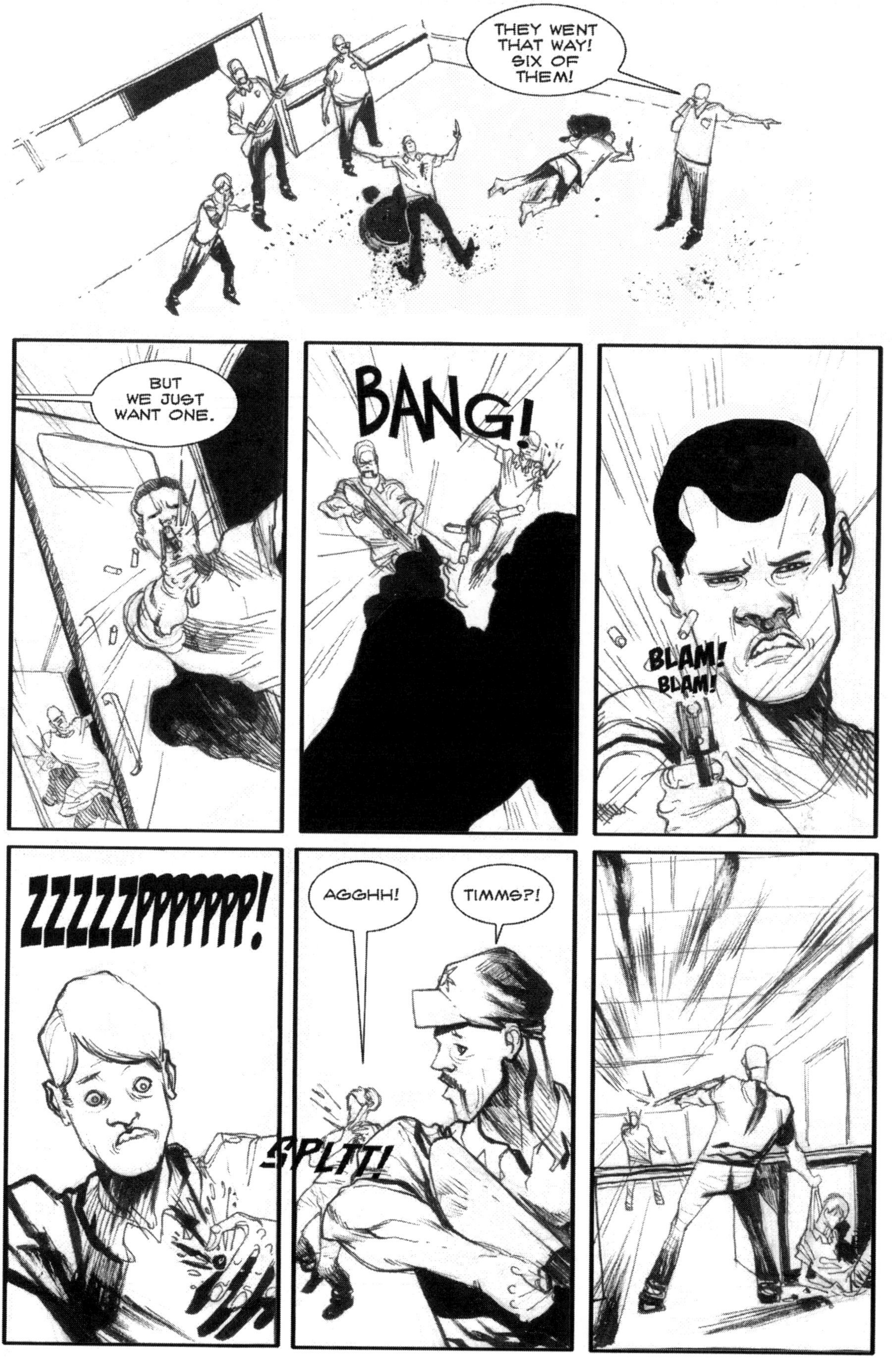
THEY WENT THAT WAY! SIX OF THEM!
BUT WE JUST WANT ONE.
BANG!
BLAM! BLAM!
ZZZZZPPPPPPP!
AGGHH!
TIMMS?!
SPLTT!

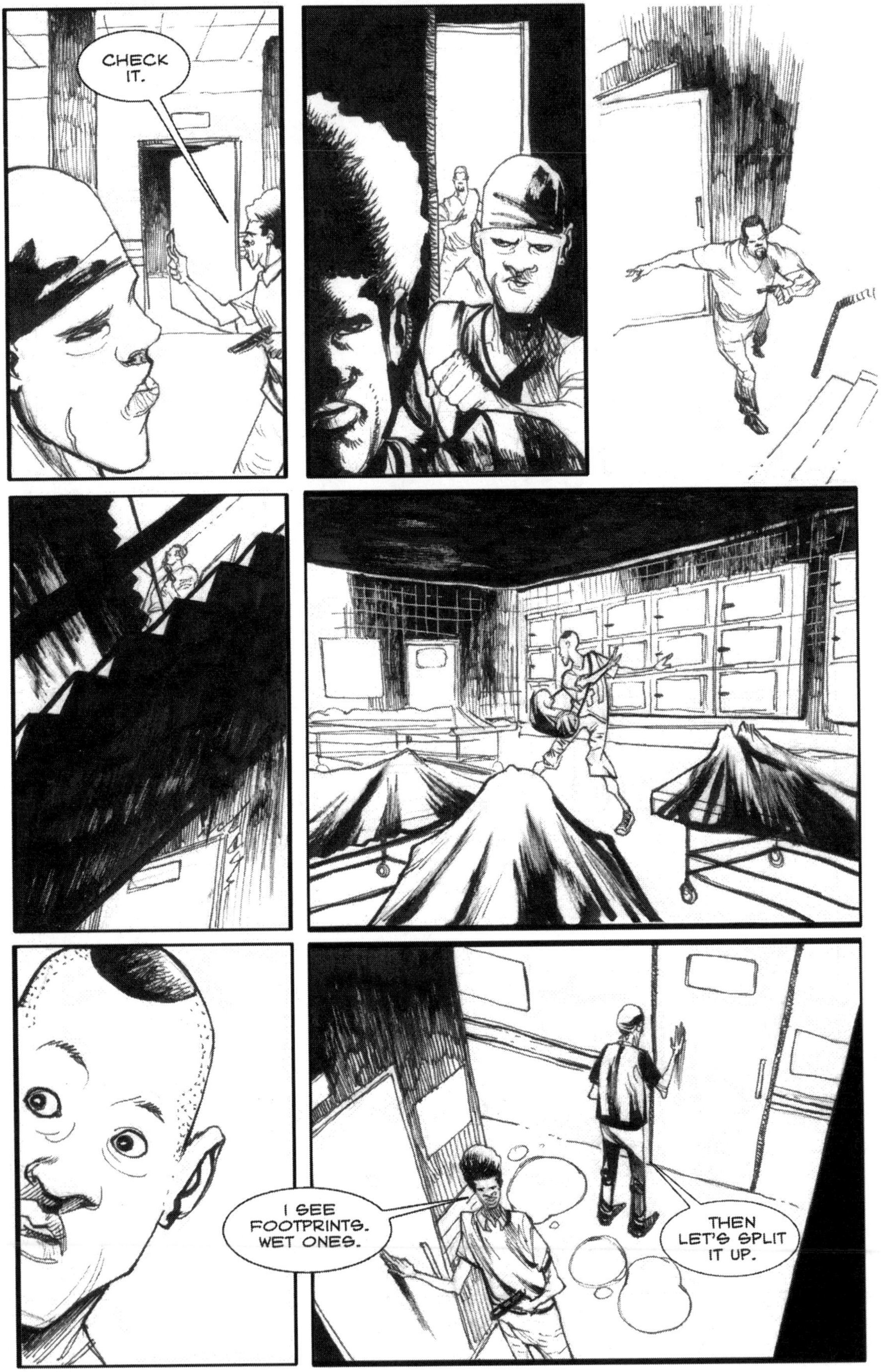
CHECK IT.
I SEE FOOTPRINTS. WET ONES.
THEN LET'S SPLIT IT UP.

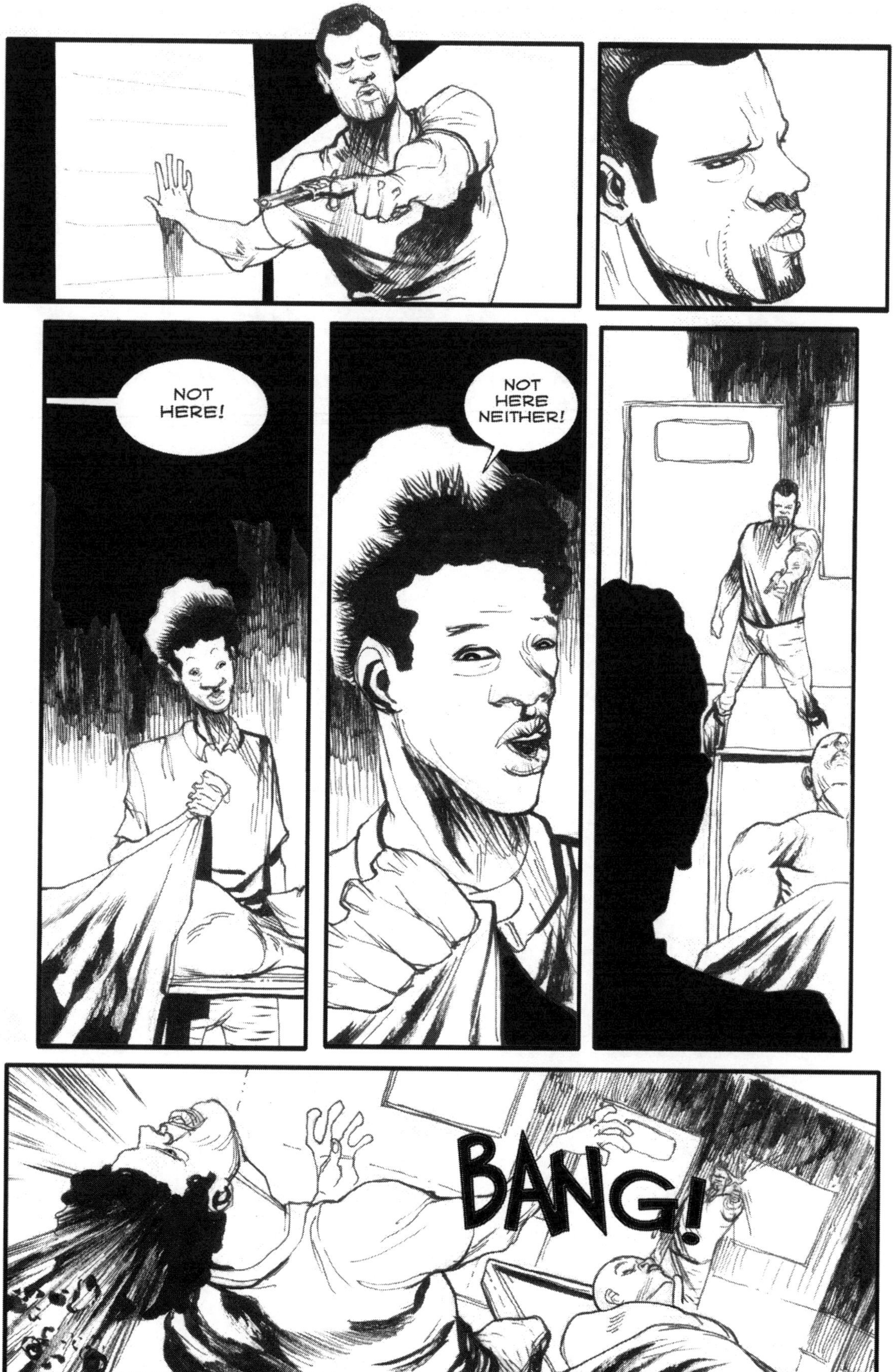
NOT HERE!
NOT HERE NEITHER!
BANG!

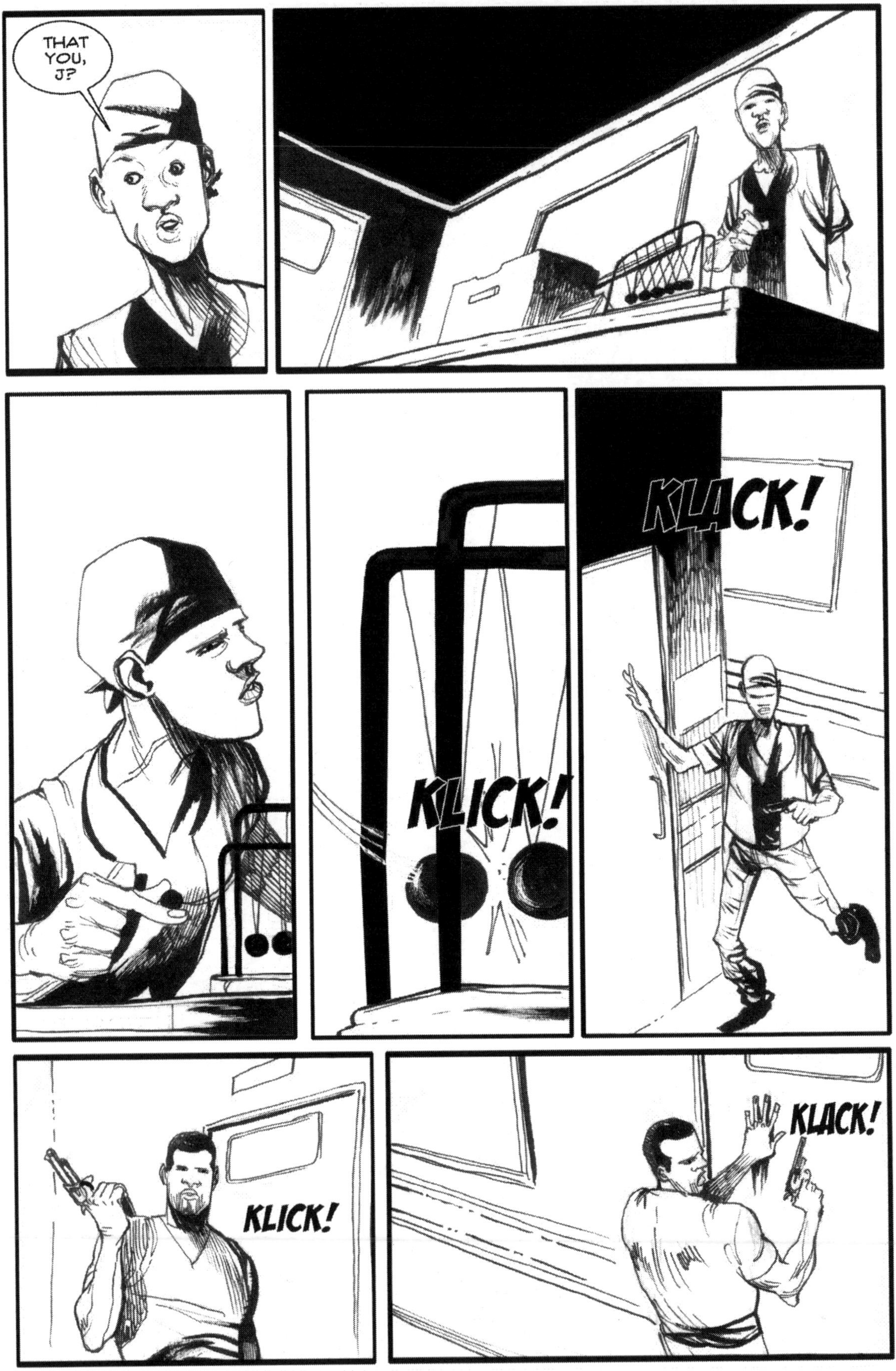
THAT YOU, J?
KLICK!
KLACK!
KLICK!
KLACK!

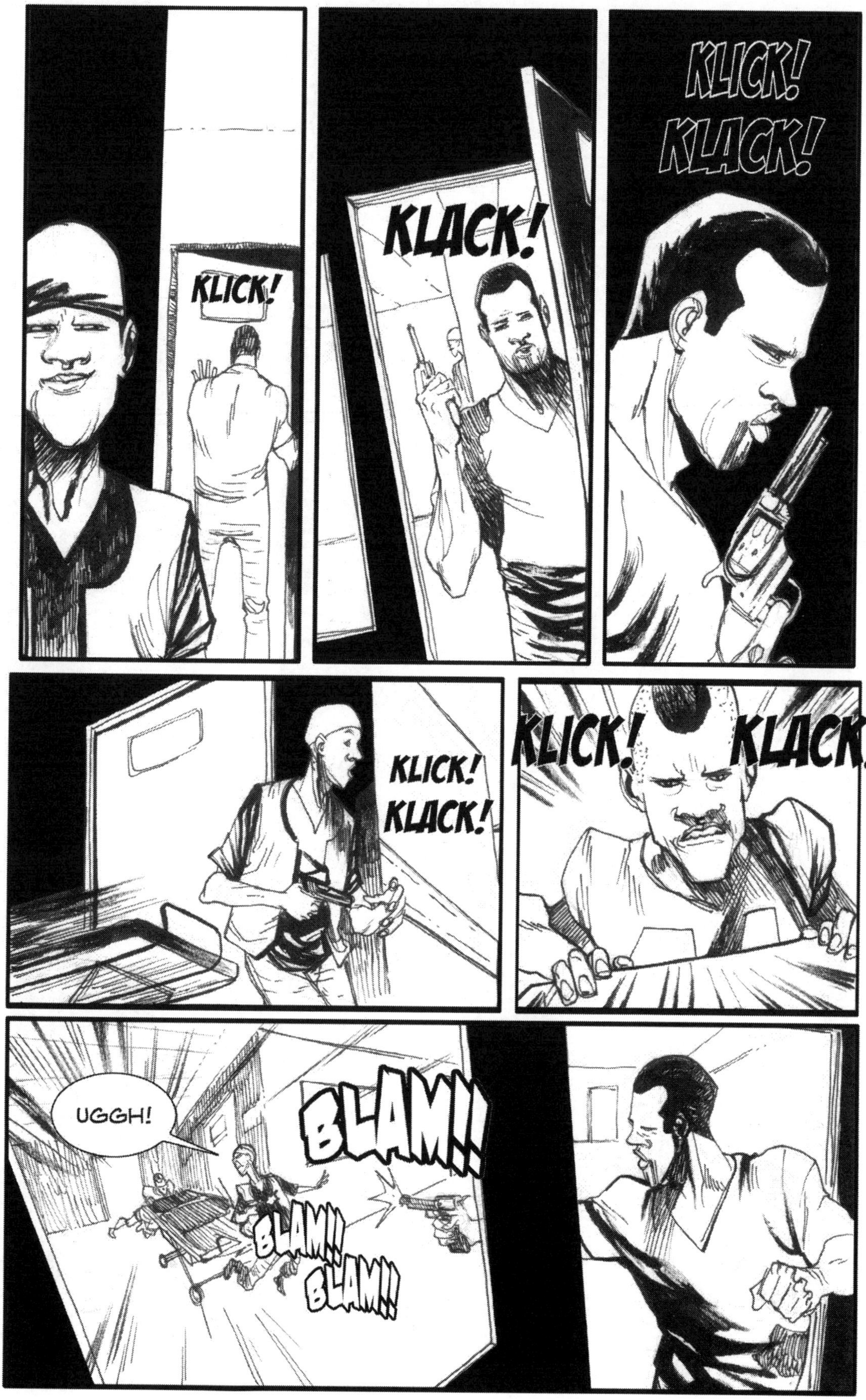
KLICK!
KLACK!
KLICK!
KLACK!
KLICK!
KLACK!
KLICK!
KLACK!
UGGH!
BLAM!!
BLAM!!
BLAM!!

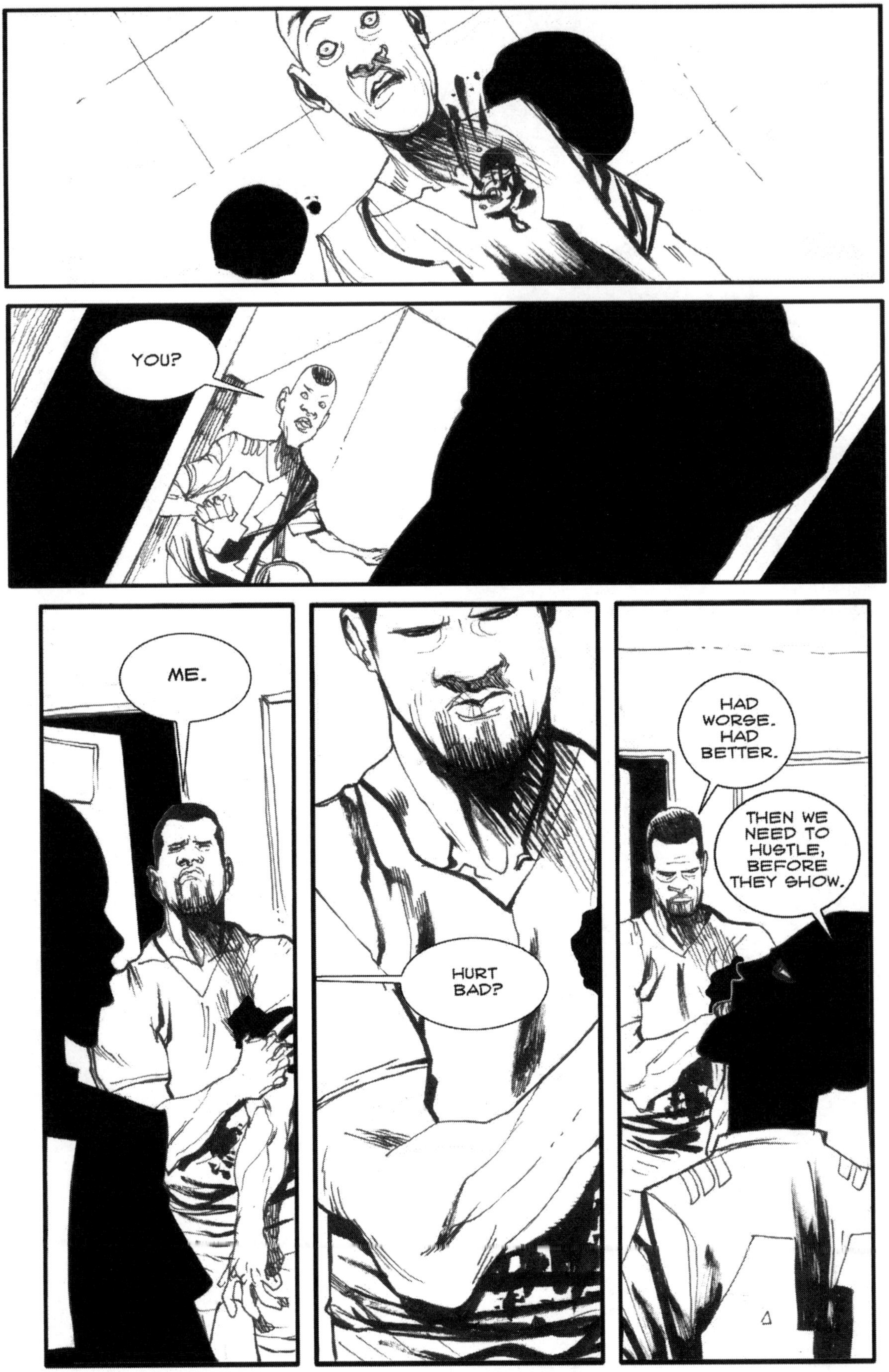
YOU?
ME.
HURT BAD?
HAD WORSE. HAD BETTER.
THEN WE NEED TO HUSTLE, BEFORE THEY SHOW.

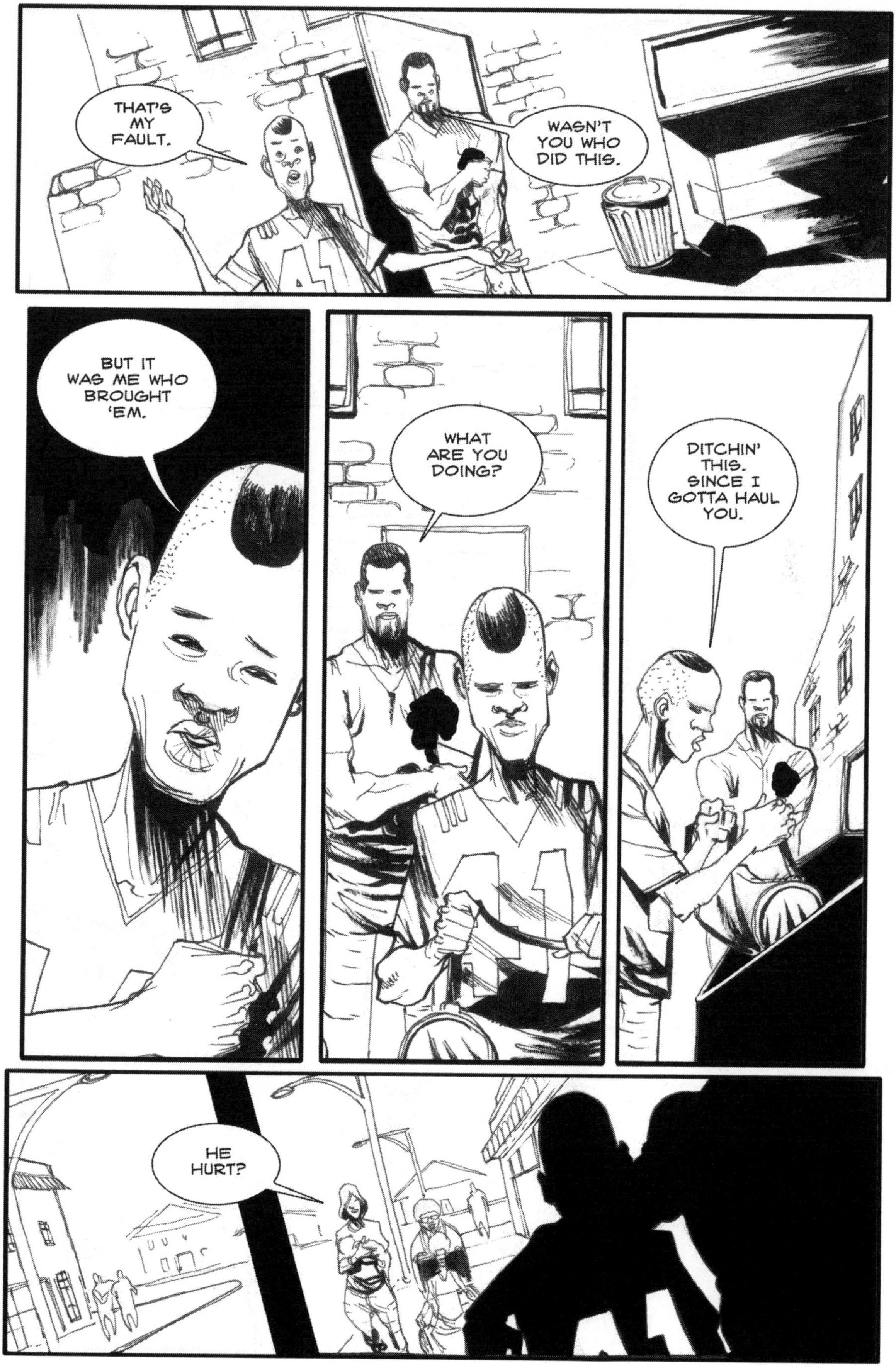
THAT'S MY FAULT.
WASN'T YOU WHO DID THIS.
BUT IT WAS ME WHO BROUGHT 'EM.
WHAT ARE YOU DOING?
DITCHIN' THIS. SINCE I GOTTA HAUL YOU.
HE HURT?

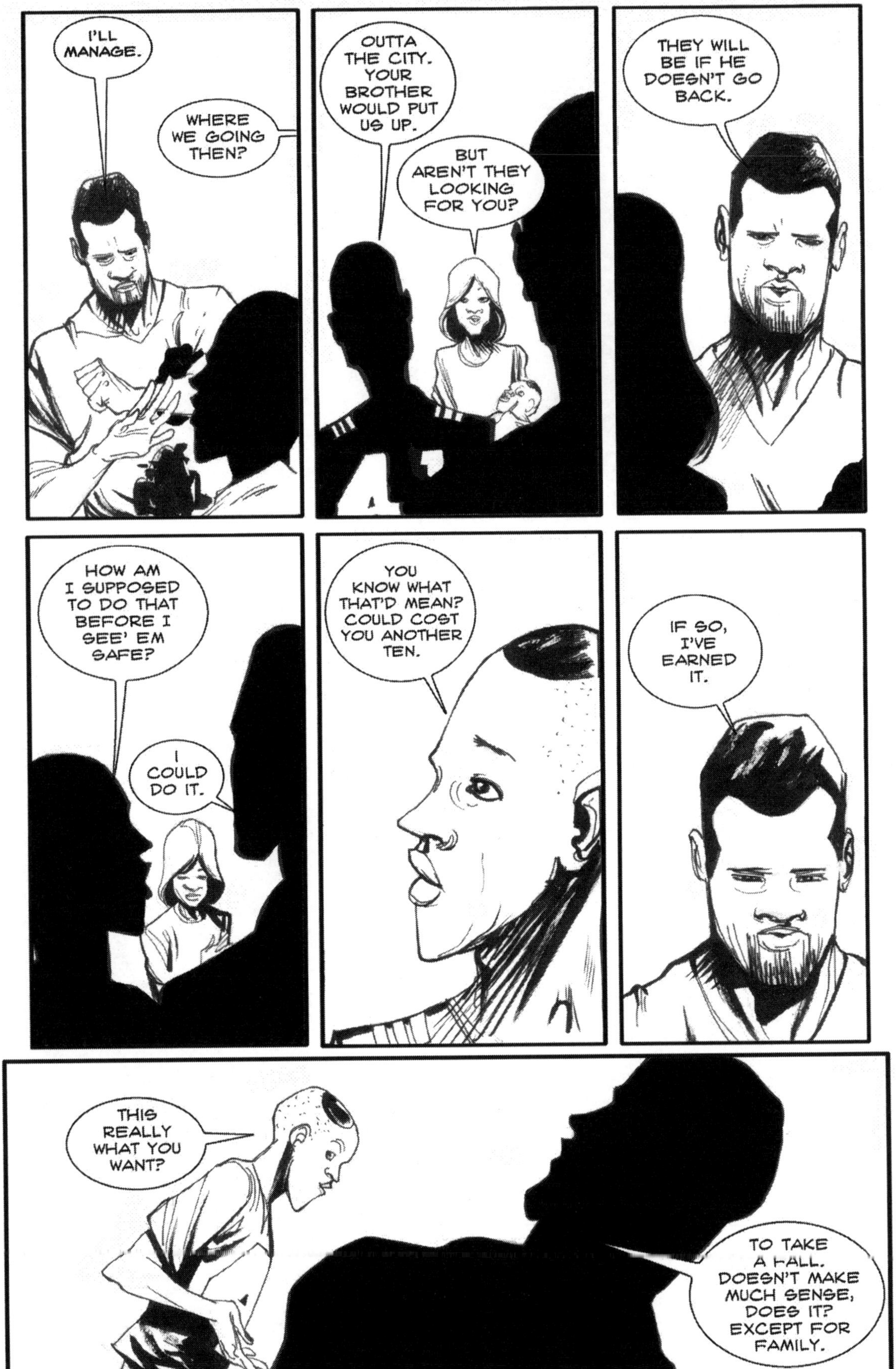
I'LL MANAGE.
WHERE WE GOING THEN?
OUTTA THE CITY. YOUR BROTHER WOULD PUT US UP.
BUT AREN'T THEY LOOKING FOR YOU?
THEY WILL BE IF HE DOESN'T GO BACK.
HOW AM I SUPPOSED TO DO THAT BEFORE I SEE' EM SAFE?
I COULD DO IT.
YOU KNOW WHAT THAT'D MEAN? COULD COST YOU ANOTHER TEN.
IF SO, I'VE EARNED IT.
THIS REALLY WHAT YOU WANT?
TO TAKE A FALL. DOESN'T MAKE MUCH SENSE, DOES IT? EXCEPT FOR FAMILY.

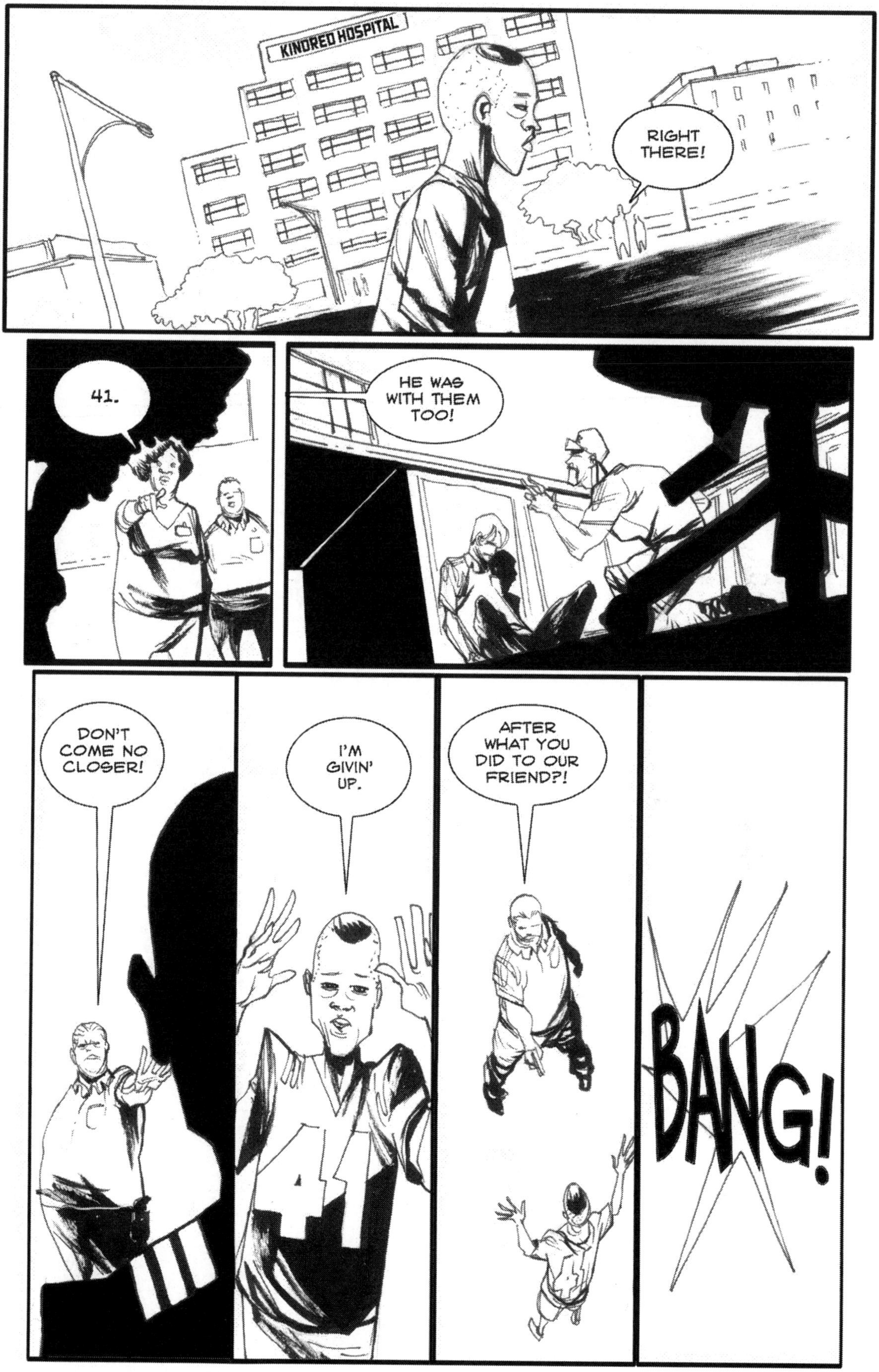
KINDRED HOSPITAL
RIGHT THERE!
41.
HE WAS WITH THEM TOO!
DON'T COME NO CLOSER!
I'M GIVIN' UP.
AFTER WHAT YOU DID TO OUR FRIEND?!
BANG!

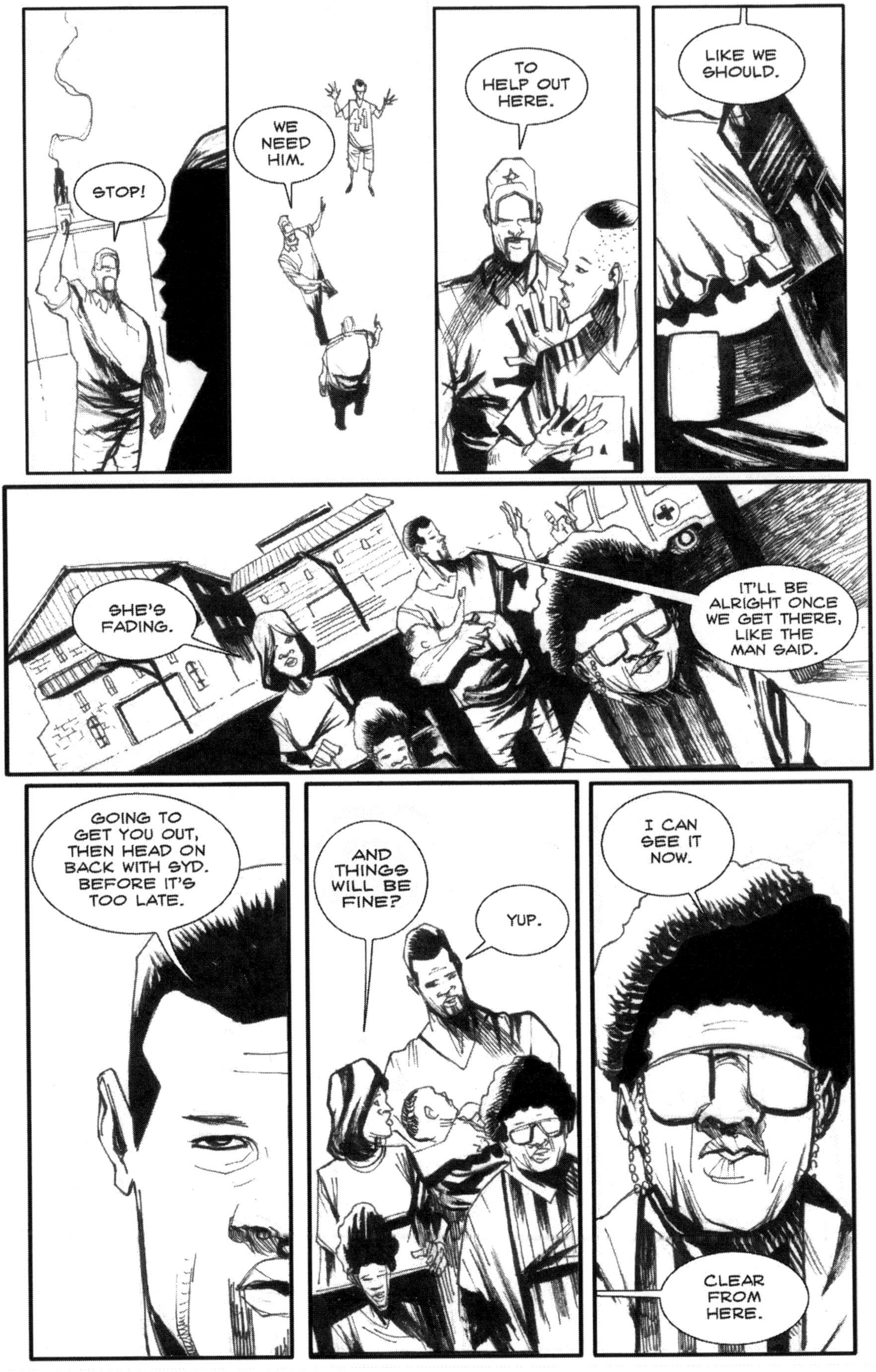
STOP!
WE NEED HIM.
TO HELP OUT HERE.
LIKE WE SHOULD.
SHE'S FADING.
IT'LL BE ALRIGHT ONCE WE GET THERE, LIKE THE MAN SAID.
GOING TO GET YOU OUT, THEN HEAD ON BACK WITH SYD. BEFORE IT'S TOO LATE.
AND THINGS WILL BE FINE?
YUP.
I CAN SEE IT NOW.
CLEAR FROM HERE.

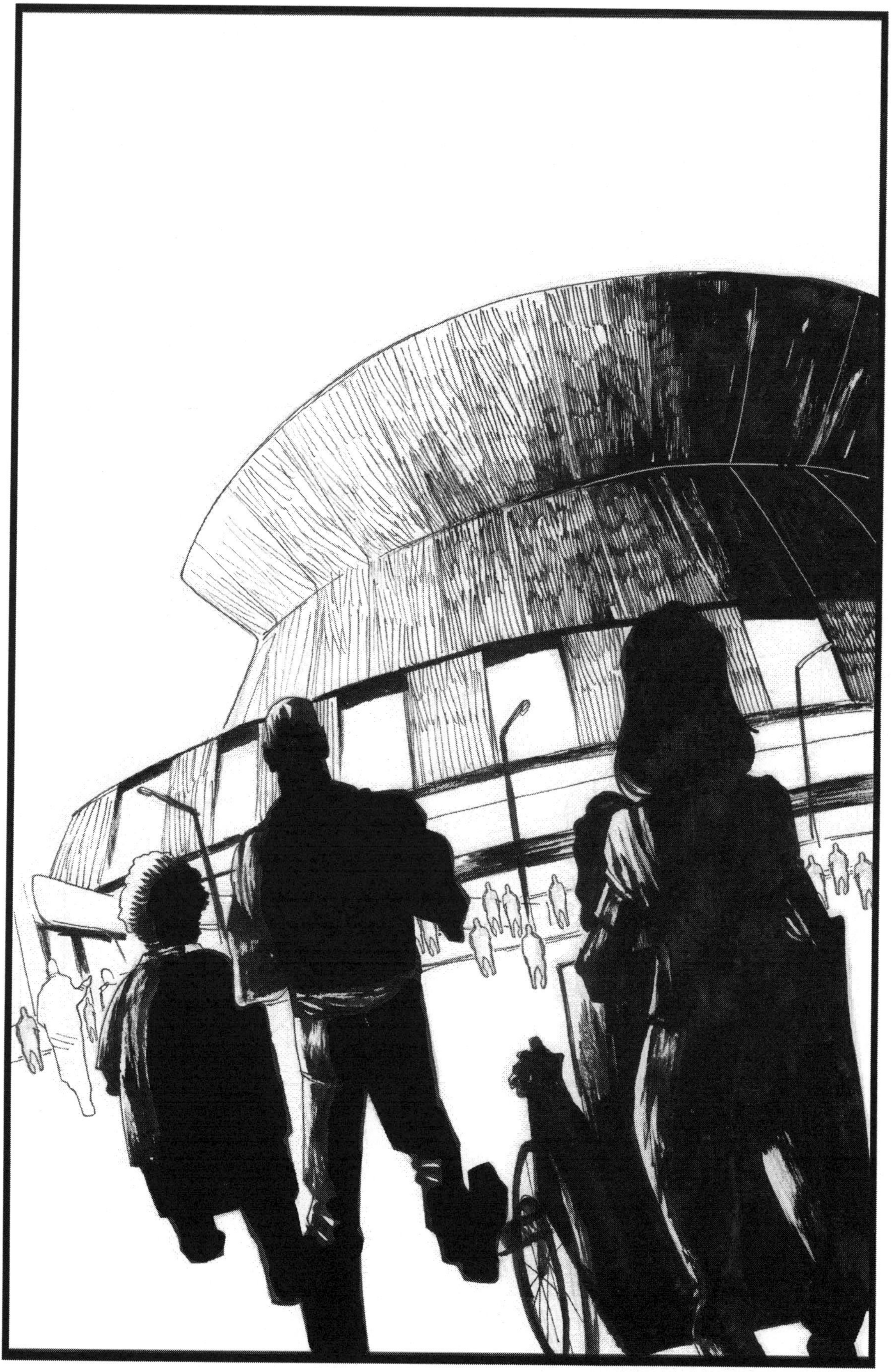

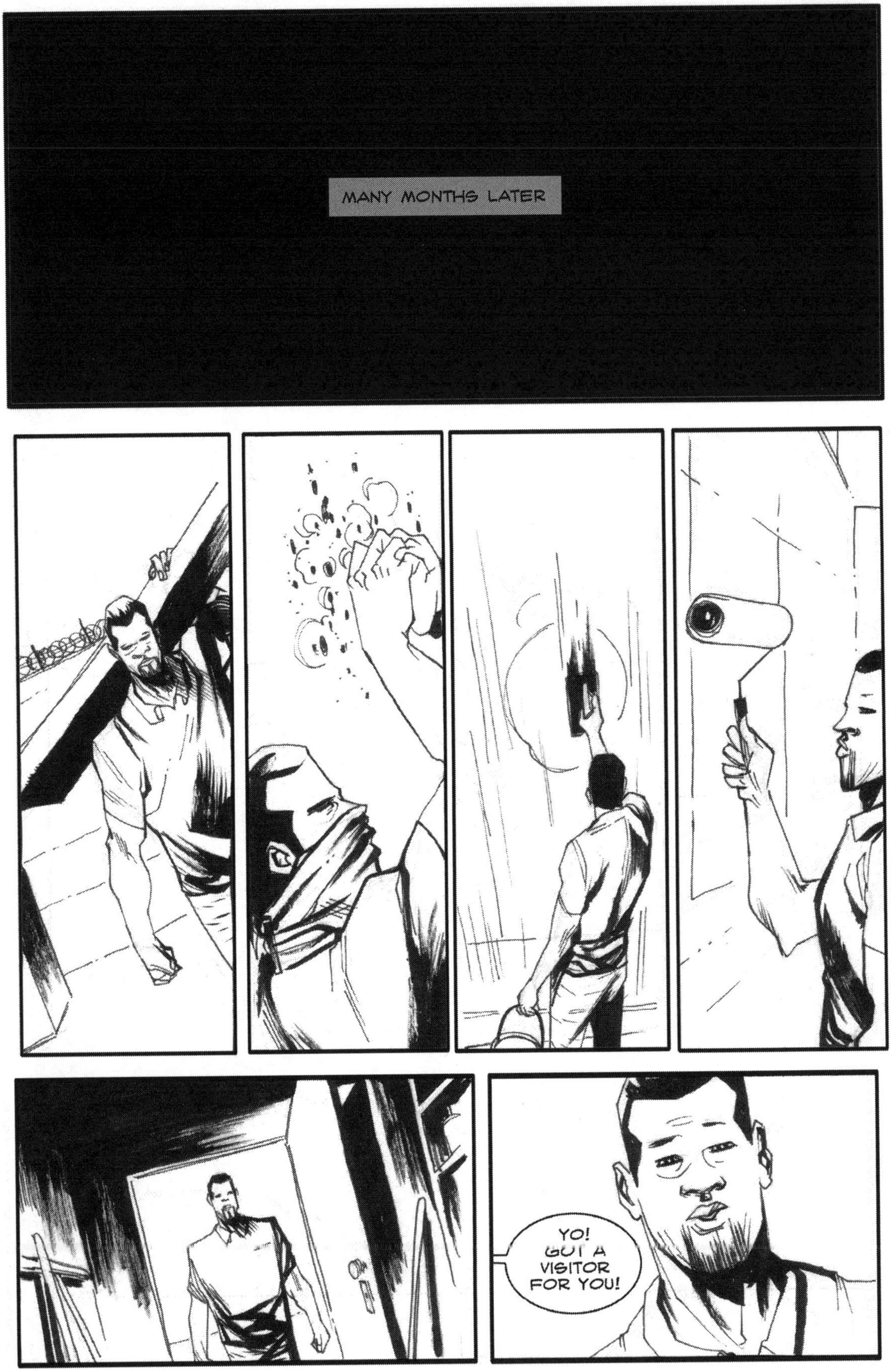
MANY MONTHS LATER
YO! GOT A VISITOR FOR YOU!

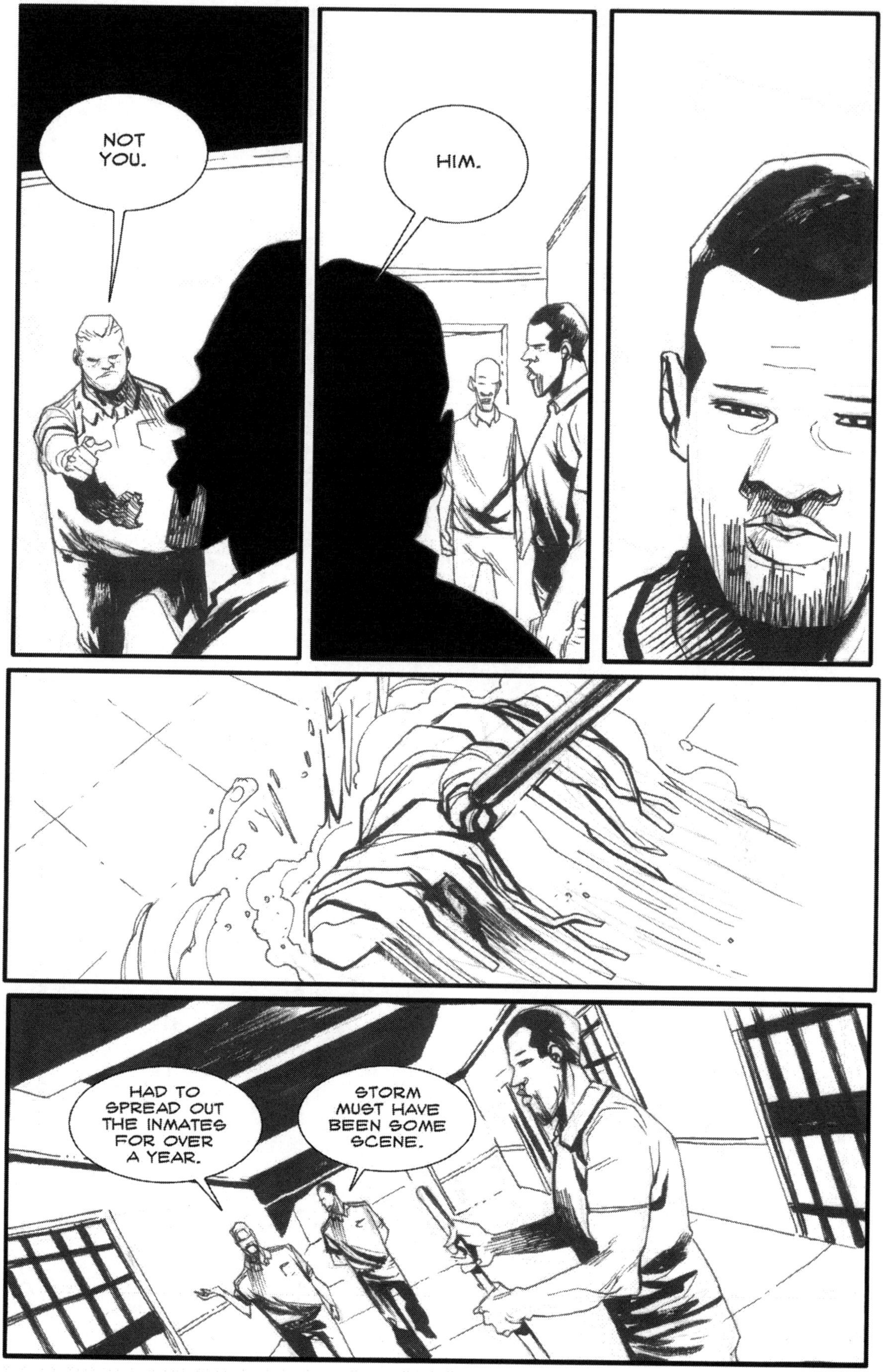
NOT YOU.
HIM.
HAD TO SPREAD OUT THE INMATES FOR OVER A YEAR.
STORM MUST HAVE BEEN SOME SCENE.

COME OVER FOR SUPPER, AND I'LL TELL YOU ALL ABOUT IT.

MY WIFE'S A HELL OF A COOK.

RUSS.

WHY YOU SMILING?

JUST BECAUSE.

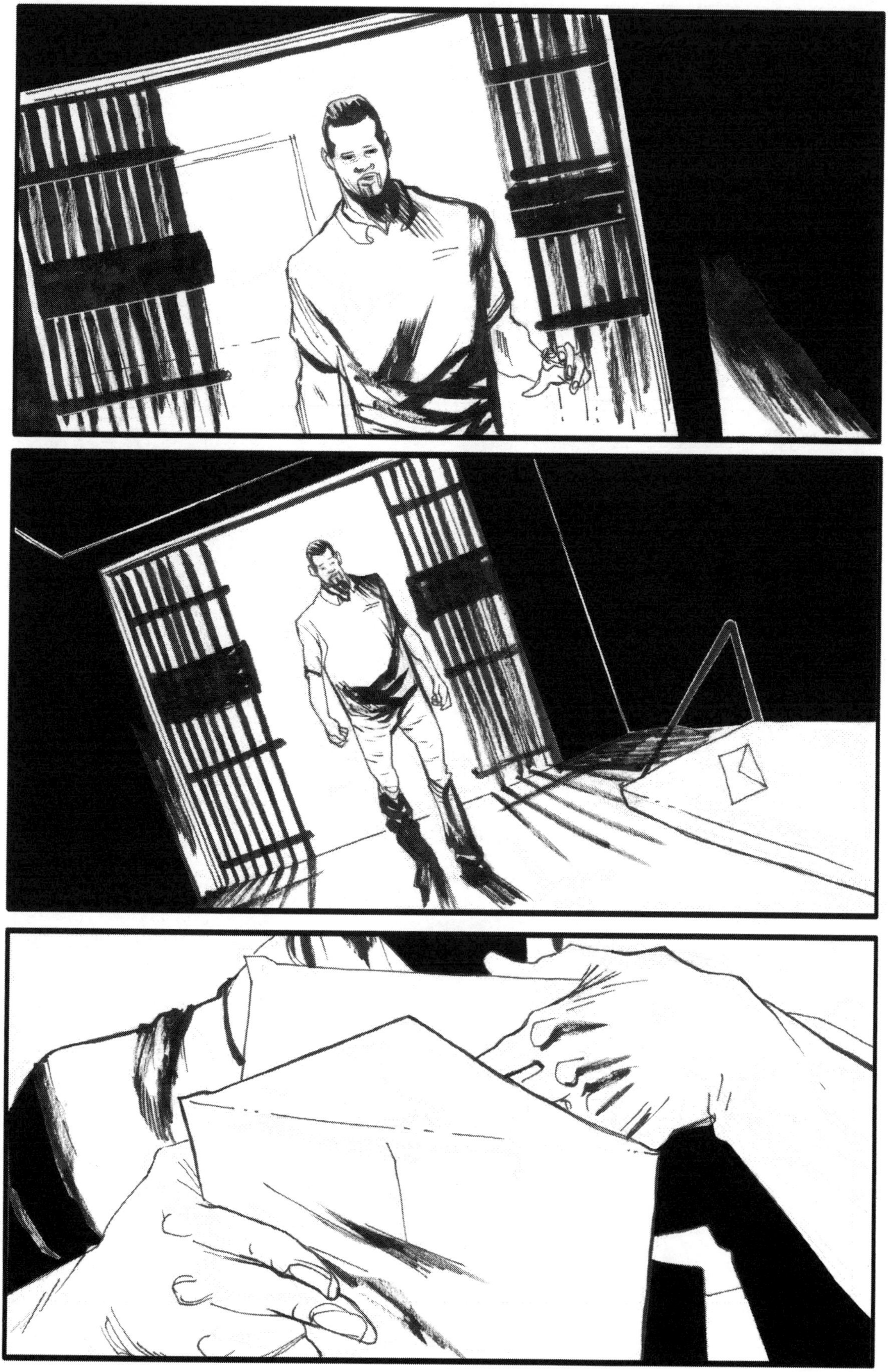

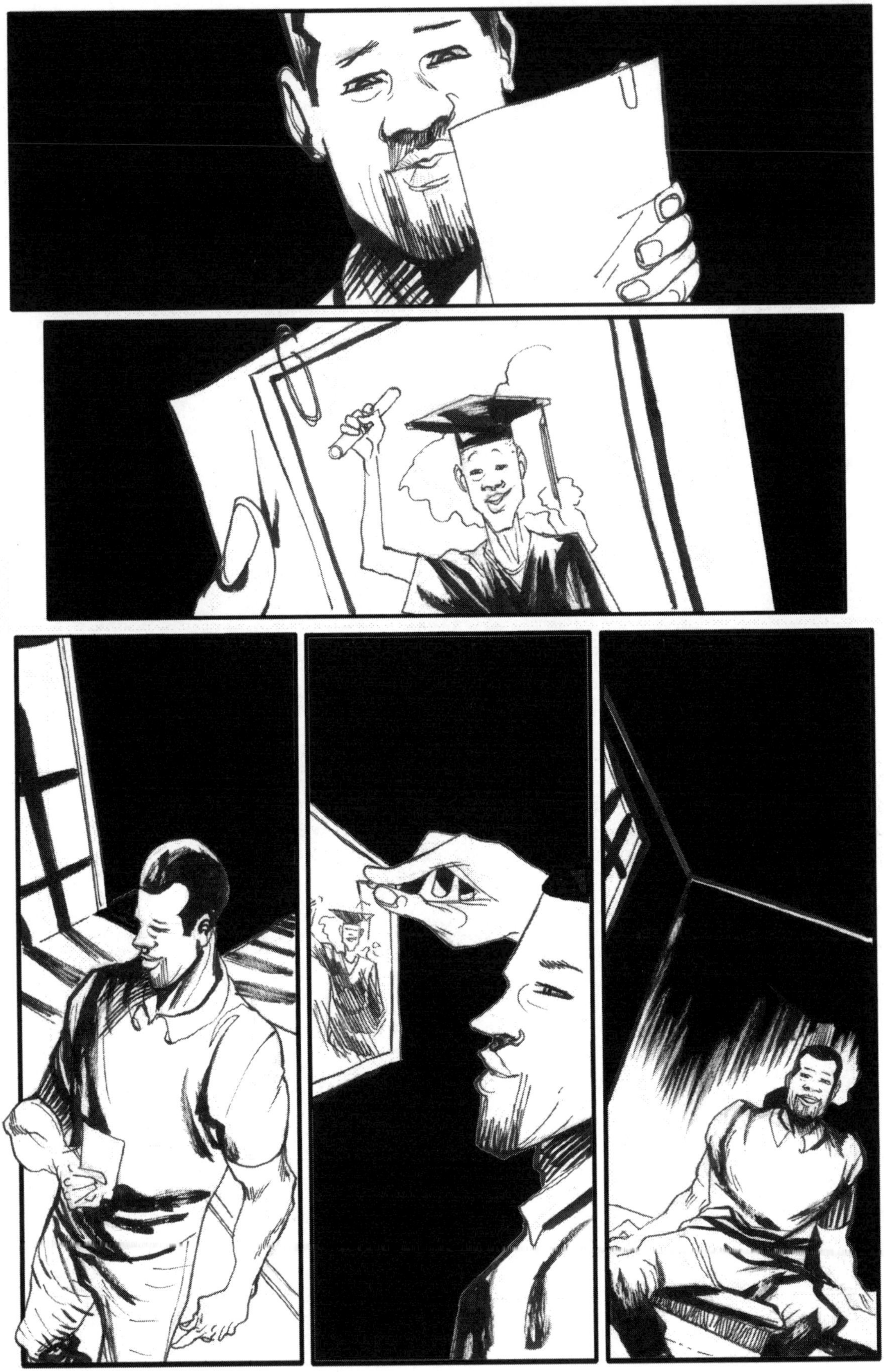

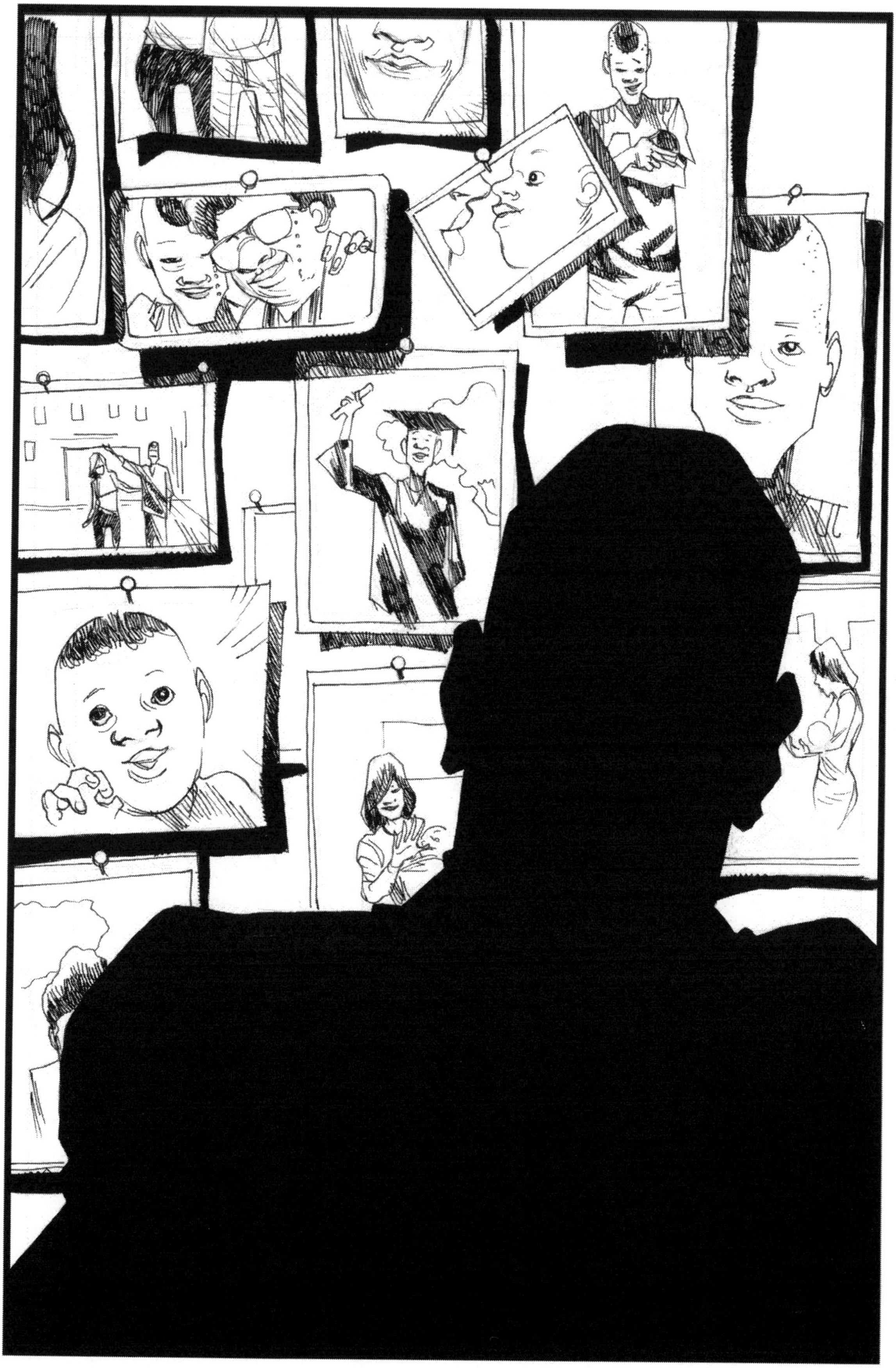

EPILOGUE

AT LEAST 14 PRISONERS ESCAPED FROM THE ORLEANS PARISH PRISON COMPLEX DURING HURRICANE KATRINA. THE CONVICTS AND JUVIES HELD THERE DURING THE STORM WERE DISPERSED ACROSS THE REGION IN THE AFTERMATH. INMATES REPORTED DOZENS OF DEATHS INSIDE THE COMPLEX. YET THE STATE HAS NOT CONFIRMED THESE FATALITIES. INSTEAD IT TORE DOWN THE MAIN TEMPLEMAN FACILITY WITHOUT ALLOWING AN INSPECTION BY THE PRESS.

FOR MORE INFORMATION ABOUT THESE EVENTS, CONSULT THE ACLU REPORT ON THE INCIDENT:
ABANDONED AND ABUSED:
ORLEANS PARISH PRISONERS IN THE WAKE OF HURRICANE KATRINA
HTTPS://WWW.ACLU.ORG/REPORT/ABANDONED-AND-ABUSED

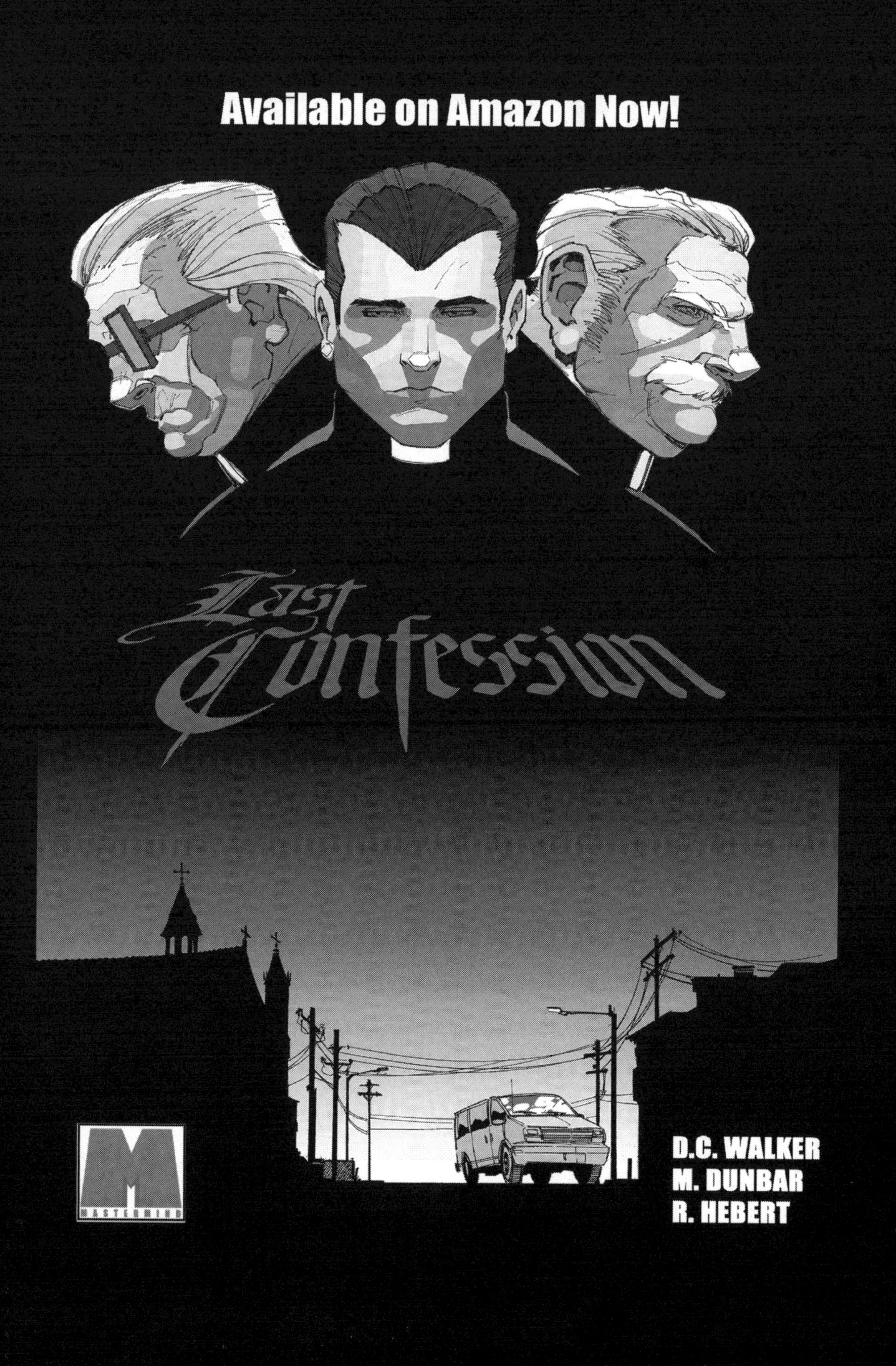
Available on Amazon Now!
Last Confession
D.C. WALKER
M. DUNBAR
R. HEBERT

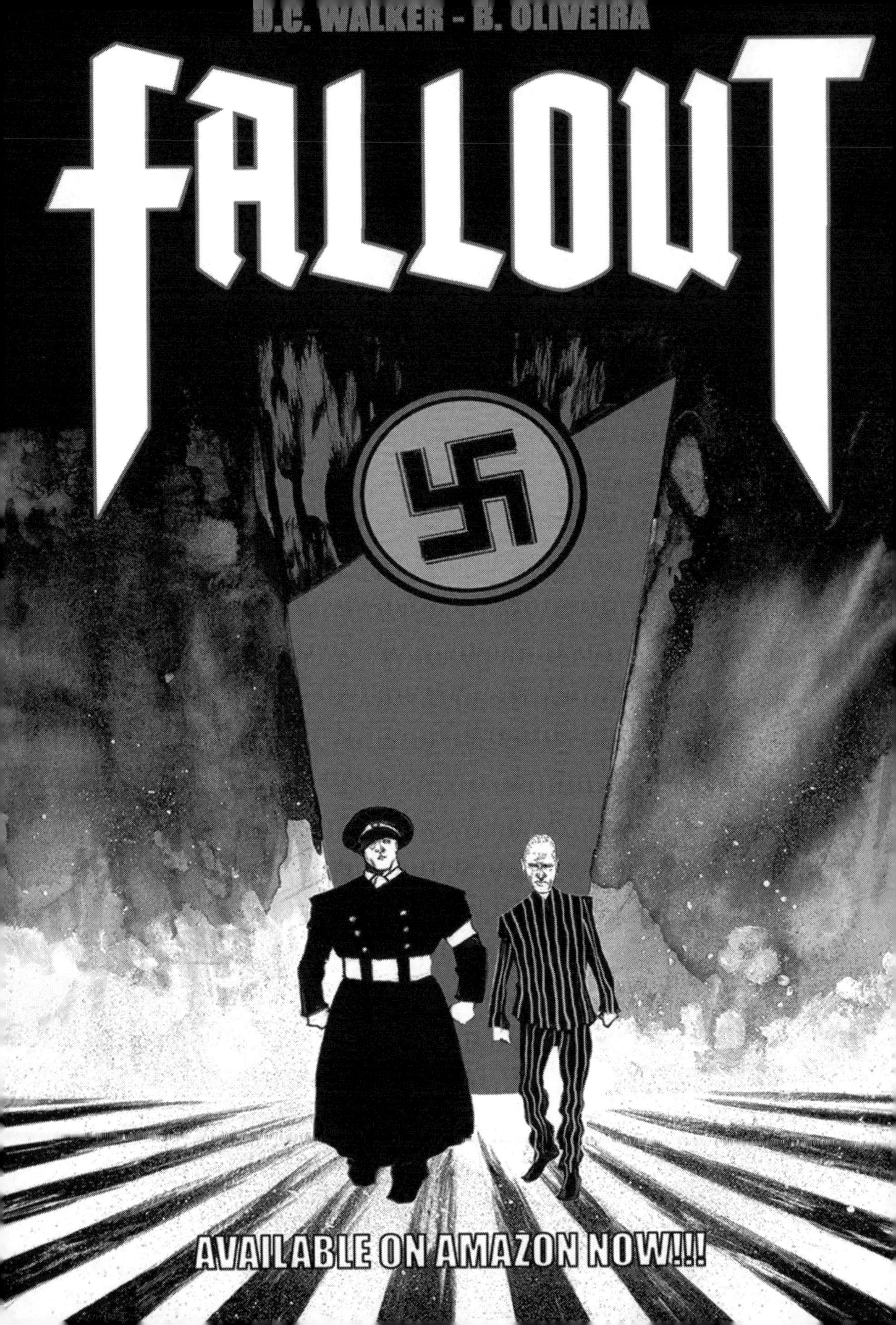

D.C. WALKER - B. OLIVEIRA
FALLOUT
AVAILABLE ON AMAZON NOW!!!

50514670R00096

Made in the USA
Lexington, KY
28 August 2019